The British Business Elite

First published in 1981, *The British Business Elite* is a study of the attitudes to class, status and power of top businessmen in Great Britain, based upon first-hand interviews with chairmen, chief executives and other directors of Britain's largest industrial, banking and insurance companies: men of genuine wealth and power. Dr Fidler produces important empirical data in a field of study which has been plagued with problems of access; a field in which much of the theory has been based on assumptions.

The book includes a careful examination of the background and career of those interviewed; a discussion of the way in which businessmen see the objectives of their companies, particularly relevant to the long-standing debate over the ownership and control of corporations; their views of class and status and of the power of businessmen in Britain. Finally, Dr Fidler considers the implications of the research for future theory and investigation.

The British Business Elite

Its Attitudes to Class, Status and Power

John Fidler

Routledge
Taylor & Francis Group

First published in 1981
by Routledge & Kegan Paul Ltd

This edition first published in 2024 by Routledge
4 Park Square, Milton Park, Abingdon, Oxon, OX14 4RN

and by Routledge
605 Third Avenue, New York, NY 10017

Routledge is an imprint of the Taylor & Francis Group, an informa business

© J. Fidler 1981

Publisher's Note
The publisher has gone to great lengths to ensure the quality of this reprint but points out that some imperfections in the original copies may be apparent.

Disclaimer
The publisher has made every effort to trace copyright holders and welcomes correspondence from those they have been unable to contact.

A Library of Congress record exists under LCCN: 80042214

ISBN: 978-1-032-91386-5 (hbk)
ISBN: 978-1-003-56302-0 (ebk)
ISBN: 978-1-032-91387-2 (pbk)

Book DOI 10.4324/9781003563020

THE BRITISH BUSINESS ELITE
Its attitudes to class, status and power

John Fidler

ROUTLEDGE & KEGAN PAUL
London, Boston and Henley

First published in 1981
by Routledge & Kegan Paul Ltd
39 Store Street,
London WC1E 7DD,
9 Park Street,
Boston, Mass. 02108, USA, and
Broadway House,
Newtown Road,
Henley-on-Thames,
Oxon RG9 1EN
Printed in Great Britain by
Biddles Ltd, Guildford, Surrey

British Library Cataloguing in Publication Data

Fidler, John

The British business elite.
- (International library of sociology)
1. Executives - Great Britain
I. Title
306'30941   HF5500. 3G7   80-42214

ISBN 0-7100-0770-1

To Joan

CONTENTS

Preface   xv

1 Strategists, ideologists and influentials:
  the business elite in sociological theory   1

  1. 1 Introduction   1
  1. 2 A terminological note   3
  1. 3 The business elite in sociological theory   4
  1. 4 The economic role of businessmen   5
  1. 5 Businessmen and industrial relations   13
  1. 6 Businessmen in the class structure   15
  1. 7 Diversity in class imagery   17
  1. 8 The business elite as ideologists   25
  1. 9 The business elite as political influentials   31
  1.10 Conclusion   38

2 The meaning systems of top businessmen   39

  2. 1 Introduction   39
  2. 2 Sources of businessmen's meaning systems   41
  2. 3 The director as a member of the middle class   42
  2. 4 The director in touch and out of touch with the
        working class   43
  2. 5 The director as a member of the upper class   44
  2. 6 The director as ex-public schoolboy   45
  2. 7 The director as adherent of Tory party ideology   47
  2. 8 The director as creator and recipeint of business
        ideology   48
  2. 9 Conclusion   51

3 Design of the research   53

  3. 1 Some preliminaries to research   53
  3. 2 Objectives of the research   57
  3. 3 Methodology   58
  3. 4 Details of method   59
  3. 5 Critique of the methodology   68
  3. 6 The context of the study   74
  3. 7 The interviews   76

4 Reserved seats: family background, education, career
  and present lifestyle of top businessmen   78

4. 1   Introduction   78
4. 2   The elite were well placed by birth   79
4. 3   Early life experiences: the contribution of the
        public schools   82
4. 4   Higher education: the universities and
        professions   83
4. 5   Comparisons with other studies   87
4. 6   An index of social status   91
4. 7   The careers that led to the top   95
4. 8   Service experience   98
4. 9   Management training   99
4.10   Main experience in the firm   100
4.11   Income and wealth   104
4.12   Home life and the drift to the south   109
4.13   Community life   112
4.14   Clubs and leisure activities   113
4.15   Summary   114

5 The company comes first: the responsibilities and
   objectives of directors   117

5. 1   Introduction   117
5. 2   Goals for the firm   117
5. 3   Capitalists and managers   124
5. 4   Family connections   127
5. 5   Long-term and short-term goals   130
5. 6   The director's responsibilities   131
5. 7   On growth   137
5. 8   The chief executive's audience   139
5. 9   Conclusion   143

6 The view from Mount Olympus: conflict, consensus
   and participation in the firm   145

6. 1   Introduction   145
6. 2   The board and industrial relations   146
6. 3   Sharing the objectives   147
6. 4   A psychological boundary in the firm?   151
6. 5   Consensus and conflict   153
6. 6   Multiple images of the firm   160
6. 7   Issues: (1) trade unions   162
6. 8   Issues: (2) employee participation   163
6. 9   Conclusion   166

7 Not a society person, not at all snooty: businessmen's
   views of class and status in Britain   168

7. 1   Introduction   168
7. 2   Outline of the chapter   169
7. 3   Methodology   170
7. 4   How businessmen spoke of class   171

7. 5	The number of classes perceived	174
7. 6	The criteria which separate class	176
7. 7	The upper class	178
7. 8	Self-assigned class	179
7. 9	No ruling class?	180
7.10	The low status of British businessmen	183
7.11	Status is not the same as power	186
7.12	Class imagery compared	187
7.13	Variations in images of society	189
7.14	Re-explaining class imagery	195
7.15	Some distinctive views of class	197
7.16	The themes of class imagery	205
7.17	Conclusion	209

8 An uninvented lobby: the business picture of power in Britain — 215

8. 1	Introduction	215
8. 2	Outline of the argument	216
8. 3	National versus local politics	217
8. 4	The changing nature of political involvement	220
8. 5	The business elite and political parties	226
8. 6	Perceptions of power under a Labour government	230
8. 7	The issues	232
8. 8	Channels of influence	234
8. 9	How successful is the business lobby?	238
8.10	The mass media	241
8.11	The establishment	242
8.12	Summary and conclusions	245

9 Conclusion — 249

9. 1	Introduction	249
9. 2	The assumptions of the study	249
9. 3	The findings of the study	252
9. 4	Implications for theory and future research	255
9. 5	More everyday issues	266
9. 6	In conclusion	271

Appendices — 273

1	The interview schedule	273
2	On the use of personal contacts in one's career and in influencing government	277

Notes	284
Bibliography	293
Index	305

FIGURES

1.1 Variables to be related in models of class imagery   20

2.1 The internal composition of meaning systems   41

4.1 Relationships between salary, shareholding,
     income and wealth   106

7.1 Models of class in Britain   175

7.2 Businessmen's 'picture' of society   212

7.3 An outline of some core beliefs of top businessmen   214

9.1 Some empirical findings of this study   259

TABLES

3. 1 Summary table of final achieved sample   65

4. 1 Father's occupation, tabulated in the Registrar-General's social class groupings   80

4. 2 Father's occupation - ranking on Hope-Goldthorpe scale   81

4. 3 The type of school attended by top businessmen   84

4. 4 The extent to which different groups among top businessmen had attended a place of higher education   85

4. 5 Subject read at university or technical college: chief executives only   86

4. 6 Professional qualifications obtained by top businessmen   87

4. 7 The educational background of the directors of large commercial firms as found in different studies   89

4. 8 The educational background of City directors   90

4. 9 Numbers of men graduating from university as found in different studies   90

4.10 A comparison of different groups among top businessmen using a composite social status index   93

4.11 Relationship between status of family background and university or professional training - whole sample   94

4.12 Relationship between status of family background and university or professional training - bureaucrats only   95

4.13 Extent of formal management training among top businessmen   100

4.14   Career experience of chief executives:
       commerce only   101

4.15   Areas in which the chief executives have spent
       the major part of their working lives   102

4.16   Number of organisations worked for during career   103

4.17   Age of obtaining first main board appointment   104

4.18   Gross annual income from all sources – chief
       executives – 1974–6   105

4.19   Total wealth holdings – chief executives – 1974–6   105

4.20   Correlations of salary and shareholding with size
       of firm   107

4.21   The location of company headquarters: medium
       and large firms only   111

4.22   Leisure interests of businessmen   114

5. 1   The stated objectives of company chief executives
       by ownership position   122

5. 2   The stated objectives of chief executives by sector   123

5. 3   Mean rate of return earned by companies under
       different types of control   124

5. 4   Rate of return and type of control   125

5. 5   Rate of return and chief executive's status   126

5. 6   How top businessmen see the responsibilties of
       the director   133

6. 1   Extent to which other groups in the company are
       thought to share the chief executive's objectives –
       by sector   148

6. 2   Extent to which other groups in the company are
       thought to share the chief executive's objectives –
       by size of company   149

6. 3   Answers to question: 'Do you see two sides in
       your company?' – by sector   154

6. 4   Answers to question: 'Do you see two sides in
       your company?' – by size of firm   154

6. 5 Co-variation of answers to questions concerning existence of conflict in the firm and reasons for conflict 157

6. 6 Reasons for conflict in the firm - by sector 158

6. 7 Reasons for conflict in the firm - by size of firm 159

7. 1 The basis of class 177

7. 2 References to the upper class 178

7. 3 Groups which constitute the upper class 179

7. 4 Self-assigned class of businessmen 179

7. 5 Variations in images of society as seen by different types of businessmen 191

7. 6 Self-rated class by type of respondent 192

7. 7 The bases of stratification as stated by different groups 192

7. 8 Self-rating of class by family background 193

7. 9 The bases of class by family background 194

7.10 Answers to question: 'Do you see two sides in your company?' 195

7.11 Reasons for conflict within the firm 196

8. 1 Involvement of heads of large firms in political and voluntary activities at three points in a fifty-year timespan 222

8. 2 Involvement of heads of a sample of merchant banks, insurance and property companies in political and voluntary activities over a fifty-year timespan 223

8. 3 Political and voluntary involvement of the heads of all firms in the interview study over a fifty-year timespan 224

8. 4 Political and other donations by firms in the study - by size of firm 228

8. 5 Political and other donations by type of control 228

8. 6 Total list of issues mentioned by businessmen   232

8. 7 How different types of company attempt to
      influence government   237

8. 8 Types of access to political decision-makers -
      by size of company   238

8. 9 The outcome of twenty issues on which business
      tried to influence government   240

PREFACE

This book was mainly written with sociologists in mind, especially those interested in the business corporation, elites, the power structure of capitalist societies, or the imagery of social class. However, since its whole perspective revolves around the thinking and actions of the very top executives of business firms, I hope that it will also be of interest to economists and other management researchers, and to management practitioners and more general readers.

Precisely because the activities of businessmen are of interest and concern to workers in several different disciplines, and within several areas of sociological debate, I have had to discuss a wide range of theory and previous research findings. Some readers may feel therefore that the treatment of some issues is not detailed enough, and I can only say in answer to this that the book is primarily intended to present empirical research and to discuss such theory as it is relevant to, and is relevant to it.

Others will find that the discussion of the literature and the research methodology in the first three chapters is more detailed or specialised than their own interests or concerns require. However I think that much of Chapter 4 onwards will be accessible to the more general reader and can be read without too much reference back to earlier chapters. I will say no more about the structure and aims of the book here as they are set out in the first few pages of the text itself.

I have accumulated a number of debts in the course of the research and the subsequent writing of this book, and can do no more to repay them than acknowledge them. First and foremost the research would not have been possible without the co-operation of the businessmen who were interviewed and who gave most generously of their time. I promised them anonymity, and I sincerely hope that the book in no way breaks that promise. The research was funded partly by the Science Research Council, but in the main by the Social Science Research Council.

I owe much to Professor Dorothy Wedderburn and Jack Winkler for help and guidance in setting up the project initially. Jack and I have had a number of discussions since then which I have greatly valued. I am especially grateful also to my supervisor at Aston University, Professor John Child, not only for his knowledge and experience, but for his encouragement, without which I would not have completed the research.

I must also thank Theo Nichols, who read an early draft of this manuscript, and pointed out much that was lacking in it; and

Professor Ray Pahl and David Dunkerley who read later drafts and made many perceptive comments. I have also benefited from discussions with François-Charles Mougel and Mike Useem of Bordeaux and Boston Universities respectively, and colleagues and friends at Aston, Nuffield College, Oxford, and Imperial College, London. Several of those mentioned here have differed fundamentally from me in their theoretical orientation or conclusions, and of course none of them can be held responsible for the flaws in this work.

I am also very grateful to Isla Smith, who, as well as typing the manuscript, helped to remove the worst constructions of my written English. Finally I must thank my wife, Clare, who could not have envisaged when she met me in 1974 that I would still be devoting so much of my time to businessmen six years later. Her tolerance and encouragement have been essential.

John Fidler

1 STRATEGISTS, IDEOLOGISTS AND INFLUENTIALS
The business elite in sociological theory

'The ideas of the ruling class are in every epoch the ruling ideas.' Marx and Engels, 'The German Ideology', 1970, p.74

'Only the expert knowledge of private economic interest groups in the field of "business" is superior to the expert knowledge of the bureaucracy.' Max Weber, 'Economy and Society', 1968, p. 994

1.1 INTRODUCTION

The focus of this study is the beliefs, opinions, values and attitudes of British top businessmen. It is largely an empirical study; indeed, what distinguishes it from most preceding studies is that the bulk of it is based on 130 first-hand interviews by the author with chairmen, managing directors and other directors from a range of large British companies. These interviews took place over a period of two years (1974-6); and were followed by a lengthy analysis of the resulting material.

This is not a study of managers in the wider sense, nor even of company directors as such, for the term director nowadays is used to cover anybody from a self-employed building contractor to the chairman of British Petroleum. Rather, the claim is made for this study that it is about members of the elite within the business world, men of genuine wealth and power. To illustrate this, I may mention that amongst those interviewed were four men who at some stage have headed nationalised industries, a former Lord Mayor of London, two ex-MPs, two presidents of the CBI and several members of its Grand Council, sixteen known millionaires and five of the heads of the ten largest industrial companies ranked by turnover.[1]

The perspective of the study is that of the sociologist, and this shaped the content and style of the interviews. There are many topics on which one might seek the opinions of directors; amongst them, for example, how to cure Britain's economic ills, how to run a large company, or what abilities or traits are needed for a successful career in commerce.

Whilst the research reported here is not irrelevant to such concerns, they were not its main objectives. These objectives are set out below (chapter 3), but simplifying them one may say that the research was intended to investigate the possibilities of access to top businessmen and, as far as possible, to make a study of their values, attitudes and beliefs, particularly with respect to class, status and power in Britain. I wanted to interview businessmen so as to obtain direct evidence of their attitudes and, to a lesser extent, behaviour, because so much sociological theory with respect to elite groups is based on *inferred* attitudes and behaviour.

It should be made clear at the outset that the study was conceived as an exploratory one. I did not know when I began how successful I would be in obtaining access to businessmen, nor how useful the research methodology would be. In the event, fears concerning the problems of access were largely unfounded and the research proved at least feasible. Thus the main interest in the study for both sociologist and layman must lie in the research findings. But before presenting these, I wish to show that an understanding of the values and beliefs of businessmen is of importance to sociological theory. The crux of any such argument, however, is relatively simple; it is that businessmen have power and influence in certain domains of social life, even if this extends no further than their own companies. They, more than other people, have the ability to act in accordance with their own interpretation of the world and, to some extent, some would say to a very large extent, they are able to impose their values, their opinions, their attitudes on others.

Thus I begin the study by setting out the place that the business elite have in sociological theory, and the varying interpretations of their role and importance in society. I try to show that businessmen whether as an elite, or as members of a class, or, even more straightforwardly as top managers, enter into key roles in the conceptualisations of sociologists in ways that, for example, foremen or professional employees do not. Yet, despite the importance they are given, there are few studies of any size that focus specifically on them, and those that exist are often unsatisfactory simply because the assumption has been made from the outset that businessmen cannot be studied in the way that sociologists would study other groups.

The study of how social class, status and power in society are perceived by members of society has received much attention. The reason for this is presumably that although sociologists might be able to construct models of society which bear no resemblance to the way in which it is perceived by other members, the perceptions of how society 'is', of 'why it is', and of the limits, consequences and possibilities of social action are important in guiding the actions of members of society. Amongst such studies there is a dearth of those that look specifically at those who benefit (even taken in a material sense) from existing social structures. Elite groups, we shall see, are doubly interesting in this regard, for they are groups that are part of social structures but which also have capacities to define and shape them.

Let me set out now the structure of this book. In this chapter I examine the sociological literature to which the business elite are relevant, concentrating here on the theoretical issues. In the following chapter I look in more detail at writing and research con-

cerned specifically with the beliefs, values and attitudes of businessmen. The remaining chapters then report my own study.
Chapter 3 gives a discussion of the objectives and methodology of
the research. Chapter 4 is a detailed examination of the background and careers of those interviewed, comparing my findings
with other studies.[2] Chapter 5 discusses the issue of how businessmen see the objectives of the company, a chapter which is
particularly relevant to the long-standing debate over the ownership and control of corporations. Chapter 6 asks to what extent
top businessmen believe that their objectives are shared by other
groups within the company, and produces material of relevance to
those concerned with industrial relations and industrial participation. Chapter 7 discusses the 'images of society' held by the
business elite, which was a primary focus of the study from its
inception. Chapter 8 takes up, albeit in a limited way, the question of the power of businessmen *vis-à-vis* certain state elites, and
their lobbying activities. Chapter 9 summarises and discusses the
findings of the earlier chapters.

1.2 A TERMINOLOGICAL NOTE

I have already made references to 'top businessmen' and to the
'business elite'. To avoid confusion, it may be as well to state at
this stage what is, and is not, intended to be implied by these
phrases.
 In the discussion of the literature which follows I examine various sociological debates which revolve around what I call the
business elite. By this grouping I mean those who hold the higher
positions (for example, are main board directors) in the larger
non-state-owned enterprises, that is manufacturing, service and
financial companies.
 Throughout this discussion I refer to the business elite rather
than the economic elite, though the latter is the more commonly
used term. There are important reasons for doing so. The term
economic elite implies that the group in question has a major role
in national economic affairs, and it is clear that many groups other
than businessmen have such a role. Even if the economic elite were
taken to mean the heads of large economic organisations, it should
surely include the heads of nationalised industries and the civil
servants who deal with them. However, this study is concerned
solely with non-nationalised companies.[3] Equally, I intend to show
that the business elite have important roles other than the purely
economic.
 In using the term business elite I acknowledge that it may be
construed as implying a theoretical position. Elite theory is historically linked with attempts by Pareto and Mosca to create a political science on a different basis to that employed by Marx (see
Bottomore, 1966; Meisel, 1965). Thus Marxists are inclined to
rebuke sociologists, or even, as in the case of the Poulantzas-
Miliband exchanges, each other (Poulantzas, 1969; Miliband, 1970)

for using the term elite. They appear to feel that the mere use of the word elite implies that power can reside ultimately with a group other than the ruling class, and would prefer to confine their analyses to 'fractions of capital'.

I wish to emphasise that I do not intend to prejudge the issues of whether there is a ruling class, a power elite or competing elites in society. I use the term business elite in the same way that Giddens (1973;1974) refers to 'elite groupings'. It is a descriptive phrase to designate those in the top positions in the bigger firms.

Now it must be accepted that this description is vague. The problem of being more precise is quite simply that all theory in this area has a certain circularity. The business elite are said to perform certain roles; for example, they allocate resources within the corporation and hence within the economy, they lobby politicians, and so on. But it is not possible to delineate clear points at which people do or do not perform these roles, and one is in danger of defining the business elite as those who play the roles, and perform the functions, which are ascribed to the business elite.

Thus one is forced to make a definition for practical purposes whilst recognising that, if one studies people who correspond to it, some will not in fact do some or all of things ascribed to the group. Two assumptions underlie my definition. The first is that within the corporation members of the board of directors are by and large the group who are best rewarded, have greatest status and most power.[4]

Second, I assume that men who head larger companies are more likely to play the roles of the business elite than men in small companies. In other words, it is taken as self-evident that in an advanced industrial society those heading a multinational conglomerate employing tens of thousands can have an impact through the way they allocate capital, or can be politically influential, to an extent that is of an entirely different order to that of a firm employing half a dozen. Even if we accept the existence of a ruling class distinguished by its ownership of capital, I take it that people could share a similar position as members of such a class without necessarily having a similar political or ideological role in maintaining capitalism.

Thus, for empirical purposes, the business elite are taken to include many of the following: the main board directors of the largest 250 wholly British-owned companies (using turnover as the main, but not the only measure), together with the main board directors of the merchant banks (members of the Accepting Houses Committee); clearing banks; top twenty insurance companies; top twenty property firms; top twenty investment and unit trusts.

1.3   THE BUSINESS ELITE IN SOCIOLOGICAL THEORY

It is a fact attested to by simple observation that businessmen do not affect the lives of others only by the way they run the companies they head. For whatever reasons, they are to be found in other spheres: as politicians and local councillors; on the boards and committees of Quangos, charities, hospitals and schools; as wealthy men and patrons of the arts; as members of the aristocracy and landed gentry; as members themselves, and friends, of the powerful, the notorious, the beautiful, the high-ranking, the entertaining and the 'jet set'.

For the purposes of study and theoretical development, this exciting scenario has to be systematised and perhaps deprived thereby of some of its mystery (and fun). The sociological literature suggests a number of roles played by the business elite, and I will discuss these in turn. As I see them the roles are:
(a) an economic role - the primary role of their working lives as company directors;
(b) allied to (a), a role in the industrial relations system of the company;
(c) a role as members of a certain class or classes, and status grouping, in their own right;
(d) a role as the creators and maintainers of ideology;
(e) a role in the political system, most obviously but not exclusively as the defenders of the interests of business.

1.4 THE ECONOMIC ROLE OF BUSINESSMEN

It is obvious that the actions and attitudes of the business elite are important in the economic sphere. We can distinguish two rather different aspects of this: first, they are directly important in the economy of society as a whole in the decisions that they take regarding the pricing of goods and of labour, and the allocation of capital. Second, though clearly tied to the first, they act within the economic unit of the firm, fixing wage levels, determining conditions, manning levels, and other policies; in other words, they are part of the industrial relations system.

By and large, I shall try to keep these two aspects separate, and will discuss the former first. The business elite may be considered as managers, and as having all the roles that Mintzberg[5] ascribes to managers. But directors are seen in the literature as having particular functions in the firm. A reading of a number of discussions written over a thirty-year period[6] reveals a relative consensus on these. The tasks of the director may be said to be:
(a) to see that the company carries on business in accordance with the Memorandum or Articles of Association (in America, the Charter), and to put possible changes in these to the shareholders. And to ensure the long-term success of the company which entails,
(b) the safeguarding of corporate assets, having regard to changes in the structure of them, and to,
(c) approve important financial decisions and actions, and see that proper annual and interim reports are given to shareholders (in accordance with legal requirements);
(d) select the chief executive, and possibly other executives, and

thereby ensure the continuity of management;
(e) audit the performance of management, by receiving and calling
for reports on the company, and by questioning the chief executive and other executives at board meetings;
(f) remove the chief executive when his performance is inadequate;
(g) establish the objectives for the corporation, and ensure that
there are adequate strategies;
(h) establish the basic policies of the corporation;
(i) see to the continuity of the board.
The key elements of these tasks for the purposes of the sociologist
are the establishing of objectives for the corporation, the strategies for achieving these, and the policies which will be followed
in achieving them. But this brings us immediately to an area of
debate concerning the nature of the objectives which the boards
of large corporations do pursue. This is, of course, the ownership and control debate, stemming initially from a work of Berle
and Means (1932), and we must give the course of this debate
some attention here.

Following Wildsmith (1973), one can set out four propositions
that stem from Berle and Means's book. They are, that as capitalism develops:
(a) economic power in terms of control over assets tends more and
more to concentrate in a relatively small number of corporations;
(b) as this happens, the assets come under the control of managers who do not themselves own a significant part of the shares;
(c) the constraints of the capital market become an increasingly
ineffective discipline on the managers;
(d) managers develop goals other than those of profit maximisation
(which is the essence of the 'managerialist' position of which there
are a number of variations - see below).

Since the business elite, by definition, control the largest corporations, the processes suggested by these propositions should
be furthest advanced amongst them. There should be a significant
group of the controllers of industry who are themselves free of
the control of the shareholders and the capital market, and who
have goals for the company other than the maximisation of profit.

The truth of the first of the four propositions has been well
demonstrated.[7] The second, however, has stimulated a vigorous
debate, particularly in the United States, resulting in a whole
range of estimates of how many of the largest one hundred, two
hundred or more corporations are controlled by managers as opposed to owners.

Berle, in his original work, suggested that an 'owner' should
control at least 20 per cent of the shares. On this criterion, by
1967 it was found that some 85 per cent of the largest 200 US
companies were controlled by boards whose members were not owners of the corporation but managers (see also studies by Gordon,
1961; and Larner, 1966).[8] Yet, as Zeitlin (1974) points out, how
many shares the board themselves hold may not be a good guide
to the control position: both Rochester (1936) and Lundberg (1946)
concluded that many of the managers heading firms that Berle and

Means classified as manager-controlled were, in fact, installed by owners, even though the latter took no part in running the firms.

As can be seen, the kind of evidence put forward here, and the conclusions drawn from it, revolve around the question of how much stock is needed to control a company. By using different criteria, different researchers come to very different conclusions. Unfortunately, it seems that different amounts of stock may be adequate to control corporations in different circumstances. According to Zeitlin (1974), as little as 5 per cent of the equity may be sufficient in some cases. And discovering how much equity different individuals and institutions own is not easy, granted the use of 'pyramiding' and nominee shareholders.

The third of Berle and Means's propositions, that the capital market ceases to be a constraint on managers, depends on more than the actual owners not being in control positions in the firms or in touch with those who are. It depends also on stock being widely dispersed and the managers being freed from the constraints of the capital markets (and, particularly, having access to extra capital when they want it).

Leaving aside the question of whether managers ever feel themselves to be free of such constraints, even if they appear to be from the outside, there is still the possibility of informal groupings of shareholders, especially amongst banks and other institutions, which may exercise a controlling influence. This possibility led Burch (1972) to adopt an alternative methodology to those outlined above. He searched business and financial journals looking for evidence of control by such groups (called by him interest groups) other than those indicated as controlling in the annual reports. He found that only 40 per cent of firms could be said to be probably under manager control, with a further 15 per cent possibly so controlled but probably not. In the remainder of cases, according to Burch, there were reliable indications that individuals or interest groups controlled the firms.

Berle and Means's third proposition is the most crucial for the ownership and control thesis, but the one on which there is least relevant evidence. For it must be pointed out that all the data on the amounts of shares held by individuals and groups only points to the potential for control, either by one group or another. What is lacking is data on the extent to which various groups are either aware of this potential or make use of it.

This is apparent when we come to consider the next type of evidence most frequently introduced into the argument - that of interlocking directorships. Such research is often oriented to the notion, alluded to by Marx, but made more explicit by Hilferding (1910), that corporate control ultimately passes into the hands of finance capitalists. [9]

In principle, finance capitalists are those who have no direct interest in production or in everyday control of it, but who control the means of production simply because they own large amounts of capital, or the institutions that provide such capital. It is a weakness of more recent uses that financial controllers are seen as any high official or board member of a merchant bank, investment house, insurance company or pension fund,[10] irrespective of the role that such men play within the institutions or their own personal relationship to capital.

As De Vroey's (1975) discussion makes clear, Hilferding's main contention was that the growth in size and number of joint stock companies would lead to a concentration of power into the hands of relatively few big capitalists who would now control larger economic units with a reduced proportion of legal ownership. Hilferding also interpreted the noticeable intertwining of banks and industrial companies as indicating that big capitalists would increasingly be bankers. However, De Vroey, following Lenin, points out that the merger between industrial and financial capital does not have such automatic consequences; and, where such a merger occurs, the question of who has the upper hand must be decided in each individual case. This point has often been forgotten in more recent analysis.

It is simple enough to demonstrate that the directors of financial institutions are often invited, or invite themselves, to sit on the boards of large industrial and other commercial firms. This has been shown for the British case by Stanworth and Giddens (1975) and Whitley (1973) and, with respect to the United States, by Fitch and Oppenheimer (1970), Zeitlin (1974) and Domhoff (1967). The latter concludes from the fact that a majority of directors in industrial firms, banks and insurance companies are (by his definition) upper class, and the presence of corporate interlocking that 'the corporate economy is run by the same group of several thousand men'.[11]

Similarly, a well-known paper that makes the case for widespread control by representatives of financial interests in Britain is that of Brown (1968). Brown appears to see directors from banking and other institutions as able to control industrial and service firms by voting at board meetings. He distinguishes three types of control: family or tycoon control, co-ordinator control (in effect finance control) and managerial control.

Brown found that (in 1966) 47 of the top 120 company boards were co-ordinator controlled. But, having attempted to repeat Brown's work ten years on, I would suggest that either his definition of a co-ordinator-controller differs from mine or the position has changed greatly in the intervening years, for I found only eleven companies among the top 120 that were co-ordinator-controlled in 1976.[12]

A more complex analysis has also been carried out by Nyman and Silberston (1978). After reviewing the evidence of previous studies, they suggest that to determine who controls a firm one has to take account not only of shares held by individuals, that is, by the directors themselves and outside groups, but also the presence on the board of a member of the founding family, the other directorships of directors, and 'the identities of the chairman and managing director, their career history and the manner by which they came to be appointed'.

They made their own analysis of the control of the top 250 wholly British firms, using a more complex classification than those of previous studies. On the basis of this they concluded that approximately 56 per cent of the firms they looked at were still owner-controlled.

More direct evidence of the actual processes of control within companies suggests that management may play a much bigger role than research of the type undertaken by Brown or Nyman and Silberston would indicate. Pahl and Winkler (1974) investigated nineteen companies by observing each of the main board directors for a full day. They concluded that control of the firm often did not lie with the board as such but with a cabal or clique. This meant that control might lie partly with board members, partly with members of management outside the board. Pahl and Winkler suggest, contrary to most previous assumptions, that the more directorships a person has the more easily they may be manipulated and kept in the dark by other directors or managers. The writings of Mace (1971;1972) also suggest that on boards where there is a preponderance of non-executive directors, control may pass to the management.

Both Nyman and Silberston (1978) and Scott (1979) in his comprehensive review of the literature are aware of this evidence, but tend to ignore it. Yet in view of the small number of concrete examples that they produce of firms which are controlled by outsiders although apparently controlled by management, this would seem to be an important point. [13]

Turning to the fourth of Berle's propositions, we see that it suggests that managers will pursue different goals from those of owners. Berle's hope is that they will become responsive to the needs of society and pursue socially desirable aims as well as, or instead of, profit.

Even amongst those who accept that ownership has become separated from control there has not been agreement as to the aims which managers will have for the firms they control. It is possible to argue that managers are just as constrained as owners ever were and will pursue profit in a very similar manner; that they will attempt to pursue purely selfish ends, such as higher corporate salaries, increasing the value of their own shareholdings, or increasing the resources that they control and, allied with these suggestions, that once they have made a minimal profit they will be chiefly interested in the growth of the firm.

Once again, the attempts to test these hypotheses have been mainly of a statistical kind, but the results have not been very revealing. Nyman and Silberston (1978) list some ten different American and British studies from which all that emerges consistently is that owner-controlled firms have higher rates of profit, though even this is statistically significant in only two cases. One is inclined to wonder also, since no two authors agree on what is and what is not a managerially controlled firm, whether such studies can expect to be conclusive.

The studies by economists summarised by Nyman and Silberston,

however, tell only part of the story. For it may be that whatever
their values, owners and managers are constrained by the capital
market to pursue the same goals, which would account for the
fact that their performance in practice is very similar. To establish this we would need to examine the values and objectives of
the two groups concerned (that is owners and managers), and to
show that they do have different objectives.

So far, there is little evidence that they do. Pahl and Winkler,
in the study referred to above, state that they repeatedly encountered the concept of the 'professional manager' and directors who
embodied and articulated it. They continue however:

> Their idea of professionalism is not that usually employed by
> sociologists but more like that of actors, the ability to produce
> a competent performance in any circumstances no matter how
> unpromising. The indicators of successful performance are
> profits, growth and return on investment. The essence of the
> professional manager is his rigorous and exclusive dedication
> to hard financial values.

Pahl and Winkler point out that amongst the directors they encountered, both owners and managers expected the professional
manager to be more profit-conscious. However, it must be noted
that not all (or possibly not even a majority) of managers who
were encountered were professional in this sense. Elsewhere,
Winkler (1975) has stated that directors were often of two kinds:
those concerned only with money and making the maximum profit
in any given situation and those concerned with the technicalities
of their jobs. The latter could include financial specialists, who
were concerned with creating good management systems, just as
much as technical directors or other specialists.

The crux of Pahl and Winkler's argument, then, is not so much
that managers are oriented to financial goals, but that managers
oriented to profit, growth and return on investment are dominant
and becoming more so. However, we must look for evidence from
a wider and more representative sample than the nineteen companies that they were able to research before accepting this point
of view.

In fact, ever since Berle's 'Power Without Property' (1969) was
published, in which he suggests that managers of firms will develop a corporate conscience and begin to think of themselves as
responsible to the public outside the firm, his ideas have been attacked by those who accept the divorce of ownership from control
as real enough, but are far from optimistic about the consequences.

Thus, both Mason (1958) and Kaysen (1960) are unhappy with
the replacement of the competition and the controls afforded by
the market-place by a reliance on the ethics of managers. Kaysen
specifically recommends the break-up of large corporations. For,
he suggests, when a management with the intention of being
socially responsible sets out to balance the interests of the various
groups that come within the corporation's sphere of influence, it
inevitably does so from within its own conception of what these
interests legitimately are. Kaysen questions whether the back-

ground and training of business leaders qualifies them to make
the kind of judgments that are involved. In any case, he maintains that on some issues business attitudes are not in accordance
with what the national interest requires.

Galbraith (1967) also sees the corporation as largely freed from
the constraints of the market-place. Control of the corporation as
he sees it is vested in what he calls the technostructure, which
appears to be an amalgam of the middle managers and technical
specialists. The technostructure seeks, according to Galbraith, a
minimum level of profits and, contiguous with that, the maximum
obtainable sales growth and technical virtuosity. To achieve its
ends, it sets out, not to respond to public taste, but to manipulate
the tastes and values of the buying public.

In the United States a number of reports have been produced to
show that business has been responsive to social needs. Its efforts in such areas as hiring and training the hardcore unemployed,
providing assistance for black businesses and involvement in urban rehabilitation are cited in this regard (see studies by, amongst
others, Flower, Cohn and Austin).[14] In Britain Shenfield (1971)
has produced a set of case studies indicating how some company
boards perceive and carry out their social responsibility.

Nichols (1969) also considered the question of whether British
managers are developing orientations towards social as opposed
to purely financial goals. He studied 65 directors in fifteen firms
in a northern city. The technique used was a questionnaire in
which sets of statements with three alternative answers were presented to those who took part and they were asked to choose
between them. This was followed up with an interview.

The forced choice questions had answers in three categories:
(a) a 'laissez-faire' set, broadly speaking in line with the goals
of profit maximisation in all circumstances and presenting directors as responsible only to shareholders; (b) a set that presented
the director as serving the long-term interests of the corporation;
and (c) a set that saw a moral responsibility on the director to
take account of social needs.

Nichols's finding was that apart from one particular firm, where
the directors did favour the third category (the social responsibility answers), the largest group of choices was made from the
long-term company interest answers. But he further found that
businessmen had difficulty in distinguishing this set from the
third set and often explained the latter in terms of the former
(pp. 179-87). He concluded that probably the majority of businessmen saw no real contradiction in the pursuit of business aims and
of social goals.

Nichols's work is an important precursor of the present study,
and it returns us once again to the question of managers' values
and orientations; and hence to the subject of ideology, which is
to be taken up below. However, it is as well to point out that the
empirical basis is fairly limited: Nichols draws much of his sub-
stantive conclusion to the answers from just four forced choice
questions, and on two of the three sets of alternatives many

businessmen saw little essential difference. Further, although
Nichols achieved a high acceptance rate (only three firms approached would not co-operate), the actual sample is not ideal,
consisting as it does of both managers and directors from firms
which are either comparatively small in size, or would have been
subsidiaries of larger groups. (This is not clear from Nichols's
account.)

The issue of social responsibility brings us to a major and largely
uninvestigated problem of the ownership and control debate. That
is that even if there is a limited move towards more control by managers, and even if we can demonstrate that the behaviour of businessmen is different from what it was in the nineteenth century,
or that new ideologies have emerged, it has still to be demonstrated
that one is the consequence of the other. We need both inter-
company and cross-cultural studies.

For as Cheit (1964) points out, the emergence of an ideology of
social responsibility may be simply the response by businessmen
to the new social pressures that they find on them, especially if
they find that these are not incompatible with the making of good
profits. Cheit mentions that business has come, in several countries, to accept governmental planning in economic affairs that
once would have been unacceptable. Businessmen also now accord
a legitimacy to organised labour that they would once not have done.
(See also Heilbroner's article in the same collection.)

This too may simply be because they no longer have any choice
but to accept it. Cheit sums this up in the heading of one of his
sections: the gospel of social responsibility is important as a conservative response to a changing environment. [15]

Let me then sum up the debate concerning the economic role of
businessmen. It is accepted that the economy is dominated by a
relatively (relative, that is, to 60 or 100 years ago) small number
of corporations. It is accepted that many of those in positions of
power in such corporations have no obvious kinship connections
with the original founders and owners, nor a high percentage of
the share capital.

From this point we have a series of open questions. Are the managers placed in control of the corporations by hidden groups of
capitalists? Does the presence of bankers and insurance or investment company directors on corporate boards indicate the existence
of hidden networks of control by capitalist interests? Do the personal values of the 'managers' differ from those of the capitalists?
And, if they do, are the managers constrained, either by the
presence of financiers on their boards or the capital market more
generally, to pursue the traditional goals of capitalism? Are such
changes as are apparent in business ideology over time merely
adaptations by managers and capitalists alike to the changing business environment?

We might be closer to answering some of these questions if there
had been more first-hand studies of businessmen, rather than the
reliance which there has been on statistical analysis. For example,
a detailed investigation of the careers of business managers might

have shown the extent to which they owe their positions to capitalist influence. And a comparison of the values of capitalists and
managers would clearly go to the heart of the debate.

Although this debate was not the starting point for this investigation, the data collected was highly relevant to it. I make no
claim to have answered the questions posed above, but the data
presented here does represent a new approach to some of them.
(See in particular chapter 5.)

1.5 BUSINESSMEN AND INDUSTRIAL RELATIONS

In theory (and, as we shall see, in practice) the main board's
concerns are said to be the setting of objectives for the company
and the determining of strategies to achieve these. When it comes
to putting these strategies into operation, we enter the realms of
management and industrial relations, and there are, of course,
numerous works which concern good practice in these fields.

The focus of this enquiry was primarily with class, status and
power at the societal level rather than within the firm. Yet it is
often held that men draw their beliefs to a large extent from their
primary group experience, amongst which the firm itself may be
of considerable importance. Thus, in considering their values and
beliefs more widely, one has to take account of businessmen's
views of relationships within the firm, their views, that is, not so
much of industrial relations in detail, but rather of the overall
climate or framework within which industrial relations takes place.

In fact the opinion has often been expressed, and is enshrined
in the recommendations of a Royal Commission, the Donovan
Commission, (1968) that industrial relations should be a concern
of the main board. [16] Thus it was certainly not irrelevant to
enquire into these matters in this study.

Alan Fox, in his evidence to that same Royal Commission, drew
attention to a divide which he saw in the attitudes of top managers
(Fox, 1966). Fox contrasts what he calls the unitary and the pluralist views of the firm. The unitary view sees the logic of the
enterprise as pointing towards a unified authority and loyalty
structure, with managerial prerogative being legitimised by all
participants. From this viewpoint, workers' behaviour in opposing
management is seen as illogical or against their own interests.
Unions are likewise regarded as a historical carry-over, the outcome of sectional greed, or as vehicles for those who seek to sub-
vert the existing social order.

Fox's contrast is the pluralist view of the organisation, a conception apparently taken from Cyert and March (1963). [17] In this,
the organisation is viewed as a coalition of bargaining groups, a
complex of tensions and claims which have to be managed so that
everybody can pursue their own individual or group aspirations.
Trade Unions are accepted by pluralists as legitimate expressions
of challenge to management rule.

Fox has been both advocate and critic of the pluralist perspective.

In a later paper (Fox, 1973), he states that the pluralist perspective represents a kind of Parsonian compromise. Collective
bargaining can take place between parties in the business enterprise because each group recognises the other's aspirations as
valid, and both sides limit their claims. Pluralism presupposes a
nucleus of shared values and norms about the aims and place of
the enterprise, but serves to screen the actual disparities of
power that exist between management and labour. It is, in fact,
the high point of enlightened managerialism.

Fox's views are not without their critics (for example, Wood and
Elliott, 1977), but that is not the point at issue here. What is of
interest is the contrast in values noted by Fox, the existence of
dual ideologies.

An interesting comment on Fox's conceptions is given by Winkler (1974) in a paper based on the observational studies made with
Pahl (1974). Winkler found that:

> Most conspicuously absent from the environments of directors
> were workers. Most directors had no significant contact with
> manual or clerical staff other than their secretaries. This
> generalisation applied with equal strength across all the com-
> panies, regardless of size or the form of the industrial relations
> system.

> Where directors came into contact with workers the contacts were
> brief, sporadic and of a ritualised kind that would not allow the
> directors to gain any insight into the workers' interests, goals,
> opinions, problems or personal situations. They conceived of work-
> ers as a cost, as, in fact, they viewed shareholders, and only
> managers were differently regarded. Thus, they tended to have a
> normative expectation that the labour-intensive functions of their
> operations would operate smoothly and without trouble.

How do directors come to know what they do know about industrial relations? Winkler lists eight sources[18] and states that directors'
views of workers were often stereotypes, and inconsistent stereotypes at that. The directors activated those conceptions of workers
which best furthered their own long-term interests.

Most important, according to Winkler, directors' attitudes to
workers as revealed in the statements they made privately amongst
themselves were strongly 'us versus them', or, in Fox's terminology, an 'extreme form of the pluralist conception'. And he goes
on to ask 'who is controlling whose image of society?'[19] for since
directors' views of workers are formed in crisis or bargaining situations, or else from the media, it is not perhaps surprising, after
a long history of socialist activism in Britain and in the light of the
view the media take of industrial relations,[20] if directors do adopt
such attitudes.

Winkler's work cannot be accepted uncritically, however. Aside
from the very high rejection rate in gaining access to firms, his
statement that his findings applied to all sizes of firm, irrespective
of size or type, is most surprising, and leads one to question the
representativeness of the sample, or the soundness of the technique for obtaining a complete picture of how people think. Winkler

criticises questionnaire and interview studies for inviting and receiving bland assurances and half-truths about directors' attitudes and behaviour in industrial relations. Yet, whilst we may accept the evidence of observation of directors' lack of contact with workers, and lack of involvement and lack of concern in industrial relations, we may also ask whether the attitudes they were seen to express are necessarily representative of their views or indicative of their image of society, as Winkler takes them to be. Could it be, perhaps, that only those with strong feelings on the subject or those who were in a bargaining or crisis situation, actually demonstrated any attitude at all? This study takes up similar issues (chapter 6) and, as we shall see, produces some similar findings, but some differences also.

1.6 BUSINESSMEN IN THE CLASS STRUCTURE

The debate over the ownership and control of corporations is ultimately a debate about the class position of businessmen. Starting from the premise that businessmen were once the bourgeoisie, the thesis of the separation of ownership and control seeks to deny the validity of Marxism by maintaining that the structure of industry is now so changed that a genuine change has taken place in the structure of society. This is particularly the claim of Berle himself (especially in Berle, 1960), but it is also evident in Dahrendorf's (1959) thesis that classes distinguished by ownership or otherwise of property are but a particular case of the more general basis of class which is now revealed to be authority relations, and in Bell's writing on post-industrial society (Bell, 1961).

Proponents of a Marxist viewpoint would perhaps regard the view of Marx's thought challenged by the thesis as oversimplified or deliberately falsified. Certainly, Marx himself recognised the growing size of companies, and the tendency towards the concentration of wealth in fewer and fewer centres. He was also well aware of the existence of the absentee landlord, the hired manager, and the joint stock corporation, and none of these appears to have led him to change his essential conclusions about the nature of the capitalist system.

It has been maintained, on the basis of certain Marx's statements on these subjects in 'Capital' and the 'Theories of Surplus Value', that in his description of the historical development of Britain, as opposed to his earlier philosophical or polemical work, Marx specifically included in his theories a middle class (see, for example, Swingewood, 1975). This middle class would include such diverse groups as the petit bourgeoisie, shopkeepers and other middle-men, managers of economic enterprises and their assistants, as well as an 'ideological' group including lawyers, artists, journalists, clergy and state officials.

If this is the case, it is not apparent how this 'middle class' fits into Marx's seemingly clear contention elsewhere that in developed capitalist societies two classes, the bourgeoisie and the proletariat,

become increasingly opposed. If a middle class is recognised within the Marxian model, it is hard to see how the essential elements
of class struggle and the two major classes can be retained; if it
is not recognised, then it leaves certain groups, and most obviously the hired managers who run economic enterprises, in an
ambiguous position.

Sociologists, of course, have not had to rely on the separation
of ownership and control or the 'managerialist' school of thought
in seeking an alternative conception of class structure, for Weber
had long before offered a refinement of Marx's analysis. Though
this is widely known, it is worth setting it down here as it indicates why there are such acute problems in studying class imagery
and class consciousness.

In Weber's discussion, class is no longer seen as resulting from
the relations of production, but from the differential life chances
that different groups have in the market. Thus, the basis of class
formation in the ownership, or lack of ownership, of property is
accepted, but alongside the classes so created there are said to
be 'commercial classes'. The latter stem from the varying extent
to which different groups have marketable skills, that is, hold
management positions or have professional, clerical or manual
skills.

Weber then distinguishes just four 'social classes', these, presumably, being groups whose position relative to the market is
roughly similar and recognised by them as being so. The four are:
the manual working class, the petit-bourgeoisie, the property-
less intelligentsia and technical specialists, and the 'classes privileged through property and education'.[21]

Alongside the social classes, Weber points out that there are
status groupings, status being an 'effective claim to social esteem
in terms of positive or negative privileges'. Status can stem from
a number of attributes, including social class position, and one
effect of the status order, Weber believes, is that it may hinder
the free development of the market. In effect, what he appears to
be saying here is that by restricting certain sorts of goods, status
groups can stand against groups whose power stems solely from
control of property.

Finally, Weber adds the formation of political parties in modern
societies as an element of power distribution. Parties are specifically oriented towards the acquisition of power, but from Weber's
definition it appears that he means more than the conventional
political party, and would include groups that are often now called
interest groups, Together in Weber's own well-known formulation,
'classes', 'status groups' and 'parties' are phenomena of the distribution of power in the community.

To this it might be added that these are phenomena of power in
society, but they are not the only phenomena of importance to its
maintenance and distribution for, as Weber's work shows, the
existence of ideologies and the position and manipulation of these
within the culture of society are also important.

Weber's analysis shows why class is so difficult to study in an advanced society. The classes that he delineates may or may not exist, or the division between the propertied and the unpropertied may indeed be the only one of significance, but class is bound up with status, and status groupings may serve to blur the edges or cut across class groupings. Classes may be well-defined, but status, a claim to esteem, can have infinite gradations. And again, there are formal political allegiances (Weber's parties) which may be formed for expediency but which can obscure class divisions.

Class would be a somewhat empty concept if it remained a purely theoretical one. Marx himself maintained that a class is only truly a class when its members are conscious of it and take action to protect its interests. The requirement that members of a class be conscious of it appears to be implicit also in Weber's move from the statements of the basis of class to the definitions of the four main social classes.[22] Thus, the links between people's position within society and their conceptions of it have been much investigated. Within Weber's conception the class position of the business elite can be seen as ambiguous: they may be property-owners or not, privileged through property and education or technical specialists. And whilst the business elite has a clear interest in defending the interests of business (and has organisations specifically for that purpose), it has not been clear what is its overt class identification, or whether within it there is some variation in identification.

The current literature, especially where it deals with ideology, sometimes implies that the beliefs and values of elite groupings concerning class and status are straightforward. In fact, a number of interpretations are available; it is suggested variously that an 'upper class' will be one of the most class-conscious groups in society (Baltzell, 1958); that their class view will be the culturally dominant one, a legitimatory ideology, incorporated into the meaning systems of the middle class and much of the working class (Parkin, 1971); that elite groups may deny the significance of class as such (Giddens, 1973); or, as we saw above in the case of directors, that they may hold a conception similar to that of the traditional manual worker (Winkler, 1974).

Since a large section of this study is concerned with the beliefs and values of businessmen concerning social class and status it is necessary to give some attention to studies in this area more generally. Thus, in the next section I take up the problems of studying 'images of society', and will return to the specific components of businessmen's thinking in the next chapter. Those well acquainted with this field will find much of the next section familiar, but it will serve to set the framework for this investigation.

1.7 DIVERSITY IN CLASS IMAGERY

Perhaps in the past it would have been superfluous to undertake the research reported later in this volume. Who the bourgeoisie, or the middle class, were would have been clear both to observers and members of the groups concerned. They were that class of

urban-based merchants who stood apart both from the rural landowning aristocracy and gentry and the mass of labourers. To those
merchants were added, as the industrial revolution proceeded, the
entrepreneurs, the founders of business and the owners of work-
shops.

Later, as Cole (1950) has discussed, a group emerged catering
to the needs of, and mixing with, this bourgeoisie: shopkeepers,
clergy, professional men of various kinds. These groupings together constituted the middle class or classes, which stood below
the aristocracy, and those few of the better-established capitalists,
merchants and financiers whom the aristocracy accepted as near-
equals, but clearly above the ordinary workmen.

Since this stage (in Britain it would have been roughly around
the middle of the nineteenth century), the advanced capitalist
societies have become much more complex. The number of administrators, managers, professional and semi-professional workers,
clerks and technicians has been greatly expanded. So too have the
cities and towns, and the number of skilled and semi-skilled workers who dwell in them.

One result of this is that sociologists and other observers find
it hard to define what the middle class is and where its boundaries
occur. Amongst British authors, Lewis and Maude (1949) gave no
definition. Cole (1950), though he specified a number of occupations which might (or might not) be middle-class, maintained
that all they had in common was an opposition to further levelling
down. Raynor (1969) too does not define the middle class as a class,
rather he refers to a 'middle stratum' of people, who fall in the
middle of the hierarchies of class, status and power.

The point here is that once we would have expected little variation in the views of members of society about the nature of the
stratification system and their place within it. When the social
order was, or where it still is, based on inherited ownership of
land or the lack of it, then whole families become socially fixed
over generations. The merchants mentioned above are a group
whose position is not based on land tenure, as are craftsmen, shopkeepers and the clergy, but with the exception of the latter these
too may be inherited positions.

Thus in rural areas there may still be what Plowman, Minchington
and Stacey (1962)[23] call 'local social status systems'. Such systems
depend for their operation and maintenance on the personal knowledge that members of communities have of other people in the
locality. In the contemporary community of this type, as described
by Stacey *et al.* (1960), the hierarchical order places the local
aristocrat at the top, together with the local members of the gentry.
One or two wealthy businessmen may mix with these, but otherwise businessmen, professionals and shopkeepers constitute a
separate rank again; workmen of various types rank below these.

In such a system people's family background, or 'breeding',
count for as much as acquired wealth or position. But such systems
seem to be declining: Stacey reported the existence of one in Banbury in the early 1950s, but by the time of her repeat study it had

all but disappeared (Stacey *et al.*, 1975).

Correspondingly, in studying urban communities, or groupings within them, sociologists have referred as much to internal disagreement as to consensus. [24] For it is clear that, if nothing else, people in different positions in the stratification order tend to perceive the nature of social class and social status in different ways; to assign different positions to different groups of people, and to vary widely in the amount of social conflict they perceive. [25]

The major distinction that has been made is between the conception generally held by middle-class groupings and those held by the working class. Empirically, these have been treated as white-collar occupational groups and manual workers, and much of the literature on the subject of images of society has concentrated on the latter. And whilst some of this research has been geared to specific problems of sociological theory, [26] there does seem to have been a belief that middle-class norms and values are so accessible as to need little direct research. But if we examine the literature concerning working-class images of society and apply similar considerations to the middle-class (or upper-class) elites, we find a far more complex situation than has so far been allowed for.

British theory concerning working-class images of society is based on a number of studies, particularly those made in the 1950s by, for example, Hoggart (1957), Bott (1954) and Young and Willmott (1957). The findings of these were, however, paralleled by research in other European countries, for example, the studies by Willener (1957) and Popitz *et al.* (1957). And whilst there are certain difference of emphasis and ideological tradition with regard to trade unionism and political parties, the picture that emerges from American research is similar. (See Lane (1961) and Hyman in Bendix and Lipset (1953).)

It appeared from these studies that a substantial minority grouping identified with a class other than the one into which it might be objectively placed, either in the label it adopted or its definition of classes or in other attitudes. And even among those who call themselves working-class, there have been found to be substantial variations in belief systems. One problem for theory has been to explain these.

The underlying premises of European theory are that a person's beliefs and values are related not only to their own particular circumstances as a manual or white-collar worker, or even the finer divisions of status and reward, but also to their whole interpretation of society, with respect to its structure and the opportunities within it. The latter are called 'images of society', although the term in practice has been used rather widely to cover almost anything from a person's social norms and values, to the specific picture of society which the sociologist extracts from him in interviews and questionnaire studies. In a slightly different terminology, which I shall adopt here, Parkin (1971) refers to 'meaning systems' which are shared sets of beliefs and values, and adaptive responses, to which individuals can refer when contemplating their own position in the stratification system.

It will be seen below that somewhat disparate elements are brought together which attempt to relate the individual or group's objective situation, norms and values, to their abstract conceptions of society and to the propensity to various forms of social action. These variables - objective situation, values, abstract conceptions and social action - can be further broken down into sub-variables, themselves interrelated (as shown in Figure 1.1). Taking just the four main categories, it is often not clear what the relationship between them is thought to be.

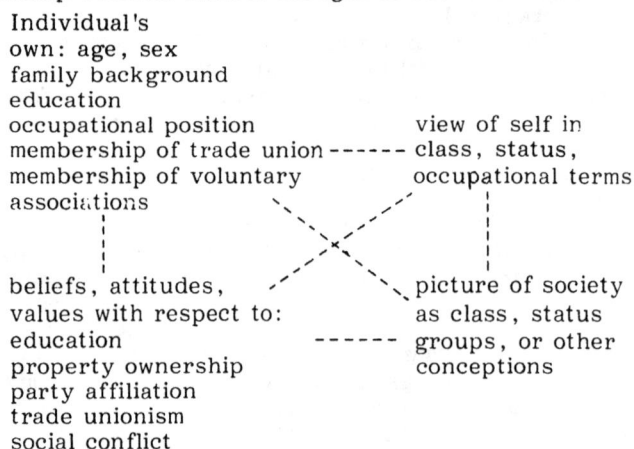

Individual's
own: age, sex
family background
education
occupational position   view of self in
membership of trade union ------ class, status,
membership of voluntary   occupational terms
associations

beliefs, attitudes,   picture of society
values with respect to: as class, status,
education   ------ groups, or other
property ownership   conceptions
party affiliation
trade unionism
social conflict

Figure 1.1 Variables to be related in models of class imagery

Perhaps the single most influential theoretical writing in this field has been Lockwood's (1966) paper. In this, a scheme is presented in which the images of society held by three groups of manual workers are related to two sets of objective variables, the work situation and the community structure. Two of the three types of manual worker, the 'deferential' and 'proletarian' had been extensively studied; the third, the 'privatised' worker was to figure strongly in a major subsequent study (Goldthorpe *et al.*, 1969).

In Lockwood's paper three aspects of the work situation were seen as important: involvement in the job, interaction and identification with workmates and interaction and identification with the employer. Similarly, the variable, community structure has three elements: the existence or lack of an interactional status system (that is a well-recognised system in which people mix socially with people of similar status); the existence or otherwise of an occupational community (in which people mix to a large extent with workmates outside work); and the extent of occupational differentiation.[27]

Lockwood attempted to explain the variations in working-class imagery which had been noted up to that time, but he also placed the middle class within the scheme, although, in his words, 'only because they give the paradigm a certain pleasing symmetry'. Middle-class occupations were thought to have all three features of work situation mentioned, and the middle-class community was likewise viewed as having the three characteristics referred to.

A rather more general approach has been developed by Parkin (1971), who discussed not images of society', but rather what he calls meaning systems. The latter are not defined, but from the text it is clear that they constitute systems of beliefs, and of norms and values, through which individuals or groups can interpret and make sense of their own personal situation in the class structure, and which will guide their action in relation to it.

Parkin distinguishes three types of value system. The first of these is the dominant value system, which promotes the endorsement of existing inequality. This is clearly the value system we expect to find amongst elite groupings, and both upper and middle classes. Parkin's conception here reverts to the Marxist notions of a ruling ideology, and he suggests that whilst there may be differences in outlook between, for example, aristocratic (traditional) and managerial or entrepreneurial elites, they are not likely to be fundamental with respect to the values underlying class inequality. The acceptance by less privileged groupings of these values is likely to result in conceptions of the class, status and reward structure in either *deferential* or *aspirational* terms.[28]

The second value system, originating in the traditional urban working-class community, is the subordinate, which is essentially that held by Lockwood's 'proletarian' worker. This value system does not suggest a version of the opportunity structure as open, nor of society as an organised unity, rather it promotes its own view of the importance of community and neighbourly togetherness, and of shared distrust of outsiders, particularly higher status groups, of 'them' as opposed to 'us'.

Parkin is inclined to be sceptical of the subordinate value system as a manifestation of emerging class-consciousness, or even of a base on which such consciousness can be built. He points to a third value system, emanating from the mass political party, as being the one that leads to such a radical, or oppositional, interpretation of class structure.

Parkin's conceptualisation, although in some ways matching Lockwood's, has some differences. It is altogether more general, and it refers specifically to value systems. The strength of this is that it allows for a more flexible interpretation of attitudes and behaviour because, as Parkin presents his scheme, it would appear that individuals might, at different times, be aware of, and be guided by, any of the three value systems. Quite possibly, only minority groupings of the population would be expected to have a value system that fits neatly into only one of the three types.

This strength, however, is at the same time a weakness, since Parkin does not detail the precise content of any of these value systems, nor their manifestations in behaviour, nor does he specify the circumstances in which any particular value system is most likely to be found. His model is not as specific as Lockwood's and, perhaps, in consequence has not been examined in the light of research specifically oriented to it. Parkin does quote similar sources to Lockwood, and he refers to Lockwood's paper itself, but he particularly neglects the work situation, which in Lockwood's conceptualisation appears as strongly as the local community as a source of orientations to class and status inequality. [29]

Lockwood's (1966) paper has led in turn to a profusion of studies which wholly or partly examine in some form the 'images of society', or the value systems of the working class. (See the work edited by Bulmer (1975) for a collection of these studies.) The exact findings are not at issue here, but if we trace the evolution of such studies in this area over the past twenty years (or even more), we notice four points of importance. First, we notice that from an early divergence of methodology, there has been in recent years a certain convergence on the technique of the open-ended interview. Amongst earlier studies, Hoggart (1957) drew on his own personal experiences and observations amongst the working class. Bott (1954) relied on very extensive interviewing of a relatively small number of people, Popitz *et al.* (1957) used open-ended interviewing, but used questions on a variety of subjects, and did not directly raise the issue of class or status, Willener (1957) did put the question directly, but allowed for open-ended answers. In a range of other studies, however, questionnaires or highly structured interviews were used. [30] In more recent research, however, researchers seem to have settled on the open-ended interview as the most suitable technique, raising a range of topics in the interview, with the specific issue of social class amongst them.

Such a methodology can be defended on the grounds that respondents are not forced into making artificial choices; they can thus discuss the topics in their own language, choose their own categories, and hence reveal their value system, and their picture of society.

It also brings its own problems, such as those of establishing any reliability for such a technique, of the extent of the validity of such answers (though this is not confined to interview technique), and of coding the data. I shall return to these in chapter 3.

A second point, however, is that a convergence of methodology is not matched by a convergence in the results. Lockwood's model described at most four types of image of society, even if one sees the middle-class viewpoint as distinct from the deferential proletarian. Willener (1957) and Popitz *et al.* (1957) had already described more, however, and, to cite some more recent studies, Davies (1967) describes five models of society, split into a total of fourteen sub-types. So too, Brown and Brannen (1970) researching on shipbuilding workers report some fourteen distinct 'images of society', though again these can be reduced to five main types. Similarly, in recent work in Melbourne, Australia, Hiller (1975 a and b) has found it necessary to describe more models, and more complex ones, than those contained in Lockwood's scheme. [31]

A third feature of the recent literature is that there has been more attention given to describing the models of society encountered by the researcher, than in accounting for how the subgroups of respondents come to hold them. This is true, for example, of the extensive work by Hiller, cited above, and claims that this is in some way a 'phenomenological approach' can in no way blind us to the fact that neither theory nor empirical research is really advanced by mere description, although, to be fair, this is not true of some of the papers in the collection edited by Bulmer, which draw our attention to factors, such as religious belief, or the extent and nature of bureaucratisation in the work setting, which can be of importance in understanding how a particular group of workers views its situation.

Finally, one might remark that the culminative effect of reading much of this research is to throw into doubt the whole idea that respondents hold some fixed pictures of society which researchers have reliably tapped. The profusion of descriptions of images of society, set against the fact that they are derived from coding open-ended interviews, leads one at least to ask the question of whether the typologies are typologies of all the images of society the researchers could think up, or all those the respondents actually held.

These problems have meant that it has not been possible to demonstrate the connections between work and community structures and ideal types of class imagery in practice. Lockwood, however, maintains that this is to be expected when reality is compared with ideal types. And it must be accepted that, whilst others have suggested factors which may be of importance, his paper remains the only one to explicate the linkages between work, community structure and social imagery.

However, the most important objection to the studies of social imagery may be the reliance on a single methodology. It can be argued that allowing respondents to state their abstract impressions of the stratification structure is artificial, and, in itself, uninteresting. Class is only relevant, it may be said, when people *are* forced to make choices.

Indeed, a number of authors have pointed out the difference between answers to abstract questions on class inequality, and other issues, and those to more concrete issues with which the respondent is concerned. Mann (1970), reviewing a whole range of studies in England and America, concluded that the working class may accept dominant values when abstract questions are put to them, but reject them or, more characteristically, give inconsistent answers on more concrete issues. Mann suggested that: 'The individual has contact with society only through primary and secondary groups and consensus in the prevailing order is *imposed* on the working class.' Thus, 'So far as the individual is concerned his normative connections with the vast majority of his fellow citizens may be extremely tenuous, and his commitment to general dominant values may be irrelevant to his compliance with the expectations of others.' Mann puts forward the hypothesis, of some relevance here, that only those sharing in societal power need to develop consistent societal values.

What Mann is saying is that to the extent that abstract conceptions of society are important and necessary to people they may accept dominant values, but in taking practical action they may act in their own self-interest. The most obvious example of this is the widespread acceptance, even by union members, of the opinion poll statements to the effect that 'trade unions in this country have too much power'. Whilst they acquiesce in this at the abstract level, they may still follow their own leaders, or support or push their leaders into positions of active militancy in practice. Parkin's conceptualisation takes account of this point, for Parkin views the subordinate value system as the result of accommodation to the facts of inequality, and in effect an acceptance of dominant values is negotiated and absorbed into an abstract philosophical acceptance. In the deferential value system, by contrast, the dominant values are reinforced by personal contact and primary relationships.

Thus the current literature concerning 'images of society' takes us to this point: we have a number of studies of working-class images of society, and a smaller number that focus on the middle class. We have theoretical models which attempt to relate certain objective factors (work or community situation) to subjective perceptions of class and status. These models are not well-validated, and we are faced with the option of either adding in more objective factors or looking for some other explanation. The most usual such explanation is that the abstract conceptions of society held by many members reflect dominant values, and these values conflict with their conceptions of their more immediate situations and interests.

The question to be posed in this study is: what precisely are the dominant values of our society? If they are to be found among any grouping, then presumably the business elite, above all, will hold them. To judge from the foregoing discussion, the 'images of society' of the business elite will contain a more-or-less uniform collection of legitimating ideas or, to give it a more usual name, it will constitute an ideology. However, one might at least wonder whether the one-way flow of values, from dominant to subjected groups is as simple as it is presented. Is there no flow in the other direction? How do elite groups react to and adapt to countervailing ideas?

In chapter 2 I will consider at some length the various sources of business elite thought in Britain and, of course, in the later chapters I will present some empirical data concerning their images of society or meaning systems. First, however, I wish to consider another role of the business elite which this section has alluded to, which is their role as ideologists.

1.8 THE BUSINESS ELITE AS IDEOLOGISTS

It was somewhat ingenuous to introduce the concept of dominant values in the discussion of images of society as though it had been invented to resolve the problems of research on images of society. Social theorists had long attached importance to legitimating ideas or ideology. Most notably, Marx and Engels saw the importance of ideology in maintaining capitalism. In their famous statement:

The ideas of the ruling class are in every epoch the ruling ideas.... The class which has the means of material production at its disposal has control at the same time over the means of mental production, so that thereby, generally speaking, the ideas of those who lack the means of material production are subject to it. (Marx and Engels, 1970, p. 64)

Though the term ideology had previously been used in France (see Mannheim, 1960), it was the use by Marx and Engels which brought the concept into prominence. They applied the term to systems of thought which are determined by some conditions outside of them, and which are not themselves ingredients of consciousness. Thus, in a number of contexts, Marx uses the term ideology to refer to social theories or thought developed in accordance with bourgeois political economy. In this sense, his use of the word is condemnatory. For, as Marx saw it, the bourgeoisie could not fully understand the contradictions inherent in capitalism, and, partly because it was not in their immediate interest to do so, could not understand how their own social consciousness was determined by their own (material) situation.

As Marx recognised, the bourgeoisie are naturally opposed to the development of revolutionary consciousness among the proletariat. And the development is hindered because, as he and Engels put it, the bourgeoisie have 'the ruling ideas'. In this formulation Marx gives an active part to ideology in cementing together, albeit temporarily, capitalist society. Yet the statement is capable of two rather different interpretations. Since Marx believes that it is primarily changes in the economic substructure - the relationships of production - that determine change in the superstructure, it could be argued that ideas concerning social reality are primarily, though not completely, so determined. Since men fail to see the arbitrary and irrational nature of social relationships, they accept what exists and explain social reality as though it has to be the way it is. Such ideas are thus 'of the ruling class' in the sense that they maintain that class.

An alternative viewpoint gives the ruling class a more active role. It could be argued that from the universe of ideas and beliefs, some conducive to their position, some unconducive, some irrelevant, they or their spokesmen, and thinkers in accordance with their values, deliberately select those protective of their position. By virtue of their ability to publicise, utilise, and impose these ideas, they ensure that these beliefs are accepted by other classes.

This problem, the problem of how ideologies arise, is exactly that posed by Weber's writings on the Protestant ethic (1930). In considering the rise of capitalism, Weber saw both a certain economic and technological development as necessary, but also pointed to the changes in values associated with it. In particular, he suggested that the values of the Protestant (Calvinist) form of Christianity, current prior to the emergence of capitalism, were conducive to the values of rationality, discipline and utility that capitalism demands (see also Birnbaum, 1953).

Without taking any particular position in the debate over religion and the rise of capitalism, one can see that the interplay between ideas and institutions is potentially very complex. On the one hand, Marx and Engels appear to take the position that relations of production determine ideas, though they do not propose a social psychological theory that adequately explains the relationship between the two. Weber's position suggests that some sets of beliefs or ideas have a relatively autonomous existence, and can have an influence on institutions. Scheler, in turn, suggested an interaction between the two spheres: existential factors do not 'create' ideas, but they do hinder or quicken the extent to which ideas are adopted, advanced or developed (see Merton, 1957, chs. 12 and 13).

Thus, the first problem raised by the concept of ideology, and one which recurs in studies of business ideology, is that of the source of ideas and their relationship to those whose interests they are said to serve. The second problem is connected and just as difficult to resolve satisfactorily. The implication of Marx's writing is that ideas concerned with social reality that arise from outside the Marxist perspective are false, and merely serve the *status quo*. Bourgeois political economy is particularly attacked on these grounds.

So we have the contrast between 'ideology' and 'scientific Marxism', and one task which later Marxist writers have set themselves is to explain in what sense Marxism is scientific. There are several approaches. Lukács (1971), directly following Marx, saw the proletariat alone as able to understand and comprehend true reality. This is because the proletariat is the rising class, the class which will put into effect revolutionary Marxism. Thus, although it is ultimately in the interest of all that capitalism should be overthrown by revolution, only the proletariat are able to come to consciousness of this. If the proletariat do not then they have a 'false consciousness'.

Lukács' writings have not been considered satisfactory by Marxist theorists, however. For one thing, he seems to take the view that the revolution depends only on the coming to consciousness of the proletariat, and ignores the other changes, economic and political, which Marx saw as leading to revolution. And he ignores the question of how ideas (even those of Marxism) come to the proletariat: how do they break out of false consciousness if ideas are not brought in from outside (say, by a revolutionary party)? And as a further problem, one might ask why the bourgeoisie, generally better educated and placed for study, are unable to develop an understanding of the alienating effect of capitalism.

More recently the term ideology has also come to play a key role in the theories of Althusser, and these in turn involve another solution to the epistemological problems of the concept. In Althusser's earlier works (1969, 1970) a specific distinction is drawn once again between ideology and Marxist historical science, the difference in this case being that Althusser sees not the whole of Marx's theoretical writings, but only those dating from the 'epistemological break' (c.1845) as being scientific.

Althusser's earlier statements as to what makes a theory scientific are both obscure, and ultimately, in my view, unsatisfactory. He rejects all attempts to consider the scientificity of theories in terms external to themselves. His own assertion of the scientific nature of Marx's works is based on what he calls a 'symptomatic' reading of them which, in turn, is made possible by the principles demonstrated by the works themselves. (A circularity which he himself has noted.) Key aspects of a scientific theory to Althusser appear to be that it is open, and capable of development and restatement, whereas an ideological theory poses the questions it wishes to answer in such a way as to arrive at predetermined answers, and is therefore closed and sterile.

In more recent work (Althusser, 1971), however, he has developed his theory of ideology to give it a specific role in relation to the state and to the reproduction of relations of production. Althusser does not see ideology as a false representation of the real, that is, of real social relationships (that is, as false consciousness). Rather, in his conceptualisation it appears to refer to the position of the subject in imaginary relationships. Ideology has the function of adapting the individual to his place in society, and, thus, Althusser's perspective is distinctive among Marxists in seeing ideology, as he uses the term, as necessary to communist societies as well as to capitalist ones.

Althusser rejects the legal form of the state as the basis for analysis of it. The state is rather defined by its function which is the reproduction of class society. In this Althusser follows Gramsci, and he does so also in his stress on the importance of ideology. Using his terminology there are Repressive State Apparatuses (presumably the police, military, etc.) which are centralised, unified, and organised; and Ideological State Apparatuses which are multiple, distinct and relatively autonomous. (The latter including the churches, schools and universities, etc.)

A full critique of Althusser's work is beyond the scope of this study.[32] It is certainly a different direction from that taken here, for in Althusser's conception, all institutions which have a socialising effect and which are correspondingly functional for the maintenance of capitalism are ideological, and are part of the state apparatus. Such a view can only follow from a prior view of the nature of the system as a whole, which, of course, is provided for Althusser by the writings of Marx.

However, even from the Marxist perspective, Althusser's solution to the epistemological problem of ideology is not entirely satisfactory, bringing with it as it does the consequence that the coming of a classless society will not mean the end of ideology.

Ideology is just as problematic, however, for social scientists who are not working strictly within the Marxian perspective. Mannheim (1960) in his development of a sociology of knowledge, faces the same difficulties. For Mannheim, all thought (apart from logic and mathematics) is culture-relative. We recognise that groups within cultures hold values and beliefs that arise from their own social circumstances. How then is the scientist, especially the social scientist, to free himself from his own values? In other words, how can we study beliefs of groups within our society, and consider them as ideological, on the basis of the values implicit in them, except from our own value-laden standpoint?

Mannheim himself comes to no single satisfactory solution to the problem. At one point, he puts his trust in the 'free-floating intellectuals', men who have no class or similar attachment other than to their position as scholars. At other times, however, he seems to feel that through the process of criticism, discussion and re-evaluation, we gradually advance to better social theories. This latter position has been characterised by Bottomore (1956) as suggesting that the latest theory is the best.

In contrast to Mannheim, Parsons (1962) has no doubt about what ideological thought should be compared with. Ideology is to be measured against social science, which is assumed to meet the necessary standards of objective, value-free, knowledge. This position, however, would appear to readopt the condemnatory aspect of ideology which Mannheim is anxious to remove. In any case, although as Geertz (1964) points out, it is one of the tasks of social science to test ideological statements, particularly statements of fact, there seems no reason to accept the results as necessarily value-free or objective, though we strive to make them so.

Another test of whether or not the thinking of a group is ideological is the purpose that may be discerned in it. Thus, Plamenatz (1970) states that for beliefs to be ideological they must be shared by a group, concern matters important to the group and be in some way functional to it. In practice, they must serve to hold it together, or to justify the activities of the members. Clearly, true beliefs can be functional in these ways. Likewise Harris (1968) comes to define ideology as 'the language of the purposes of a social group'.

Thus we have a contrast between the need for ideologies among those who espouse them as opposed to their function in convincing other groups, This brings us to a division within the empirical study of ideology, for, as Merton (1957, part III) points out, there have been two rather different traditions within the sociology of knowledge, which Merton identifies as the American and the European. The former has developed extensive methodologies for studying values, beliefs and attitudes amongst mass publics, though rarely relating them to existential or historical factors. European writers, by contrast, have often tended to take as data the evidence of a few documents, or some selected thinkers, and have been mainly interested in examining the emergence of ideas over long periods of history, and relating these to social conditions in a general way.

A striking example of this within the study of business ideology is the contrast between the work by Bendix (1956), which falls very much within the European tradition, and that of Sutton and co-workers, published in the same year. Bendix is concerned with 'ideologies of management', which he defines as 'all ideas espoused by those who exercise authority in economic enterprises, and which seek to justify and explain that authority'.

Bendix's canvas is huge: he considers three societies, England during the period of industrialisation, America in the late nineteenth and early twentieth centuries, and Russia prior to and immediately after the revolution. In each case he is concerned to relate the content of the ideologies in question to the existing institutional framework. In doing so, Bendix tends to take as the source of his data the writings of philosophers and thinkers on industry and management as well as the books and statements of entrepreneurs and businessmen themselves.

An entirely different approach is contained in the treatment of ideology by Sutton and co-authors (1956). They define ideology in a rather similar way to Bendix. It is a 'system of beliefs, publicly expressed and designed to influence the sentiments and actions of others'. But the raw material for their analysis of the content of business ideology is businessmen's writings, and speeches, as well as advertisements, magazine articles and books not written by businessmen themselves at all. The theoretical explanation of ideology given by these authors is quite different to that of Bendix. For them, it is a response by the business community to the patterned role strains inherent in being a businessman. In other words, ideology is seen as having a psychological basis, and a major part of its function is to reassure businessmen as to the morality, legitimacy, and rightness of their role.

As Samuelson has pointed out (in Cheit, 1964), Sutton and his co-authors probably exaggerate the extent to which businessmen find their role uncomfortable. However, they are surely correct in seeing business ideology as having some psychological value to businessmen themselves, although most authors would not see this as the prime function of ideology. As others have observed, their methodology and consequent theoretical explanation of ideology has the logical flaw that statements made by one group (for example, the writers of management books) are seen as the expression of the role strains felt by another.

In fact, as both Bendix (1956) and Child (1969) stress, practitioners of management may not necessarily accept the ideologies put forward on their behalf. As Bendix puts it, their reactions to such ideologies may vary from whole-hearted belief in them through cynical utilisation to unthinking acceptance.

These deliberations suggest an important distinction which must be made between what Converse (1964) calls 'belief systems' and Parkin (1971) 'meaning systems' and ideologies. I have borrowed

Parkin's term here and call the collection of beliefs, values and attitudes relating to social issues held by an individual his meaning system. Within certain groups there is a tendency for some such sets of beliefs, attitudes and values to be patterned, and it is this patterning which makes possible the study of social attitudes. In contrast, I suggest that the term ideology should be confined to statements made by spokesmen on behalf of the group in question. To reiterate: ideologies are publicly expressed beliefs put forward on behalf of groups which have, or seek to have, power or social position, and which ultimately justify that power or position.

Thus, I do not regard the study presented here as a study of ideology as such, but of the meaning systems of top businessmen. Clearly, in that some businessmen are themselves writers or spokesmen, their meaning systems serve as part of business ideology. Such a conception is compatible at least with Bendix's view of business ideology. For he insists that ideology cannot be studied by questionnaire or other methods for tapping attitudes.

Likewise, I do not regard the study by Nichols (1969), discussed above, as a study of ideology. Rather, it is a study of managers' attitudes and values (and no less valuable for that). And further consideration of the methodology of the study reinforces the point. For the directors in the study did not project an ideology of 'long-term company interest' or any other point of view. It was Nichols himself who created the statements, albeit on the basis of sound observation of what values and attitudes are implied by business ideology; the respondents themselves merely indicated the extent of their adherence to them. The fact that they could not readily distinguish two of them shows that they had no need to do so for their pragmatic purposes.

Certain consequences may be suggested on the basis of the conception put forward here. First, in so far as it can be studied, ideology is always an abstraction - something that an outside observer must re-create. Not the least reason for this is that spokesmen rarely state ideologies in a pure form; rather, ideological assumptions are introduced into writing and speeches in general, whose purpose may be only partly ideological. Second, there is something of a dialectical relationship between the shared elements of the meaning systems of a group and the ideologies expressed on its behalf. The two can be out of step, but they cannot be too far out. Spokesmen for a group will constantly restate and reformulate parts of its ideology; but because the ideology does have a psychological function for the group, it must be rooted in the group's meaning systems. Thus the study of ideology is relevant, but not synonymous, with the study of meaning systems.

This does not mean that spokesmen must always say what the group thinks. Ideologists may be the leaders of group thought as Child (1969) showed. Equally, sometimes a spokesman for a group must not state too plainly what members of it think.[33]

1.9 THE BUSINESS ELITE AS POLITICAL INFLUENTIALS

One further aspect of the position of the business elite in a capitalist society remains to be discussed, and that is their role *vis-
à-vis* the state. Again it is Marx who provides the starting point
for the discussion. In Marx's view, the state in capitalist society
is not neutral, rather it acts to further the interests of the bourgeoisie. The idea is put, for example, in the polemical style of
'The Communist Manifesto':

> The bourgeoisie has, at last, since the establishment of modern
> industry and of the world market, conquered for itself, in the
> modern representative State, exclusive political sway. The
> executive of the modern State is but a committee for managing
> the common affairs of the whole bourgeoisie. (Marx and Engels,
> 1964, p. 61)

Writing twenty years later of France, Marx further defines what
constitutes the state, and indicates that his view of its relationship to the bourgeoisie is unchanged:

> The centralised State power, with its ubiquitous organs of
> standing army, police, bureaucracy, clergy and judicature –
> organs wrought after the plan of a systematic and hierarchic
> division of labour – originates from the days of absolute mon-
> archy, serving nascent middle class interests as a mighty
> weapon in its struggle against feudalism. (Marx and Engels,
> 1968, p. 289)

And further:

> At the same pace at which the progress of modern industry
> developed, widened, intensified the class antagonism between
> capital and labour, the State power assumed more and more the
> character of the national power of capital over labour, of a
> public force organised for social enslavement, of an engine of
> class despotism. (Marx and Engels, 1968)

Yet again Weber's work offers a slightly different interpretation.
Weber regarded administration according to strictly rational principles as being as much a distinguishing feature of Western capitalism as private ownership of the means of production. He was
therefore led to the study of bureaucracy, principally in the form
of the civil service, and at one stage concludes: 'The power position of a fully developed bureaucracy is always great, under
normal conditions overtowering. The political "master" always finds
himself, vis-à-vis the trained official, in the position of a dilet-
tante facing the expert' (Weber, 1968, p. 991). And further, in
the same section:

> Only the expert knowledge of private economic interest groups
> in the field of 'business' is superior to the expert knowledge
> of the bureaucracy. This is so because the exact knowledge of
> facts in their field is of direct significance for economic sur-
> vival .... Moreover, the 'secret' as a means of power is more
> safely hidden in the books of an enterprise than it is in the
> files of public authorities. For this reason alone authorities
> are held within narrow boundaries when they seek to influence

economic life in the capitalist epoch, and very frequently their measures take an unforeseen and unintended course or are made illusory by the superior knowledge of the interest groups.

Thus, in Weber's writings we can discern a theory of capitalism that suggests the civil service bureaucracy, allied or not with the elected politicians, and the business/financial interest groups as twin and potentially competing power groups.

The possibility of competing power groups within a capitalist society is further extended in the writings of Pareto, and in more specific form by Mosca. Both believed that Marx had overemphasised the economic basis of conflict. They saw the dynamic of history and of social change not as class struggle but struggle between rival elites. The power of such elites can be drawn from sources other than their control of economic goods but, in Pareto's view at least, they correspond in some way to the needs of society, or the state of society at a given time. At its crudest and simplest, this reduces at one stage of Pareto's argument to the idea that elites may rule either by cunning or force, and an elite dependent on one may be replaced by an elite making use of the other. [34]

These theories were attempts both to refute the Marxian analysis, and to refute the democratic principle. Marx's violent revolution is seen as likely to lead to no more than the replacement of one powerful elite by another. Equally democracy is seen as a fraud, a disguise for the true power position.

But Mosca's early work, in which he is concerned only to show that democracy is a sham, contrasts with his last re-working of his ideas, 'The Ruling Class' (1938). In this, Mosca reiterates that in every society an elite (translated as a ruling class) has power, legitimating itself on the basis of a political formula. Attempts to alter this by the creation of a socialist society will involve the introduction of a state bureaucracy and give possession, status and influence to state officials.

The problem then arises for Mosca of how, if elites are always to rule, individual freedom can best be safeguarded. In this respect democratic systems are seen as offering the best hope. The true solution, however, according to Mosca, is for there to be adequate circulation of the non-elite into the elite; and, further, that amongst the ruling class 'all social forces' should be represented. Finally, those who govern via elected assemblies should be held in check, Mosca suggests, by a group of officials drawn from the middle classes of professional and managerial workers. Thus a group within the elite or potential elite are singled out as being an educated non-aligned middle class, a notion close to that of Mannheim's free-floating intellectuals (Mannheim, 1960).

In Mosca's theory, the idea of elites which compete for power and which can be a check on one another is stated as a possibility, a situation to aim for. More recently, the idea is stated as an actuality and with specific mention of the business elite in the theory of what Galbraith (1952) called 'countervailing power', but which is now more usually called pluralism or, in Bachrach's (1969)

phrase, 'democratic elitism'. The more important pluralist writers,
some of whom I will discuss below, have been American and have
drawn most directly on Bentley (1908) rather than Mosca; but the
central feature of the argument, the claim that the capitalist class
does not necessarily 'rule' a capitalist society because within the
state there are groups with power independent of them and who
are opposed to them, is the same.

As Miliband (1969) does, we must recognise that the state, leaving aside the mass of the bureaucracy that carries out its functions
and policies, consists of a number of groups: the heads of government, the administration, the military, the police and security
forces, some sub-units of central government and some members
of the parliamentary assembly. State policy on any issue is presumably the result of the interplay of influence and power between
some of these groups. This is perhaps too often ignored in analysing the relationship between the state and outside groups.

Although Marx's view of the capitalist state was clear, he made
no detailed analysis of its workings in advanced capitalist societies.
That has been left to later Marxist writers; and I will therefore
consider the various theories of the relationship of the business
elite to the state by following one particular analysis, that of
Miliband (1969). Miliband begins by asserting that the state system is not the total political system, for the latter contains a number of elements that are not in the former but have a major effect
on it. Thus we cannot assume that the dominant class actually and
directly controls the state, and is thus a ruling class.

The argument used to show that it is a ruling class consists
first in rejecting the managerialist position. In the terms of this
study, this is an attempt to show that the business elite has aims
and objectives which are in the interest of the capitalist class.
Miliband's arguments were outlined above: managers are themselves
wealthy; and have industrial capital. They are connected to each
other, and holders of capital, through ties of kinship, experience,
and friendship. In any case (and this being so, other arguments
appear somewhat superfluous), they are constrained by the system
to pursue the creation of surplus value at or close to the maximum
possible level, and the motivation of individual controllers of industry is therefore irrelevant.

The aims of the state elite are not automatically synonymous with
those of the business elite. However, in order to pursue national
economic stability and growth, members of the state elite are forced
to encourage the pursuit of profit. This, in turn, is reinforced by
the shared background, education, cultural milieu and social connections of the two groups.

Routes to elite positions are to a great extent barred to those
who would be most likely to effect a change in the system: the
working class. If they are to succeed, they themselves must change.
And the class opposition of the working class is stifled by the
ability of various elites to manipulate communication and to control
and make effective use of the media. [35]

Miliband's argument primarily rests on the evidence of recruit-

ment of the elites, their opportunities for social interaction, and
the persistence of inequalities that benefit them. We may note that
not all Marxists are happy with this kind of analysis and evidence.
Poulantzas, for one, has criticised Miliband for using the term
elite, and for maintaining in effect that plural elites constitute
the ruling class. (Though Miliband would say perhaps that that
is not his argument - that is, to argue that the state elite are connected by education, social mixing and shared values with the
ruling class is not to argue that they are merely a component of
it - see Miliband, 1970). Poulantzas has been concerned to argue
that there is an objective relation between the state and the ruling
class and it is such objective relationships we should be studying
(Poulantzas, 1968; 1969). Arguments about the extent to which the
'economic elite' or even various types of capitalist, are directly
involved or influential are thus irrelevant. Indeed, it is unclear
that Poulantzas would see any evidence as admissible, other than
historical evidence.

An alternative conception to that of Miliband which also stresses
the unity as opposed to the conflict among power-holders is that
of C. Wright Mills (1956). The crux of Mills's argument is that the
major decisions in the United States rest within three institutional
areas: the military, the large corporations and the government.
Those who hold the highest positions in these fields are thus in
positions of power. Mills specifically rejects the notion of a ruling
class (and thus implies in his analysis no particular objective
relationship between the economy and the polity), in favour of
the concept of an elite:

> The power elite is composed of men whose positions enable them
> to transcend the ordinary environments of ordinary men and
> women: they are in positions to make decisions having major
> consequences. Whether or not they do make such decisions is
> less important than the fact that they do occupy such pivotal
> positions: their failure to act, their failure to make decisions,
> is itself an act that is often of greater consequence than the
> decisions they do make. For they are in the command posts of
> the major hierarchies and organisations of modern society.
> (Mills, 1956, pp.3-4).

It might be thought that the first part of Mills's analysis would
then consist of showing that the major decisions are taken in the
three areas he names, and that such decisions are not taken in
other areas. In fact this is difficult to do, and Mills hardly attempts it. He contents himself with saying that the major decisions
are those of 'war and peace, boom and slump'. Not only is this itself vague, but Mills's argument requires not only that he demonstrate that the three groups he mentions take such decisions, but
also that their failure to take decisions is not due to action by
other important groups, or even a lack of anyone to take socially
important decisions.[36]

Mills does not contend that all decisions are taken by the power
elite - many of more minor, or purely local, importance are taken
at the 'middle levels of power'. But much of Mills's concern is to

show that the three elite groupings are not independent of one another, but are largely interlinked and overlapped to give a relatively homogeneous power elite. In this, he calls on similar evidence to that employed in European elite studies. The business elite are conceived clearly in this analysis as having a major role in the power structure, and indeed Mills seems to suggest that they are the dominant of the three groupings. However, Mills makes no attempt to distinguish the managers and capitalists, for he produces evidence to show that 'the chief executives and the very rich are not two distinct and clearly segregated groups. They are both very much mixed up in the corporate world of property and privilege'. As we shall see (chapter 4), this contention is very much less obviously true in the British case.

The challenge to the work of such theorists as Mills (1956), Hunter (1953; 1959), and Domhoff (1967), has come from the pluralist school. Essentially, the pluralists maintain that although the United States may not meet the highest tests of a democracy, it is not run either by a cohesive, interconnected elite. Most pluralists would probably see more groups as being of political importance than the three which Mills focuses on, but, more than this, they would see the power of each group as being limited to rather specific areas. Thus, Riesman *et al.* (1950) put forward the idea of veto groups, and Keller (1963) refers to strategic elites. Some pluralists go further: they would see the different groups as being in competition with one another, and thus no single group being able to gain ultimate control, a view with clear antecedents in Mosca's writings. [37]

As important as the pluralists' view of the power structure is their defence of their methodology, and this is most clearly seen in the work of Dahl. In his 'A Critique of the Ruling Elite Model' (1958), Dahl argues that if a power or ruling elite exists it must be a well-defined group, able to get its way on a fair sample of cases of political decisions in which the preferences of the theoretical elite run counter to those of other groups. Like Mills, Dahl sees it as a distinguishing feature of a powerful group that they take important decisions, and he suggests that a study of power must therefore consist of a direct study of decision-taking.

Dahl put his approach into practice in a study of the city of New Haven. Here he studied decision-making (though, it should be said, retrospectively) in three areas: public education, urban redevelopment and nominations for political parties. He showed that no elite was able to dominate all three areas, except for the very highest elected officials (Dahl, 1961).

Dahl's study of New Haven, however, may be considered, in fact, as concerned with what Mills would regard as the 'middle levels of power'. An attempt to refute the Mills thesis at the national level has also been made by Rose (1967). His argument is very similar to that of Dahl: there is no cohesive power elite, and certainly not one dominated by the economic (business) elite. Rather, different elites compete for power in different areas. They may form alignments with one another on different issues, but this makes it

harder for any one of them to be dominant, with the exception of
the highest elected officials who are subject, in any case, to periodic reconsideration by the electorate. Elites organise different
publics on different issues; and thus Mills is wrong to refer to
the non-elites as 'mass society', for most members of society will
find themselves canvassed for support by one elite or another from
time to time. Rose is thus one of the few theorists to give weight
to public opinion, rather than seeing the public as passive or manipulated by the media.

Rose calls on a broad range of evidence to support his case,
including a number of studies of lobbying at the national and local
level. However, he does see the economic elite as an extremely influential one, though he points to a number of enduring divisions
within it - for example, the division between the representatives
of small businesses and the heads of larger companies.

A further point made by Rose is that the economic elite can mis-
understand what their true interests are just as much as the
working class or other groups in the population. By way of example, he points to positions taken by business representatives
in response to legislative proposals which he maintains were not,
in fact, in accord with their true interests.

Although this may be a valid point, the evidence that Rose puts
forward to support both this, and his wider contention that there
are many issues on which businessmen do not get their own way,
is not wholly convincing. Aside from Kennedy's action to prevent
price rises by the steel companies (which was only temporarily
successful), most other legislative action mentioned by Rose concerned welfare proposals of some kind. Rose shows that some
businessmen opposed these and that their opposition was unsuccessful, but he does not show that they were against the interests
of businessmen, or that there were not other businessmen in passive or active support of the proposals.

A better test of business strength in the political process would
be the outcome of issues in which business interests were directly
threatened; and, with the possible exception of the activities of
the Anti-Trust Division of the US Department of Justice, it is difficult to think of any such legislation or action during the period
from which Rose draws his examples.

This raises the whole question of how power is to be conceptualised and studied. As we saw, Dahl's definition of power, drawn
from Weber, sees person or group A as having power over person
or group B if A can get his or their way in the face of opposition
from person or group B. As a consequence of this definition, Dahl
is only able to demonstrate a power relationship as existing when
open conflict between two parties is apparent.

As Bachrach and Baratz point out (1962; 1963) the problem of
this conception in practice is that groups with an interest in, or
a grievance over, the topic on which a decision is being taken
must be represented in the political process before the conflict
which their particular interest creates can be apparent to the political scientist. However, it is arguable that much disaffection with

the political process arises because certain groups are cut off from access to the decision-making process and thus have no chance to air their grievances (the position of coloured people or the urban poor in either Britain or the United States are perhaps good examples). As Bachrach and Baratz put it: '...power is also exercised when A devotes his energies to creating or refining social and political values and institutional policies that limit the scope of the political process to public consideration of only those issues which are comparatively innocuous to A' (Bachrach and Baratz, 1962).

Bachrach and Baratz propose that we should also study the process of non-decision-making, that is, the process in which certain issues are prevented from being considered by elites as issues on which they must take decisions.

Lukes (1974) has attempted to take the argument a stage further, with what he calls a radical view of power. As Lukes defines power, a power relationship exists whenever A can affect B in a manner in accordance with A's interest, and contrary to B's real interest. B's real interest is seen as being what B would choose were he able to make a free choice unaffected by A.

It is clear what lies behind Lukes's conception: there are groups which benefit from the institutional arrangements of society, and others which do not, and the ability of some groups to go on benefiting does not depend only on their ability to prevent certain issues entering the decision-taking arena, but on their ability to maintain the whole system (more particularly the capitalist system).

However, Lukes's conceptualisation does not appear to be easily applicable in practice. It falls between the position of, for example, Poulantzas (1968), in which the continued existence of capitalism is seen as a priori evidence that the state exerts power in the interests of the bourgeoisie, and the perspectives of the other political scientists mentioned here. Lukes's only concrete example of his approach, Crenson's (1971) study of air pollution in American cities, would seem to be easily accommodated within Bachrach and Baratz's framework.

If we accept the existence of a unified state elite as such, which, as I have suggested, is something of an assumption, then the essential questions concerning its relationships with the business elite would seem to be as follows. To what extent do the two groups have differing objectives and values? If there are differences, to what extent are the business elite able to exert power (through the use of sanctions) or influence so as to avert action detrimental to their aims, or promote state activity favourable to these aims? If they have such power or influence, what is the basis of it, that is, how important is their control of economic assets, the organisations which they have to promote their interests, or their shared background and access to state officials through clubs, friendships and family? I will return to this, the consideration of the need for businessmen to influence state officials, and the methods they use to do so, with some empirical evidence, in chapter 8.

1.10 CONCLUSION

I have tried to outline here the five main areas in which current theory suggests prominent roles for the business elite. In three of these roles, the economic role, the industrial relations role and the role as political influentials, the literature abounds with references to them. To this I have added the class/status position of businessmen and their view of it as being of interest in itself, but also quite clearly related to their economic role. Their position as ideologists stems from their position as a group which is part of, or close to, the dominant class or classes, but I will give further attention to the content of business ideology because, as we shall see, the issues and areas which are the subjects of business ideology are fairly circumscribed.

What I have tried to show here is that focusing on just one group, businessmen, involves consideration of many of the major debates concerning the structure, functioning and possibilities for change within capitalist society. Clearly, all that I have been able to do in this chapter is to indicate what the major points of debate are, how and where the business elite are relevant to these, and the kinds of evidence that have been brought to bear on them. I freely admit that in no sense have I offered a full discussion of the debates concerned. For example, there are a number of books and monographs on the subject of ideology and it remains an extremely complex and difficult topic; my intention here was merely to show that the study of business ideology raises the more general problems and that we must be aware of these.

What I have also attempted to show is that when businessmen enter the various theories discussed, and the same is true for other elite groupings, assumptions are made about their behaviour, and even more so about the motivations for that behaviour, from very little direct evidence. It is widely, though not universally, held among sociologists that to understand the behaviour of social actors requires an understanding of how they view the social situations which they are part of, and that this entails some understanding of their value system more generally. In the case of businessmen, I would maintain that this understanding is to an extent lacking, and in commencing this study I was particularly interested in uniting two areas which separately have received considerable attention in British sociology in recent years: the study of elites and the study of 'images of society' or, in the terminology I will adopt here, 'meaning systems'. Accordingly, in the next chapter I will consider the sources of the meaning systems of the business elite.

2 THE MEANING SYSTEMS OF TOP BUSINESSMEN

'The ingredients, the raw materials of class ideology, are
located in the individual's various primary social experiences
rather than his position in a socioeconimic category.'
Elizabeth Bott, 'Family and Social Network', 1971, p. 163

2.1 INTRODUCTION

Before turning to the specific examination of the sources of businessmen's thought which forms the subject of this chapter, I
wish to discuss my understanding of the term 'meaning system',
which, as was stated above, is taken from Parkin's (1971) usage.
The reasons for preferring the term 'meaning system' to 'images
of society' are as much semantic as theoretical. The phrase 'images
of society' conveys the idea that what we are talking of are merely
the pictures that individuals hold of society, though in practice,
as here, the term has usually referred to much else.
I define the term 'meaning system' to be a set of beliefs, values
and attitudes held by an individual concerning social issues. I
thus see the social actor's meaning system as a guiding and inter-
preting mechanism through which he or she understands the social
world and interprets it, which shapes his or her actions and which
can become a justification for these actions.
I follow Rokeach (1968) in seeing values and beliefs as varying
along a continuum of centrality, such that the more central a value
or belief, the more firmly it will be held. Thus, where two beliefs
(or values) in practice are brought together and found to be conflicting, the less central one will be dropped. However, individuals may hold inconsistent beliefs if the inconsistency is not made
apparent to them.
The term 'meaning system' relates only to the actor's social
values and place in society. An individual may have other more
personal values which might be of greater importance in determining behaviour in particular situations. For example, a person may
not see private education as desirable, but may have a strong
wish to provide advantageous education for their child (assuming,
for this example, that such a purchase is an advantage). This
clash of values may well be resolved in favour of the more personal
ones.
This is an important point, since it can be argued that the study
of people's meaning systems as they are defined here often does
not give a simple explanation of a particular individual's behaviour.[1]

However, it is certainly the intention in studying meaning systems that these should be related to behaviour and experience. And, indeed, attempts to explain the formation of meaning systems have stressed the relationship between these and personal experience.

Elizabeth Bott, for example, on whose work, among others, Lockwood[2] drew for his paper on working-class imagery, stated: 'The ingredients, the raw materials, of class imagery are located in the individual's various primary social experiences rather than his position in a socioeconomic category' (Bott, 1971, ch.6). Whilst accepting this, I would also add, and this is of particular importance in studying higher managers, that the ingredients are not only current primary group memberships and experience, but also past primary group memberships and past experience. For example, it may be suggested that when businessmen think of man management, they draw not only on their day-to-day experiences, which to some extent are with peers, but also on past ones.

Aside from this, I suggest that it is partly implicit in the sociological literature, and I intend to take it as an explicit hypothesis here, that the images of different institutions, institutional arrangements and of society as a whole which are held by people 'match up'. By this I mean that, in this context, the view of relationships in the firm that an individual has will reflect his own value system, but will also have an echo, a parallel, in the way he sees relationships and groupings in society. Thus, a worker who views the firm as split between 'us' and 'the bosses', will likewise view society as split between 'us and them'. Meaning systems comprise not only a picture of social groupings in society, but also of the distribution of power in society, of the relationships at work, values with respect to these, and the appropriate action that the individual should take. Thus I assume that these are related, interconnected at the cognitive level, and represent this as shown in Figure 2.1.

In Figure 2.1 certain direct connections have been drawn in: clearly, for example, how an individual views the structure of society will be related to his own view of his position within it. However, it is a consequence of my understanding of the literature that all the parts are to be thought of as connected in a manner that endures over time. Naturally, some connections may be stronger than others: to value achievement may only be loosely connected with seeing society as run by a power elite.

A further assumption made here is that first-hand experience - that is, experience gained in primary groupings, in direct relationships - will be of more importance in shaping beliefs and values than indirect or secondary experience. Thus, in the case of businessmen, I assume, for example, that their view of the lower groupings of the class/status structure is formed by such contacts as the businessmen have, or have had at first hand. I assume that secondary sources (reading books, reference to the media, or stereotypes circulated by fellow businessmen) are used in the absence of first-hand knowledge, or where first-hand knowledge is assumed to be no longer relevant (for example, being born in a slum, but believing that slums no longer exist).

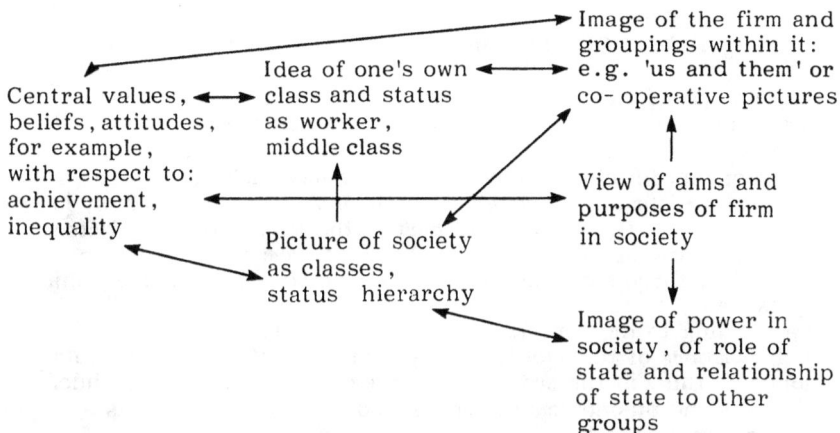

Figure 2.1   The internal composition of meaning systems

2.2 SOURCES OF BUSINESSMEN'S MEANING SYSTEMS

I pointed out above (p.17) that a variety of attitudes to class and status have been ascribed to elites. I wish to look more specific- ally here at the potential sources of these in the case of the bus- iness elite. I defined the business elite as the main board members of large industrial and financial companies. Although we have many detailed studies of the background of such directors, our evidence about their attitudes and values must be assembled from a number of disparate sources. Doubtless this assembly is incom- plete, and much of the literature is journalistic, insubstantiated or out-of-date. Nevertheless, it does serve to show the complex- ities of elite thought.

In what follows, it must never be forgotten that businessmen owe their rewards, their power and their status to their position with- in capitalist enterprises in a capitalist society. This, above all, is what they have in common as a group, and whatever else influences them, this must be a big factor colouring their thinking. It would be strange indeed if businessmen did not believe in capitalism and seek to defend it. The influences cited here mainly concern the terms in which they will seek to do so.

I have identified here, and will discuss in turn, the following conceptions of the director in the current literature:
(a) the director as a member of the middle class;
(b) the director in-touch and out-of-touch with the working class;
(c) the director as a member of the upper class;
(d) the director as ex-public schoolboy;

(e) the director as adherent of Tory party ideology;
(f) the director as recipient, and creator, of business ideology.

2.3 THE DIRECTOR AS A MEMBER OF THE MIDDLE CLASS

The position of the top businessman may be ambiguous in class terms, but for much of their careers they may well have been what many would call, without hesitation, middle class. For the larger group of top directors are managers who have achieved their positions by climbing through the company hierarchy.[3] Thus, for a time at least, they have been part of the group to which Watson[4] gave the name 'spiralists' - men who move from post to post in a hierarchy, these same moves necessitating some geographic mobility as well.

According to Raynor (1969), the most characteristic value of such members of the middle class is achievement, though he sets alongside this, in the case of the upper middle class, independence. So far as the businessman is concerned, it is clear that it is through work that he will assuage his desire to achieve.

The director, then, and many managers below him (or her), is dedicated to career achievement. But, though Pahl and Pahl (1971) found the same dedication, they also remark on the conflict in the lives of the managers whom they studied between the demands of work life and the desire of managers to spend time with their wives and families. The wives of the managers tended to resent the amount of time they spent away from home, and Pahl and Pahl were inclined to doubt whether achievement was so total a value as Raynor had presented it. Young and Willmott (1973) came to similar conclusions in their study of the work and leisure interaction of managing directors. But in the case of the latter, they appeared to be adamant that their wives simply had to accept the demands of the job.

Possibly more attention has been devoted in America to the study of the mobile group of managers, administrators, and professionals. They figured in studies of American suburban life[5] to such an extent that Berger (1961) maintained that a distorted picture had been obtained of the suburb. Perhaps the best known such study is that of Whyte (1957), which examined both the work life and the social lives of American middle-class men (whom one supposes to be mainly middle managers). Whyte suggests the rise of a new 'social ethic', replacing the Protestant ethic. The suburban Americans are committed to teamwork and social cohesion in the firm, rather than aggression or competitiveness. They are rootless - prepared to move anywhere at the firm's behest, and they are adept at fitting in with wherever they are. They show a strong predilection for joining voluntary organisations and to ostracising outsiders who will not join in such activities.

Such studies of American suburban estates suggested that they were relatively homogeneous. In Britain, at least, the middle class as a whole can choose more varied environments. Bell (1968) found a mixture of types (spiralist, burgesses and spent spiralist) in his study of a Swansea housing estate. Similarly, in south-east England at least, the better off middle class may leave the housing estates and move to commuter villages. But both here in the towns and in the city suburbs they dominate the local voluntary organisations (see, for example, studies by Pahl and Musgrove[6]).

Because the middle class are mobile, they have to forsake the very close ties which many of the working class have with their local areas. This means that kin cannot be relied on for everyday companionship and help (though as Bell (1968) shows relationships with kin remain strong and kin can provide very important assistance). Thus the middle class become 'joiners' - partly to meet people, partly because membership of voluntary associations means that they have new areas in which to achieve.

Even leaving aside those directors who have inherited their position or built up their own firm, we can only partly extend the picture we have of managers to directors as well. First, because many have long got past the 'spiralist' stage, and have been directors for a long period of time and thus resident in the same area. Indeed, those who get to the top may well have had central HQ jobs even before they became directors. Second, because Whyte's view of the compulsive mixer, enjoying teamwork at work and committee and voluntary work at home, clashes with the other stereotypes of the achievement-oriented manager. Indeed, Whyte himself stresses that business executives may be different from the organisation men he is discussing. Third, because those bureaucrats who make it to the top may be so achievement-oriented at work for much of their careers that they have no time to devote to voluntary activities. Such activities may come after they have achieved that directorship.

Finally, one must stress (and this will be taken up in chapter 4) that the business elite are very largely based in the home counties, and work in London. The ties they are represented as having in elite theory are with other directors and other elites (for example, civil servants and politicians) not with members of their housing estate or their village. The elites may take their values and their experience from one another.

2.4 THE DIRECTOR IN TOUCH AND OUT OF TOUCH WITH THE WORKING CLASS

In the last section I referred to the idea that top managers may have climbed through the company, and may have experienced either personal social mobility or a period of their careers in which they were in close contact with lower class or status groupings either in their community environment or working life. I have also suggested that the present community life of the top businessman is unlikely to involve contact with such groups. Indeed, this is summed up in the phrase 'stockbroker belt'.

There is little to suggest, correspondingly, that main board directors have any real contact with the working class in the work environment. For, as I pointed out in the last chapter, overriding among the tasks of the director is the creation of long-term strategies and the policies to achieve these strategies. Inevitably, much of this work consists of financial and market planning in conjunction with those technical specialists within the firm who can supply the information on which such long-term strategies must be based. The importance of the main board in the strategic process can thus become a prime justification for not involving oneself with operational matters. The structure of many companies, with a holding company board and a number of divisional or subsidiary company boards, completes the isolation of the main board director.

And, indeed, Winkler's (1974) research, referred to in the last chapter, and his conclusion that 'most conspicuously absent from the lives of directors were workers' suggests that a desire to avoid operational matters, and contact with workers, is characteristic of British top management.

If we accept this evidence, it means that businessmen do not have contact in any meaningful sense with lower white-collar or manual workers in day-to-day life. In drawing on experience of such groups, they must either revert to earlier memories of times in their working life when they did have such contact, or else judge by what they hear from other sources: their own middle management, hearsay or the media. They may also, as Winkler suggests, intervene in crisis situations, and have contact with union officials in times of conflict.

Thinking back to what was said about meaning systems earlier, and the importance of first-hand contact as opposed to less direct evidence, then it follows that experience of man management early in directors' careers may strongly affect the view that they take of relationships later on. It thus becomes of some importance to establish just what the extent and nature of such experience is.

2.5 THE DIRECTOR AS A MEMBER OF THE UPPER CLASS

Even a superficial examination of the British business elite indicates that amongst company chairmen and directors there are a number of the British aristocracy, and others who would perhaps be considered, by virtue of background or wealth, as 'upper class'. Sociologists have not, however, differentiated the values of either the wealthy or the aristocrat from those of the middle class. The exception is Veblen (1899), but his 'The Theory of the Leisure Class' was written in another age and a different culture, and one feels that, though the phrase 'conspicuous consumption' was appropriate to the Morgans, Vanderbilts and Guggenheims, it is less appropriate in contemporary Britain.

Two books concerned with the aristocracy and gentry, those of Perrott (1968) and Sutherland (1968), comment on their value systems, but both concentrate on landowners. Amongst such people, it is said, the ownership of land is regarded as a trust, and large landowners feel a responsibility both to preserve and pass on their estates, and to those who rent and farm them. More generally, Perrott remarks that the aristocracy is marked by a confident assumption of leadership, derived from education, breeding and wealth. Along with attachment to the land goes a sense of patriotism and a regard for the idea of England and the empire. All of this is tempered, however, with an extreme degree of self-interest and, as Perrott puts it, a dislike of 'dark industrial areas'.

This dislike of 'dark industrial areas' may go much deeper, and be part of a dislike of the whole business of making things and of being 'in trade'. Mant (1977) identifies it as among a number of factors contributing to the poor status, poor quality and ultimately poor record of British management over the past century. [7]

Yet the dislike of the aristocracy may not just be for industry as such, it may also be for a wholly different value system. The split between the 'traditional/aristocratic' and 'managerial/entrepreneurial' value systems, has been identified by, amongst others, Parkin (1971). The nature of the split would seem to be as follows.

On the one hand, the aristocratic view of society emphasises the rights of property, the hereditary principle, and the desirability of leaders who have been 'born to rule'. The managerial/entrepreneurial or meritocratic viewpoint, however, emphasises the importance of routes to leadership positions being open to competition for them, and of those who lead being the best fitted by virtue of ability.

Turner (1966) compared Britain with the United States in this regard, maintaining that the 'contest' norm, in which leadership status is earned, not given, characterises the latter, whereas in Britain one is invited to attain leadership status by those who already have it, and by virtue of having similar qualities and characteristics to theirs. According to Turner, among British elites, manners, courtesy, altruism and academically, the classics are valued.

It might seem that managerial values are now so dominant in British society as to make the aristocratic/traditional values largely irrelevant. But it should be remembered that many of the current business elite were not, for the most part, educated, trained or entering industry in current society but the society of the late 1930s, 1940s and early 1950s, when older values may have been more dominant.

The split between managerial and aristocratic elites in British society might appear quite fundamental, but two institutions have historically served to unite the two: they are the public schools and the Conservative party.

2.6 THE DIRECTOR AS EX-PUBLIC SCHOOLBOY

Numerous studies have shown that top directors are most likely to have received their education at public school. For this is a unique feature of British upper-class and middle-class life, and the middle-class desire to provide a good education for their children is often reinterpreted as providing a public school education, if not for all one's children, then at least for the sons.

It is the values and beliefs which such schools inculcate in which we are interested here. It is, of course, impossible to know the extent to which values implanted in adolescence are maintained in later life, but it is reasonable to suppose that the parents of children at public schools reinforce and sustain certain values; and, indeed, if one were able to isolate them, that such values would be more characteristic of the upper middle class than the middle-class values that were found on the Swansea housing estate studied by Bell (1968) or in Willmott and Young's study of Woodford (1960).

Lewis and Maude (1949) see the public school historically as having two functions: fusing the old nobility and gentry with the rising monied groups into a single ruling class, and the production of a cadre of empire-builders and administrators. Translated into the twentieth century, the new function of the public schools may have been (or still be) to fuse the sons of capitalists, professionals and administrators into a relatively homogeneous group of 'managers' who are the business elite forty years on. Thus the culture of, say, the son of a small Leeds businessman, who was educated at a local school, and whose company is now in the top 200 may be more different from that of the son of another capitalist than the sons of professional employees and other middle-class groups.

No single study adequately encapsulates the values of the public school: drawing on several,[8] they would appear to be:

(a) the public schools emphasise self-reliance (cf. Raynor's (1969) stress on independence as a value of the upper middle class). The boy is separated from his family and sent to stand 'on his own two feet';

(b) the public schoolboy is taught to accept an authoritarian organisation: discipline is rigid and military-like. A respect for discipline, 'fair play' and 'the done thing' is inculcated;

(c) the schoolboy undergoes a transition from the most servile position to a position of responsibility in a relatively short time. Unique to Britain is a system of education in which parents pay large sums of money for their children to be other boys' servants (fags). Within four to five years, though, the boy in turn has his own servant;[9]

(d) the public school places great stress on the taking of responsibility - as would be expected for schools whose function was to train a corps of administrators for the empire. Perhaps more than other schools, public schools provide opportunities to do this in a variety of situations: as a school prefect, a house prefect, in the military corps, in a variety of societies, in a wide range of sports teams. The intention would seem to be that everybody should take responsibility somewhere;

(e) boys' public schools, until recently, were male-only institutions. The justification for this would seem to be that adolescents should not be diverted from legitimate pursuits by sexual activities.

What the effects of this are in later life is difficult to know, but
ex-public schoolboys seem to favour it: many directors can leave
their all-male boardrooms for all-male clubs;
(f) lastly, the public school curriculum has traditionally emphasised the classics and history at the expense of science and
languages. Thus they were better suited to educating administrators than engineers. This too may have changed in recent years.

2.7 THE DIRECTOR AS ADHERENT OF TORY PARTY IDEOLOGY

Until 1964 the Conservative party was, in effect, the ruling party
of this country, and several authors (for example McKenzie and
Silver, 1968, Guttsman, 1963) have pointed out that it had by then
been in power for the great majority of the past hundred years.
If the ideology of any party in any advanced capitalist country
expresses the ideology of the ruling class, the dominant class, or
the power elite it should be this one.
The ideology may be viewed in different ways. Harris (1972 and
1968) sees it as being to a large extent pragmatic, shifting as required to keep the party in power. Other commentators, notably
McKenzie and Silver (1968) in the introductory passage to their
book on working-class conservatism, [10] detect certain continuous
strands of philosophy, though they admit this has always been
coupled with a pragmatic appeal based on various social welfare
provisions, aimed at improving the lot of the working class, which
the party has introduced from time to time.
As McKenzie and Silver see it, Conservatives conceive man as
basically sinful and prone to wickedness, or at least greed. Society is an organic partnership which has evolved over time; it is
a framework constraining man's brutishness. If it is to be dis-
turbed, the onus is on the reformer to prove the necessity of
change. Conservatives make no secret of their belief in the inequality of man; a system of classes is inevitable, even desirable.
Yet this belief in the virtues of the class system is combined with
an aversion to class conflict. Thus the Conservative appeal is
that of 'the party of the whole nation', the party that will deal
fairly with competing claims, give the country strong leadership
(and there is a tendency to look to leaders 'bred' for the task by
both the party and voters), and social cohesion.
Harris, in his discussion, is more concerned with the party's
economic policies. He emphasises that the party has supported
different elites at different times: currently its support is for the
managerial capitalist, and its ideology wavers between two forms
of corporatism: (a) étatist, in which the state takes a strong control of the economy, directing the operation of the managerially
controlled firms (this is the form of corporatism which Winkler
(1976) refers to), and (b) pluralist, in which the state promotes
competition between different interest groups and different capitalist enterprises. The latter represents a harking back by the
party to the period of liberal laissez-faire capitalism. Harris (1972)

does not clearly distinguish between a laissez-faire ideology and pluralist corporatism, but possibly he would argue that the party itself fails to. This tendency of the party to waver between philosophies is of some interest, as it parallels the competition between different strands of business ideology.

2.8 THE DIRECTOR AS CREATOR AND RECIPIENT OF BUSINESS IDEOLOGY

I pointed out earlier (p.30) that business ideology has to reflect the values and beliefs of businessmen, and itself comes to be reflected in these values and beliefs. Despite the problems of conceptualising ideology adequately, there has been much less dispute over the content of business ideology. However, I should point out in advance that much of the literature in this field is American, and it is quite possible that the statements and beliefs of business spokesmen in the United States differ in style, tone and content from those of their British counterparts. [11]

However, it does seem that some trends of ideology and managerial thinking in one country have been paralleled in the other, and that similarity of language and a conscious desire to emulate good practice have reinforced the extent of this. [12]

I therefore start this consideration of the content of business ideology with Bendix's (1956) study of the prevailing ideologies during industrialisation of two Western nations and Russia. Bendix's main concern is to compare the different types of ideological appeal made in the three countries and to relate these to the differing social structures.

Of more direct interest for our purposes is Bendix's analysis of the course of British and American ideology, even though this stops short of the present day. He indicates the existence of two themes of business ideology, the first associated with the earlier entrepreneurs, the other with the larger bureaucratised enterprises that developed later.

In summary: the entrepreneurial ideology was itself a break with an earlier tradition. It held that all individuals in society must depend only on themselves, and that the higher classes are not, and cannot be, responsible for ensuring employment, or the relief of the poor. Such views found their apotheosis in the 'social Darwinism' of Spencer, which had wide circulation in the United States in the late nineteenth century.

As industrialisation progressed, and small enterprises developed into mature firms, the ideology began to change. The managers themselves became more interested in the attitudes and psychology of the worker. As firms grew increasingly larger, and became more bureaucratised, an emphasis on teamwork and collectivity, as opposed to competition, developed. There was less stress on individual leadership and more on individual adaptability and style.

It is to be emphasised that these changes are never complete, nor are they the result of a change from owner to managerial control. Old values often co-exist alongside new ones, and reassert themselves (Child (1969) also remarks on this). Sutton and his co-authors (Sutton *et al.*, 1956) also point to the presence of a duality of themes within business ideology. On the one hand is the 'classical' creed, which sees devotion by businessmen to profits as necessary for social welfare; that emphasises that the businessman is subject to the laws of the market and directs him to attend only to the interests of the shareholder.

On the other hand, there has developed a managerial ideology, in which the businessman is presented as a professional, who is not guided solely, or even principally, by a desire to make profits. The businessman has moral claims on him, amongst them ensuring satisfactory working relationships among those who work with or for him. As Sutton *et al.* put it, in terms which will become very familiar in the later course of this study (especially chapter 5):

These are, in truth, moral responsibilities which it is your duty to assume. You, the manager of a business, are responsible to your stockholders, your employees, your customers, and the general public. You must balance their competing claims on the fruits of the enterprise, and determine fair wages, fair prices, fair dividends and prudent reserves.

This eloquently bland solution to the conflicts of industrial life is seen by Sutton *et al.* as a 'managerial ideology', although as I pointed out in the last chapter it may merely have arisen in parallel with the increase of managerially run corporations, rather than as the result of it. Nichols uses a very similar statement as one of his 'social responsibility' set of responses in his questionnaire study (Nichols, 1969). I myself prefer to call it the 'ethos of balancing interests'.

Other writers have also noted the co-existence of the two themes of business ideology. Monsen (1960), for example, points to the existence of six variants of American capitalist ideology, but, as Samuelson points out (in Cheit, 1964), these again are essentially variants of old style maximising capitalism operating in competitive markets, and managerial capitalism in which the corporation is responsive to the interests of all parties it deals with. Seider (1974) also distinguishes classical ideology from the trusteeship role in which the manager balances the interests of all those connected with the enterprise. He found two further important ideological themes - one of nationalism, stressing the importance of working together for the national good, the other specifically spelling out the place of business in promoting social welfare projects.

Perhaps the most incisive discussion of the ideology of modern-day business spokesmen is that made by Heilbroner (in Cheit, 1964). He uses as source material a series of lectures given by six leading American businessmen and subsequently published. Heilbroner points out not only the contrasts in content between the ideology of contemporary businessmen and their forebears but also in style. For where the nineteenth-century captain of industry was secure, self-confident and self-righteous, his latter-day counterpart is quiet, apologetic and thoughtful.

Once again, however, the contrast is made between classical and managerial thought; but Heilbroner points out that it is also specifically drawn by the spokesmen themselves. They contrast the old exploitative capitalism and the new socially aware responsible capitalism. The hallmark of the new capitalism is the professional responsibility exercised by those charged with power in business.

There is, too, an acceptance and statement of the need for large-scale organisation, but equally a stress on human values. Thus, much mention is made of employee relations, which has its echoes is the earlier human relations movement. Finally, Heilbroner points to a contrast between the modern businessmen and those of the past which is often overlooked: a new legitimacy is accorded to both government and organised labour. Yet, says Heilbroner, though the tone is reasonable, on reading the businessmen's statements there is no doubt that they are ideological (meaning that they are clearly intended to defend a position of power and inequality).

Rather less has been written about business ideology in Britain. Child's (1969) work has already been referred to several times, although Child states that the body of thought he is concerned with is only partly ideological. However, his book does trace the evolution of very similar themes to those already mentioned. The work by McGivering, Matthews and Scott (1960) has a section on ideology, but has the drawback that it bases it predominantly on the work of one author. As has already been mentioned, Nichols (1969) contrasts three sets of themes of ideology, the laissez-faire, the 'long-term company interest' and the social responsibility themes, though practitioners could not differentiate the latter two. Finally, one may mention again the contrast noted by Alan Fox between the unitary and pluralistic view of the firm which was discussed in the last chapter.

To summarise, then: the tension running through business ideology throughout almost all periods is between the need for aggressiveness and competition between individuals and groups, and the need for co-operation, teamwork and harmony. This tension is to be found both at the level of the organisation, and in the business view of society at large. Thus early business ideology stresses the 'survival of the fittest', and pictures society as a jungle in which the most successful are successful because they have the qualities needed. Free trade and competition are vital to the interests of the economy. Yet later, after the rise of Taylorism, of the mass production line and, later still, the 'human relations' movement, a greater need for teamwork and co-operation enters ideology. Whyte (1957) goes so far as to suggest that in recent times a social ethic has replaced the Protestant ethic amongst junior and middle management.[13] Paradoxically, while social Darwinism was the dominant view of society, the view that business ideologists and practitioners took of the firm was often that called by Fox (1966) unitary: workers who went on strike were seen as being disloyal to the firm and acting against their own interests. Conversely, Fox's pluralist perspective would somehow have to be superimposed on the harmonious, teamwork view of the company taken by managers who see themselves as 'socially responsible' professionals.

Thus business ideology is a source of competing themes; some of these have had their day and gone, others wax and wane with the fortunes of the country and of businessmen.

2.9 CONCLUSION

In this chapter I have tried to treat the business elite as any occupational group might be treated by a sociologist, and to trace the potential sources of its meaning systems. I began by defining what constitutes a meaning system in this context and making plain the assumptions which are implicit in theory as it stands. To recapitulate: meaning systems first and foremost reflect the situation of the individual: businessmen are well-off and powerful and have high status (though not, it seems, as high as they would like). Their meaning systems must somehow reflect an awareness of their power and their position. I stated also that meaning systems reflect primary group experience both past and current. I assume that they are also to some extent internally consistent and that personal experience is more important in shaping them than what is learnt at second hand.

The present literature suggests several sources of businessmen's meaning systems: the businessman may be a member of the middle class, adopting its values and cultural influences, or a member of the landed gentry or aristocracy, whom many would see as the traditional upper class in Britain. He may be an ex-public schoolboy, with the values peculiar to those institutions, an adherent of Tory party ideology, or the recipient, and perhaps creator, of business ideology.

I do not wish to run through all the themes and values that have been discussed in this chapter, but rather to point out the dualisms, the contrasts, that have recurred. The first of these was between the values of middle-class or managerial elites and those of aristocratic or traditional elites. The great prime value of the middle class is said to be achievement, and thus their view of the firm and of society is that it should be meritocratic, that advancement should be through ability, work and attainment, Turner's (1966) contest system in fact. In contrast, the aristocratic, traditional value system stresses the need for leaders bred to the job, the hereditary rights of such leaders, and the duties and obligations that go with them.

A further dualism is evident within Tory party ideology, which vacillates between an adherence to laissez-faire capitalism and a belief in the state as a necessary, directive force in the economy and society. And a dualism appears again within business ideology: on the one hand, we have traditional, profit-maximising capitalism,

on the other, managerial capitalism in which directors are presented as professionals, the arbiters of competing interest groups.
A lesser dualism occurs again at the level of the firm, which can
be seen as a tight unified team or a coalition of separate and partially conflicting interest groups. This latter contrast has been
applied to relationships between management and workers, but it
poses a problem for the aspiring member of middle management as
well. What is his stance toward the corporation to be? At one level,
he is told that he must be a member of the team, and work together
for the benefit of the company, he must be an 'organisation man';
at the same time he knows that success, and achievement, means
doing better, standing out from the team. He must be part of the
team but compete with them.

The competing themes set out here are to some extent in competition, of course, because one is declining in strength, the
other ascendant. It seems that the managerial ideology has taken
over from laissez-faire as the more predominant business ideology
for example. But older ideologies can and do reassert themselves.

There are numerous influences which this discussion has not
taken account of. The values of the public school should perhaps
be counterposed to those of the grammar school, or secondary
school; and the effect of the universities, both Oxbridge and red-
brick, should not be ignored. I have referred to middle-class
values, and those of the aristocrat, but do these adequately encompass the entrepreneur, or the person who is upwardly mobile
from the working class?

Nevertheless, the discussion serves to make clear the variables
and relationships we will have to take note of in studying the
values and beliefs of businessmen. We must look at the extent of
their social mobility, and thus, in turn, at their origins. We must
examine the types of education they have received, and their early
career experience, paying particular attention to their man-
management experience. We must look at their present work and
social situation. Most importantly, we must ask how wealthy they
are - are they all to be considered as capitalists or is there some
division within them? And what do they do in their work lives,
what are their aims and objectives for their companies, how do
they understand these? Finally, where do they live, who do they
mix with, what is the extent of their contact with other elites? We
have also seen some themes, and some ideologies, to which we have
been alerted and which we expect to find in their thought.

In the next chapter I will discuss the objectives and methodology
of the empirical study that forms the subject matter of the rest of
this book.

3 DESIGN OF THE RESEARCH

3.1 SOME PRELIMINARIES TO RESEARCH

I have covered much theoretical and empirical ground in the last two chapters, some of it in outline, some of it in depth. Whilst I have covered the main debates of relevance to the business elite, without claiming to have given a full discussion of these, it must be said that there is an extensive literature, both academic and populist, which has not been mentioned.

There can be no doubt that the upper echelons of corporate life have a certain mystique, and this has inevitably invited the writing of books that offer advice to those climbing corporate hierarchies, or speculate on what happens at the top of them. Some of these (for example Packard, 1963; Mant, 1977) draw more or less straightforwardly on social or management science. Others are more fanciful, looking for insights into company life in the writings of Machiavelli (Jay, 1967), or some dubious uses of anthropology in which the executive becomes 'the company savage' (Page, 1972) or again by reference to the 'new biology' (Jay, 1972).

I take the view that much of this literature is not useful to the serious study of the business elite, though it may be to those studying ideology. This is not because these works contain no interesting or valuable insights, although some certainly draw their conclusions from rather slender evidence. Rather, I maintain that if the business elite are to be studied properly, then it is necessary to focus specifically on them and to be aware of the major divisions both within the business elite and between them and other groups.

I would argue in particular that it is necessary:
(a) to study members of the main boards of companies, and preferably those who are known to take resource allocation decisions;
(b) to study the heads of sufficiently large firms. The multinational, divisionalised conglomerate is not the small firm writ large; and
(c) to distinguish within the business elite between entrepreneurs who begin companies, the families which inherit them, and the managers who may later come to run them. It is necessary also to distinguish between firms in the finance sector and those in manufacturing or service industries. (And further distinctions between sectors may be relevant.)

The failure to make these distinctions adequately at the outset of many studies, leads one to doubt the relevance of much of the evidence that is presented, and indeed serves often to conceal the fact that much of the necessary evidence is lacking. Thus, in a work written some time ago, Lewis and Stewart (1958) state firmly that though they divide the businessman from the manager, they refuse to divide big businessmen from small, and they do not draw the distinctions between businessmen in terms of ownership position made here.[1] They refer often to the lack of evidence on businessmen, and in its absence they are forced to make use of newspaper and magazine articles, business history and a few studies of managers' and directors' backgrounds. In a study written sixteen years later, Jervis (1974) refers equally vaguely to 'bosses', and draws largely on the same sources.

The discussion of the previous chapters should have made clear the importance for theory of the distinctions I have suggested; but there is in fact ample empirical evidence to show their necessity.

To take the first proposition – that it is essential to study main board directors rather than managers lower down in the firm: I have already indicated that writer after writer has seen the members of the board as having, as a collectivity, a set of tasks that are quite distinct from those of managers, even though some directors also have managerial roles. As Pahl and Winkler (1974) discovered, not all directors can be expected to play the most important role of the board, the allocation of capital, which may be in the hands of a clique extending outside the board. Thus, in studying top managers we must seek out those whom we can be sure, or at least have good reason to believe, will be involved in this process, otherwise we fail to study those who have real power in the firm.

It could be argued that if we are concerned with how businessmen think, especially with how they think on social issues rather than their behaviour in the processes of corporate strategy formulation, then, simply because managers at all levels aspire to move upwards, they will think in similar ways. This could be a dangerous assumption.

First, it follows from studies of social mobility in industrial societies, the general results of which have indicated that the majority of individual social mobility from one generation to the next is over a short range, that top managers are more likely to come from elite social backgrounds than are those lower down. In the British case this means that we would expect those at higher levels of management to be more likely to have fathers in similar positions in managerial or professional hierarchies, and to have attended public schools and elite universities. And, as we shall see in chapter 4, there is evidence that this is so.

However, it may well be that the psychology, the personality, of the top businessmen is different from those in middle levels of management. Of course, it is difficult to sort out cause and effect here: are they different because they are at the top, or did they get to the top because they are different? The point, however, is that there *is* a difference. We may cite, for example, the work of Ghiselli in the United States, repeated in Britain by Margerison and Elliott (1975). They used a questionnaire technique to study the motivation of managers and found clear differences between those at different levels. Those at the top gave more importance to achievement, and less to both security and rewards for the job, than did those lower down. Need for power was not found to vary much. Such results could be taken to indicate that top managers, who actually do have higher rewards and more security than those lower down, feel less need for them. More interesting is that top managers rated themselves higher on initiative and supervisory activity than lower managers, but saw themselves as less decisive and self-assured than those below them.

The high need for achievement amongst top managers has been stressed in other studies, such as those of McClelland (1953;1961). That top executives are different from men in the middle is also made clear by Whyte (1957). Although as we saw in the last chapter, Whyte maintains that managers are becoming increasingly more conformist, less competitive, and much more given to teamwork within the corporation, and are encouraged in this by those at the top, he also emphasises that the men at the top are quite different. The top executive is said to resent the control of the company and have a fierce desire to control his own destiny. Thus the evidence available does suggest that top managers differ in social background and personality from those below them.

My second point was that one must study sufficiently large firms in order to study the business elite. Clearly, the small firm is more likely to be run by a founding entrepreneur or a founding family than a larger one, where managerial or finance control becomes more likely, and in the light of the ownership and control debate this is of obvious importance. Again, it is the very large oligopolistic corporation that is in the situation, if any company is, of being able to control its markets, to be a price-maker not a price-taker, as Baran and Sweezy (1966) put it. Equally important, the large firm is more likely to be multinational, that is, both selling and manufacturing in a number of markets. This is said by critics of the multinationals to give them advantages over the entirely home-based firm, but it also poses particular problems of control for those who head them, and puts additional strains on them.

Company size affects much more than the environment in which the corporation operates and its ability to alter it. It could be argued that the bureaucracy is so well-developed in the large corporation that the processes by which people at the top get things done are qualitatively different from those in small companies. Weber, the first to discuss the concept of bureaucratisation rigorously, suggested that the larger the organisation the more it would approach the ideal-type of a bureaucracy. Despite disputes over the extent and nature of centralisation in the large company, his predictions have largely been demonstrated, most notably in the work of Pugh and associates. One of these workers has summarised their findings: 'Larger organisations tend to assign their greater number of employees to more specialised roles within a greater range of different departments; to have more standardised procedures and documentation; and to delegate decisions to further down their more extended hierarchies' (Pugh and Hinings, 1976, p. 152).

This being the case, one has to ask whether those who flourish and succeed in such hierarchies are likely to be similar to those who, one way or another, come to be running small firms. [2]

Whatever the differences of life within the large organisation as compared to the small company, one may also point out that those who head small firms are likely to come from quite different social backgrounds. The chief executives studied by Boswell (1973) in his study of small firms were far less likely to have parents in white-collar or professional occupations, or to have been to public school than the men in this study. It also seems likely that they will not have had the opportunities to work in the range of specialist functions - for example, personnel, operations research, financial analysis - that exist in the large company.

The third distinction amongst businessmen may well be the most important of all. We have seen that, in considering the business elite, we cannot ignore those who primarily work in the finance sector and control firms in banking, insurance or investment. Yet this group is likely to have followed quite different career paths, and to be doing work of quite a different nature from those in the manufacturing sector, or the service and transportation industries. This, then, is a primary division amongst the elite.

And we may also have to consider entrepreneurs as a different group from those who are essentially managers. Not only are the former likely to be much wealthier, but there is some evidence that they have rather different personality characteristics. The major study in this area, that of Collins, Moore and Unwalla (1964), has the drawback that it looked at firms only in the Michigan area, so many of the firms were small. Nevertheless, some interesting conclusions arise. [3]

The entrepreneurs investigated by Collins *et al.* were very often found to be men who came from marginal groups, such as religious minorities or immigrant groups. They tended to be men who had found it hard to make progress through conventional educational channels. This was not only the result of their marginality, or poverty; often it was their personalities that were the problem; they tended to be too restless to accept the discipline of school, or later of established organisations or professions. In this they contrast with other business leaders.

Collins and his co-workers used thematic apperception (TAT) tests to indicate the personality characteristics of their sample. Thus, the entrepreneurs could be compared with the businessmen studied by Henry (1949) and Warner and Abegglen (1955). The two groups, entrepreneurs and bureaucrats, were found to have a number of personality differences. Those who had successfully climbed the bureaucratic ladder were found, by Henry, to have a high drive for achievement and for increasing status; they had very positive attitudes to authority and their own bosses; and they were men who found great satisfaction in their own work.

By contrast, the entrepreneurs were found to have little drive for status as such; nor did they submit to authority easily, and were least effective in their relationships with authority figures. Further, they tended not to work smoothly and easily but in sporadic bursts. [4]

Thus, it is clearly wrong to discuss the business elite as though they are a homogeneous grouping. The founders of businesses among the heads of the largest hundred or two hundred companies may be few, but they are quite clearly likely to differ from the bureaucrats. And there is a third group, the sons of founding fathers, and the grandsons, nephews and other relatives, who are quite likely to be different again, but of whom there has been virtually no study in the whole of the literature.

3.2 OBJECTIVES OF THE RESEARCH

I will now set out the objectives of the research which forms the subject matter for the remainder of this book. These were as follows:

(a) to attempt to obtain access to top businessmen and, if possible, to the elite among businessmen (as defined above) to establish the extent to which such access is possible and the extent to which the methodology of the personal interview is a useful and valuable one in investigating certain topics of interest;

(b) the primary focus of the research programme was that of the meaning systems of businessmen. As discussed above, such meaning systems are taken to encompass beliefs and values concerning class, status and power in society and to embody assumptions about, and attitudes to, the workplace and the local community.

Thus, taking as a first task of sociology that of making accurate and detailed descriptions of society, one objective was to make a description of the meaning systems (or images of society) held by businessmen, amongst whom may be members of a middle social class, a dominant class or a power elite, and whose viewpoint may be compared and contrasted with that of other groups in society;

(c) the relationship between the objective situation of members of society and their subjective perception of it has been much discussed in sociological theory. Thus, one could also apply the assumptions of such theory to the case of businessmen and, in asking how far that theory was able to predict the values and beliefs apparent among them, to test that theory itself;

(d) in addition, arising from the reading of theory set out here, I wished to consider the position of the business elite in playing two key roles within the capitalist system: an economic role, particularly as allocators of resources, and a role as political influentials or power-holders, and to use the interview methodology to study businessmen's own perceptions of these roles and the way they play them.

Now it can be seen that these objectives are interdependent, to

the extent that the later ones depend on the first, the achievement of satisfactory access to businessmen, and to the elite within businessmen, and the opportunity to question them on subjects
of interest. The study was envisaged as an exploratory one, and
was extended to encompass new objectives and to take account of
earlier findings during its course.

3.3 METHODOLOGY

The first objective was that of 'examining the possibilities of
access to the business elite'. As I have remarked several times in
the discussion of the last two chapters, elite studies in Britain
have generally fallen into a pattern in which the elite in question
is studied from afar. The position has been well summarised by
Ivor Crewe, who characterises British elite studies thus:
(1) Make no attempt to analyse the whole of the British elite
structure, study only one elite group at a time. (2) Select
the single elite group on grounds of accessibility and the
clarity of its boundaries rather than its importance within
the power structure of Britain. (3) Focus on the elite group's
collective biography - on who they are (or more likely, were)
not what they believe (ideology) or what they do (roles).
(4) Exclusively focus on its economic, educational and demographic origins. Thus the typical conception of an elite group
for British social scientists consists of the incumbents of the
top echelons of clearly structured and bounded social organisations which appear to possess manifest power or prestige;
and the customary way of understanding its nature is to
analyse its social origins...... This is a caricature of British
elite studies, but not an unreasonable one. (Crewe, 1974,
pp. 12-13)
In view of the objectives of this study, and the interest in what
businessmen think as individuals, rather than the statements put
out on their behalf, direct access to businessmen was felt to be
essential to this study. I did not expect this to be easy, especially
as one prominent British social scientist declined to discuss his
research on elites with me, stating that the proposed research had
been refused funds on the grounds that access to businessmen
would not be possible.
However, there were enough precedents in the work of Hunter
(1953), Dahl (1961) and more pertinently Bauer, Pool and Dexter
(1963, see also Dexter, 1970) in the United States; [5] and Nichols
(1969) and Child (1972) in Britain to make it worth investigating
the possibilities of such access. [6]
Nevertheless, it was expected that some methodologies would be
more successful than others. Pahl and Winkler (1974) found that
only 15 per cent of the firms they approached agreed to co-operate
in a study in which each of the company's directors was to be observed at work for one complete day, and this despite the fact
that the study had the backing of the Institute of Directors.

Similarly, businessmen are not responsive to questionnaire studies. Heller (1973) reports a 55 per cent response rate in a survey concerned only with directors' educational and other characteristics. In other such studies, Hall and Amado-Fischgrund (1969) had a 25 per cent response rate, and Peterson (1971) received back 177 out of 571 questionnaires (31 per cent) sent to chief executives in 42 countries.

Thus it was decided to use open-ended interviewing using a semi-formal schedule as the main method of data-collection. Questionnaires left behind with respondents to fill in themselves were used at one stage to research one aspect of perception of social status in Britain on which it was found difficult to ask questions in the interviews. This was not a successful strategy, mainly because of the nature and design of the questionnaire. The reasons for settling on the open-ended interview as the method of data-collection were:

(a) since no comparable study had been done, and since I was prepared for a high rejection rate, this was seen as an exploratory study, and the technique of asking open-ended questions was seen as allowing respondents maximum scope to put their own views, and to utilise their own frameworks of values and norms, rather than one imposed from the researcher;

(b) I wanted to treat the elite as other groups have been treated in studies of 'images of society'. The open-ended interview has become probably the most widely used technique in such studies, and I could therefore hope to make some comparisons with such studies.

(c) I wanted to obtain all shades of business opinion, and to obtain correspondingly the maximum response rate. The invitation to businessmen to 'hold a discussion' or be interviewed seemed the most likely way of achieving this, in view of the studies mentioned above.

(d) The most obvious alternative to interviewing was direct observation, and at least one researcher has maintained that the latter is by far to be preferred, as businessmen make different statements in public to those they make in private (see Winkler, 1974). However, it seemed unlikely that observation of businessmen would reveal them in situations where they would make references to one of the central topics of the interviews, that is, social class and status. Thus, very extensive observation would be required to collect sufficient data that would be relevant. I accept the need for more observation of the business elite and return to the issue of how far one can accept what businessmen say, that is, their sincerity, below.

3.4 DETAILS OF METHOD

Construction of Sampling Frame
As a result of the initial fears concerning access to businessmen, interviewing took place in four stages. It should further be noted

that the interview schedule was altered by the exclusion of some
topics and the inclusion of others after the first sixty interviews.
This puts some limitations on the final analysis of the data, most
particularly in the analysis of lobbying and political influence
made in chapter 8, an unavoidable consequence of making such a
study in an area where there was little research experience to
call on.

The sampling frame was constructed from 'The Times' lists of
1000 largest companies. It consisted of two sections, one taken
from the main list of commercial and industrial firms, the other
from the tables of largest merchant banks, insurance companies,
and property firms. Throughout this study I refer to the first
group as the 'commercial companies' and to the second as the
'financial companies'. Amongst the former I make a crude distinction between those with at least some manufacturing interests,
and those which are completely, or very nearly completely, service companies (for example, retail chain stores, importers/ex-
porters, publishers, advertising agencies). Clearly, since a
number of large firms are now divisionalised conglomerates, sometimes with one division in manufacturing and others in service
sectors, all I have done is to sort firms with no manufacturing
activity from the rest. However, because I was concerned with
possible contacts by businessmen in their careers, or currently,
with manual workers, I wanted to discriminate between firms where
this was at least possible and those where it was not. (Construction, building and mining were therefore classified as manufacturing activities on the same basis.)

Amongst all types of firms I wanted to discriminate between
directors by their relationship to capital. I therefore utilise
throughout this study the following distinctions between bureaucrats, family businessmen and entrepreneurs:
(a) Those whose fathers, grandfathers, or other relatives began
the firm they now head, or a substantial part of it, and who hold
substantial capital holdings in the firm, are called family businessmen. To establish which were such men required investigation
both of the man's shareholding and something of the firm's history.
(Examples of such men are the Cadburys, Sainsburys and Lord
Cowdray.) Not included among this group are those men whose
fathers headed the firm they now head, or were directors or senior
managers in it, but who were not founding families, or who do not
hold controlling shares (for example, Sir Reay Geddes of Dunlop).
I regard the family·businessmen as the group most likely to hold
the attitudes, such as they are, of the capitalist; more likely even
than the founding entrepreneurs because their families have held
wealth over generations.
(b) The second group is the bureaucrats: they are men who began
their careers at the bottom, or more usually as graduates or in a
professional capacity, and have climbed to the board through the
management hierarchy. (Examples: the heads of ICI, GKN, Tube
Investments.) Needless to say, the term bureaucrat is not used
with pejorative intent.

(c) The third group is the entrepreneurs; men who began the company they now head, and have built it up over the years; or who by merger and/or takeover have put together a large firm. Deciding who should come into this group can in some cases be difficult, since some men who seem prima facie to fall into this category turn out to have begun with small family businesses. Thus, Sir Jules Thorn, Sir Isaac Wolfson, and the late Charles Clore are obvious candidates for inclusion; but Sir Arnold Weinstock or Sir Frederick Wood of Croda are perhaps more doubtful cases.

The distinctions drawn here are similar to those used by Bendix (1956) and Clements (1958), although the latter further distinguishes between bureaucrat managers by their career patterns. The relevant information to make the categorisation used in this study can be difficult to find in practice for smaller companies, but for the purposes of this study it was a very useful one to make.

The third way of categorising firms was by size. Multiple criteria are available here: turnover, assets, numbers employed and so on. The following procedure was therefore adopted. I took all wholly British-owned firms outside the top 250 by turnover as being small firms (that is firms in the range 251-1000 of 'The Times' 1000), and where I refer to small firms in this study it is this group that I mean.

Amongst the top 250 I used multiple criteria. Again foreign-owned firms were first excluded. Then I took firms in order of size by turnover excluding those not also in the top 150 by size of assets, to give a list of 90 firms which are called here large firms.

The remaining firms were then excluded if their assets fell outside the top 250 in order of asset size, to give a list of 98 firms which are called medium sized firms. The effect of this is to place with the small companies those such as commodity brokers or importers which have a very large turnover relative to their assets.

A breakdown of the top 188 wholly British-owned companies as defined here (that is, 'large' and 'medium sized' firms) indicated that 129, or 69 per cent, are headed by bureaucrats; 42 (22 per cent) by family businessmen and just 17 (9 per cent) by entrepreneur-tycoons. No equivalent analysis was made for financial companies, nor was any attempt made to order them by size, although data on the numbers they employed was collected.

In view of the lengthy discussion in the literature as to the extent of shareholding required for control (see chapter 1), and the possibilities of control by hidden interest groups, I must point out that the breakdown of the bigger firms by type of control, that is bureaucrat, entrepreneur, family, was done primarily with a view to position vis-à-vis personal holdings of the top one or two executives, whom I hoped to interview. If hidden control is exercised by interest groups or financial institutions then there may be, amongst the firms apparently controlled by bureaucrats, a number that are subject to such control. I discovered no instances of such control.

The financial firms were all placed together as part of the same sampling frame, although banking, insurance and property are in principle quite different activities. However, in the examination of the interview material, men from the three different areas were analysed separately.

The Four Stages of Interviewing
The four stages of interviewing were:
(a) As an initial sample, and in order to establish that a study of this kind would be possible, a random sample was taken of chief executives from the commercial and financial sectors. I took both sectors because I hoped to compare them, but almost twice as many commercial firms were sampled because I also wanted to compare the heads of manufacturing and service companies. This initial sample was made on a completely random basis, except amongst small (that is, below the top 250 by turnover) firms, where only firms based in the south-east were taken. This made the heads of smaller companies more nearly comparable to those heading most large firms, as the latter tend to live in the south-east.

The respondents' co-operation was obtained simply by writing to them. The letter explained the purpose of the research as to investigate 'the career and backgrounds of Britain's top business-men' and to discover their views on a number of topics, which were set out as being 'the aims and goals of the men at the top for their companies; the responsibilities of the director, the re-lationship between business and government; and rewards, con-flict and consensus both within the firm and wider society'.

The letter went on to request an interview with the researcher to last about one hour, at some time convenient to the respondent. It was stated that the interviews would be confidential, and that no names would be revealed in any of the research publications. This was clearly important in obtaining access, as was the promise of a short report on the research. The letter was brief, compris-ing only three paragraphs.

The initial approach was made to 133 chief executives, 87 from the commercial sector, the remaining 46 from the finance compan-ies. Of these, 63 (47 per cent) accepted the invitation to be interviewed, and it was found possible in fact to interview 60 of these (45 per cent). Thirty-nine of these chief executives worked in the commercial sector, twenty-one in financial firms.
(b) The response from the first stage was considered to be en-couraging, and a preliminary analysis was made of some of the material. At this stage it was hoped that the study could be dev-eloped by comparing directors in different functional specialities in the firm, such as marketing, finance, production and so on. Therefore, a short report on the interviews was prepared and sent to those who had taken part, asking them to suggest direct-ors on their firms' boards who would also be willing to be inter-viewed. It was hoped that, as the chief executives had already proved co-operative, they would be sufficiently interested to per-suade their fellow directors to take part.

This was not a successful tactic. In the event only nineteen such interviews with full-time directors in ten different companies were obtained, and three of the latter were financial firms. The men came from a variety of specialities. All the sixteen commercial company directors came from firms within the top 250 by turnover.

These men were interviewed, and extensions to the questionnaire were piloted on them. However, they were a group which was both self-selected to a greater degree than the original sample was, and yet was too small to allow for comparisons of men working in different functional specialisms which had been the intention. Thus, throughout this study much more weight has been placed on the evidence obtained from the chief executives, and in many of the tables they are shown separately.

(c) All the interviews in the first two stages were with men at the workplace and were limited by constraints of time. I now decided to see if I could obtain longer, in-depth interviews, which possibly would give some insight into the home life of the businessman.

I therefore contacted all the eleven chief executives of large firms (again those in the top 90 as defined above) who had retired in the year May 1974 to April 1975 and asked them for interviews. I obtained interviews with nine of the eleven.

These interviews were very useful, in that I was allowed considerable lengths of time, in some cases most of a day, and they thus provide almost case-study material. In practice, however, I went to the men's homes in only five cases; the others I saw at their clubs, or offices of firms where they retained non-executive directorships.

Again these men are not strictly comparable to men who are still working full-time, but it has been felt to be justified to include them for most of the discussion. Although retired, they had left office in all cases within months of the interviews, and usually retained some business interests. More important, it seems very unlikely that men can change on retirement the pattern of thought of a lifetime, and the study was concerned with their patterns of thought. Clearly, there was little point in asking questions about the current strategies or policies of their companies, and some questions had to be left out or rephrased. Otherwise, this group showed little apparent difference from the other chief executives of similarly sized firms.

(d) In the final stage of the study it was decided to concentrate on the chief executives of medium and large commercial firms, and sampling was done only amongst these. There were several reasons for this. First, it was by now clear that access was as easy to the heads of large firms as small ones, and since I was interested primarily in the business elite it was clearly sensible to take only those men who most clearly held that status. Again, experience of the second stage had showed that choosing just one man from each firm gave better results than appealing for help from the directorate as a whole.

However, the decision to approach chief executives posed a

difficulty with regard to men in the finance sector, as, having approached 47 in the first stage, there were very few left in the original sampling frame, and no suitable additions. I therefore decided not to approach any more men from this sector. This leaves only a small comparative sample in this study, which must therefore be considered primarily as a study of men in industrial and service companies, excluding the City.

However, I still wished to be able to compare 'capitalists' with 'managers', or 'bureaucrats' as the latter are called here. I therefore wrote to all the entrepreneurs and family businessmen heading firms amongst the top 188 (on the multiple criteria) who had not been hitherto approached, plus a number of bureaucrats chosen at random. It was now that one particular problem of access became apparent: of thirty-seven bureaucrats successfully approached (that is, those confirmed as receiving the letter), twenty-one, or 57 per cent, agreed to be interviewed; likewise of thirty-eight family businessmen receiving letters, eighteen (47 per cent) were interviewed. But of fifteen entrepreneur-tycoons approached, only three accepted. Clearly, then, it is the latter group which presents the true problems of access for the social scientist. We may therefore summarise the final sample of men who were interviewed in table form, and this is done in Table 3.1.

I do not claim that this is a representative sample of the British business elite. It does, however, contain a balance of men from manufacturing to men from service firms, there being 66 of the former and 39 of the latter. Further, as it happens, amongst the 111 chief executives 9 per cent are entrepreneurs, 22 per cent family businessmen and 69 per cent bureaucrats, which corresponds to the overall breakdown of the 188 largest companies as given above. The balance is similar amongst the chief executives of commercial firms taken separately also. However, it must be remembered that whilst there was relatively good response from the entrepreneurs heading small firms, it was poor amongst the comparatively well-known men who have built up firms so large that they come into the top 188.

What I do claim for this sample is that all types of men, all shades of opinion and viewpoint are likely to be present in it. Certainly there can be no doubt that a very high proportion of those interviewed are members of the business elite by most definitions, and that they may be assumed to play (or did) the roles ascribed to the elite in chapter 1.

As can be seen from Table 3.1, 47 chief executives from the 90 largest British firms were interviewed (although some of these were retired), and this included five of the heads of the top ten companies by turnover. (And see the second paragraph of chapter 1 for some of their other offices of note.)

Design of the Interview Schedule
The interview schedule, which is reproduced in Appendix 1, was intended to allow the executives who were to be interviewed to reveal in their own words their picture and values concerning

Table 3.1   Summary table of final achieved sample

			Chief executives		Other directors
		Entrepreneurs	Family businessmen	Bureaucrats	All bureaucrats
Total		130	10	24	77	19

		Entrepreneurs	Family businessmen	Bureaucrats	All bureaucrats
Total		130	10	24	77	19
Large	Manufacturing	1	5	27	11
	Service	1	5	8	0
Medium	Manufacturing	2	4	6	0
	Service	0	4	5	4
Small	Manufacturing	3	1	6	0
	Service	1	3	8	0
All	'Commercial'	8	22	60	15
	Insurance	0	0	9	3
	Merchant banking	1	2	6	1
	Property	1	0	2	0
All	'Financial'	2	2	17	4

inequalities of reward, opportunity, status and power, first in the firm, and then more widely in society. The schedule consisted of a series of standard questions which were always asked as far as possible with the same wording. However, additional questions were used as necessary. Further, when issues were raised by the respondent spontaneously these would sometimes be discussed prior to their usual place in the sequence of questioning. This helped to give the interviews more of the feel of an informal discussion which set the respondents more at ease.

The original interview schedule began by asking the person being interviewed to outline his career from the time of leaving full-time education. Aside from the intrinsic value of this as part of the data-collection process, it was felt that it would serve to get the man concerned talking freely. This section was retained throughout all the interviews.

The first main section of the interview questioning dealt with aspects of conflict and consensus in the company. The interviewee

was first asked to set out the goals towards which he was directing the organisation at that time. In later interviews this was
augmented with questions concerning the responsibilities of the
company director, and of the effect or lack of it of a family connection with the company.

Following the statement of their own goals for the firm, the executives were asked to what extent they saw other groups as
sharing these goals. The discussion then moved to areas of potential conflict within the firm, especially that between management
and other employees.

Further aspects of the original schedule dealt with the basis on
which people are, and should be, rewarded in the firm; with the
question of whether the executive was aware of a boardroom cabal
or clique (a question prompted by the work of Pahl and Winkler,
1974) and in a crude way with status and power in the firm. Finally, the interview moved specifically to a discussion of class and
status in wider society.

After the first sixty interviews some parts of the schedule were
analysed and these, in the main, dealt with the questions of the
goals for the firm, of some aspects of industrial relations, and of
power within the firm. A preliminary report was made.

However, it was clear that while some parts of the schedule were
producing interesting data, those dealing with the executive's own
rewards or rewards more generally in the firm, and of status and
power in the firm did not justify their inclusion in their original
form. Thus on the question of rewards in the firm, the executives
either affirmed their belief in the free market for wages, or else
of a job evaluation scheme, or sometimes both. The questions on
status and power produced little more than an advocacy, or affir-
mation, of the necessity and correctness of the firm's formal hierarchy. [7]

The interview schedule had presented another difficulty which
was not originally foreseen. This was that in the discussion of
class and status in society, the statements made by businessmen
revealed little about them as a politically influential grouping. It
seemed that this issue, the issue of power in society, was perceived by businessmen as being distinct from the topic of class,
or else that they did not see themselves as a political elite,
although they may in fact have such influence. I therefore wished
to add a section to the schedule dealing with the power as businessmen saw it of themselves relative to other groups, and of ways and
issues on which they might seek to influence state officials. The
decision was taken to cut the less useful sections of the schedule
and to add in this new area of questioning.

Thus not all those who were part of the sample were asked all
the questions set out in Appendix 1; specifically, the first sixty
men interviewed were not asked in any depth about influencing
government. This is to be regretted, but it was clearly desirable
to make the change in the schedule.

A consistent problem was the choice of wording in the basic
interview schedule, and this can be seen most clearly with respect

to questions about social class. Here, as elsewhere, it was thought desirable not to use any terminology that would suggest an 'image of society' to the respondent, and various forms of wording were experimented with in which the word 'class' was not used in the question at all. It was soon found, however, that only questions phrased in a relatively direct form produced a useful response here. In this particular case a modification of the question used in the 'Affluent Worker' studies (Goldthorpe *et al.*, 1969) was used, which in this case was: 'People talk of there being classes in our society, how do you see this?' Elsewhere other questions were taken from studies concerned with similar topics, with suitable modification.

Details of Method
Once the interviews were arranged, a programme of research was undertaken on the personal histories of the men to be interviewed, and the nature and history of the companies. It was clearly impor- tant to be well informed in this respect. Kincaid and Bright (1957) have pointed out that this does make research of this kind rela- tively expensive and time-consuming. Indeed, they report that they could only average three interviews per week. A higher rate of interviewing was achieved in this research. 130 interviews were done in the two-year period from May 1974 to May 1976. There was some transcribing of tape-recording after this date, however.

The tape-recording of the interviews which has not yet been mentioned was a very important part of the research method. I always asked permission to tape-record the interviews and in the majority of cases received it.[8] After the interview a full transcript was made of the interview, and it is on the basis of the content analysis of these that the businessmen's beliefs, values and atti- tudes are reported.

The procedure thus adopted was extremely time-consuming. (Estimates of the time it takes to make a transcript have ranged among researchers from three to seven times the actual interview time.) I believe, however, that it is very rewarding; and the only acceptable way, other than transcripts from shorthand, to use the open-ended interview technique. It allows for repeated resifting of the interview material, and ensures that respondents are at least not misreported.

The length of the interview requested was one hour; in only a few cases was this cut short. More usually, longer was allocated, in some cases as much as two and a half hours with men working full-time, and even longer with those who were retired. The first two interviews were done by myself and a colleague; and I then did all the remainder except for five with chief executives which were done by another researcher.[9] All transcribing and analysis is my own responsibility.

The format in which interview extracts are reproduced may be noted here. I have stuck to the use of ordinary punctuation, feel- ing it to be adequate for the rhythm of ordinary speech except

that I have also used dashes to indicate pauses for thought.
Usually I have not reproduced sounds such as aah, um, ugh, etc.
I have never changed the respondent's words, but sometimes
sections, or identifying names, are left out. Where such a break
in actual flow of what was said is made it is indicated by a series
of dots:.... Proper names, especially of companies, are shown
as (-------).

3.5 CRITIQUE OF THE METHODOLOGY

General
In outline, the methodology of this study consisted of contacting
people who were defined as being top businessmen, that is, members of the boards of the largest British firms or financial institutions; interviewing them on a number of topics, and by content
analysis of the resulting transcripts attempting to extract a synthesis of their views of their companies, of relationships within
them, and of class, status and power more generally in society.
This methodology parallels that used in other similar sociological
investigations with one difference of some importance, and others
of perhaps lesser import.

The difference that will appear of overwhelming importance is
that those studied were men of power and some wealth rather than
manual or clerical workers. At best, we suspect them of being
better able than other groups to construct a plausible story, that
is, to put across a picture of beliefs that is internally consistent,
and founded in testable fact, or even knowledge to which they
may claim privileged access, than we find elsewhere. At worst, we
suspect them of insincerity, and this specific difficulty is taken up
in the next section.

There are other problems: first, it was necessary to make the
discussion always appear relevant to questions of industrial life,
or at least to business, or politics connected with it in some form.
I could not discuss in any detail the men's social lives, patterns
of friendship, their prominently or lowly placed relatives, their
membership of voluntary associations, their relationships with
their wives and neighbours - in short, their community situation.
I offer some information on these topics, but it is, of necessity,
limited and, in consequence, limits the explanations of how images
of society are generated amongst this group.

Open-ended interviewing also raises certain problems concerning
the reliability and validity of the data gathered. Taking the first
of these, the question may be phrased 'would those interviewed
have said the same things at a different time or in a different situation?' I certainly would not deny that some of those interviewed
would express some views on some topics that would differ from
those I found if they were interviewed again in different circumstances, and I specifically argue this point on the basis of my
findings. As to whether repeat interviews would produce different

results, we simply do not know. There are clear difficulties with obtaining repeat interviews with such a group, and I did not attempt it. Perhaps this is an area on which future research will improve.

The question of validity is also difficult to answer. This is a study primarily of beliefs and values, and I would argue that the open-ended interview is the best way of allowing a respondent to display his beliefs with minimal interference from the researcher. The onus is then on the researcher to make an analysis of the resulting statements that adequately takes account of what was actually said, and of the range of variation within it. To this end I have never hesitated to test my own impressions of what the businessmen said by counting and analysing just how many of the total, or of relevant sub-groups, did make such statements. This technique does provide a constant check that the researcher has not built too much on the odd, unusual or striking statements of individuals or small minority groups.

Against this, however, it must be said that simple word-counting or even phrase-, sentence-, or concept-counting, cannot be adequate in itself as an analysis of belief systems. It is necessary to look for whole patterns of belief, of sets of linked concepts, or even sets of shared but implicit assumptions. To some extent this has been attempted, but inevitably the personal viewpoint of the researcher intrudes into such research. The only corrective must be re-analysis of the same material by other researchers. This I would welcome. [10]

Sincerity
The most widely repeated criticism encountered in connection with this study, one made by both academics and laymen, concerns the sincerity of the men who were interviewed. How do we know that businessmen were telling the truth in the interviews, and were not just putting across a good picture of their activities? Did they perhaps tell only part of the truth, keeping the darker side of their activities hidden? At worst, do they tell outright lies?

Before considering the question, one may perhaps point out that in almost any other sociological study of this kind it would be extraordinary for the researcher to raise such questions. Substitute coalminer, foreman, lorry-driver, clerk, or shop steward where the words businessman or director or chief executive appear in this book and it would be most unusual, almost, indeed, in bad taste, to wonder if one's respondents were liars.

For some reason, however, it appears that businessmen are often thought to be engaged in some kind of activity that is in some respects shady, or, at best, distasteful. The businessman, by implication, is of the kind of character that can cope with the subsequent disjunction between public morality and private acts, under which more sensitive souls (especially those of academics who are to a man honest, scrupulous, and non-materialistic) would wither. It has been most extraordinary to encounter such expectations amongst middle managers, who might themselves be expected to aspire to high company office.

One comfort is that there is no consensus as to the direction or nature of business falsehoods: some have it that businessmen evince a false concern for employees, social welfare, and the values of the 'soulful corporation', whilst in reality being concerned with profit at all costs. Others have it that they conceal behind the veneer of talk of the need for profit, efficiency, and the importance of entrepreneurship, a desire for the easy life, empire-building and personal gain. Some see the men at the top as ruthless and hard - the men who elbowed every one else out of the way; to others they are those who always did the conventional, who were the 'yes-men' and took no risks in their rise through the bureaucracy.

Businessmen in this study did not, when interviewed, volunteer tales of tax havens in the Cayman Isles, or of bribing politicians, or insider trading, or of the forming of secret cartels (though some, it transpired from other sources, were doing or were aware of some of these things). Despite this, it is my belief that the great majority were sincere in the answers they gave on most questions. It is, of course, virtually impossible to produce evidence to back up this impression. On those topics where I did have independent evidence - their careers, or their wealth or income - I found a few errors, but these could as well have been genuine mistakes.

This is not to say there were not inconsistencies amongst the views that businessmen gave, or even statements that appeared to be contradicted by the person's own behaviour either before or subsequent to the interview. I have pointed to some of these in the analysis, but, again, these may in fact be situations where a generalised statement is contradicted by a particular instance. For example, a director may maintain that it is a director's responsibility to look after the welfare of employees, and to provide security of employment; they may sincerely believe this, but acquiesce when employees are made redundant at a particular factory if they feel that circumstances compel such redundancies. In such situations it is not easy to differentiate between pious talk being used to cover a different attitude to practical cases, and a general but sincere belief being contradicted by a particular but unusual circumstance.

Certainly, if businessmen do tell deliberate falsehoods then my observation is that they have become so adept at it they do so in most cases without even pausing to work out their evasions. They may well use cruder language amongst themselves, and no doubt they did on occasion search for the delicate or bland phrase, but it will be seen that the interview transcripts contain many instances of blunt and straightforward talking.

My conclusion, that those interviewed were on the whole sincere, is reinforced when we come to ask what would be the motive for insincerity. It must be remembered that businessmen were giving up their time, which is often very short, to assist in research, in all reports of which they were to be nameless. None were to benefit from public acclaim for their views, or the picture they presented in the interview. It would seem unlikely that men in such positions gain much in self-esteem by spinning yarns to academic researchers; indeed, it would seem a priori more likely that a shop steward or foreman would do so than a captain of industry.

Businessmen may, of course, hold beliefs that conflict with the facts as sociologists view them; they may behave in ways that are contrary to their own beliefs or values; they may act in ways which they are not aware of or in the reverse of the way they think they act; they may, in short, deceive themselves. This, however, is not the same as being insincere, and is certainly not confined to businessmen.

More Fundamental Considerations
This research attempts to throw light on certain problems of sociological theory by studying the behaviour and attitudes of people who are seen as occupying key roles within the capitalist system. The most fundamental criticism of it that might be made is that it is not relevant to the problems of theory which it addresses.

This criticism may be seen as part of a wider critique of sociological research which attempts to understand the actor's 'frame of reference', which is the starting point for many sociologists working within the traditions of Weberian thought. The criticism comes, figuratively speaking, from the right and the left. On the one hand, and specially relevant to this study, Milton Friedman has remarked that 'asking businessmen to explain their [economic decisions] in this way has about the same validity as asking octogenarians to account for their longevity' (taken from Friedman, 1953, and quoted in Shackleton, 1978). A similar criticism is made by some Marxists, who would maintain that the capitalist system is not to be understood by reference to the beliefs or personal behaviour of individual capitalists. We must examine these claims.

The economist's argument here is that economic systems have their own laws which govern such factors as the price of goods, the level of interest, the rate of investment, and so on. Individual agents within the system can make their own decisions, but only within the framework of the laws. For example, a company does not charge the wrong price for its goods because, one way or another, if it does it goes out of business. Thus, what can be learned from asking businessmen about their decisions is either trivial and obvious, or else is not capable of refutation or proof, except when examined in the context of the economic system as a whole, and with the use of 'objective' measures.

The argument is a powerful one, but it is so only as long as we accept that the assumptions of economic theory are met. Controllers of business enterprises would only be subject to economic laws if there were in fact a free market economy, free from restrictions, and with perfect competition. It may be argued (see chapter 1) that these conditions do not exist in any economy dominated by very large oligopolistic firms, in which consumers buy on the basis not just of price but perceptions of value for money, which in turn may be mediated by deliberate marketing strategy; in which governments maintain monopoly industries, and subsidise certain firms, sectors, and geographic regions; and in which a strong trade union movement may be able to obtain wages above the 'economic' level. It is true that economists have attempted to incorporate some of these factors in their analyses, but it seems doubtful that they are able to do so without giving to the controllers of large firms some element of choice as to how they behave.

It may be argued, therefore, that the problem with 'positive economics' is that it is no longer adequate when applied to the economy of advanced industrial nations. We may take as an example here the ownership and control debate, which has been considered by both economists and sociologists. The foundation of the debate is the contention that the managers of very large firms are freed from any direct control over the level of dividend they pay out, or the disposition of the firm's resources, and so are able to develop alternative goals to profit maximisation. Such a debate could not take place if firms were bound by rigid economic laws. And as we have seen, positive economics has not provided a successful resolution to the debate. All that we have is a plethora of studies, some of them conflicting, as to whether or not owner-controlled firms do have higher rates of profit or growth or whatever. Indeed, economic theory alone seems unable to provide us with a successful definition of what an owner-controlled firm is, for in more recent studies it is suggested that we take account of such factors as the history and identity of the chairman and chief executive.

One can do no better in summing up these arguments than to quote from an article by Edith Penrose, written over twenty-five years ago, in which she attacked biological analogies of the firm (then more prevalent than they are now):

Our knowledge of why men do what they do is very imperfect, but there is considerable evidence that consciously formulated human values do affect men's attitudes, that many considerations are reached after a conscious consideration of alternatives, and that men have a wide range of choices. The information that we possess about the behaviour of men, small as it is, does furnish us with some plausible explanations of what firms are trying to do and why. (Penrose, 1952)

Marxist theories encompass far more than the economic, and the Marxist critique goes further. The argument here is similar in suggesting that by asking businessmen about their place in the system, their behaviour and their roles, and by accepting their accounts as true, we give a false place to the ideas that men hold. Men are not free agents but constrained by the material conditions in which they live. Further, understanding the actions of individual capitalists does not contribute to an understanding of the system of capitalism, which has its own internal and pervasive logic. And Marxists believe that one result of the relationships in which men find themselves within the capitalist system is that the system itself appears to them in a mystified guise, so that their ideas about it are no clue to its true nature.

One's view of such arguments depends partly on one's view of Marxism as a system of thought. As a sociologist, one might reply that Marxist reasons for wanting to understand capitalism (the understanding being largely given in the works of Marx), which is to explain it and to expose its contradictions and the exploitation inherent with it (as a spur to class action), are not necessarily those of the sociologist. As a sociologist, one might well be interested in how men adapt to the conditions in which they live, and the explanations that they give for their conduct.

But certain problems of Marxist theory suggest that the understanding of the ideas that men hold is not irrelevant. One such problem is explaining how it is that the revolution has not occurred in the most 'advanced' countries economically, which is where Marx predicted it. Another is to explain how classes, which are economic divisions, can come to be social ones as well; and this in turn is related to the wide problems of explaining the connections between the economic, the political and the ideological spheres.

The economistic interpretation of Marxism, which views social, political and ideological phenomena as mere epiphenomena, more or less directly controlled by the substructure, the relations of production, has looked increasingly unconvincing as more and more countries have emerged calling themselves communist, without having developed completely through the stages of feudalism and capitalism. That leaves two alternative strands of Marxist theory.

The first draws upon the distinction between class-in-itself and class-for-itself, made by Marx in some of his writings. This sees the failure of the revolution in Western capitalist countries as attributable to the failure of the working class to develop the necessary consciousness of their position and of the nature of the system. As Hindess (1978) points out, such a position, which sees class action as possible on the basis only of shared consciousness, has the consequence, which Weber recognised, that there may be important kinds of action which are not based on class division at all (but on distinctions of, for example, race or religion). Such an interpretation of Marxism is not incompatible with sociological studies of the kind presented here, but is clearly problematic from the Marxist perspective.

An alternative conception is advanced by Althusser (1965; Althusser and Balibar, 1970). In this system, the distinction between class-in-itself and class-for-itself is repudiated. Rather, the 'relative autonomy' of the economic, the political and the ideological instances is asserted, but via the notions of structural causality and overdetermination it is stated that the economy determines all three. However, it does so, in the overworked phrase, only in the last instance.

Althusser's complex (and obscure) writings are not without problems of their own. As both Hirst (1976) and Hindess (1978) point out, the concept of relative autonomy is a way of avoiding the trap of economism, towards which Althusser tends because he

rejects as ideological Marx's earlier writings in which consciousness, especially in the theory of alienation, does play a part. A
difficulty of Althusser's writing, however, is that it fails to give
any clear guidelines as to how we can know what the limits of
economic determination in the political or ideological spheres are.
And, indeed, Hindess and Hirst accuse Althusser of failing to
face up to the consequences of the autonomy of political and ideological phenomena which are 'that such phenomena cannot be
evaluated solely in terms of their representation, or failure to
represent the essential interests of classes' (Hindess, 1978).[11]

From Althusser's structural perspective, then (and Poulantzas,
1968, 1969, employs similar arguments), studies such as this one
have no validity. As I argued with respect to positive economics,
I personally doubt that the development of social theory can be
completely successful without reference to the ideas and beliefs
that participants, whether as members of classes, or other groupings hold. However, in no sense do I regard such data as the only
evidence that can be brought to bear on any theoretical problem;
the conclusions of this study have to be taken in conjunction with
other evidence of all types.

3.6 THE CONTEXT OF THE STUDY

It may be of some help, especially in chapter 8, which is partly
about political lobbying, to recall for the reader the atmosphere
in Britain when these interviews took place, especially among
businessmen, for there was a certain change in their attitude over
the two years.

Interviewing began in May 1974, just four months after Mr
Heath's government had ended following the miners' strike. Initially, as was clear from the interviews, the passing of the Tory
government greatly alarmed heads of business companies. So did
the personnel and the avowed intentions of the incoming Labour
government. From their manifesto, and statements of members
of the cabinet, it seemed that there was to be more nationalisation
of companies in the private sector, together with the creation of
the National Enterprise Board; there would be an attempt to direct capital investment through the enforcement of planning agreements; the Conservatives' Industrial Relations Act would be replaced by something more favourable to the trade unions and
measures to introduce industrial democracy would be made law.

Thus, at the start of the period of interviewing, businessmen
were far from happy with the prospects for the country or themselves. In fact, of course, these intentions came to very little.
The government was largely preoccupied with the economy and its
most draconian measures were directed at curbing inflation. However, even its efforts in this direction did not always please businessmen. At one stage the government was controlling prices,
wage rises, and dividend increases, and was apparently intending
to control investment as well.

In the face of the apparent strength of the Labour left *vis-à-vis* the government, the genuine problems faced by many businesses, and the effect on their own rewards of inflation and wage control, businessmen did attempt to counter, at least by propaganda. Thus, they took all opportunities to emphasise the need to raise profitability levels, or to refer to the drain, real or apparent of managerial talent caused by the restriction of salary levels, or the low morale of the country's managers.

Perhaps it is just this writer's own sensitivity to such issues, but it did seem that business's attempts to put its case were hampered, both during the Heath government and subsequently by a succession of events that were, if not scandals, certainly unfortunate publicity from the business point of view.

To name some of these: there was the property boom, during which some highly publicised deals, in which enormous profits were made, took place (symbolised by the huge and empty Centre Point). There was the refusal by Distillers to pay compensation to thalidomide victims, until public (and, so I was told, private) pressure forced them to. There was a boardroom row at Lonrho, and subsequent revelations, which moved Mr Heath to the memorable description of the events as 'the unpleasant and unacceptable face of capitalism'. At the end of the property boom, there was the collapse of several so-called fringe banks, together with one or two not-so-fringe merchant banks. And, in turn, came the demise of Slater Walker, together with revelations of illegal deals in the Far East. There were reports that numerous British companies in South Africa paid wages below the 'poverty datum line'. There was the departure of the chief executive of the Rank Organisation, and the attendant publicity given to the amorous activities of the chief executive and chairman. More recently, the chairman of Scottish and Universal Investments resigned after allegations of insider trading. And, in common with American nultinationals, a number of British companies admitted to paying bribes for business in various countries.

Most of the businessmen interviewed in this study would dismiss these stories, indeed did dismiss these stories, as being unrepresentative of the bulk of business activity or behaviour by business leaders. But the stories alluded to, though some in isolation are trivial, can hardly have served to impress on the general public that the behaviour of those who head large corporations is, in the phrase of the Advertising Standards Authority, 'legal, decent, honest, and truthful'.

But the period was not one of continuous gloom for businessmen, and indeed, by the time of the last interviews, in late 1976, a distinct change was noticeable in their feelings. There were two aspects to this.

First, the immediate crisis of 1974 passed away, and inflation was (in 1976) slowing. Second, it was by then clear that much of what the Labour government had promised, or threatened, depending on your point of view, was not going to happen. For instance, the price and dividend controls which were being applied in 1974 were relaxed; the Industry Act had little effect, the government's intentions to introduce measures to establish industrial democracy went into abeyance, and Mr Healey's promise to 'squeeze the rich until the pips squeak' resulted in a Royal Commission on the Distribution of Income and Wealth but little more.

Thus, the changing climate may be summarised as being one in which business was initially worried, and in which it was continually on the defensive, but in the event few of its worst fears were realised.

3.7 THE INTERVIEWS

Lastly in this chapter, it may be of some interest to readers to describe what actually took place at the interviews. The vast majority took place in London, and with the exception of the retired men, at the offices of the directors themselves. Suitably clad, and clutching my cassette recorder, I made my way to company headquarters, first to one receptionist, and very often to another on another floor. Although a high percentage of the appointments made initially were changed because the man in question had some other engagement, I was rarely sent away once the arranged meeting time had come. The businessmen were usually on time, and seemed to live a life of meetings scheduled and controlled by their secretaries.

There was some variety of office design and decoration, but there are, in principle, two kinds: the director's suite at the top of the massive modern block, and the older period building with antique furniture, which is often smaller, perhaps housing only a small staff and some of the main board. It should be noted that only a very few of these executives had their offices on a factory site.

It seems that the more senior the manager or executive the more he is allowed, or desires, to make his office look as though it is not an office. Thus the top man's desk is often empty of papers; he may have a television in the room; and very frequently he has a sofa, armchairs and a small table.[12] It was here that we would sit for the interview, often taking tea at the same time. I was rarely offered alcohol and lunch only once, but tea or coffee very frequently.

I found the businessmen personally to be very much as one would expect a largely random selection of 130 men, but, of course, better spoken, more articulate and self-confident than average. Most were pleasant in their manner, some even charming; some were very interesting, one or two slightly dull, and a few were hostile or aggressive for whatever reasons (one or two became aggressive in the course of the interview). It is only fair to record that there were some men of obvious and impressive intelligence. Aside from this, I can offer no tips to aspiring chairmen except that it seems to help to be tall.

The interviewees themselves asked surprisingly few questions about the purposes of the research. The explanation they were given which stressed little more than its academic value seemed to satisfy them. And they rarely queried the direction and nature of the interview, until the questioning touched openly on social class (see chapter 7).

Initially, it was a somewhat daunting task to attempt to interview men of the sort of experience of those in this study, but, as with all performances, I believe it improved with practice. The results of it must be judged by the findings it produced, and to these I now turn.

4 RESERVED SEATS:
family background, education, career and present lifestyle of top businessmen

'Any attempt to deny that my own seat in life was reserved for me would be ridiculous.' J. Paul Getty: 'As I See It', 1976, p. 20

4.1 INTRODUCTION

It was noted at the start of the previous chapter that elite studies in Britain have, with a few exceptions, depended heavily on reference works to describe the business elite. The major problem of doing so is that the information contained in such works is always incomplete. Further, it is at least arguable that the data from such sources will tend to be biased towards inclusion of those who are from high status familes by birth.

To take one example, 'Who's Who', a major source book for many such studies, has information nowadays on all but a few of the chief executives of the top 100 companies. In the past, however, such men were not included automatically, and those who were were often those with aristocratic connections, or else those who had achievements to their names from spheres outside business, such as being a member of parliament. Thus one suspects that men were far more likely to appear in 'Who's Who' if they were part of a family that controlled a firm over some generations than if they were men who worked their way diligently through it to arrive and spend a few years in the top position.

Inevitably, too, the amount of information contained in reference works is limited, and there are certain areas of interest which are not included in them.

The interview methodology adopted in this study, together with the additional research into the backgrounds of the men who were interviewed, allows us to fill in some of the gaps. And whilst the information presented here is not always as full as one would wish, it is in some ways a more complete description of the origins, careers, and other aspects of businessmen's lives than has so far been available.

Thus this chapter has several purposes. First, it brings together most of what might be called the factual, as opposed to the attitudinal, data collected in this study. By doing so one is able to compare the men studied here with the characteristics of the business elite as a whole, so far as these are known, and ask whether there are any obvious biases in the sample, or at least the sample of chief executives. My conclusion in this regard is that in almost all characteristics the men in my sample were typical of top business-men apart from the absence, mentioned earlier, of entrepreneur-tycoons heading large companies.

I also try in this chapter to give a full picture of the sort of men who come to head Britain's big firms, the career paths that took them to the top, the rewards of being there and the lives they now lead. In drawing this picture I make use of my own data and those from previous studies.

Inevitably there is a mass of largely statistical information to present here, and one must be conscious that the detailed dis-cussion of this can be very indigestible to anyone who is not en-gaged in compiling such data himself. However, much of it can be easily gathered from the tables, and the summary at the end of the chapter, whilst the text itself should make clear any particular points of interest to the reader.

The chapter falls essentially into four parts: the first concerns the social background and educational experience of the business elite (sections 4.2-4.4); the second compares the interviewees with those surveyed in other studies of directors and managers (sections 4.5, 4.6); the third examines the careers of the respon-dents (sections 4.7-4.10); and the last summarises what is known of their present lifestyles (sections 4.11-4.14).

4.2 THE ELITE WERE WELL PLACED BY BIRTH

Paul Getty (1976) remarks in his autobiography that 'any attempt to deny that my own seat in life was reserved for me would be ridiculous.' Those who have investigated the business elite have long been conscious that the majority of seats appear to be reser-ved - if not for individuals, then at least for those whose fathers already occupy rather similar seats. Such conclusions have usually been drawn on the basis of the kind of education the elite have received. We may begin here, however, by considering the occu-pations of the fathers of the men who were interviewed. This is set out in the Tables 4.1, 4.2. The first of these uses the con-ventional categories of the Registrar-General's social classes; the second uses the recently devised Hope-Goldthorpe scale (see Gold-thorpe and Hope, 1974). The latter was specifically designed to be used in studies of social mobility. It is based on the subjective judgments of large numbers of people as to the relative 'goodness' or desirability of different jobs. Several dimensions enter into such judgments, and it should be noted that the scale is contin-uous, the lowest ranked occupation receiving a score of 17.52, and the highest receiving 82.05. Further, on this scale some kinds of manual job rate more highly than some white-collar jobs, which may reflect the change of relative rewards in occupation in recent years.

A glance at the tables is enough to confirm that top businessmen, even if they are not born into founding families, are drawn over-whelmingly from the sons of those in white-collar occupations. Only

Table 4.1   Father's occupation, tabulated in the Registrar-General's social class groupings

| | | | Type of respondent | | | | |
		Whole sample	Bureaucrats (commerce)	Bureaucrats (City)	Family Businessmen	Entrepreneurs	Chief Executives
Total		130	75	21	24	10	111
Category of father's occupation[a]							
I		17(13)	12(16)	2(10)	0	3(30)	13(12)
II		88(68)	42(56)	17(81)	24(100)	5(50)	77(69)
III	Non-manual	8(6)	7(9)	1(5)	0	0	8(7)
III	Manual	9(7)	8(11)	0	0	1(10)	6(5)
IV		0	0	0	0	0	0
V		0	0	0	0	0	0
Not known/deceased		8(6)	6(8)	1(5)	0	1(10)	7(6)

[a] Father's occupation is taken at age sixteen. In this table, and throughout this book, figures in brackets are percentages, usually based on the total at the top of the column.

Table 4.2   Father's occupation – ranking on Hope-Goldthorpe scale[a]

Scale range of father's occupation	Whole sample	Bureaucrats (commerce)	Bureaucrats (City)	Family Businessmen	Entrepreneurs	Chief Executives
Total	130	75	21	24	10	111
70 and above	29(22)	15(20)	8(38)	3(13)	3(30)	27(24)
60-69.9	55(42)	26(35)	9(43)	19(79)	1(10)	46(41)
50-59.9	21(16)	15(20)	1(5)	2(8)	3(30)	18(16)
40-49.9	6(5)	5(7)	0	0	1(10)	5(5)
30-39.9	11(8)	8(11)	2(10)	0	1(10)	8(7)
Below 30	0	0	0	0	0	0
Not classified/ deceased	8(6)	6(8)	1(5)	0	1(10)	7(6)

Type of respondent

[a] For comparative purposes it may be noted that, on this scale: most professions fall in the range 70-80; the businessmen would rank around 70; a farmer is at 58; an industrial company foreman around 47; the most highly graded manual worker at 45; other skilled workers in the 30-40 range; and completely unskilled workers around 18.

nine of all those interviewed were known definitely to have fathers in manual occupations, and none of these men in turn was completely unskilled. It is a feature of both the Registrar-General's classification and the Hope-Goldthorpe scale that professional men (doctors, lawyers, opticians and so on) rank higher than men in business. This may well reflect attitudes to business in Britain, but it produces the result that the (often very wealthy) members of business dynasties are classified lower in father's occupational class than the sons of some bureaucrats.

It should also be said that the men whose fathers were part of the founding family were not the only men with fathers in the firm they headed when interviewed. Six of the 60 men who were chief executives in industry, and are classified here as bureaucrats, in fact had fathers who were chairmen or managing directors of the same company. Likewise, one man in the commercial sector had a father who was a merchant bank director, and three of the merchant bank bureaucrat chief executives had fathers who were merchant bank directors.

A comparatively high percentage of the bureaucrats outside the City, in fact, eleven of the 75 (15 per cent), had fathers who owned and ran small businesses; these range from cloth mills and a wholesale furniture business to small builders. Overall, twenty-three (31 per cent) of the 75 had fathers who were directors or managers of big companies, or owners of small ones.

4.3 EARLY LIFE EXPERIENCES: THE CONTRIBUTION OF THE PUBLIC SCHOOLS

Seven men in this study were not born in Britain or educated here. These include three of the entrepreneurs and one family businessman, and these men perhaps fall into the category of the marginal groupings which Collins et al. (1964) found to make up a high proportion of entrepreneurs. Yet as Tables 4.1 and 4.2 indicate, the British-born entrepreneur who began from really poor beginnings and built up a large company within his lifetime is either comparatively rare or else is not adequately represented in this sample. Sometimes, though, it is the sons of such men who push the firm into the large company league, and this was true of two of the family businessmen.

We should also note that the men in this study largely grew up during the late 1920s and the 1930s, a period of depression in Britain when social welfare provision was very much more limited than it is today. There were six men whose fathers died before they were sixteen, leaving their families relatively poorly off, and in two cases this cut their education short. One entrepreneur and four other men in all were forced to leave school before the age of seventeen.

For most of those in this study, however, it can be argued that they not only received full schooling, but that they received enormous advantage from it. For this study indicates once again that a majority of the business elite attended public schools.

Because the figures are sometimes disputed, public school has been defined with care here: it is taken to mean all schools which are (i) fee-paying, (ii) members of the Headmasters' Conference, and (iii) require admission at age thirteen via the Common Entrance examination. These criteria differ from those of Wakeford (1969) who includes only boarding schools. The difference in practice is small, but Wakeford would exclude, for example, St Paul's, which is in fact one of the so-called Clarendon schools.[1] For purposes of comparison with other studies the latter are also separated off here, but it should be noted that the Clarendon schools, with the exception of Eton, are no longer the most successful producers of future business leaders. Apart from Eton, none of the schools produced more than three men, a number equalled by Oundle, and exceeded by Clifton, which produced six. Boyd (1973) uses the category 'major public schools', but it appears to be a somewhat arbitrary choice. Table 4.3 summarises the educational background of the men in this study.

As can be seen, there is some variation in the extent to which various sub-groups of this sample of the business elite had been to public school. We can combine categories in the tables to compare the numbers going to Clarendon, other public schools, and to either state or direct grant schools. On doing so and applying the Chi-square test we find that family businessmen were more likely to attend Clarendon schools. (Chi-square = 12.4, df = 2, significant at the 1 per cent level. Comparing chief executives only, the same level of confidence applies. Chi-square = 13.0, df = 2.) Comparing bureaucrat chief executives in the City with those in the industrial/commercial sector we find that 47 per cent of the former attended Clarendon schools, and overall 71 per cent attended a public school, compared to just 12 per cent and 50 per cent respectively for the industry men. These differences are also statistically significant at the 1 per cent level (Chi-square = 10.0, df = 2).

4.4 HIGHER EDUCATION: THE UNIVERSITIES AND PROFESSIONS

There has been some comment on the extent to which British top management has higher educational experience compared with that of men in similar positions in other European countries. It has been suggested that top managers in Britain are less likely to have been to university and that this in some way may contribute to Britain's poorer rate of economic growth (see, for example, Fores and Clark, 1975).

It is of some interest, therefore, to examine the extent to which the men in this study had been to university. The data (see Table 4.4) suggest that in fact the very top men are very likely to have such education, especially when one takes account of the fact that for two groups - the family businessmen and the entrepreneurs - such qualifications would not have helped them in their careers.

Table 4.3   The type of school attended by top businessmen

(a) All those interviewed

	All	Bureaucrats	Family Businessmen	Entrepreneurs
Total	130	96	24	10

Type of school

	All	Bureaucrats	Family Businessmen	Entrepreneurs
Eton	15(12)	8(8)	7(29)	0
Other Clarendon	12(9)	9(9)	3(13)	0
All other public	47(36)	33(34)	11(46)	3(30)
Other independent/ direct grant	7(5)	7(7)	0	0
State	42(32)	36(38)	2(8)	4(40)
Foreign	7(5)	3(3)	1(4)	3(30)

(b) Chief executives only

	All	Bureaucrats Commerce	City	Family Businessmen (commerce)	Entrepreneurs (commerce)
Total	111	60	17	22	8

Type of school

	All	Bureaucrats Commerce	City	Family Businessmen (commerce)	Entrepreneurs (commerce)
Eton	15(14)	3(5)	5(29)	6(27)	0
Other Clarendon	10(9)	4(7)	3(18)	3(14)	0
All other public	41(37)	23(38)	4(24)	10(46)	3(38)
Other independent/ direct grant	6(5)	5(8)	1(6)	0	0
State	33(30)	23(38)	4(24)	2(9)	2(25)
Foreign	6(5)	2(3)	0	1(5)	3(38)

In addition, it appears that a relevant professional qualification, most usually accountancy, has been regarded as an alternative to a degree, and the data do not confirm the premise that the men at the top are predominantly arts graduates.

The tables indicate that although 58 per cent of all the elite went to a place of higher education, those of a high social status background were more likely to go to Oxford or Cambridge. Indeed, the City men and the family businessmen were not likely to go to university at all if they did not go to Oxbridge.

Table 4.5 indicates clearly that the picture of the leaders of industry and commerce as being arts graduates is not true of the

Table 4.4 *The extent to which different groups among top businessmen had attended a place of higher education*

(a) *All those interviewed*

	All	Bureaucrats	Family businessmen	Entrepreneurs
Total	130	96	24	10
Oxford/Cambridge	49(38)	33(34)	15(63)	1(10)
All other universities	19(15)	16(17)	1(4)	2(20)
Technical/commercial college	6(5)	4(4)	0	2(20)
No higher education	56(43)	43(45)	8(33)	5(50)

Note: When categories of technical/commercial college and of no higher education are combined, a Chi-square test indicates that family businessmen are more likely to go to Oxbridge than bureaucrats, at 5 per cent confidence level.

(b) *Chief executives only*

	All	Bureaucrats (commerce)	Bureaucrats (City)	Family businessmen (commerce)	Entrepreneurs (commerce)
Total	111	60	17	22	8
Oxford/Cambridge	56(50)	22(37)	8(47)	14(64)	1(13)
All other universities	15(14)	12(20)	0	1(4)	1(13)
Technical/commercial college	6(5)	4(7)	0	0	2(25)
No higher education	44(40)	22(37)	9(53)	7(32)	4(50)

men at the very top. At least as many men have science or engineering degrees, although, as will be seen from Table 4.6, only around a third practised for long enough to obtain an engineering professional qualification. Overall, a degree consisting entirely or in part of economics was the most favoured one, and this was possessed by 46 per cent of all chief executives with a degree, and by 25 per cent of all the 90 chief executives heading commercial firms in this study. Indeed, this may indicate that many men had some intention prior to going to university of entering commerce and chose their degree accordingly.

It will be clear from Table 4.5 that of 74 men entering university, eight did not obtain degrees, which indicates that 'Who's Who' entries can be misleading in this area. Two of the eight left through lack of funds, the remainder being either family businessmen or men who went into City firms, who had perhaps not taken higher education too seriously (confirmed by their own accounts).

Table 4.5   Subject read at university or technical college: chief executives only

	All	*All chief executives*	Commerce	
			Bureaucratic chief executives	*Family businessmen*
Number entering a place of higher education	74	57	38	15
Number qualifying	66	50	36	11
Number who read				
Science/engineering	14(21)	12(24)	10(28)	2(18)
Any arts	14(21)	9(18)	7(19)	2(18)
Economics/commerce[a]	28(42)	23(46)	16(44)	4(36)
Law	4(6)	3(6)	0	3(27)
Other/not known[b]	6(9)	3(6)	3(8)	0

Percentages are based on those who obtained a qualification.
[a]   Includes PPE at Oxford; B. Comm.
[b]   Other: for example, printing diploma; hotel and catering diploma.

One alternative preparation for entering on a career in business is that of obtaining a professional qualification of some kind, most frequently accountancy or law. Table 4.6 shows the extent to which the businessmen had such qualifications. However, it will be recognised that such professional qualifications are not always obtained at the start of one's career. In the case of the accountants, they usually did obtain their qualifications by taking articles as an alternative to going to university. The engineers in this study had all been to university first. The men in insurance firms had the relevant qualifications of the professional institute and this had been obtained during their careers.

These figures show again the importance of economic or financial training in a successful business career: a fifth of all bureaucrats were trained accountants. And taking *all* the bureaucrats in commercial, as opposed to City, firms in this study together we find that thirty of the 75, that is, 40 per cent, had either a degree with an economics or commerce content or an accountancy qualification. The equivalent figure for the small group of City bureaucrats is eight out of twenty-one - 38 per cent.

It would be wrong to conclude from this that 'industry is controlled by accountants' or that the percentage of technologists at the top is overtly low, for in many of the companies which the men headed science or engineering knowledge would not be relevant. Equally, however, the idea that British companies are run by men with completely non-relevant (that is, arts) degrees, is not supported. The most frequent qualification for the very top posts of commerce appears to be one that gives some knowledge of economics, finance or accountancy.

Table 4.6 Professional qualifications obtained by top businessmen

| | Chief executives | | | |
| | | | | |
	All those interviewed	*Bureaucrats (commerce)*	*Bureaucrats (City)*	*Family businessmen (commerce)*	*Entrepreneurs (commerce)*
Total	130	60	17	22	8
Accountancy	23(18)	12(20)	5(29)	0	1(13)
Law	11(8)	5(8)	1(6)	2(9)	0
Engineering	9(7)	5(8)	0	2(9)	0
Other[a]	10(8)	1(2)	6(35)	0	0
None	80(62)	37(62)	6(35)	18(82)	7(88)

[a] Other: surveyor, Fellow of Institute of Actuaries, F.C.I.I., but does not include business degrees or Ph.Ds — there were three men with the latter.
Some men have more than one qualification.

4.5 COMPARISONS WITH OTHER STUDIES

Because previous elite studies have focused so much on the social background and educational experience of elites, the data presented so far in this chapter provide a useful means of checking the extent to which the selection procedure has introduced unrepresentativeness into the sample. However, it must be remembered that whereas the bias in this study is that the men who took part were self-selected, in most others it occurs because of the incomplete data to be found in reference books.

Also, other studies rarely make the distinctions between types of businessmen (entrepreneur, family businessman and bureaucrat) which have been used here; and it must be remembered that I deliberately over-sampled some of these groups. Thus the comparisons are inevitably crude.

Two types of comparison are made here. I compare the characteristics of the business elite's background as indicated in this study with those of other studies. And I make a comparison of the internal variation within this sample that accompanies the type of the company.

We saw earlier that of the chief executives in industry, only nine in number, and ten in percentage terms, had fathers in manual occupations, and a further 7 per cent had fathers in clerical or lower supervisory jobs (that is, R-G class III, non-manual). Over four-fifths of this group in fact had fathers from the Registrar-General's social classes I and II.

These figures are certainly in rough agreement with previous

studies. In Hall and Amado-Fischgrund's (1969) study of 120 of
the top 500 chief executives, just 7 per cent were found to have
fathers in the manual worker category. They quote 8 per cent of
men as being from white-collar occupations, but differentiate a
category of people in sales, including retailing, so their figures
are not directly comparable. Nichols (1969) found rather more men
from manual worker backgrounds - 18 per cent - in his sample of
65 directors in a northern city. His figure for men in clerical and
supervisory jobs, 6 per cent, is similar, however.

Copeman (1955) published a study of over 1000 directors from
companies with assets of £1 million or more. He found that just 8
per cent of them had fathers in manual, clerical or lower supervisory occupations, compared to 16 per cent here. Thus it is
possible, if the two sets of figures are comparable, that there has
been a change over twenty years, though a relatively slight one.
Copeman found, incidentally, that 19 per cent of all directors had
fathers who were directors in the same company; for the sample
of chief executives here the figure is 29 per cent.

The present study is in line with and confirms other studies
with respect to the family background of business leaders. The
high proportion of men in the business elite with fathers who had
directorial, managerial or professional occupations, or who were
business owners, is partly due to the continuing representation
of family companies among the bigger firms. It is also due to the
fact, which is more or less true for all advanced capitalist societies, that though there may be considerable social mobility at all
levels, the bulk of it is over a short range.

This being the case, a working-class family has a higher chance
of moving one of its members into the elite strata in two generations than in one. Thus Hall and Amado-Fischgrund (1969) found
that more of their 120 executives had grandfathers in manual occupations than had fathers, and more had fathers in professional or
executive positions than had grandfathers. [2]

It seems, then, that in most families a member must enter what
Payne and Ford (1977) call the 'lieutenant class', that is, the professional, managerial and senior administrative personnel who run
the big organisations, public and private, before his son or sons
(and, more recently daughters) can go on to enter the elite positions. Payne and Ford maintain that recruitment to the lieutenant
class is now relatively open. If this is so, it may mean that future
generations of the business elite will be more likely to have grand-
parents from working- or lower-middle-class backgrounds. Such a
transition should have been aided by the 1944 Education Act and
the increase since the last war of university places. The indications
are, however, that the elite has not changed much in composition
in this period (c.f. this study with Copeman's of 1955).

I have made use of data from various sources concerning the
educational background of directors as a further means of examining how representative of top businessmen the men in this study
are. This is done in two tables: 4.7 and 4.8.

Table 4.7 indicates that the men who were interviewed in this

study fall well within the range of previous findings of the percentages of men who had attended public school amongst top
directors. Different researchers utilise different definitions of
public school and this accounts for some of the variation in the
figures, but it is clear that between 50 and 60 per cent of all top
directors (and probably closer to 60 per cent) have been to public
schools; and that this has changed very little over time. Likewise,
the Clarendon schools, especially Eton, provide a disproportionate
percentage.

*Table 4.7   The educational background of the directors of large commercial
firms as found in different studies*

Study	Sample	Percentage at public school	Percentage at Clarendon schools	Percentage at Eton
Glennerster and Pryke (1973)	Top 100 chief executives in 1938	57	–	–
Copeman (1955)	Directors of large companies	58	–	–
Farrow (1963)[a]	Top 100 chairmen	64	–	–
The Director (1965)	Directors	62	–	–
The Director (1966a)	Directors	44	–	–
Heller (1973)	Directors of top 200 firms	71[b]	–	–
Whitley (1973)	Directors of top 50 firms	66	–	13
Stanworth and Giddens (1974a)	Company chairmen over 100 years	54	15	6
Fidler (1975)[c]	Chairmen of top 100 firms	52	17	11
This study	Chief executives interviewed	59	23	15

[a]   Quoted by Glennerster and Pryke (1973) includes direct grant.
[b]   May include all fee paying.
[c]   Data collected for this study not published elsewhere.

The same picture emerges from studies of the directors of City
institutions, who are even more likely to have a public school
education (Table 4.8). Again it appears that those in the interview sample have a similarly elitist background to those in the two
quoted studies.

To complete the comparisons with other studies I have drawn up
one final table (Table 4.9), showing the percentage of directors
in this study and others who had been to university. It may be

Table 4.8   The educational background of City directors

Study	Sample	Percentage at public school	Percentage at Clarendon schools	Percentage at Eton
Whitley (1973)	Directors of financial institutions	80	–	35
Standworth and Giddens (1974a)	Clearing and merchant bankers	83	59	35
This study (1975)	Chief executives – merchant banks, insurance, property	82	53	35

noted in this regard that it is to be expected that studies working from published data will exaggerate the number of directors who are graduates. This is because, as shown above, some of those interviewed did not, for various reasons, obtain degrees, even though their 'Who's Who' entry recorded them as having attended university.

Once again, the percentage of graduates in this study is not far outside the range found in other studies, but it is higher than other quoted figures, as is the percentage with Oxbridge degrees.

Table 4.9   Numbers of men graduating from university as found in different studies

Study	Sample	Percentage attending any university	Percentage attending Oxbridge
Copeman (1955)	Directors – 1,000 largest firms	36	20
Clark (1966)	Directors (Northern Area)	37	16
Nichols (1969)	Directors ('Northern City')	47	29
Guttsman (1963)	Officers of business organisations (FBI, etc.)	46	34
Hall and Amado-Fischgrund (1969)	120 chief executives	38 (approx.)	–
Heller (1973)	Directors – firms in top 200	49	29
This study (1975)	90 chief executives – commercial companies	57	41

It is possible, of course, that men with university experience are more disposed to assist university research.

When one turns to consider professional qualifications one finds there are less comparable data available. We saw earlier that of 90 chief executives in commercial companies, twenty-eight, or 31 per cent, had some kind of professional qualification, though these men may have been to university first, as, for example, all the engineers had. Quoted figures in other studies are lower: Hall and Amado-Fischgrund (1969) give a figure of 23 per cent; Barritt (1957) of around 22 per cent. Betts (1967) studied directors in companies in five specific industries (radio and TV, food manufacturing, industrial plastics, retailing and construction). He found 61 per cent of them either to have a degree or a professional qualification, which compares to a figure of 25.8 per cent quoted by Barritt. The equivalent figure in this study for chief executives in commerce is 69 per cent, and for all those interviewed 78 per cent.

Thus, the men in this study appear to be more likely than directors in general to have either a degree or a professional qualification. Of equal interest, however, is the areas these qualifications were in. Copeman (1955) found that 42 per cent of the directors in his study with qualifications had them in science or engineering, 35 per cent in business subjects or economics, 14 per cent arts and 9 per cent law. Likewise, 34 per cent of the directors studied by Betts were qualified in science/engineering, and 21 per cent were accountants, though these figures may be biased by the industries he chose. The chief executives in this study, however, were trained as scientists or engineers in only 13 per cent of cases, though there were plenty of manufacturing firms in the sample. 14 per cent were accountants, but, as we saw, 38 per cent had either an economics degree or accountancy training. This seems to confirm that it is above all knowledge of finance that qualifies one for the very top posts.

4.6 AN INDEX OF SOCIAL STATUS

As we have seen, family businessmen as a group are more likely than the bureaucrats to have the educational experience traditionally associated with high social status in Britain, for example, to have attended an elite public school or an Oxbridge college. In this respect the City men, especially the bankers, stand between the family businessmen on the one hand and the 'managers' on the other.

The education one has received in Britain is very often a guide to the social status of the family one is born into. However, just as there are several positions with respect to ownership of capital, so do these positions enclose a certain variation of family social status. Thus, while some men have experienced social mobility through the acquisition of capital (that is, the entrepreneurs), so others amongst the family businessmen have experienced it through the expansion of capital.

Clearly, too, some managers have been socially mobile by virtue of the process of rising to the top of their companies. For the purposes of this study, therefore, it was found useful to develop an index of the social status of the families into which respondents were born.

The problem of existing indices of social standing is that they are not fine enough for the purposes of elite studies. The scale developed by Goldthorpe and Hope (1974) may be excellent for examining social mobility in the population as a whole. However, when it is applied to this sample of businessmen, we find that the highest position that a businessman heading the largest industrial firm can attain is 69.11, which is the position accorded to the manager of a firm employing 25 people. Using this scale, the son of a doctor in general practice who attains the chairmanship of ICI is said to have achieved a small amount of downward mobility. Likewise, the multi-millionaire head of a firm employing 50,000 ranks no higher than the manager of a firm employing 50.

Correspondingly, when one applies the Hope-Goldthorpe scale to this sample of businessmen, because of the almost total absence of men with fathers in unskilled and semi-skilled manual occupations, the extent of upward mobility within the sample is found to be very small. Yet in looking at the question of different life experiences within the group it may be more sensible to ask which men have experienced an appreciable upward mobility by the standards of the group themselves, rather than those of the population at large.

An alternative to the Hope-Goldthorpe scale or similar scales based on father's occupation might be to take the type of school a man has attended as an index of family social status. This has some merits, but is not completely satisfactory for two reasons. First, there are amongst those interviewed some seventeen men who were members of the landed gentry, aristocracy or baronetage (according to the latest available editions of 'Burke's Peerage' (1970) and 'Burke's Landed Gentry'[3]). In the British social status system these men are probably still to be considered of the highest social status in origin. Of the seventeen, thirteen were educated at Eton, but the others are arguably of no less high an origin. Second, there are a very few men who, as the result of circumstances (scholarships or private benefactors) attended elite schools despite being from manual working class, or lower white-collar families.

At the other end of the scale, the men who attended state and direct grant schools range from those who came from very poor homes to those whose fathers were in professional or managerial occupations.

Therefore I suggest, for the purposes of British elite studies, a composite index of father's social status. The index is based on father's occupation, schooling and relationship to the gentry and aristocracy. The four positions on the index as applied in this study are:

Status IV (the highly upwardly mobile): all those whose fathers ranked at or below 45.57 on the Hope-Goldthorpe scale. This is the level of the highest ranked manual worker, but below it come some supervisory and white-collar workers. Also included here are men whose fathers died before they were sixteen, and whose family circumstances forced them to leave school before the age of sixteen. This group is considered to be all those in the study to have experienced upward mobility, requiring at some stage the acquisition of appropriate accent, lifestyle, conversational topics, dress and so on to enter the elite; all, in fact, of what Bourdieu and Passeron (1977) have called 'cultural capital'. Number in whole sample: 18

Status III: men who attended any schools other than public schools as earlier defined, and who do not appear in group IV (or I). Number in study: 30

Status II: men who attended public school other than the Clarendon schools, left at age sixteen or over, and are not members of the aristocracy, landed gentry or the sons of baronets. Number in study: 47

Status I: men who attended one of the Clarendon schools, other than men classified in group IV by father's occupation, plus all members of the aristocracy, gentry or the sons of baronets. Number in study: 29

Note that men born and educated abroad cannot be classified on this scale. There were six such men in this study.

Table 4.10   A comparison of different groups among top businessmen using a composite social status index

		Chief executives		
	All those interviewed	*Family businessmen (commerce)*	*Bureaucrats (City)*	*Bureaucrats (commerce)*
Total	130	22	17	60
Social status index				
Group I	29(22)	11(50)	8(47)	7(12)
II	47(36)	9(41)	5(29)	22(37)
III	30(23)	1(5)	3(18)	18(30)
IV	18(14)	0	1(6)	11(18)
Not classifiable on this scale:	6(5)	1(5)	0	2(3)

The advantage of utilising a scale such as this is that it allows a comparison to be made of the effects of simply having capital with those of being born into a position of high social status. As we shall see, the two are related, but having money is not always the same as being well born, and vice versa.

As one would expect from the foregoing discussion, family businessmen tend to rate more highly on the index than bureaucrats, and City bureaucrats rate more highly than those in commerce (see Table 4.10).

Let us return briefly to the question of university and professional qualifications. Frequently during the interviews the respondents gave as their opinion that there was no bias towards selecting public school men for senior management positions; and it was sometimes also said that what would be more important to career success in industry in the future was the possession of a degree or other relevant training. Whatever the truth of these arguments, in the case of this sample it is clear that schooling and other qualifications are not independent. In the last two tables in this section I show the extent to which men at different levels on the social status index obtained either a university degree or a professional qualification.

Both these two tables indicate that it is the best placed, and the worst placed in terms of family social status, who obtain the most qualifications, when all the latter are considered together. Oxbridge, however, appears to have been much more the prerogative of the social elite in the past.

Table 4. 11   Relationship between status of family background and university or professional training – whole sample

Social status index	Number in sample	Number and percentage with university or professional qualifications	Number and percentage with Oxbridge place
Total	124	97(78)	49(40)
I (elite)	29	28(97)	24(83)
II	47	32(68)	16(34)
III	30	21(70)	5(17)
IV (mobile)	18	16(89)	4(22)

One suspects the finding here is the result of two trends: in the case of the more elite groupings, they found it easy to obtain qualifications and did so, even though such qualifications were not particularly necessary for them. For those who did not begin well placed, however, the system is probably highly selective: only a small group of the exceptionally bright obtain qualifications and succeed in business. [4]

But overall, the principal conclusion about the educational background of British-born top businessmen must be that not only did they start well placed, they took no chances, and in the majority of cases (78 per cent) obtained high qualifications as well.

Table 4.12   Relationship between status of family background and university or professional training – bureaucrats only

Social status index	Number in sample	Number and percentage with university or professional qualifications	Number and percentage with Oxbridge place
Total	94	77(82)	33(35)
I (elite)	17	17(100)	13(77)
II	34	26(77)	11(32)
III	27	19(71)	5(19)
IV (mobile)	16	15(94)	4(25)

4.7 THE CAREERS THAT LED TO THE TOP

Getting In: Bureaucrats
The men who came to be studied here are considered important because their careers led them to the positions of highest responsibility. In this section I consider some aspects of this career experience, particularly those of relevance to later sections of the study. Once again, family businessmen and entrepreneurs will be considered separately from the bureaucrats, and I begin with the latter.

In what is probably the most comprehensive study of managerial careers in Britain so far, Clements (1958) delineated five major career routes. Consideration of the careers of the men in this study, and of the typology itself, suggests that these are in fact best considered as ways into management. In practice, as Pahl and Pahl have pointed out (1971), careers often do not follow regular and simple patterns of progression up a hierarchy or hierarchies. As many of those who were interviewed in this study accepted, luck does play a part in success, most especially in the form of opportunity to prove oneself, to get in on a new venture at the beginning, or be noticed by those higher up the company. Careers may have false starts, changes of direction, or sidesteps.

However, it will be shown below that a very high proportion of those at the top of industry have worked for three organisations or less; and that many spent the longest period of their career with just one company, which is the one in which they entered higher management, the board, and consequently were heading when they were interviewed.

Thus, the crucial part of a career may in fact be the early stages - the stages when potential top managers are emerging, as one of those interviewed put it, 'from the ruck at the bottom of the pyramid'. Once one is in middle management, or the lower echelons of senior management, a career may follow more on the pattern of an orderly progression from post to post. In saying this, however, I would stress that these early stages may last only a few years or for a very much longer period, involving moves through several organisations and occupations while the man searches for the niche that fits him.

This interpretation of the men's careers was reflected in their accounts of them. Although no attempt was made to quantify this, the majority did seem to spend the greatest part of this section of the interviews explaining how they came to be in a particular firm, and in some cases their particular speciality, rather than detailing the various management positions they had held. However, one can put little weight on this as the respondents were often aware that the facts of their later careers were available to the author from reference books and the press, whereas their earlier careers were not.

To return to the Clements typology, one may suggest that what it actually tells us is the several routes that men can take in obtaining their earlier positions of managerial responsibility. On this basis one may classify the 75 bureaucrats in manufacturing and service firms as follows:

(a) *Self-made men (9)* There were nine men who went into firms straight from school, and thus started in effect at the bottom. Only a small minority of the business elite at present, such men may become even rarer in the future, as university or business qualifications come to be regarded as minimal requirements for higher management.

(b) *Managerial trainees (17)* Seventeen men were graduates, and could be considered the equivalents of what Clements calls management trainees. He characterises them as having arts degrees; as we have seen, amongst my respondents, economics was more common.

(c) *Pre-qualified experts (31)* The largest category is that of men with some particular training obtained before entering commerce. Included here are science and engineering graduates and trained accountants. It is the latter who are the larger group - there were fifteen of them, with just four scientists and six engineers.

(d) *Special entrants (9)* Apart from men whose families actually owned a significant proportion of the equity, there were a number of men who began their careers in firms in which their fathers were already directors. We may assume they had sponsors for their careers, and apart from the eight in this category, there was one other man with an admitted sponsor.

(e) *Others (15)* Finally, we are still left with a group, fifteen in all, whose careers simply do not fit into these categories. These are men who have moved through several occupations, in some cases spending a large part of their lives in other fields before entering business. This group includes a man who had been an accountant in a firm of accountants, a solicitor, two ex-civil servants, and men who at some stage had been MPs, academics, teachers, journalists, PR men, or had worked for banks or nationalised industries. It may be noted, however, that even among chief executives only a very small minority can be said to have come from financial institutions.

If we turn now to the bureaucrats in the City companies we find their experience to be rather different. There are basically two types of City director in this study: the man who has worked his way up through an insurance company to be general manager (or sometimes chairman), and the merchant banker.

Within insurance the career route for all seems to have been to enter the firm near the bottom, with graduates starting a couple of rungs up, and progress up the ladder. The professional qualifications, either as an actuary (F.I.A.) or as a member of the Insurance Institute (F.C.I.I.) were taken en route. Thus, there was only one accountant amongst this group and he was a chairman who had come to insurance from elsewhere in the City. Contrastingly, apart from two bankers whose fathers were also bankers, all the bureaucrats in banking or property were qualified in either accountancy or law. The City men tended to have more straightforward careers than the men in industry; the great majority entered their respective firms when comparatively young and remained with them, although some bankers collected outside directorships (and chairmanships) along the way.

Family Businessmen and Entrepreneurs
So far as the family businessmen (Clements's 'crown princes') were concerned, there was, of course, no problem of where to get into industry, or how to do it, except for those who were not directly descended from the founder of the firm (that is, who were nephews or sons-in-law). The family businessmen seem to have undergone an initiation period into their firms that often involved working on the shopfloor, or its equivalent, and moving round from department to department before taking on a management position.

Regrettably, the number of entrepreneurs in this study is too small for it to be possible to make any generalisations about them. Of the eight in the industry and commerce sector, four were either immigrants or Jewish, and this is in line with the conclusion of previous studies that a relatively high proportion of businesses are founded by men from marginal groups who find it more difficult to succeed in established companies. (Similarly, five out of eight second-generation family businessmen were either Jewish or the sons of immigrants.) However, the entrepreneurs in this study appear to have spent only relatively short periods in doing what Collins et al. (1964) call 'basic dealing', that is, struggling through bankruptcies and other failures before getting their firms established.

4.8 SERVICE EXPERIENCE

In considering the amalgam of events and experiences that constitute the careers of the men studied here, and relating them to
other studies, one might easily overlook the one particular experience that in the case of this group may be of great importance.
That is of serving in the armed forces in the war.

Since the average age of the men in this study was 56 (in 1975)
and 60 per cent of them fall within six years of this, it can be
seen that many had the experience of having just joined a firm,
or being at some stage of university education when the war broke
out, and of having to break off their careers to do wartime service. This could well mean that six years of a man's business
career were lost, and men joining the services as late as 1943
were sometimes not demobbed until 1947. The younger men had at
least to do national service, and some men who did not join the
forces spent the war years engaged on war work.

Altogether it was known for certain that 58 per cent of the men
in this study did wartime service in the forces, and 11 per cent
did two years national service. (One man had fought in the First
World War.)

There was much in the accounts of the men to suggest that the
experience of the forces was of far wider significance to them
than the enormous disruption it caused. Very many of the men
felt it had been of personal value. There are several sides to this.
For some of the upwardly socially mobile it was the forces, and
the opportunity to obtain a commission, that first released their
ambition. One retail chain store head recalled that:

'I consider that I completed my education in the army. I
learnt what ambition was all about. When we were called up
we vowed we would not take a commission, but our paths
took different courses. I was responsible for training, I saw
the advantage of being commissioned as opposed to non-
commissioned.'

In the services in wartime promotion was often rapid. Men who
had just begun their business careers at the start of the war
returned six years later often with the rank of major or above.
Often they would be placed in comparatively senior management
positions. In the case of family businessmen and a few others,
they would go straight on to the board. [5]

We will see below that the management training of this generation
of businessmen was comparatively limited. The growth of British
business schools came too late for the majority of them to benefit
from it. But a number of those with no other training referred to
the courses they were sent on by the army or other branches of
the services in approving terms. Here are some answers to the
question 'Did you have any formal management training during
your career?'

'None - except in the forces, a very good training in man
management.' (Chairman of a large engineering company)

'No - but I appreciate that the experience and training one got doing staff jobs in the RAF was as good a management training as any other.' (Chairman - small service company)

'In the war with BOAC I ended up a captain, so I had a number of technical and training courses. They were relevant in due course.' (Chairman - medium sized service company)

Perhaps the most important aspect of service experience, however, was that it gave many of the businessmen in this study their first, and for many their only, experience of managing people as such rather than a finance, sales, or a commercial department. We will also see below that most of these top businessmen have not had any experience of shopfloor management. Their contact at work with those at the bottom of the hierarchy has been severely limited, but they may well have found themselves leading similar sorts of people while commanding a platoon in the army, or serving on a ship in the Royal Navy, or in the RAF.

Perhaps some day social historians will be able to tell us the extent to which the services of the Second World War correspond to the picture that one is left of them from British films of the 1940s and 1950s. That picture is largely of ex-public schoolboys leading cheerful and unprotesting working-class men (frequently Cockneys) into battle, either on the ground or from the bridge of a destroyer; or else jumping into Spitfires prepared for them by working-class mechanics, and flying off to engage the enemy, using jargon culled from fox hunting.

Whether or not that caricature is an honest picture of the social structure of the armed forces in wartime, or the relationship between ranks, it is probably true that some at least of top businessmen draw on experience of man management that took place in organisations very different in structure, and internal power relationships, from those of modern industry. The same point has been alluded to by Fox (1966), in making a contrast between the 'unitary' view of the firm which takes the army as a model, with that of the 'pluralist' viewpoint.

4.9 MANAGEMENT TRAINING

As has been stated, this generation of businessmen received little formal management training. The position is summed up in Table 4.13. Training here is split into three types:
(a) full diploma or degree courses, of at least six months duration;
(b) courses external to the company, of at least a week's duration, which may be at business schools, or run by management consultants, professional associations or other bodies;
(c) in-company, or very short courses.

This typology is crude, and ignores the fact that some very large companies now have their own management schools, in which the training may be as good as that received at a state or consultancy school. However, this does not affect the main point which is that what stands out in Table 4.13 is the fact that a majority have had no training at all, and 62 per cent have had no exposure of this kind to ideas external to their companies. This is not to say that the men themselves did not believe that such training is useful, for in many cases they said that they did think it valuable.

Table 4.13   Extent of formal, management training among top businessmen

| | | Bureaucrats | | | | |
	All	*Chief executives (commerce)*	*Directors (commerce)*	*Chief Executives (City)*	*All family businessmen*	*All entre-preneurs*
Total	130	60	15	17	24	10
(a) Business degree	9(7)	5(8)	1(7)	1(6)	1(4)	1(10)
(b) Short external courses	29(22)	13(22)	8(53)	2(12)	3(13)	0
(c) In-company/ very short courses	8(6)	4(7)	2(13)	0	2(8)	0
(d) No training	81(62)	35(58)	4(27)	14(82)	18(75)	9(90)
Not known	3(2)	3(5)	--	--	--	--

A Chi-square test shows significant differences at the 1 per cent level between directors in commerce and other groups.

4.10 MAIN EXPERIENCE IN THE FIRM

I have already pointed out the difficulties of making generalisations about managerial careers - right from their beginnings such careers can take diverse paths. However, certain aspects of such careers are of importance here. In particular it was suggested in chapter 2 that experience within the firm of working with groups from other class or status positions may well be very important in creating images of wider society. Of prime importance might be experience of manual workers, and their lifestyles, aims and aspirations.

With this in mind, I have attempted to summarise the areas in which the men in this study have spent their working lives. The analysis here is confined to chief executives in the industrial and other commercial sectors, because the career paths of the City men were usually a relatively straightforward progression through the wholly white-collar environment of the bank or insurance firm.

The careers of the chief executives are summarised in two ways in the following tables. First, in Table 4.14 I show how many executives have had any experience of working in certain functional

areas. These are:
(a) production, meaning the management of factories or production within manufacturing units;
(b) finance, including corporate planning;
(c) sales, marketing or commercial; and
(d) staff positions, which include personnel, company secretary,
PA to the chairman or another director; solicitor and so on.
   Finally Table 4.14 shows how many men have any experience
outside the business world; such experience includes working in
the accountancy or law professions, in the City, the civil service,
journalism and so on (category e).

Table 4.14   Career experience of chief executives: commerce only

	All	Bureaucrats	Family businessmen	Entrepreneurs
Number	90	60	22	8
Percentage with any experience of:				
(a) Production/works management				
in manufacturing firms:	24 } 27	22 } 24	36 } 41	13
in service firms:	3	2	5	–
(b) Finance	23	33	0	13
(c) Sales/marketing	40	53	9	25
(d) Other staff functions	29	37	14	13
(e) Civil service/City/ professions	48	43	14	13
Inadequate details	4	7	–	–

See the text for details of categories (a) to (e). Figures add to more than 100 because some
interviewees have experience in more than one functional area.

   In Table 4.15 is shown where the men spent the greatest time
during their working lives. The most important category here
turns out to be 'general management', which means running a
complete firm, a subsidiary or a large group or division. It would
also include running retail chain stores. It is meant to refer to all
positions in which the persons concerned had ultimate responsibility for more than one functional area.
   Table 4.14 is shown here in percentages to simplify it and make
comparison of the different kinds of men easier. In some cases,
especially that of the entrepreneurs, it will be clear that these
refer to very small numbers. Nevertheless, the tables show some
interesting differences between the groups.
   Most notable among these is that only a minority of these men at

the very top of British industry have any direct experience of managing shopfloor employees. In all, only twenty-four out of the 86, 28 per cent, on whose careers there are details, have this experience. What is of more interest is that nine of these twenty-four are family businessmen, and this group were thus more likely to have this experience than the bureaucrats. The reason for this is that often, in the past at least, the way in which the family businessman learnt the business was by spending some time on the factory floor, and then taking over first the supervision, and then the management, of one of the firm's factories.

In contrast, the bureaucrats were more likely to have come up through the sales/marketing functions (53 per cent of all bureaucrats had some experience here) or finance (in which 33 per cent had worked). In addition, 43 per cent have at some stage worked outside the world of commerce, either in the professions, though this includes accountancy, or the City or the civil service.

As can be seen from Table 4.15, five out of 60, or 8 per cent, of the bureaucrats had in fact spent the majority of their working lives in some occupation outside the sector they now work in. This table emphasises again that taking charge of the productive side of industry is not the route to the top for bureaucrats, even in the thirty-five firms with significant manufacturing operations.

Table 4.15   Areas in which the chief executives have spent the major part of their working lives

	All	Bureaucrats	Family businessmen	Entrepreneurs
Total	90	60	22	8
General management	64(71)	37(62)	19(86)	8(100)
Production/works	2(2)	0	2(9)	0
Finance	9(10)	9(15)	0	0
Sales/marketing	5(6)	4(7)	1(5)	0
City/civil service/ professions	6(7)	6(10)	0	0
Insufficient details	4(4)	4(7)	–	–

What this would seem to imply is that non-contact in the present-day work situation, which has been described by Winkler (1974), is in the case of the chief executives merely the continuation of the pattern of their careers. In the great majority of cases they cannot draw on first-hand experience for their impressions of the thinking and behaviour of manual workers. Paradoxically, the capital-holders are more likely to have had such experience, but they provide a minority of the business elite in any case. And, of course, the knowledge that they were to take over control of the business in time may have modified the behaviour of the workforce when they were in direct contact with them.

In the final tables of this section I examine the number of organisations the men have worked for, and the age at which they obtained their boardroom place.

From Table 4.16 it is clear that among bureaucrats there is not a great deal of movement from firm to firm. Four-fifths of all chief executives have worked for three firms or fewer, and in the financial sector the percentage is even greater. By and large, also, the men in the commerce sector obtained their board places comparatively young: 67 per cent were on the main board before the age of 45 (financial sector - 63 per cent).

Table 4.16   Number of organisations worked for during career[a]

| | | Chief executives | | | |
	All	*Bureaucrats (commerce)*	*Bureaucrats (City)*	*Family Businessmen (commerce)*	*Entrepreneurs (commerce)*
Total	130	60	17	22	8
Number of organisations					
One	54(42)	18(31)	8(47)	18(82)	2(25)
Two	33(25)	20(34)	4(24)	2(9)	4(50)
Three	22(17)	9(15)	3(18)	2(9)	2(25)
Four	9(7)	5(8)	1(6)	0	0
Five or more	10(8)	6(10)	1(6)	0	0
Not known	2(2)	2(3)	0	0	0

[a]   This table does not include service in the armed forces.

What this means in practice is that after they have begun to rise into senior management future chief executives do not move from firm to firm but stay with the same company to obtain a boardroom place, and after further experience (as much as ten years in some cases) they take over the chief executive position.

As can be seen, and would be expected, family businessmen rise to the board in general rather faster than bureaucrats. And five out of the eight entrepreneurs had founded their companies by the age of thirty. In the case of the directors who were not chief executives, some appear to have arrived at the board rather later than the chief executives did, and may be too old to make the chief executive position. (But one of them has become a chief executive since the interview with him.) Note that the present ages of all the groups in the table have very similar means - around 56 - and so we are comparing similar groups here (leaving aside retired chief executives).

Table 4.17   Age of obtaining first main board appointment

	All	Bureaucrat chief executives finance	Commerce		
			Bureaucrat chief executives	Family Businessmen	Entrepreneurs[a]
Total	130	17	60	22	8
Below 30	14(11)	0	1(2)	5(23)	5(63)
30-4	15(12)	1(6)	3(5)	9(41)	1(13)
35-9	27(21)	6(35)	14(23)	5(23)	0
40-4	33(25)	4(24)	21(35)	2(9)	1(13)
45-9	18(14)	1(6)	9(15)	1(5)	1(13)
50-4	16(12)	2(12)	8(13)	0	0
55+	4(3)	3(18)	1(2)	0	0
Not known	3(2)	--	3(5)	–	–

[a] Refers to age of founding present firm or obtaining control.

4.11 INCOME AND WEALTH

When we turn to consider the director's life outside the firm I am able to produce rather less relevant information and can offer only a partial description of the community situation of the businessman. What one can say is that there is a certain amount of variation: there are members of the landed gentry who retire to country houses at the weekend; there are men who live in houses in the midst of suburbia; there are those who come into London from a ring of commuting towns and villages round it; and those who live in the better preserved parts of inner London; and with such variations may go a range of interests and involvements in the local community.

One of the first points to make is that the business elite do have considerable choice as to how their out of work hours are spent. That choice is provided by income and wealth holdings that put them comfortably into the top brackets; and this despite their own distress at their falling real incomes at the time they were interviewed, resulting from a combination of inflation, pay curbs, and high taxation.

In the next two tables the income and wealth holdings of the chief executives are summarised. These figures are the result of self-reporting by the men themselves (and there are thus a number of gaps due to refusals), supplemented by estimates made from known share and other capital holdings. These are inevitably underestimates, but they give an idea of the range of wealth holdings. In the case of incomes, inflation will already have pushed

these considerably higher in absolute terms.
  As would be expected, family businessmen and entrepreneurs
are on the whole considerably wealthier than the bureaucrats.

Table 4.18   Gross annual income from all sources — chief executives — 1974-6

	All	Bureaucrats	Family businessmen	Entrepreneurs
Total	111	77	24	10
Annual income £ thousands				
100 or more	9(8)	0	8(33)	1(10)
70-99.9	8(7)	2(3)	3(13)	3(30)
50-69.9	11(10)	6(8)	3(13)	2(20)
30-49.9	31(28)	22(29)	5(21)	4(40)
20-29.9	23(21)	21(27)	2(8)	0
10-19.9	6(5)	4(5)	2(8)	0
Not known/refused	23(21)	22(29)	1(4)	0

Table 4.19   Total wealth holdings — chief executives — 1974-6

	All	Bureaucrats	Family businessmen	Entrepreneurs
Total	111	77	24	10
Wealth in £ thousands				
Greater than 1,000	16(14)	0	10(42)	6(60)
500-999	6(5)	0	4(17)	2(20)
200-499	11(10)	7(9)	2(8)	2(20)
100-199	21(19)	14(18)	7(29)	0
50-99	23(21)	23(30)	0	0
25-49	9(8)	9(12)	0	0
15-24	2(2)	2(3)	0	0
Not known/refused	23(21)	22(29)	1(4)	0

  I also collected data from company reports of the salaries and
shareholdings (in the principal firm in which the man was chief
executive) of all the chief executives. Some interesting conclusions

can be inferred from this data.

First, using four measures of size of company - assets of the firm, turnover, profit, and number of employees - I correlated both size of salary and value of the shareholding with the size measures and found that whereas salary is related to size of firm, the amount of shareholding the executive has is not. This conclusion holds both for bureaucrat chief executives in the commercial sector (data available for 57), and for entrepreneurs and family businessmen (data available for 31). The exercise was not undertaken for men in finance firms because of the lack of suitable measures of size.

It would appear then that the larger the firm a man heads the more his salary goes up, which is entirely what one would expect. However, size of firm makes no difference to value of shareholding in the case of bureaucrats, and gives only a small correlation, significant with two of the four measures, for the capitalists (see Table 4.20).

Some further interesting results are obtained when we categorise the salaries of the men into the same bands as their incomes, and likewise their shareholdings into the same bands as were used for their wealth holdings. We can use Kendall rank order correlation coefficients to give an indication of the links between salary, annual income, shareholding and wealth holding for the men who are capitalists, and those who are managers. The results can be shown in two diagrams (Figure 4.1).

(a)   Bureaucrat chief executives: number = 55

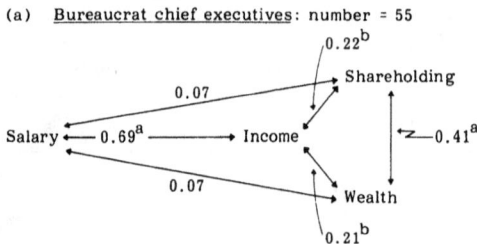

All correlations are Kendall Tau-Beta.

a = significant at 1% level   b = significant at 5% level

(b)   Entrepreneurs/family businessmen: number = 30

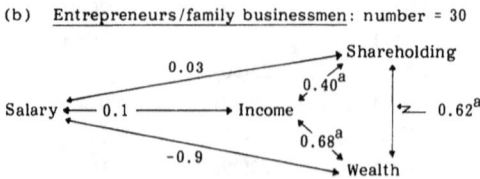

All correlations are Kendall Tau-Beta.

a = significant at 0.1 per cent level

Figure 4.1   Relationships between salary, shareholding, income and wealth

Table 4.20   Correlations of salary and shareholding with size of firm

	(i) Correlation coefficients of salary with:			
	Assets[a]	*Turnover*	*Profit*[b]	*Number of employees*
57 Bureaucrat chief executives	0.58	0.54	0.58	0.52
31 Family/Entrepreneurs	0.51*	0.54	0.64	0.53*

All coefficients significant at the 0.1 per cent level of confidence, except * significant at 1 per cent level

a Assets are taken straight from 'The Times' 1,000 list of companies
b Profit is profit in absolute terms; figures are for 1975

	(ii) Correlation coefficients of value of shareholding with:			
	Assets	*Turnover*	*Profit*	*Number of employees*
57 Bureaucrat chief executives	-0.9	-0.11	-0.08	-0.13
31 Family/Entrepreneurs	0.16	0.33	0.19	0.35[o]

All correlation non-significant, except o significant at the 5 per cent level

One may infer from the above relationships that the bureaucrats' incomes are composed to a large extent of their salary, and that this accounts for the strong relationship between them. A weaker relationship indicates that the more wealth they have, the greater the shareholding in the firm of which they are chief executives. Again this is not an unexpected conclusion, and one would not expect the relationship to be very strong as bureaucrats have other places in which they may invest their wealth, and also because, as many pointed out when assessing their own holdings, their house or houses are often a very large part of their personal wealth, and this is presumably a variable fraction of their total wealth.

In contrast, the entrepreneurs and family businessmen do derive their income from their wealth, and a considerable section of this wealth is liable to be shareholdings in their own firm. Salary, however, shows little relationship with income.

These relationships indicate that the distinctions between types of businessman do encapsulate valid distinctions among the business elite between capitalists and managers. However, this kind of data once again lead to no very clear conclusions in the context of the ownership and control debate.

To take the bureaucrats first, it is clear that their income is related to their salary, and their salary in turn is related to the size of company they run. This would seem to be a stimulus towards expanding the company. However, since income at the higher levels is severely taxed, the small amount of real income the executive receives in turn for the salary increase he can justify on the basis of the company's growth may not be thought worthwhile. If wealth is the aim, then it seems that men heading small firms may do as well as those running larger ones (Table 4.20). Once a man has a shareholding in his firm, then expanding the assets would logically seem the best way to expand the value of that shareholding. (Dividends produce a relatively small income flow after tax unless one's shareholding is very large indeed.) But again, how is that expansion best achieved - by making more profits, or in some other way?

In contrast, the capitalists obtain their income to a large extent from dividends. Their salaries it may be noted in the case of this sample had a mean at £25,100 (standard deviation 13,100), rather lower than that of the bureaucrats (mean £32,400, standard deviation 13,200). Again, they face the problem that their dividends are highly taxed. Thus it may depend very much on the individual whether a high rate of profit or an expansion of the asset base is desired. In fact, of course, the actual value of the shareholding depends on the share price, which in turn will be related to the profit performance.

It may be noted that the mean value of the bureaucrats' shareholdings in their firms was £50,500; but it shows a wide variation - the standard deviation is 210,800. The capitalists had mean shareholdings of £1,360,000, standard deviation of 2,488,000. (This was calculated using stock market prices for mid-December 1975, taking an average of the year's high and low values at that time.)

Differences between groups must not blind us to the most obvious fact about the business elite as a whole: by most standards
these are all wealthy men. Using the by now very dated figures
of the Royal Commission on the Distribution of Income and Wealth
(1974), we find that all the chief executives have incomes that
place them amongst the top 1 per cent of the population, and this
will probably still be so even though inflation will have vastly
raised the qualifying figure of £6,236. Likewise all the chief executives are in the top 10 per cent of wealth-holders, and four-
fifths of them come within the top 1 per cent (see the Royal
Commission figure, p.80, but note the assumptions made in arriving
at the estimates).

4.12 HOME LIFE AND THE DRIFT TO THE SOUTH

I have indicated above that many of the business elite have had
careers that afforded them little contact with manual or other
lower status workers and in background they themselves came
predominantly from white-collar families.

It may be suggested, however, that at previous stages of their
careers many of the elite will have lived in occupationally mixed
communities, and these will have given them the contacts they
have not had at work. On this I have no evidence. What I will
suggest is that such contacts are some way behind them. Most men
in this study had been on the boards of their companies for some
time. Leaving aside the retired directors, the average time spent
on the board for all men in the study is fifteen years, and for
bureaucrats alone, 12.9 years. I wish to show now that taking up
such a main board place usually means moving to the south-east,
and living in a community which is anything but mixed.

A drift of population to the south of Britain is often remarked
on. I wish to point out here its consequences for the pattern of
directorial life. One is that whereas in the past many firms had
their headquarters in the area in which the firm grew up, often
on the original factory site (as the HQ of, for example, Pilkingtons
still is), there are very strong pressures on medium and large
firms to move their headquarters to London, or at least to move
most of the directorate there.

The desirability of having the company headquarters in a large
city, from the point of view of the directorate, has been well recognised by geographers, both in Britain and elsewhere. With
regard to the British case, both Westaway (1974a, 1974b) and
Parsons (1972) have pointed to the tendency for large companies
to site their headquarters in the south-east, to the detriment of
other regions and in the face of government policies to develop
other regions.

Westaway draws on the work of Tornquist (1970) and Thorngren
(1970) in arguing that firms above a certain size need to have
their administrative and head office staff in large cities to perform
the functions of scanning the environment, adapting to it and

planning for future change. Information flow via direct contact between members of different organisations is a very important reason for firms to have their head offices in London. In this context, one might specifically draw attention to the importance of the City as an international finance centre to which company directors may wish to have ready access, and to the fact that London is to an extent at the centre of transportation systems, particularly international ones.

Other factors mentioned by Westaway are the opportunities a city gives to make use of shared services (for example, computers), the need for a ready supply of staff with the right skills, and interlocking directorships.

All of this suggested that firms in this study might not just have happened to have had their headquarters in the London region, they might have deliberately located them there. A simple test was made of this hypothesis, and the findings are shown in Table 4.21. Here the location of the company headquarters of medium and large companies in this study at three different times over a fifty-year period is examined. Information came mainly from the 'Stock Exchange Yearbooks' for 1925, 1950 and 1975. There was no question of course of including small firms in this analysis because they were originally only included in the study if they were based in the south. (Also I do not check on the alternative hypothesis that the arguments above suggest: that is that firms with a London headquarters will grow faster than those outside and therefore are likely to come to represent a disproportionate percentage of large firms.)

The resulting table serves as a comment on the structure of British industry, rather than proof of the hypothesis of the drift to the south. So many firms were already based in London by the time they were publicly quoted that only a small amount of movement is indicated. But the table does show that only 16 per cent of firms were based outside London at the time of the interviews. And the results are in line with Young and Willmott's conclusion that the proportion of professional, managerial and clerical workers in the London region is rising faster than in the country as a whole. (Young and Willmott, 1973, ch. 1.)

I suggest that the resulting structure of large British firms has two consequences for directors. First, on obtaining a main board place they cease to be what Watson (1964) called spiralists, and spend the rest of their working lives in the London region. As a result of this they move to one of three geographical areas to live: one of the 'better' parts of London, or its suburbs; one of a ring of commuter towns; or one of the small, previously rural villages of the kind described by Pahl (1965). In none of these cases does it seem likely that the businessman spends his out-of-work life in a mixed occupational community.

The second consequence will be developed in more detail in chapter 8. It will be suggested there that businessmen, because they are closer to the capital, because they live in white-collar areas, and because of demands on their time and their own inclination,

Table 4.21 The location of company headquarters[a]: medium and large firms only

Date of public quotation	Companies now London-based			Companies based outside London
	Moved by 1925/always London-based	Moving 1925-49	Moving 1950-75	
Before 1925 38 firms	22	1	8	7
1925-49 21 firms	13	0	3	5
1950-75 16 firms	16	0	0	0
All 75 firms (at 1975)	51	1	11	12

[a] In the case of firms built by merger I have considered the separate parts as separate firms throughout their history. Thus a firm based outside London merging with one with a London HQ and adopting the HQ as the headquarters of the conglomerate, counts as one firm moving to London, one that has always been there. There were no examples of firms moving the other way. Thus the 12 firms quoted as being outside London are in fact nine composite groups, since three had merged with the others.

are less involved in local voluntary affairs than they were in the past, and more involved in affairs of a national character that are directly relevant to business.

4.13 COMMUNITY LIFE

To complete the arguments of the previous section I have examined the location of the homes of those men whose homes were in the south-east of England. Placed on a map, they could serve as a guide to the more expensive areas of London and its suburbs. Of the 85 addresses that were known, twenty-three were in the Greater London area, but only five of these were in the band between the North and South circular roads and the edges of the GLC area. Eleven were in Kensington or Chelsea, with others in Hampstead, Highgate, St John's Wood and Belgravia. Sixteen men had flats in London as well as homes outside and these followed the distribution of first or only homes. The remaining men commuted in from the suburbs, a ring of commuter towns, or from rural villages up to as far as 75 miles away. Thus there is some variation in the communities in which businessmen live, and it would be possible for some to have quite wide contacts with groups outside the upper middle class, while others could not.

Whether there is such contact, and the nature of it, one cannot say. The interview data, when examined, give the impression that businessmen's friends are drawn overwhelmingly from the middle class, and that when there is contact with lower status groups it is with people who, in effect, work for the businessman in some capacity - what one might call 'hired deferentials'. When the limits of time permitted, I did ask the men who were interviewed to give the occupations of five friends. This was successful in the case of sixty men of all types (that is, bureaucrats, family businessmen and entrepreneurs). Here is the result. Of sixty men giving the occupations of five hundred friends:
42 (70%) mentioned directors and managers of their own and similar companies;
17 (28%) said doctors;
15 (25%) said clearing or merchant bankers;
14 (23%) said lawyers;
17 (28%) referred to other professional groups, including those employed by business firms;
11 (18%) said farmers;
8 (13%) said MPs or cabinet ministers;
7 (12%) said civil servants;
7 (12%) said proprietors of small businesses;
5 (8%) said shopkeepers including art or antique dealers;
3 (5%) said peers (including a duchess). [6]
Contrastingly, I have collected all references to contacts with non-middle-class groups made outside work that the men made during the interviews; there were the following categories: 'labourers on my farm', 'game keepers' (or 'gillies'), 'gardeners', 'my PT

instructor who is also a scaffolder', 'the man who sweeps the road
at Sunningdale golf course', 'the professional at my golf club'.
   The evidence here is slight, but in uncharted waters any map
used with caution may be better than none. I would contend that
far from living in mixed occupational communities, top businessmen live in isolation from lower status groups. From the interviews
it seemed that there is a small group who do have more extensive
contacts outside the middle class; and one might mention, for example, men who do political canvassing, or have been MPs or local
councillors. But it is a small group.

4.14 CLUBS AND LEISURE ACTIVITIES

To round off the picture of the top men of British business I offer
some information on the clubs they belong to and their leisure interests. This is mainly included for the sake of completeness, but
it is not without its importance, since meeting in exclusive clubs
is said to be one of the ways in which the different groups that
together comprise the 'power elite' or the 'ruling class' communicate and co-ordinate their power.
   In practice, this would seem to have been greatly exaggerated.
In chapter 8 we will see that businessmen make almost no reference to meeting politicians or civil servants in such clubs, although
they are quite open about their extensive contacts with such
groups. Here I shall merely indicate the extent of such membership.
   I used here only documentary sources, and thus have information
on only 87 of the 130 who were interviewed. The rest are less well-
known businessmen who are less likely to be members of such clubs.
I took the following as comprising 'exclusive London clubs', though
several of these are probably not particularly exclusive: Brooks's,
White's, Turf, Junior Carlton, Carlton, Boodle's, Garrick, Pratt's,
Athenaeum, Bucks, Bath, Reform, City Livery, Beefsteak, Caledonian, Naval and Military, Travellers, Savile, United Oxford
& Cambridge.
   The most popular clubs with businessmen in order are Brooks's,
Boodle's, Bath, Caledonian, City Livery. Of the 87 men, only 41
were known to be members of any one of these listed above, which
is 47 per cent. It is unlikely that more than a handful of the remaining men in this study were members of such clubs. Since the
41 men were spread among twenty clubs, it would seem a poor way
of co-ordinating the activities of the business elite, who could
probably have far more contact through interlocking directorships
or the CBI.
   Turning to leisure interests, those that are found among the
business elite are very much what one would expect among the
middle/upper class of middle age. Golf emerges as the favourite
sport, but in fact gardening is the most frequently stated pastime.
Probably the data of Young and Willmott (1973) is superior here.
They studied a group of managing directors, most of whom would
have come from smaller firms than those in this study, but their

methodology consisted of asking the respondents which of a list of activities they took part in. From their study it emerges that watching television is the most indulged-in activity, but this is hardly ever recorded in reference books. Some of their data are given here for comparative purposes.

Table 4.22   Leisure interests of businessmen

1 *Sport* 60% of all the 83, that is, 50 men, claim some kind of sport as a leisure activity. Most popular are:

This study		*Young and Willmott (1973)*
Golf	played by 29%	33%
Sailing	played by 16%	20%
Tennis	played by 10%	20%
Fishing	played by 14%	14%
Ski-ing	played by 7%	
Shooting	played by 8%	
Riding	played by 5%	

2 *Other Outdoor* Gardening: 30%; walking: 7%; Farming: 7%

3 *Cultural* Reading, music, theatre, ballet, opera, etc., mentioned by 24%; most popular: reading: 10%; music: 12%

4 *Indoor Hobbies* Photography, winemaking, handicrafts, bridge, etc.: 17%

5 *Travel* 8%

4.15 SUMMARY

In this chapter the family background, education, careers, and present community life, other than political involvement, of the businessmen who took part in this study were examined.

In chapter 2 it was suggested that the life and career experiences of the businessman or senior manager are potentially very wide. The generalisation remains true for this group, who come from a wide range of companies, both financial and commercial, have a range of educational, professional and managerial training and have worked for their firms in a range of capacities.

In some respects, however, the generalisation may be modified. One consistent aspect of the lives of businessmen in this group is that neither in their career nor their family life nor present community life have they of necessity had to become involved with manual workers or people from lower status groups. The extent to which such a generalisation can be more widely made is difficult to judge, but it would seem likely to be true of all those main board directors who do not have and have not had direct experience of shopfloor production management or certain kinds of personnel work.

A review of the evidence of this chapter may bring home the point. It was found, as in previous studies, that the majority of the businessmen were born into white-collar families, usually of professional or managerial status (Table 4.1). A majority had attended a public school (Table 4.3).

As a group businessmen are very likely to have received higher education at a university or technical college (Table 4.4), or else a professional training (Table 4.6). Indeed, whether it is the case that men of high status background are highly likely to receive such education and to succeed in business, or whether such education is a positive asset for success, it was found that a high proportion - 78 per cent - have either education beyond school or professional training.

The evidence of this chapter was that the distinctions between bureaucrats, family businessmen and entrepreneurs were valid ones. Aside from the great differences in wealth and income of capitalists and managers, it was possible to show differences between two of these three groups (the bureaucrats and family businessmen) in terms of education, professional and management training and career experience.

It was concluded on the basis of comparison with other studies that the respondents in this study were not untypical in terms of background of the business elite as a whole.

Businessmen of this generation were likely to have had their education or early careers disrupted by wartime service in the armed forces. The group as a whole had not received extensive management training. I hypothesised that for some the former may have acted as a substitute for the latter.

The most striking feature of these top businessmen's careers is that the majority of bureaucrats, and thus of all those studied, had no direct experience of managing manual workers. Family businessmen were more likely to have had such experience, but they are a minority. The most common career experience of all groups, that is, where they have spent the major part of their careers, is in general management. Amongst the bureaucrats, the most important experience in a management function was that of sales or marketing.

Businessmen who are going to the very top of their firms must expect to obtain their main board place early. Seventy per cent of those interviewed had a seat on the main board by the time they were forty-five.

We saw that a move to the main board usually entails settling in the south-east of England, and I suggested that this is the result of the tendency of large firms to have their headquarters in the London area or to have moved them there as they grew. I examined the location of the homes of the businessmen and questioned the likelihood that they lived in occupationally mixed communities, as these have been presented in sociological theory. This in turn suggests that most contacts by businessmen outside work are with members of the professional and managerial groupings. Such evidence as is available on the occupations of the friends of the businessmen in this study, and the extent of their contacts with lower white-collar and manual working-class groups, tends to confirm this.

5 THE COMPANY COMES FIRST: the responsibilities and objectives of directors

'We were a professional team, all of whom had risen from the ranks. I do not think any of us felt that our first duty was to the shareholders. The company came first and we were intensely proud of Beechams and of what we had made of it. We believed in its destiny and were dedicated to building a great international company capable of competing with the powerful U.S. corporations which dominated so many of the markets in which we were involved. Profits were the measure of our success and the means by which we had to grow. The proportion retained in the business had steadily increased until it exceeded that paid out to shareholders.'
H. G. Lazell, 'From Pills to Penicillin', 1975, p. 191

5.1 INTRODUCTION

We come now to the central focus of this study, the beliefs, attitudes and values of the business elite; and I start here with the organisations that consume the major part of businessmen's time and energies, that is, their own companies. I am thus concerned here with the economic role of the businessman; and because of the attention it has received in the literature, I consider it specifically within the terms of the ownership and control debate.

In the discussion which follows I will first consider how the heads of the various companies in the study conceptualised their general objectives for their firms. I then compare the attitudes and performance of 'capitalists' and managers and look briefly at how these top businessmen saw the responsibilites of the director. Finally, I consider how the long-term goals of businessmen are likely to be translated into more short-term aims, by asking which groups inside and outside the company are likely to influence the chief executives.

5.2 GOALS FOR THE FIRM

As a guide to the sections that follow, I will outline the position that the evidence presented here leads to with respect to the ownership and control debate. I will suggest here that what appear as alternatives to social scientists appear rather differently to businessmen themselves. For them, the 'soulful corporation', to use Berle's (1960) phrase, has already arrived. But 'soulfulness', social responsibility or socially desirable ends, are seen as being compatible with, and to be pursued, via the very traditional route of making profits. An ethos has been evolved, and I believe that adherence to it is wide and still spreading, that presents other goals (growth, serving the interests of customers or of employees) as only short-term alternatives to the long-term pursuit of profit; and, indeed, these may be seen as the means to long-term profitability. About the short-term goals that result from this and the process of strategy-formulation it is more difficult to generalise. I incline to the position that, in the absence of complete knowledge, businessmen will seek to increase profits on a year-by-year basis, which clearly may not require the maximisation of profits in any given year.

The evidence on business goals comes from an early section of the interviews in which the businessmen were first asked quite simply to state the principal objectives which they saw their company as pursuing.

This relatively naive line of questioning takes little account of the varying levels of complexity on which it could be answered; of the very different situations which existed with respect to the market, competition and type of product or service produced, or the varying size and structure of firms in the sample. Yet from the majority of the respondents it did produce a set of statements that define in a general way what businessmen feel they are there for; what they are trying to do, and why: in effect, a business philosophy. Thus we have such statements as:

'There's no doubt at all what our objective is - we're here to increase the wealth of the nation.'

(Q. How do you know you're doing this?)

'The simple and sensible way to recognise that you're doing this is to add annually to the funds of the company in real terms.' (M.D. - large engineering group)

'The primary responsibility of the board is to shareholders to assure the business is run profitably in their interest. The second responsibility is to the community at large, that where one can develop the company for the country's advantage in overseas fields one should do it. Thirdly, certainly staff and employees play an important part in my thinking, because [-] is a service company and success is dependent on our ability to find the right people and motivate them.' (Chairman - medium size service company)

(Q. What were your objectives in building up the company?)

'Oh we were definitely interested in growth, we wanted to be the best and the brightest. We wanted to be rich, powerful and all the rest of it. When I took over the company twenty-five years ago we were small beans - affected by rich and powerful competitors and we said one day we will be as big and will be able to affect our environment in some way.'

(Q. You say growth - in what sort of terms?)

'Well you can measure it in all sorts of ways. ... Earnings per share, that's one measure, they have grown, - profits have grown, - the number of employees has grown, - assets have gone up ....' (entrepreneur, medium size capital intensive firm)

'This is not an easy one. I think in general terms the objective is to run an efficient company. The problem comes when you try to measure it. We see it primarily in terms of increasing profitable growth subject to a number of constraints. [How are you measuring that?] Until recently we were basing it on the previous year. But recently we've been trying to take a five year forward look.' (M.D. of insurance company)

'[The objectives are] to make a proper return on the capital employed; to protect the deposits, bearing in mind the nature of our business, and ... to maintain the quality image of our name.... And to create a satisfactory and enjoyable work environment for the chaps here, because if you don't do that the thing doesn't tick, bearing in mind we're in the people business.' (merchant banker)

'Let's be clear the objectives are not new .... What has been introduced is a thorough strategic planning process which establishes the business the company is in, and where we will be in ten years in terms of quality, quantity and cost [discussion of planning process follows].... The objectives come right back to the classical things - but basically to grow and profit by the handling, processing and distributing of commodities, our own and other people's. Our success is measured in terms of beating inflation by 5 per cent. A growth of profits, etc. in real terms of 5 per cent.' (M.D. in family firm)

Taking all these statements and analysing them shows that statements couched in terms of profits, serving the interests of shareholders, or a steady growth of profits are by far the most common objectives for these top businessmen. Indeed, statements of such a form were made by over 80 per cent of the 103 active chief executives (see Table 5.1). Profit was by far the most frequent word used in statements of business objectives.

It is worthwhile considering briefly why profit, and more usually steadily rising profits, should be seen so clearly as the objective of the business enterprise. There are several reasons. The first, which was for obvious reasons not alluded to by those interviewed, is that maximisation of profit has simply been handed down over generations as being the essential aim of the business manager. According to Henry (1949), those who succeed in business hierarchies have a strong orientation to acceptance of authority, and of the goals of those above them. Put more crudely, it would seem unlikely that managers will succeed to positions of the highest level if they have doubts over the profit maximisation objective, nor will they in turn promote those who do.

Additionally, as we saw (chapter 4), a high proportion of the chief executives have economics, commerce or accounting education, in which they are likely to have imbibed classical economic theory.

Second, it is recognised, even by those who suggest alternative goals for a corporation's directorate, that certain minimum levels of profitability have to be satisfied if the firm is to continue in operation. This is, naturally, well-recognised by businessmen themselves. Two related factors are of importance in this regard. The first is that in the modern enterprise the minimum profit is not that which allows the firm to break even, nor even the same level allowing for inflation and depreciation. In most large firms a secure level of profitability is seen as one that allows for a certain amount of research and development, for investment in new ventures, advertising, diversification, product substitution, and so on. The second factor is that businessmen themselves see profit as the route, or the means, to goals which theorists propose as alternatives, most conspicuously the goal of growth. From the interview material it becomes clear that profit and growth are not usually perceived as alternatives; indeed, whilst classical theory refers to maximisation of profit, many businessmen appear to think first of maximisation over the long term, and hence a steady growth of profit. An additional factor in such a transformation is that businessmen in practice have to operate with only limited knowledge of the market-place, and of likely future trends, and cannot themselves know when profit has been maximised (a point made also by Newbould and Jackson, 1972).

A third reason for perceiving the organisational goal in terms of profit is that it does allow, year by year, some kind of quantifiable target to be set, against which success or failure of the firm and its constituent parts can be measured. It is on the basis of such reasoning that Ansoff (1969), after reviewing the work of other theorists on the goals of managers, decides to take the maximisation of profit as the aim in his discussion of corporate strategy (but again not necessarily maximisation in any one year).

But a final, and most telling, reason for profitability to be seen as the major aim of the business organisation emerged also from the interviews. It is that a sizeable proportion of top businessmen have at the forefront of their minds an ethos which combines the objective of profitability, or of maximising shareholders' return, with that of the idea of the director, or the board, as the arbiter of conflicting interests. According to this ethos (hereinafter called the ethos of balancing interests), the director must arbitrate between the interested parties that are bound up with the firm: those most usually named are the shareholders, the employees and the customers; but the company's suppliers and the community, both at the local factory level or in the form of central government, may also be included. According to the ethos, however, the directorate only arbitrates in the short term: for in the long term the interests of all concerned with the company coincide.

It may be remarked that the ideas behind this 'ethos' are not new. Child has indicated how early British thinkers on management

put forward the idea of the manager as the balancer of interests
between labour and capital. Rowntree and Elbourne put forward
such ideas in the early 1920s, as did Sheldon in his 'Philosophy
of Management' (1923), Lee in 'The Social Implications of Christianity'
(1922) and even Sir Alfred Mond in a section of his 'Industry and
Politics' (1927) headed Seeing Fair Play. [1]

What is interesting is the way in which, to capital and labour,
various other groups are now added to the balance which the manager holds. Further, the notion of balancing interests is bound in
with the concept of the director's role as being, as Nichols (1969)
put it, to pursue the 'long-term company interest'. [2] A very similar amalgam is to be found amongst American management thinkers
and can be found explicitly stated in, for example, the reports
of a symposium of businessmen, academics and management consultants which met as long ago as 1954. (See Brown and Smith
(eds), 1957, pp. 21-2.)

Here are some versions of the ethos as put forward by the interviewees, starting with a former president of the CBI.

Q. What do you see as the responsibilities of the board?

'I've tried to spell this out in the last few years - it's a bit
like putting a record on. To serve the needs of those to whom
the company sells its products, to constantly have regard to
the interests of the employees. It has to understand and react
to its responsibilities to society at large, both local and national. And it has to show both present and potential investors
that it is making adequate use of its resources. Now I don't
know that I can expand on that - that, in my view is the job
of the board of directors.'

And the head of one of Britain's top five firms said:

'A great deal of rubbish is talked about these objectives. First
of all if you don't serve the customers you go out of business.
If you don't serve the shareholders you're in trouble. If you
don't look after labour you're sunk. Your responsibility is to
look after those three at the same time. Each is always wanting
more, but there is no such thing as a company which pays no
attention to its troops, its shareholders and its customers.'

In very similar vein, the chairman of a small manufacturing company said:

'We in management of this group are in there for achieving a
profitable return on the capital that we employ, but the profit
must be made by methods that are acceptable to the community.
Following on from that we have an objective to see that employment policies are right, that if we are set out to give a service
to customers that we give them that service, and if there are
any community problems - we recognise our responsibility to
the community.'

And in the financial sector, we have this from the M.D. of a bank:

'I think they [the objectives] are changing towards being
multi-objectives rather than being a single objective. I think
we have come away from the maximisation of profit as a single
objective, and we now have that objective as the test of

efficiency, and it is obviously broken down into sub-objectives, such as maximising the return on capital employed and doing better than your competitors, which I think is a very good inter-firm comparison; but they are subsidiary to the profit objective. And we have introduced as well an objective to be measurably the best employer in banking – I think one can begin to measure it in terms of staff turnover, pay disputes, and the treatment one gets from the trade union. So very much the question of staff – staff involvement. And I'd go further even than that because I think it isn't just profits and staff it's the place in the community – it's the sort of role the bank has to play in the national scenery.'

With the ethos of balancing interests the soulful corporation has arrived: if the competing interests are somehow reconciled in the short term then all prosper in the longer term. In an attempt to measure how widespread the ethos is, I have tabulated in Table 5.1:

(a) all those who referred in their objectives, or amongst their responsibilities, only to profits, shareholders, or growth of profit;

(b) those who stated some versions of the balancing interests ethos, referring at very least to profits/shareholders, customers and employees; together with some other combinations of objectives (c)–(e).

The balancing interests ethos turns out to be the single most widely formulated statement of the executives' objectives for the firm, and there is also a smaller, though sizeable group, who mention employees and shareholders together. Yet, overall, one must emphasise again that profit or serving shareholders was quite clearly at least part of the objectives of 81 out of the 103 executives giving any reply.

Table 5.1 shows that 'capitalists' and 'managers' differ little in the distribution among them of stated objectives. A chi-square test shows no differences of statistical significance between the two groups (at the 5 per cent level). The Table 5.2 compares men from different sectors of industry.

As can be seen, six men from City firms expressed their objectives entirely in terms of providing a service for the customer. Three of these were from insurance companies, two of them mutual funds. The other three were merchant bankers, who expressed the view, which occurred also amongst other bankers, that the banks provide services akin to those of the law or accountancy firm. In effect, they were asserting a view of themselves as professional men rather than businessmen, and it would be interesting

Table 5.1   The stated objectives of company chief executives by ownership position

	Bureaucrat	*Family businessman*	Entrepreneur	*All*
Number giving reply to this question	70	23	10	103[a]
(a) Number who saw their objectives only in terms of profit, serving shareholders, etc.	21(30)	6(26)	2(20)	29(28)
(b) Number giving a version of 'balancing interests ethos'	27(39)	6(26)	3(30)	36(35)
(c) Number saying profits and employees	10(14)	6(26)	3(30)	19(18)
(d) Number saying service to customers only	5(7)	1(4)	0	6(6)
(e) All other	7(10)	4(17)	2(20)	13(13)

(As in other tables, figures in brackets are percentages.)

a Amongst retired executives 2 were non-executive chairmen at the time they were interviewed and their views are included. Those of other retired chief executives are not.

Table 5.2   Stated objectives of chief executives by sector

	Sector			
	Manufacturing	*Service*	*City*	*All*
Total	55	35	21	111
Giving classifiable answers to this question	49	34	20	103
Saying profits alone	15(31)	10(29)	4(20)	29(28)
'Balancing interests'	19(39)	11(32)	6(30)	36(35)
Serving the customer[a]	0	0	6(30)	6(6)
Profits and employees	9(19)	8(24)	2(10)	19(18)
All other	6(12)	5(15)	2(10)	13(13)

a Customer only mentioned.

Chi-square tests do not indicate differences between sectors at acceptable levels of confidence.

to interview a very much larger group to discover how widespread this self-portrayal is, or how seriously it is meant to be taken.

5.3 CAPITALISTS AND MANAGERS

As we saw in chapter 1, the ownership and control debate has partly been concerned with whether in firms which are manager-ially controlled the directors will have different aims from firms in which families or entrepreneurs remain in control. We have already seen that in terms of their overall objectives for the firm, or their responsibilities as company heads, we get a similar pattern of responses from the family businessmen and entrepreneurs as we do from the bureaucrats.

On the basis of the statements made in the interviews, I would suggest that in practice the objectives, aims and even styles of management of family controllers are not likely to differ greatly from those of bureaucrats. (Indeed there were indications that family businessmen were sensitive to charges of inefficiency in the firm, and were keen to demonstrate that they were as competent as managers would be in the same position. Thus they would refer specifically to the openness of promotion in their company, their own management training, and the use of various management techniques.) It should be noted that these generalisations are being applied only to family men controlling larger firms. That is, those that came into this study, not small firms as referred to by the Bolton Committee (1971) or Boswell's (1973) study. Equally, I do not include entrepreneurs with second or subsequent generation family controllers.

In this context it is of some interest to compare the firms in the study using a more objective measure. Therefore the next table (Table 5.3) compares firms in the commercial (that is, non-City)

Table 5.3   Mean rate of return earned by companies under different types of control

		Type of control		
	All	Bureaucrat	Family business	Entrepreneurial
Number in sample	84	54	22	8
Mean rate of return: %	22.9	23.1	21.7	25.2

Rates of return used were taken directly from those given in 'The Times' 1000 list of companies. The rate is that before payment of interest and tax, based on assets of the company at the beginning of the financial year. Analysis of variance indicates that groups cannot be said to differ at acceptable levels of confidence.

sector on the mean rate of return on capital earned in two years, 1974-5.

As can be seen from the table, rather than the capitalists *per se* making the higher rates of profit, it is the entrepreneurs who do. In fact, the family businessmen obtain, taking the mean, a lower rate than the bureaucrat-controlled firms, although this is not statistically significant because the spread of rates of return is so wide. The next table (Table 5.4) shows the actual distribution of rates of return.

Table 5.4   Rate of return and type of control

		Type of control		
	All	*Bureaucrat*	*Family business*	*Entrepreneur*
Number of firms	84	54	22	8
Rate of return				
35% and above	8(10)	5(10)	2(9)	1(13)
25-34%	17(20)	7(13)	6(27)	4(50)
15-24%	45(54)	34(63)	10(45)	1(13)
Less than 15%	14(17)	8(15)	4(18)	2(25)

Chi-squared 9.69, 6 degrees of freedom, not statistically significant at acceptable levels of confidence.

There are clearly many criticisms that can be levelled at these tabulations. They compare firms across sectors, when certain sectors may have a concentration of one type of control or another. The sample of firms is small, and rates of return have been taken for only two years. Equally the rates may not be properly standardised and thus comparable.

Nevertheless, the data as it stands points to only one conclusion, which is that amongst firms under different types of control the rate of profit varies and no type of control can be said definitely to produce higher rates. The evidence here is not in line with that of previous studies (for example, those of Florence, 1961; Kamerschen, 1968; Monsen, Chiu and Cooley, 1968; Radice, 1971). However, the review of such studies by Child et al. (1975) makes it clear that there is little agreement among them.

Of course, one explanation for the slightly greater rate of profit earned on average by bureaucrat-controlled firms would be that some are misclassified. A refinement of this would be to see firms as falling into a more complex pattern of control types, as recently suggested by Francis (1980). In such a pattern, aside from managerially controlled firms, we would also expect to find firms under the control of financial controllers, who might represent the institutions, or hidden interest groups. It is certainly not clear from the interviews which firms if any were miscategorised. However, one might suggest that if such control operates, then it is very likely that the chief executive himself is such a financial controller, especially if he is the chairman.

Again it would take some investigation to establish just which such chairmen are. But from the discussion in chapter 4 it may be suggested that they are likely to be men born into high social status families; that is men who would rate in the top section of the social status index proposed in the previous chapter. Thus it is of interest to compare the mean rate of return of firms with executives of varying social status, as measured by the index.

Table 5.5   Rate of return and chief executive's status

Social background of chief executives	Number of firms	Mean rate of return %
Social status I	18	19.7
Social status II	34	20.2
Social status III	16	23.9
Social status IV	10	27.0
Foreign-born executives	6	38.2

Analysis of variance shows no significant difference between groups for groups I to IV.

Now on the index as it was developed (chapter 4), position I contained the men of high social status in family background, position IV those of the lowest social status. According to the hypothesis just advanced, group I should be most in contact with and most nearly the traditional capitalist class. But this group achieves the lowest rate of return on average, whilst the men of the lowest social status achieve the highest rates of return (and the foreign-born men do better still).

However, the variations between groups are not different at an acceptable level of statistical significance. Nevertheless, the trend in the figures is striking, and suggests either that men who have close family or traditional connections with the upper class are no more likely to pursue high profits than those who have moved into the business elite from situations of lower status; or else that they are no better able to achieve them.

One explanation for the trend in the figures may be that men who are born of lower status parents find it easier to get to the top in newer, and more expansionist sectors (for example, electronics or services) than in older, less successful sectors (shipbuilding, engineering). However, the data collected here is not suitable for testing this hypothesis.

5.4 FAMILY CONNECTIONS

In the final stage of interviewing the sampling was specifically
designed to give a comparative sample of family businessmen/
entrepreneurs and managers (bureaucrats). And members of each
group were specifically asked about their own position in relation
to shareholdings in their companies. The answers were revealing
in that each group appeared to see its own situation as most favourable to the long-term success of the company.

Family businessmen and entrepreneurs were asked whether they
thought that they would see their responsibilities as directors in
a different light if they did not have the specific personal attachment of a family connection with the company. In reply, the family businessman gave three types of answer:

(a) it makes no difference;

(b) we're more concerned with people;

(c) we're more concerned with the long term.

The third type of answer is particularly interesting in the context of the debate over ownership and control, for in some cases
the family businessmen were suggesting that managers would be
more likely to sacrifice the long-term stability or success of the
firm in pursuit of high short-term profits. Here are some of the
replies:

'I think it [having a family connection] makes a difference in
that in so far as the family is concerned they're interested in
the total financial viability of the company much more than an
individual independent manager of a company is. I think when
you are taking long-term decisions, you take decisions that
are different from those you would take if the family were not
there - if you are taking action to prevent a merger, or taking
action that is short-term policy rather than long-term policy.'
(chief executive - large service company)

'No I think the particular edge it gives is the question of timespan. You tend to take a longer view. You expect the family
connection to continue. It has gone on for, since whenever
so on normal - eh - extrapolating techniques you will expect
it to continue. You take a longer view - you're very concerned
not to run the business down, to sacrifice the future for the
present - whereas so many of the other pressures are the
other way.'

(Q. They're to produce a high dividend, or high earnings per
share?)

'Right - or possibly to sell the business.' (chief executive -
large manufacturing company)

'Well things have changed slightly .... Sir - has been away,
he's just come back and he's saying, "How dare you say to a
newspaper I come into meetings when they're nearly over, and
the family connection isn't there." And in a way it isn't. You
see we've now got a non-family M.D. and a non-family finance

director. I really look at it as a company. I've got a lot of
shares in it. But I've got responsibility to 100,000 shareholders. It's a non-family board, so it's gradually moving.'
(chairman - service company)

'No - not at all - this company has been through the rather
fraught transition from a family-owned company to a widely
owned multinational. I knew it would take at least two years
for the change to take place. There are certain advantages
to the family firm. Before I took up the appointment I talked
to twenty-four chief executives - mixed - from family run and
other companies. Our researches show that there is more
concern for people in family run businesses.' (M.D. - large
manufacturing company)

Whatever the truth of this last statement, it seems that family
businessmen are not immune to the pressures of business and may
find the drive for profits coming from their own family or even
their managers. One family company chairman stated he was
pleased to retire because:
'The tensions and pressures within a business that are based
on cold rational logic are getting greater and greater. And
when emotionally you know that it's a wrong decision what can
you do - you know, I think a manager today when he's
considering redundancy, lots of professional managers treat
this as a necessity in a business. The only thing to do is cut
down and wield the axe. I think that ought to be the last
thing he ought to be doing. But it's very difficult to argue
against when he's got a profit target and he's going to attain
his figures, and this is the way by which he succeeds.'
Both the bureaucrats and family businessmen questioned along
these lines came from firms in the top 250 by turnover. The former, however, were asked a slightly different question: would
they personally desire a bigger shareholding in their company,
and would it be an incentive or change their objectives? Here the
pattern of answers was again straightforward: the chief executives
replied that naturally they would like more shares because they
would then be richer men. But they did not see such shareholdings
as an incentive, nor did they think that such shareholdings would
lead them to work harder or improve their performance:
'Honestly, I don't see shareholding as giving an added
incentive .... Same thing with options. Options [here] are
open to everybody. I can't see why top people should have
options and not the office boy. I've had it put to me that
because Joe Bloggs has 20,000 shares he might make a different decision from if he didn't. He's a bloody poor director
in that case.' (chairman - large engineering group)
The same men summarised the arguments against large shareholdings:
'If you have a large shareholding you can never afford to do
anything about it. Now I get letters from shareholders saying
why don't you have many shares. If I had a hundred thousand,

and I sold ten, a shareholder would write and say "why have
you sold ten - don't you have any faith in the company?" And
as my old chairman used to say, and we do now have an employee scheme, the workers have quite enough risk working
in the company without risking their savings in it.'
The point concerning the psychological value of demonstrating
one's faith in the company by putting some of one's savings in it
was made by several men. On the same topic a retired executive
said: 'I quite honestly would think that the vast majority of chairmen and directors of big companies they haven't a big stake in
the company, I think they'd just consider they'd got a job to do.'
(This attitude to shareholding should not be taken as betokening
any widespread lack of desire for greater financial rewards, since
there were frequent complaints about the low level of British managerial salaries, and high taxation.) And one final quote here
from a manufacturing company chairman, perhaps sums up the
managerial position to shareholding amongst those who did, in
fact, see it as desirable:
'I don't think it makes me feel the responsibilities more keenly.
It gives me an added incentive but I don't honestly think it
would make any difference to any decisions. But at least it's
something one hopes by one's own efforts will improve and
give a capital gain in these days. I don't think it affects our
decisions. I think it's a good thing to have it because I think
people look at it more and think this is our money. So you
look at it more and think would I put my money in this venture. It brings it home to you.'

(Q. Would you want a much larger shareholding, as American
directors often have?)

'I don't think so. We need a balance here. The majority of
shareholdings are institutions'. They have a medium and long-
term interest. If directors' shareholdings were too great I'd
always be a bit worried that then they were making short-
term decisions, instead of what we've got to do. Anybody can
make a profit over the next two or three years - we've got to
have a balance between the short and long term.' (chairman -
manufacturing company)
As some of the quotes above demonstrate, there was no sign that
the bureaucrats regarded themselves as part of the capital-owning
class. For all but a small minority, the bulk of their income comes
from their salaries (see chapter 4). In a number of cases when
they were asked about their shareholding, or to estimate their
wealth, they pointed out that their house would always form the
greatest proportion of their savings. Thus there was little evidence that at any stage in their careers they might have changed
from seeing themselves as managers to being capitalists.[3] In any
case, as one or two said, their own shareholding acquired over a
lifetime would always be very small compared to the size of holding
that, for example, a pension fund could build up in a short time.
The retired executives were specifically asked whether they had

as chairman/chief executive, regarded themselves as primarily
the representative of shareholders or the most senior manager;
their answers reinforce the point:

'Well both. I always thought I was the boss. Nobody dared to
argue with me on the line management. On the board I had
to be democratic. On occasion I changed my mind after list-
ening to the board's views.' (retired chairman - electrical
firm)

'Certainly not a representative ... just somebody with a job
to do.' (M.D. - engineering group)

'Very much the first [a manager]. To try and make a success
of the company with responsibility for everybody who worked
there, and to customers. The shareholders were one group,
but there were others. And I suppose to me it was always the
people who worked there that I felt the major responsibility
to.' (M.D. - engineering group)

'Oh it's a very theoretical sort of question. It's not black or
white. I regarded myself as responsible for all that [the
company] did even if I didn't know it was being done. I certainly accepted that if shareholders weren't satisfied I was
the man who had to answer them, and be answerable to them.
But I wouldn't say that was the predominant moving force. It
was that there was a great enterprise and you sought to see
the enterprise performing well. That was the first thing.'
(chairman - chemicals)

If we turn now very briefly to the third group, the entrepreneurs, then this, admittedly small, sample presents a different
picture again. They tended to view both second generation family
businessmen and professional managers as lacking their own dy-
namism and flair. Thus, one specifically mentioned the lack of
opportunities for entrepreneurs as the cause of Britain's economic
problems.

In contrast to those who have risen through established firms,
this group may well see themselves as capitalists, One opined that,
'I always say that if we had another 100 millionaires in this country
we wouldn't be in the mess we're in.' Another spoke of industrial
relations in his firm as 'relations between labour and capital'. And
a third, talking of his own motivation, said: 'I never thought I
would do anything else but come into industry. My heroes in my
youth were the robber barons in the States, the Vanderbilts, the
Mellons, the Jim Fisks. My bedside reading was always *Fortune*
and so on.'

5.5 LONG-TERM AND SHORT-TERM GOALS

I have suggested that the evidence of the interviews leads to the
conclusion that businessmen do not have goals for their firms that
differ fundamentally from the traditional goals of the capitalist

enterprise and no consistent division was apparent in the goals
of 'managers' and 'capitalists', though as I have just shown there
were some differences of attitude between bureaucrats, family
businessmen and entrepreneurs.

I have tended so far to talk rather generally in terms of profits,
or long-term profits. So did many of those interviewed. However,
it must be readily accepted that this defines only the formal aims
of the organisation. In Perrow's (1970) terms, this is the 'system
goal' of the organisation, but as Perrow remarks (p. 151),stated
at this level of generality, knowledge of these goals would not
help us to understand any one particular organisation. [4]

Perrow discusses several case histories of corporations which
had clear system goals (maximising the immediate return to investors, extreme cost-cutting). One can produce similar ones for
individual corporations in this study. But the question remains
as to whether it is possible to generalise about system goals in a
more specific way. That is, if maximising long-term profitability
is the overall goal, what do businessmen do from year to year, or
month by month? What sort of short-term goals do they formulate?

I believe the answer to the question has been best expressed
by Newbould and Jackson (1972), and will put forward the hypothesis here that whilst much of top businessmen's time and energy
is expended in taking decisions whose results will not be apparent
till several years have elapsed, what they are likely to do in the
short term is to attempt each year to make a bigger surplus than
in the previous one (if they can a bigger surplus allowing for
inflation). The issue here is a complex one, and I can offer only
limited evidence, [5] but in support of the proposition, it is worth
considering:

(a) the way in which the interviewees regarded their responsibilities as directors, and

(b) what I will call the 'audience' of the chief executive.

5.6 THE DIRECTOR'S RESPONSIBILITIES

In chapter 1 I discussed the responsibilities which management
thinkers, and practitioners, have suggested should be the provenance of the main board director. In the interpretation of these
by the main board, the over-arching objectives must become
translated into practical objectives and a division of labour amongst
top management. A consideration of these, and of the comments of
the respondents, indicates that in the comparatively large companies with which we are concerned, the attention of the full-time
executives of the main board is mainly concerned with taking
strategic decisions that will produce revenue for the company only
in the long term. Directors appear to conceive of their responsibilities to a very large extent in terms of taking long-term strategic
or policy decisions.

Taking the responsibilities of the director (pp. 5-6), it will be
recalled that apart from the legal responsibilities, the requirement

to safeguard the assets, and to report to shareholders, they were to:

(a) audit the performance of management;

(b) remove the chief executive when his performance is inadequate;

(c) establish the objectives of the corporation and ensure there are adequate strategies;

(d) establish the basic policies of the corporation.

When reviewing the first set of interviews in the light of the issues discussed here, it became clear that it was of some interest to devote part of the later stages of the study to a consideration of the directors' responsibilities and questions on these lines were included in the interview schedule (see Appendix 1). The topics were thus discussed with nineteen main board directors, nine retired chief executives and forty-two full-time chief executives, 70 men in all from companies in the top 250 turnover.

The first conclusion from these discussions must be that the directors' responsibilities, as set out by management thinkers, are not to the forefront of practitioners' minds (if they are actually known and accepted at all). Although two-thirds of the interviewees mentioned at least one of the points above (discounting purely legal responsibilities), it was usual for only a few to be mentioned and then in vague and unspecific terms. The third who did not formulate their responsibilities in the theorists' terms tended to refer to looking after the long-term success of the business, for such things as 'total responsibility for what goes on in the company' or else their responsibilities to shareholders, employees, customers, the community, as discussed already.

Table 5.6 summarises the answers which were received. The most frequently stated responsibility was that of creating long-term strategies or policies, which was mentioned by 46 per cent of the 68 appearing in the table. This was closely followed (often after probing the interviewer) by 'resource allocation', an answer given by 42 per cent. Altogether forty-two of the 68 (62 per cent) giving any classifiable answer mentioned either strategy or resource allocation, and this rises to 70 per cent if we exclude the nineteen directors who were not chief executives. In tabulating these answers, no attempt has been made to separate the functions of strategy and policy formulation. Whilst one may agree with Ansoff's (1969) argument that the two areas are conceptually distinct, they have not always been distinguished in writings on corporate policy-making, and most respondents did not draw a distinction.

Thus long-term strategy, or policy, and the resource allocation process are the functions of the director which come most readily to the minds of practitioners. One must state that whereas by 'resource allocation' one is inclined to think of the forward investment, planning and budgeting process, the men who were interviewed tended to insist that they meant also the allocation of key personnel, manpower more generally, and, in some cases, materials, plant or other resources.

Those interviewed did also include, from time to time, a selection

of other possible directorial responsibilities of the chairman or
particular directors. These included:
(a) responsibility for the cash structure of the company and for
setting dividends;
(b) policy and planning on acquisitions and divestments;
(c) communication inside and outside the firm;
(d) choosing the board and successors to it;
(e) setting top salaries;
(f) maintaining 'company values';
(g) home government contact and lobbying;
(h) taking account of government policy in various countries of
the world and its effects on the business, in particular of legislation and currency rates;
(i) short-term investment of spare company funds.

Table 5.6   How top businessmen see the responsibilities of the director

	Main board director	Bureaucrat chief executive	Family owner/ entrepreneur	All
Number giving classifiable answer	19	28	21	68
% mentioning as a board function				
1 Long-term strategy or policy	32	54	55	46
2 Resource allocation	21	50	55	42
3 Monitoring management performance	11	18	40	22
4 Selecting senior management	21	17	30	22
5 Morale/well being of employees	26	11	10	15
(Any of 1-4)	42	75	75	66

Figures in this table are percentages other than the top line.

Clearly, we do learn something from the answers which businessmen give to the questioning here, but what must first strike the
observer is the very limited extent to which the answers to open-
ended questioning correspond to the list of directorial responsibilities prepared on the basis of management theory. There would
seem to be four possible explanations for this, none of them mutually exclusive, which it may be worth considering in turn.
    The first is that directors do not in fact do the things that
theorists think they do, whether the theorists are academics or
thoughtful practitioners. This point of view has been argued very
convincingly by Myles Mace (1971;1972), who maintains that

American board members do not perform duties imputed to them. In his view, boards do not, and cannot, establish broad objectives, corporate strategies or policies, rather what they do is to approve these in the form of accepting (or rejecting) proposals for capital allocation. Mace also maintains that in practice directors fail in their duties of asking discerning questions of the president or of selecting the president (chief executive). Mace's view of the board pictures it as following the lead of the chief executive and senior managers. Thus it offers advice to the president, adds specialist knowledge to management discussions and acts, if it must, in crisis situations.

Mace's arguments are compelling, though they are more readily applicable to American company boards in which non-executives are often in the majority. But they would not appear to explain the vague or limited nature of the interviewees' replies. For one thing, the men in this study were asked to comment on the responsibilities of executive directors, who presumably are involved in putting strategies to the board. Further, the functions most frequently mentioned, strategy and policy formulation, are amongst those that Mace says are not performed by the board as such.

An alternative explanation is that whilst boards do the things they are supposed to, not all members of the board act as 'proper' directors. This would perhaps be the view of Pahl and Winkler (1974), who found in the firms they studied that many board functions were performed by cabals or cliques. Indeed, some of the members of such cabals were drawn from men right outside the boardroom. It is implied, though not explicitly stated by Pahl and Winkler, that the key function of such cabals is the allocation of resources in the form of capital.

This being the case, it would presumably be possible to interview main board directors who were not involved in capital allocation, but purely in operational or technical activities, and so could not give a specific account of a director's responsibilities. However, this explanation seems unlikely to apply to a sample so heavily weighted with chief executives, and indeed this was the point of concentrating on this group.

Related to this second explanation is a third possibility, which is that it is found desirable by those who run large company boards to leave the functions of the board largely undefined. Certainly, one cannot imagine that senior managers are sent away to management school to learn how to be directors. Nor, so far as one can tell, are they likely to be handed a piece of paper on joining the board detailing the principles on which the board will operate, or telling them how to behave. Directors perhaps learn how to be directors by watching and taking part. Thus chief exexutives may well know in practice what the board does, but never define it and may even find it desirable not to do so.

For if many directors do not act as directors in practice, then clearly the collective responsibility of the board to which management thinkers refer may be a myth. That this can be the case was most obviously evident in the discussions with the entrepreneurs,

who were in some cases not in the slightest attracted to the idea
of collective management, preferring rather to regard themselves,
together with one or two lieutenants, as controlling the firm. Thus
one said: 'The chairman [himself], the managing director and the
finance director are responsible for the direction of the group as
a whole. The other directors are in effect technical directors,
they look after the divisions.' Another echoed this comment:
'I don't think there is a distinctive role of the director. One
problem of British business is that the title of director is so
much desired. So I prefer not to talk of directors but of the
leaders of the business - it could include someone who isn't
a director but is management .... We do tend to regard the
board that way, we give membership as a reward. We give it
either because the bloke is running a large enough bit of the
group, or to assure a part of the company they are being
adequately represented.'

A third said he saw the director's responsibilities as protecting
the shareholders' interests, paying an adequate dividend, and
seeing that the firm paid correct salaries. But about his own role
he was more specific:
'All the directors except two have responsibility for some area
of the business or some function. Then there is the chairman
and M.D. at the centre keeping a taut ship. You must have a
good centre where policy is watched and monitored. Despite
the policy of decentralisation we centralise the control of
finance. Every Monday morning there is a statement of every
bank account of every company of ours in the world, so that
I can see what the position is. The executive directors are
not involved in that, except at board meetings, where it's
discussed of course.

We also negotiate bulk buying ... we co-ordinate finance,
lend money on a short-term basis ... we look at world trade,
consider present businesses and expansion .... and nowadays politics enters into business a good deal, we spend 10
per cent of our time on the political side.'

The fourth explanation for the answers here is that the question
was incorrectly designed or the probing inadequate or the interviewing poor in some way. Thus only generalised and rather
simplified answers were received. Without entirely accpting this,
there may be some partial truth here, given the equally important
point that businessmen are essentially pragmatic, and may not
have previously given the questions much thought. Thus, as
Table 5.6 shows, some of those questioned reached automatically
for the stock phrasing of the 'ethos of balancing interests', and
in effect defined to whom they feel responsible, rather than for
what.

Overall, a surprising number (twenty of the 70 - 28 per cent)
of those interviewed specifically said that main board directors do
not perform a role distinctively different from senior managers
below them, or else saw it as a concern for a longer time span, or
a concern for the whole company rather than just one division.

Thus a director of a large multinational said:
'I think in many ways a director is just a senior manager,
although he has certain other legal obligations which a manager, in terms of one division, doesn't have. He also has
the inherent status of a director which obviously must vary
from one company to another and from one country to another.
A director in Germany means something slightly different
from a director in Sweden, from the point of view of the way
it's perceived locally. But basically I would say he's a senior
manager who - he shouldn't think on a functional basis only
whatever his damn job is, he's got to think across the total
company to a greater extent than a senior manager would.'
One argument in favour of a view that poor questioning or the
limited time given to the topic do not account for the limited nature of the interview responses is that some respondents did produce very full answers that do correspond to the management
books. There was a bureaucrat who stated:
'The executive director is a member of the board and a manager. As directors they have the same responsibilities as
non-executives. They are all responsible collectively as members of the board for: one, the future policy of the company,
its future plans and growth. Two, ensuring that top executives are properly appointed. Three, providing the resources
to the managers that they need. Four, monitoring the progress of the company. They are legally responsible to the
shareholders, but they have wider responsibilities to give
maximum satisfaction to employees.'
Likewise, a family company chairman who had extensive management training gave an almost textbook answer:
'Basically the directors in my opinion are the trustees of the
company, whose business it is to ensure the company is a
responsible corporate body, and to be aware of the needs of
its employees, customers, shareholders, the communities in
which it operates and the national interest. Their duties are -
to judge the performance of the chief executive officer. To
accept from the executives ideas and strategies for the future
and to decide on these. To establish certain basic policies,
for example a policy on insider trading, or to purchase from
at least three suppliers, or to sell no more than X per cent
to one customer. To decide to keep some authority - over the
appointment of the chief executive, and possibly other senior
people, and probably over major expenditures.'
To sum up, then, one must say that those best placed to say
what are the duties of directors seem to find it difficult to articulate them; and over a quarter see no real distinction between
what top managers and the directorate do.
One should also mention that when these points were made in a
report to the respondents themselves, a few wrote to the author
suggesting that when asked outright directors would find it difficult to give an account of all that they did. What they were likely
to do was to talk about their major activities, or those they had

most recently been doing. Thus they would only refer to selecting the chief executive if they had in fact been recently involved in doing that.

There may possibly be some truth in this explanation. If this were so, then it would indicate that directors not only conceive of their duties primarily in terms of long term strategic planning, but actually are most frequently engaged in doing just that. This being the case, it probably makes little sense to refer to the goal of 'maximum profits', since there is comparatively little that the men at the top can do in any given year to affect profits without deleterious effects in the long term. In very large companies short-term profits are in the hands of men further down the line (though if profits fall short of expectations in a given year, top businessmen could perhaps initiate a search for extra revenue, or try to conceal the real profits, perhaps through hastily drummed-up business, or the cancellation of investment programmes, or devices such as stock revaluation). What the men at the top do is to choose between different areas for investment and expansion, though probably also setting guidelines as to acceptable rates of return on capital investment as well as targets for annual profits.

That the heads of large companies operate in this kind of way is demonstrated when we consider the accounts they give of their current objectives in terms more specific than 'profits' or 'balancing the interests of all concerned with the firm'. Here are two, the first from the chief executive of a multinational:

'We're saying currently, the rate of growth of production in the UK is half anywhere else, so, thinking internationally, the areas of growth are Europe, America and Japan. Therefore the investment pattern will change. We'll be putting more money into Europe, America and to a lesser extent Japan .... The other dimension - in products X we'll be providing only sustenance capital, and may be cutting down. On products Y, a growth area, we'll be expanding in several different areas. So there are two dimensions.'

The second from a retail chain store executive:

'Our long-term objectives are to develop firstly much bigger stores on the edge of towns, or in town centres so long as we have sufficient parking. There are still 450 towns where we have small shops where we would like big ones. Secondly, we'd like to develop the non-food side further. Thirdly we are still looking at the Continent. We have friendly associations with firms in France and Germany. We'd like to expand there. Those are our three objectives.'

5.7 ON GROWTH

The view put forward here then is that when those who run large firms try to achieve their long-term objectives, they seek expansion, whilst 'satisficing' in the short term on profits (cf. Simon, 1964).

However, it is important to note that businessmen only do this because they have to plan for the long term (cf. Simon, 1964; Newbould and Jackson, 1972). Nevertheless, they do not regard growth as an alternative to profits. For when interviewed, they tended to justify the desire for growth with such statements as 'you can't stand still, if you don't grow you decline', 'managers like to see growth', 'if the company's growing there's more for everyone to do, so they're all happy', and 'it's easier to manage growth'.

Businessmen use the word growth to cover both physical expansion, growth of assets and growth of annual profits. They may well assume that these go together. Theorists have suggested that businessmen pursue growth as an alternative to profits - so as to control the market, reduce uncertainty or provide positions for managers beneath them. Growth may have such effects - but when I analysed the statements of all those twenty-nine men from non-financial firms who referred to growth as an objective, it was found that in twenty-six cases they either emphasised that growth must be at the same rate of profitability, or that by growth they meant growth of profits.

On this point it is worth illustrating from two interviews just how overriding objectives of the kinds discussed so far are translated into practical strategies. The first case is the family head of a partly financial conglomerate. His objectives for the firm were, he said: 'to keep the maximum number of people employed'.

'I feel we have a moral responsibility to keep the business going. The business is essentially a service business, and thus we depend on customers, so it's easy to say the objective is to serve the customers, but in fact it is to continue the business as a living operation.'

But also: 'The business has been growing, and we want it to go on growing steadily. 'Thus growth is an objective because: 'if you're not growing you're standing still and then you decline'. Yet the way of measuring growth turns out to be: 'Profits still is the best criterion. Don't let it be overwhelming but it is the best criterion.'

So from an objective of keeping the maximum number of people employed, we move to a tangible objective of a steady growth of profits. To take another case, an entrepreneur, head of a conglomerate, had as his objectives: 'to look after stockholders, customers, employees at all times. I've left out the national interest, which might come in and could be said to come in in any case.' Later, however, asked if management shared his objectives, the same man said: 'they might, but we would not be worried if they did not', for their objectives are to produce 'growth of assets per share, growth of earnings per share' and to maintain 'quality of earnings'. Here again the interests of all concerned with the firm can be combined and reconciled with strategies aimed at growth of profits.

5.8 THE CHIEF EXECUTIVE'S AUDIENCE

We have suggested that the majority of businessmen conceive of their objectives for the firm in terms of long-term growth of profits, however measured. To do so, they must create strategies that not only include plans for investment, but also set targets for the short term. What is the nature of these targets likely to be?

I believe that Newbould and Jackson (1972) have summed up the most likely way in which businessmen will solve the problem. They write:

It is when one considers textbooks in economics and finance that the disparity between the accepted view and the reality is really marked .... The objective can be regarded as a maximising exercise: with sufficient information (which is always implicit in economics and finance) all decisions can be aimed at producing the greatest possible residual over several years. In reality, of course, the managers choose a course dictated by the fact that less than complete information is available, or a course that lessens the complications of ensuring that every decision should lead to maximum profit: they aim at an increase of the residual compared with the previous year's achievement. It is the growth ethos again, or the contents of economics and finance books as interpreted by managers. (pp. 186-7)

On the basis of the interviews I would also hypothesise that another reason why chief executives and their boards will aim to increase the 'residual' every year may lie in the values of the financial analysts of the press, and of stockbrokers, and other investment analysts. This group, one may suggest, is not powerful in the sense of being able to exert direct pressure, but rather because it acts for the chief executive as an audience. At the end of each financial year the audience can applaud or dismiss publicly the chairman's performance, and that of his team. Pahl and Winkler (1974) spoke of profit conscious managers as employing a concept of professionalism, akin to that of the actor - 'the ability to turn in a competent performance in any circumstances, no matter how unpromising' - I suggest that actors need an audience.

There are a number of groups who may have an interest in the profits that a company makes. Employees and their representatives, of course, will wish to know for their own sake that the company is doing well. Senior managers will be very interested, but are much too involved themselves to be considered as objective judges.

This leaves external groups of three kinds: (a) non-executive directors; (b) shareholders - both the so-called 'small shareholder' and the institutions - and (c) the financial analysts. Let us consider these groups in turn.

So far as the non-executive directors go, we saw in chapter 1 that a considerable body of the literature has pictured them as the watchdogs of capitalism; they are the representatives of the institutions, or of hidden interest groups or else just of the capitalist

class *per se*. In practice there was little evidence that the executive directors in this study felt the scrutiny of the non-executive
directors at all keenly. And whilst only a few expressed opinions
in the other direction, where they did they were vehement, as
for example, the retired executive of thirty years' experience on
several major company boards who remarked:
> 'You go to board meetings for a year or two and you don't
> contribute anything. I mean you ask questions and all the
> rest of it .... The important man is the non-executive dir-
> ector who looks after the shareholders' interests. They are
> the only ones who can sack the chief executive. The others
> are the slaves, their contracts, their holidays, everything
> depends on the chief executive .... The important thing is:
> how should the non-executives be appointed? Half of them
> are appointed by the chairman or chief executive because
> they're friends of his and they'll keep him in power till he's
> 90 if he wishes. That's the wrong way of doing it. I don't
> know what the answer is.'

Or the merchant bank director who said:
> 'I have been absolutely astonished on most of the major boards
> on which I have sat at the absolute acquiescence of quite
> senior figures in their own right, who when sitting on another
> board say very little. Now this is partly a function of the
> strength of the chairman concerned, partly a function of the
> way they are appointed; it is partly a function I think of the
> fact that most of them don't have enough time to give the
> attention to the job as I see it being done'.

These men echo Mace's (1971) and Chandler's (1975) comments
on the functioning of American boards. So, in an unintended way,
did the many executives interviewed in this study who insisted
that their non-executives were playing a valuable role on the
board. For what the value of the role almost always consisted of
was their experience, or the helpful advice they could give
particularly in specialist skills brought from other fields. Non-
executives are not regarded by full-time executives as the controllers of British industry.[6]

That the small shareholder now has little control over the giant
corporation is a well-worn theme. The problems that many thousands of individual shareholders face in taking co-ordinated action
to coerce management are obvious. Winkler (1974) has stated that
in his experience managers regard shareholders as costs. Likewise a number of those interviewed, including some quoted here,
stated that they felt closer to the employees than to the shareholders.
The small shareholder can vote on annual motions, but if his company's performance is bad he is most likely to vote with his feet
and move his investment elsewhere.

The best illustration of the problems facing the small shareholder is to be seen when one attends the annual general meeting
of the large firm. The author attended three, all from very large
companies. The three could conceivably be unrepresentative, but
they do account for hundreds of thousands of investors. One can

only say that until one has seen it, one cannot comprehend the
difficulty which the average small shareholder has in even getting
questions answered. At none of the three did shareholders ask
for or gain information on the performance of the company. Nor
were there present the 'professional shareholders' whose activities
at the AGMs of American firms have been vividly described by
Brooks (1971).[7] Indeed, the meetings seemed to have a considerable representation of senior employees of the firm, and their
wives, who looked unfavourably on pointed questioning. Such
questioning as there was came from what are, in effect, outside
pressure groups concerned with such issues as smoking and
health, experiments on animals, pollution or South Africa. Small
companies may be different in this regard, but their chairmen's
reports of them did not make them appear so.

Of course, there can be occasions when the small shareholder
is courted, as when a board splits into two factions over a takeover bid (for example, the first attempt by P & O to take over
Bovis in 1972), yet even these are rare situations.

The increasing percentage of shares owned by institutions, now
according to Prais (1976) as high as 40 per cent of all quoted
equity, would seem to make them the most likely controllers of
industry. And certainly their own analysts do visit firms to talk
to the directorate. Yet whilst they might intervene actively in
firms which were in trouble, it was not apparent in talking either
to the commercial company businessmen, or the directors of financial firms, that they were actively pushing firms in any particular
directions. There would seem to be a certain reluctance on the
part of the institutions to use their potential power. Certainly, no
chief executive referred to conflict with such shareholding groups.

There was reference, however, to other company watchers - in
particular the analysts of the stockbrokers and the press. One
may suggest that for many company chairmen these provide the
yearly index of performance. Their comments are public recog-
nitions of the directorate's performance. Thus the head of one
large multinational said:

'If we were really in any trouble, or having boardroom squab-
bles, the institutional investors would come round .... They
have their own analysts and we're under that scrutiny. We're
under scrutiny of course from the stockbroker analysts, and
the financial journalists.'

And a retired chairman spoke in similar terms:

'I always saw myself as chief executive with the widest con-
ceivable responsibility, obviously aware of the shareholders,
actually more aware of ————— [laughs]————— actually
more aware in a sense - to the extent that you're playing to
the gallery you're playing to Patrick Sergeant of the *Daily
Mail*, playing to Lex of the *Financial Times*. You're playing
to the press commentary. Actually it was most disheartening -
you couldn't get shareholders along to attend the meeting.
For years at [-] we had great difficulty. You couldn't get
the vote of thanks seconded - the AGMs a formality. I regret

this. It's a fact of life one has to accept that the ordinary
shareholder doesn't count. I don't think one's very conscious
of the shareholders directly as people. One's very conscious
of the institutions, of the stockbrokers, the press.'

The press can also make those who are free from potential pressure from institutional shareholders, that is, the family businessmen and entrepreneurs with high personal stakes, feel that they
are under pressure. This was the case with one family businessman, who ran a company in which a proportion of the shares were
not enfranchised. His firm's poor performance had attracted considerable comment of which he said:

'I must be honest and say that, although we are highly self-
critical, no one could call us smug, the obnoxious publicity
we have had is a form of pressure one can't totally ignore.'

(Q. The press then have an impact?)

'Yes they do.'

(Q. Is there more direct pressure from the City?)

'Well no - direct pressure from the City would be if our bankers were to say your overdraft's too high you've got to get it
down. That hasn't happened in any way at all. There's been
no City pressure at any stage at all. Rude remarks from
stockbrokers one puts in the same category as remarks from
the press.'

Even relatively successful businessmen can find the attention of
the press less than enjoyable. One bureaucrat, chairman of an
engineering company, put it:

'I never worry about the bloody City and the stockmarket
because that's one thing I have absolutely no control over
whatsoever, is it. You come out with your results and pick
up your *FT* and they can be [the company] up, or down, or
[the company] better than expected, and I think, well how
the hell did they know what to expect because I didn't know
myself till last week. No I talk to the brokers, and the merchant banks, though we tend to have a low profile Citywise.
But so what, would it really make us any more profit, I
doubt it.'

If, as I suggest, the stockbrokers' and institutions' analysts,
and the press, provide the chairmen and chief executives with
their audience, then part of the answer as to the short-term aims
of the latter will be found in what the former look for. Clearly the
institutions, because they are obliged to make regular payouts of
insurance, or pensions, require and look for a constant flow of
dividend. As to how the other analysts judge companies, one
simply does not know. But a judgment at any stage can only depend on past performance, particularly immediate past performance,
and what is known of future prospects. One may suggest yet again
that the minimum way to satisfy these groups, and the one that
company directorates will always aim to comply with, is to produce
an increase in profit year by year.

5.9 CONCLUSION

Let me now summarise the course of the argument of this chapter concerning the ownership and control debate and then draw some conclusions from it. I attempted to ensure that the sample of business leaders in the study contained sufficient numbers of entrepreneurs, family businessmen and bureaucrats, and a sample of directors of financial as well as industrial firms. In the last chapter I indicated that although the men in this study were all well off by any ordinary standards, there was a difference not of degree, but of order, between the wealth of the bureaucrats and that of the men with family holdings, and especially in their corporate holdings.

I have also attempted to show in this chapter that there were apparent differences of attitude between the three groups. The groups were conscious of their identities and the differences between them. Thus the family businessmen were keen to be seen as being as 'professional' or 'able' as the managers with whom they might be compared, but at the same time liked to feel that the family tradition gave them a commitment to the long-term future of the firm which managers might not have. The entrepreneurs, naturally, have an even greater personal identification with the companies they have founded; and, in many cases saw themselves as quite clearly the people who ran the company, and ran it with military control. The bureaucrats, perhaps trying to look on the good side, would portray their relatively low stake in the company as giving them a more dispassionate, or reasoned, approach.

Thus, as I argued in an earlier chapter, the business elite is not homogeneous. But in overall business philosophy there is a trend in thought, and one which I believe will be maintained or strengthened. That trend I called the 'balancing interests' ethos. The main board director is portrayed as balancing the interests of the shareholder, the employee, the customer and even the nation; but these interests are seen to clash only in the short term; in the long term, they coincide and the long-term pursuit of profit is seen as being to the benefit of all parties.

All three ownership groups appeared to maintain a roughly equal allegiance to the ethos, and I pointed out its antecedents in earlier business ideology; and its parallel manifestations in the US (and probably elsewhere).

It was also apparent among the directors of some financial institutions. And it is worth noting again that among merchant bankers, the supposed finance capitalists, an ethic of the banker as a professional providing a service can be discerned (and granted the status accorded to the professions relative to business in Britain that may not be surprising) which is somewhat at odds with the concept of the banker as the ultimate controller of industry.

Not only is the 'balancing interests' ethos widespread, but it and other strains of business thought specifically cling to the notion of profits as the objective of business. There was no sizeable group of businessmen who would admit to the pursuit of growth for its own sake; where growth was mentioned it was conceived in terms of growth of profits.

Since the posited split in the aims of capitalists and managers does not seem to exist, the ownership and control debate loses much of its point. But in saying this I am not claiming to have ended all interest in the objectives and strategies of higher managers. For one thing, there do seem to be differences in the rates of profit achieved by different groups; and it may be that differences of philosophy are partly responsible for these. It appeared here, for example, that the family businessmen were less successful than the other groups; and it may be that their feeling that the company is entrusted to them makes them cautious; perhaps they are also unwilling to dilute their holdings by raising capital on the open market and this limits their ability to take advantage of business opportunities, and so on.

Thus the contention that businessmen of all types have generally similar aims, and that these are not at odds with those of traditional capitalism, in no way diminishes business strategy as a fertile field for study. Here my own conclusions were less clearcut. The question is: if businessmen are engaged in the long-term maximisation of profit, what can they do to achieve it? In the very large companies, with which this study is mainly concerned, the businessmen's answer seems to be that their main concern as executive directors must be with long-term strategic planning and policy-making. Whether this is a correct reflection of what they do, or a 'correct' approach to running a company is another matter. But it does mean that businessmen do not necessarily concentrate on short-term profit maximisation.

It is sometimes suggested that various pressures: the AGM, the price of the shares on the stockmarket, the City in the form of bankers or institutional holders, or the non-executive directors (who, of course, may be bankers or institutional representatives), contrive to keep the executives on the road to profit maximisation. But the executive directors interviewed here did not seem to regard such pressures as particularly pressing or constant on them, indeed some asserted the reverse. Curiously, the most obvious pressure on chief executives seemed to be the annual (or thereabouts) scrutiny of the press, and similar analysts, when the results came out. Such scrutiny is rather like school reports; though no threat or sanctions is automatically attached to them they can make you feel quite uncomfortable.

How does one maximise profit in the long term, in the absence of complete information and in a complex and variable environment? How does one simultaneously please the company watchers? A minimal way, I suggested is to aim for a year on year increase in profit.

6 THE VIEW FROM MOUNT OLYMPUS:
conflict, consensus and participation in the firm

'All our chairmen have been very conscious of the need to move round the company, and to get to see people, and not be a remote Olympian figure.'
Retired businessman

6.1 INTRODUCTION

The discussion of the objectives of the business enterprise has obvious relevance to sociological theory. In the interviews it also provided a route to another purpose which was to examine the picture that the respondents had of relationships within their companies. This forms the subject matter of this chapter.

I will suggest in the following sections that businessmen heading large companies may hold several images of the firm. For much of the time 'directorates', 'dominant coalitions', 'cliques' or 'cabals' are concerned with resource allocation. As we have seen, strategic decision-taking, and the resultant capital allocation process, are the most widely accepted concerns of top directors. In this process only a small group at the top of the firm are involved. And for much of the time other groups within the firm, particularly those way down below in middle or lower management, and in clerical, routine or shopfloor jobs, can be ignored. The dominant image of the firm is largely that of a compliant mass.

The top businessman has another role, that of communicator to groups outside and inside the firm. Few deny the importance of this role. However, to the extent that businessmen play it, I suggest that it can lead once again to an image of the firm as the 'core company' and the mass. But in this image the core company is not the dominant coalition, or resource allocators, but a somewhat wider group – those, in effect, who have access to top management and can be expected to develop a full understanding of the aims and objectives of top management.

Businessmen's images of the firm as compliant, or as being in greater or lesser access to top management and maximum information, coexist with experience of, or at least knowledge of, conflict within the firm. The most obvious of such conflicts is that of the shopfloor worker and management. Such conflict can create an additional image of the firm, one of opposed sides, of 'us and them'.

It would seem that such multiple images do not necessarily create problems or tension within those who hold them. Theories of cognitive dissonance may suggest that conflicting ideas need

resolution, and some businessmen are indeed able to make reso-
lutions of their multiple images. However, many others articulate
different images of the firm in different circumstances. There are
yet still others, of course, whose viewpoint remains wholly consistent, but I suggest they are not the majority.

6.2 THE BOARD AND INDUSTRIAL RELATIONS

As we saw (chapter 4), the majority of the businessmen studied
here come from white-collar backgrounds. In their careers they
moved through functions that did not involve them in direct contact with shopfloor workers. Though they may well have personnel
specialists, production directors, or other men with a reputation
for understanding factory workers on their boards (Winkler (1974)
calls these 'one-man chains') their personal knowledge may be
expected to be slight.

Directors' personal conceptions of their role in the firm lean
towards roles which keep them away from operations, and involved
with long-term strategy formulation and resource allocation. As
Winkler points out this conception of their role provides a justification for lack of contact with all but a select section of the
company. In my discussions with businessmen of their responsibilities, industrial relations entered into the frame of reference of
a minority only, and then under the guise of looking after the
morale and happiness of employees.

Thus, my evidence so far in no way contradicts Winkler's (1974)
findings (see chapter 1). But to those not so well acquainted with
boardroom practice, the lack of concern with industrial relations
amongst British directors may well seem surprising. For a long
time it was the fashion to see industrial relations as a key factor
in Britain's economic malaise. Fashions, and understanding,
change, of course, and other factors are now as frequently blamed
(over-taxation, high government borrowing, low industrial investment). Nevertheless, the concern with industrial relations did
produce a Royal Commission,[1] which, in turn, suggested that
industrial relations should be a boardroom concern.

It is thus of some interest to examine the views of the businessmen studied here on conflict and consensus in their firms. All
sizes of firm are represented here and all types (except for the
nationalised industries) of industry and commerce. And with the
spread of white-collar unionisation, even the City firms do not
find the questions entirely academic.

The concern in what follows, however, is not so much specific
issues (such as the conduct of wage negotiation, or trade union
recognition) but the general climate of understanding, and of
conflict and consensus that is perceived within the company. To
quote the metaphor that has been used elsewhere in research (for
example, Goldthorpe et al., 1968a), is the company seen as a football team, with all playing on the same side, or do the top men
themselves see two (or more) sides? The question was approached

in two different ways in the interviews: first, by enquiring into the extent of understanding and acceptance of the directorate's goals within the firm, and second, by a more specific discussion of conflict in the company. Both trade unionism and employee participation were also discussed.

6.3 SHARING THE OBJECTIVES

It will be recalled from the previous chapter that all the chief executives interviewed were asked to give an account of the primary objectives that their company was pursuing. Beyond the statements about making a profit, looking after employees, serving customers and so on, I was told of plans to reduce borrowing requirements, of investment, of expansion and growth in new markets, and new geographical areas, of new products to be launched and other changes peculiar to the individual company.

Each respondent was later asked: to what extent do other groups understand and share the objectives you have outlined? And I asked in turn: do all the board? Do the members of management? And to what extent do employees below management? (see Appendix 1).

The results are most meaningful considered in the light of statements by the chief executives, since they will tend to play the most important part in formulating the objectives. Not unexpectedly, very few of them were inclined to admit that their boards were not either in whole understanding or whole agreement on the corporate objectives. But there were some: for example, a few chief executives said that some members of their board tended to think in terms of sales, or technical proficiency, rather than profits.

As one might expect there were more who felt that probably much of management would not be aware of the board's objectives. This is not to say that managers were expected to disagree but, as a number of those interviewed said, they would have their own objectives or targets. Similarly, employees outside the board would not on the whole disagree with the objectives, but they simply would not be aware of them, or often would not be concerned with them.

Tables 6.1, 6.2 summarise the position. Note that a sizeable minority were unwilling to generalise or said they quite simply did not know what their employees thought.

Now it must be conceded that the chief executives were asked to make difficult generalisations here. Clearly, it is hard for a person to make statements about what is in the minds of the other members of the board, and how can they tell what thousands of employees understand and think? It is not surprising that some choose not to generalise, and say that they cannot or do not know.

Even so, some broad conclusions emerge; there is a greater expectation that groups outside the board will know what the company aims are in the City firms than in industry and commerce. Likewise,

Table 6.1   Extent to which other groups in the company are thought to share the chief executive's objectives – by sector

		Non-retired chief executives only		
			Type of company	
	All	Manufacturing	Service	City
Number answering	103	50	32	21
(i) Do all the board?[a]				
Yes	97(94)	48(96)	30(94)	19(91)
No	5(5)	1(2)	2(6)	2(10)
Don't know	1(1)	1(2)	0	0
(ii) Do a high proportion of management?				
Yes	62(60)	27(54)	19(60)	16(76)
No	31(30)	17(34)	11(34)	3(14)
Don't know	10(10)	6(12)	2(6)	2(10)
(iii) Do the majority of employees?				
Yes	36(35)	16(32)	7(22)	13(64)
No	48(47)	26(52)	18(53)	4(18)
Don't know	19(18)	8(16)	7(25)	4(18)

Figures in brackets are percentages. For question (iii), chi-squared = 10.5, with four degrees of freedom, significant at the 5 per cent level.

[a] For the exact form of the questions see Appendix 1.

the larger the firm the less the men at the top feel that they know what men down below them think, and the greater the expectation that lower level employees will not understand or share the objectives. However, these variables are to some extent related. The relevant tables are not reproduced here, but there is no significant variation between types of owner, or men of different social background, except that all the family businessmen, and all the entrepreneurs, thought that all their board would understand and share their objectives.

More important than the statistics is the actual nature and content of the discussions by the respondents of this question. One should make clear two aspects of these: first, that when the businessmen say their employees do not know, or share, the objectives they are not implying by this a state of conflict, or a perception by themselves of widespread opposition in the firm. Rather

Table 6.2 *Extent to which other groups in the company are thought to share
the chief executive's objectives – by size of company*

		Size of company (number of employees)			
	All	Less than 1,000	1,000 to 4,999	5,000 to 14,999	15,000 or more
Number	103	17	21	24	41
(i) Do all the board?					
Yes	97(94)	15(88)	20(95)	22(92)	40(98)
No	5(5)	2(12)	1(5)	2(8)	0
Don't know	1(1)	0	0	0	1(2)
(ii) Do a high proportion of management?					
Yes	62(60)	13(77)	13(62)	16(67)	20(49)
No	31(30)	4(24)	6(29)	7(29)	14(34)
Don't know	10(10)	0	2(10)	1(4)	7(17)
(iii) Do the majority of employees?					
Yes	36(35)	11(65)	8(38)	9(38)	8(20)
No	48(47)	4(23)	11(52)	10(42)	23(56)
Don't know	19(18)	2(12)	2(10)	5(21)	10(24)

they picture the employees as being uninterested in the objectives; or more subtly, only being interested in them to the extent
that they impinge on their own lives, that is, to the extent the
company objectives may affect job security, wages or promotion
prospects.

This then is one of several pictures of the state of the firm. The
employees below a certain level are presented not as being an opposed group, nor one necessarily in willing consensus, but as one
that is uninterested. Such a picture can take many variations,
depending partly on the level at which one defines company objectives; for example, employees can be represented as self-centred
– tied only by the cash nexus to the firm, and only interested in
their wage packet.

'So far as shop floor workers are concerned, I can only give
you a personal philosophy .... They are not interested at all
in whether or not the company makes a profit, they are much
more interested in what their take-home pay is, and whether
that allows them to meet their bills and obligations and keep
up a certain standard of living.' (M.D. – small service firm)

'I think when you get below a certain level to be honest,
they couldn't care less, so long as they know there'll be
fifty quid in their pay packet on Friday night.' (M.D. -
medium size manufacturing firm)

Or they can be seen as uneducated, unsophisticated, or *unable*
to comprehend the subtleties of company policy.

'Clearly there can only be an understanding of why we're a
growth company in those people who are nearer to the action
as it were. When I say that, I think managers do, but the
involvement of people in the very fabric of their community
would not allow them to have a complete understanding. We
try to preach the gospel .... The company has become bigger
and that makes it more difficult for us to talk to everybody
and make sure the message gets through. I think it's more a
lack of understanding than acceptance.' (chairman of large
firm, objective - 'profitable growth')

More frequently than either of these, the workers are presented
as a group unaware of the objectives, but a group who would
share in them if they only knew them. In other words, management
faces a communication problem.

'I think people do agree with the need for profit - but one
can't know - but what else could they think.' (family businessman - medium service company)

'We employ 30,000 in this country, 25,000 overseas. You can't
communicate with all of them. My object in doing this is to
tell these emissaries, if you like, to go to base and tell 'em
what I've said. And I do tell 'em in some detail. What's in the
bank. What the capital expenditure is. They can tell them anything. Also we send out a version of the annual reports to
employees and shareholders .... I wouldn't mind if each man's
wife read it. Because I think there's an awful lot of misconceptions about this.'

(Q. What about?)

'About profit. And what happens to it. There's still this conception, you know, that there are big fat men lying about the
place investing millions, and taking millions out of the business.
- I think we've finally got rid of this.'

(Q. How?)

'Just by talking to people and getting our managers to talk to
people.'

(Q. Do you think it's important that workers understand your
objectives?)

'Absolutely.'

(Q. Even though you feel there are some things you must keep
from them?)

'Well they might not materialise. Why worry them unnecessarily.'
(chairman - large engineering group)

'Twice a year I get all the subsidiary directors together, and
do a briefing with them. Did the company meet its objectives
or not - really on my own performance. So those managers
certainly understand what [the company] is all about. Beyond
that I think there are some people, economists and planners,
who understand it, but so far as the line managers go it's too
abstract for them. They have more concrete objectives in
their own jobs.

But we have been trying to communicate to all the employees
the need for profit and the creation of wealth. The chairman
has been on a television film and we produce these newspapers.'
(M.D. - family firm)

We may note, in passing, that these ideas of what employees can
or cannot understand, are or are not interested in, confirm the
top men in the belief that there is little need or demand for more
knowledge or participation in top level decision taking. Put crudely, the attitude is often that if they did know what we're doing,
and did understand it, they would accede to it, so there's no need
to involve them. To this point I shall return.

6.4   A PSYCHOLOGICAL BOUNDARY IN THE FIRM?

It becomes clear from the interviews, then, that those at the top
of large companies expect to have the full understanding of only
a comparatively small group of employees. This is the group that
they personally can know. The size of the group in practice may
vary - it may be only the members of the board and a few top
managers below them, or else it may be the top hundred or two
hundred managers. It may also include some staff men, or it may
be a larger proportion of management. In saying 'can' know I do
not necessarily imply that the man in question does. Rather, this
is the group which he can, and on occasion may, communicate
directly with, a group whose names may be marked as being intended for top management positions, who may even appear in the
annual report in a list of senior management.

It is this group, I suggest, that those at the top think of when
they think of 'the firm'. It is this group of whom they are sure,
this group from whom they expect consensus on the company objectives, this group to whom the strategies and policies can be
revealed. In other words, within the formal boundaries of the
firm (or the more variable boundaries of the organisation theorists)
a psychological boundary is drawn, and the firm constituted in
the minds of the elite which runs it. Beyond the boundary, of
course, they know the firm exists. They have visited its locations,
spoken with a handful of managers, shop stewards and occasionally
factory workers. Some decisions, say to close a factory, may sud-
denly bring to their awareness other groups. But it is the core
grouping which constitutes the firm in an everyday sense.

Its existence is revealed in the interviews:

'We ought to be able to motivate the management like the

army - straight down the line. But I've never been able to get it down below the third level crust - there's a crust there of real dead ends. People I only saw about once a year at some Christmas party or something. The top fifty people I probably saw once a month.' (retired chairman - large manufacturing firm)

'Last year I got the top 150 people together and told them where we are going. And I had them together for a whole weekend a few weeks ago. This is the way we disseminate on broader policies.' (M.D. - large manufacturing firm)

'There are senior staff of about 160 out of 30,000 who are the people who have a direct relationship with me. I settle their salaries with top management. I write to them directly on anything of importance that's occurring. We have a meeting not less than twice a year, usually more.' (chairman - large manufacturing firm)

'We have a share option scheme confined to those thirty-five men who we feel can have a direct influence on policy - but of course the government has made it not worthwhile ....
I've got 60,000 chaps in this business and if I wanted every one of them to be aware of the corporate objectives, I'd have to send them all to Harvard for a year and then some of them might. And I don't particularly want management to be aware of the central objectives .... The vast majority of people will make their careers within one division. A tiny minority eventually make their careers outside, and to raise expectations to a level that will not be met is neither kind nor sensible.' (M.D. - food processing firm)

What I am suggesting here may seem strange, but in fact I would go further and suggest it is the way most people cope with large organisations. After all, an organisation, and a company even more than, say, an army, is an abstract concept. It cannot be seen, or easily defined. (Is a company a group of men, or a collection of plant and machinery, and offices, or the shareholders? It is, of course, none and all of these, and all are constantly changing.) A factory worker is liable to regard the factory where he works as 'the company'; head office and other factories are far less real to him, and may be viewed with suspicion. Likewise, members of an army regiment may well regard that regiment as the 'core'. Anyone who doubts this should ask himself how, when he comes to think of them, he views the very large organisations of which he or she is a part.

This concept of the 'core company', or the psychological boundary of the firm, is important in understanding how large companies are viewed by those who run them. For example, several men made statements indicating the importance amongst their responsibilities of attending to the morale and happiness of their employees. Yet the same men had or were about to make quite large numbers of men redundant - the act seems inconsistent with the good intentions. The inconsistency does not arise if one sees that these men were concerned with the well-being of those they regarded as the firm. The decision to regard a small part of the firm as the firm is an unconscious, not a deliberate one, but it is a useful protective device.

Thus top businessmen see consensus in the core company. Beyond that is unknown territory ('one can't know what the workers think'). To map it they resort to devices which, viewed from the outside, may seem less than satisfactory: reports in the media, the tales of guides such as personnel managers who are thought to have explored it well, or talks with those people they regard as being from the outer regions, but with whom they do have some contact - the hired deferentials: secretaries, chauffeurs, waitresses in the directors' dining room (see Winkler (1974) on this point).

In some cases, one must hasten to add, the firm is so small that everybody is known - in my sample there were the merchant banks and property companies. Here consensus is believed of all but a small minority.

6.5 CONSENSUS AND CONFLICT

Probably no phrase is used more frequently in everyday and media discussions of industrial relations matters than the 'two sides of industry'. The concept generally applies to two potentially opposed and certainly mutually suspicious groupings. Winkler's (1974) observation that directors exhibit attitudes which are markedly 'us and them' prompted an exploration of this topic in the interviews. The question was usually posed in the form: 'we often hear talk of the two sides of industry, do you see, or are you aware of, two sides in this company?'

Once again the responses vary greatly according to the type of company a man works in, and to a lesser extent, its size. As one would expect, amongst the chief executives, those in the bigger firms and in the manufacturing sector were the most likely to see two sides. However, there were also a number who either said they simply did not know, or, more frequently, that they could not generalise: either conflict was perceived as varying from plant to plant (for example, 'at Aylesbury there's no two sides, at Liverpool there most definitely is'), or from time to time. The latter was particularly associated with those who saw the firm falling into two sides for wage bargaining purposes (Table 6.3).

All in all, then, we see that the percentage who do see two sides in the company varies from 59 per cent of men heading companies in which there is a manufacturing operation of some sort, to around 20 per cent of men heading completely service firms. The insurance sector raises the percentage who do for City firms. A similar variation is found amongst companies of varying size.

Of more interest again, however, is the reasons that are given for there to be two sides of industry. They can be placed into

Table 6.3   Answers to question: *'Do you see two sides in your company?'* —
by sector

	All	Manufacturing	Service	City
Number answering	106	54	31	21
Yes:	44(42)	32(59)	6(20)	6(29)
No:	41(39)	12(22)	15(49)	14(67)
Don't know/can't generalise:	21(20)	10(19)	10(32)	1(5)

Chi-squared for this table = 22.3, four degrees of freedom, showing significant differences
between groups at the 0.05 per cent level of confidence.

Table 6.4   Answers to question: *'Do you see two sides in your company?'* —
by size of firm: chief executives only

		Size of firm – number of employees			
	All	Up to 1,000	1,000 to 4,999	5,000 to 14,999	15,000 or more
Number answering:	106	16	20	25	45
Yes:	44(42)	4(25)	6(30)	9(36)	25(56)
No:	41(39)	10(63)	10(50)	11(44)	10(22)
Don't know/can't generalise	21(20)	2(13)	4(20)	5(20)	10(22)

four broad categories.
(a) A group which points to the British class system as a source
of divisions penetrating industry as well, or to 'historically entrenched social attitudes', a divisive educational system or mis-
understandings by workers of what happens to profits. In other
words conflict at the company level is seen as the result of misguided or misdirected class feeling.

Two quotes may be cited as examples:
'The management and labour - there is always that to some
extent. We are fortunate in our industry, we don't have too
much of it. We all get a bit removed from it, but I would say
it's not really a problem in our industry.'

(Q. What's it based on?)

'I would say, a little bit on education in this country. The
problems in Germany, for example, are a great deal less.

Certainly it's a bit historic here - they built up from the war.
The educational system over there gives people the belief
they've all got the same chance to a greater extent than in
this country. This is something here, people always feel they
didn't have that chance, or their parents couldn't give it to
them.' (M.D. - large manufacturing company)
Another put it very similarly:
'Let me put it like this. The nation is socially divisive, isn't
it? And you have to go back to the first half of the nineteenth
century ————— I mean, if you're first into the industrial
revolution, if you lose your share of the world markets, you
live with the sickness of the past. And if at the same time you
build up a socially divisive public school system you're bound
to have two sides. But I really think industrial managers are
damned and denigrated too much.' (chairman - large manufacturing company)
(b) A second kind of explanation also tends to view conflict as
somewhat inevitable, but here it is viewed as a feature of industrial life, proceeding either from an inevitable tension between
the managers of an organisation and those they manage, or from
the existence of trade unions. Since unions are regarded as a
functional necessity in large firms, these explanations may be
grouped together. They are not usually an attack on unions as
such. A banker put it as follows:
'I think it's almost impossible to avoid some "them and us"
feeling between the managers and the managed, in just the
same way as there is an inherent division between officers
and other ranks. I think it is impossible to have organisation
on the basis of no conflict because people don't on the whole
altogether like being told what to do - and I would have
suspected that you would have anarchy if you had a no-
conflict situation.'
(c) A third viewpoint maintains that there are not two sides in
the company for most of the time, but that of necessity there is
when it comes to wage-bargaining. This explanation enables the
person in question to both maintain that there is consensus over
the objectives of the firm but conflict over the 'sharing of the
cake'. As the chairman of a large engineering company said:
'Most days of the year they are on the same side. There are
periods and situations when they move to opposite sides of
the table and are in negotiating and bargaining situations.
But the underlying and continuing factor accepted by both
is that management should manage, and management does not
always mean doing the popular thing.'
(d) The most frequent explanation of the two sides of industry
however, is to regard it as avoidable, an aberration from what
should be occurring. Thus, conflict may be regarded as the result
of large plants, of poor communication by the managers concerned,
of militant unionism, or deliberate agitation by politically motivated
minorities, and so on. Here are some variations on the theme:
'I come back to the question of size - when you get a large

unit, when communication ceases between management and worker, if that's the right word, I always object to the definitions on principle.'

(Q. But anyway it's a question of communication?)

'Yes I come back to the problem of size - I think that in a large company it is bound to be a problem.' (M.D. of medium size manufacturing company)

'There shouldn't be two sides in our group - we've encouraged people to improve their position, and made it possible for them to get right to the top. Let me give you examples... We don't think in terms of two sides, we're one organisation.... Remember we're not a bit labour intensive, in this company there's only a few thousand of us, and very few on the shop floor. Even those people I meet at the staff dance and have a drink with them. You can't do that if you're employing 20,000 people - it's impossible.' (chairman - medium sized service company)

'We don't have any of these conflicts - we don't just sit up here and nobody ever sees us. I go round twice a year to all the plants. Up to twice a year. [Management-worker] conflict is not necessary - it's stirred up by outside forces. The average Englishman doesn't want to upset society.'

(Q. You mean union militants?)

'Well I think they're professional stirrer uppers.' (M.D. - small service company)

'We tend in this country to employ jumped up union men as foremen, who very often are promoted because they are bullies. Most of the industrial problems I've come across in my career have been associated with that kind of management taking an attitude which is not the company attitude at all, it's his own attitude which provokes naturally a reaction from the union men.'

(Q. So it's poor leadership in the plant?)

'I think so, yes, well poor leadership - it's probably poor communication from the top as well.' (M.D. manufacturing firm, formerly a works manager)

Now the first point to note here is that how people explained conflict in industrial life varied according to whether they thought it occurred significantly in their own firm. This is best shown by tabulating the answers as is done in Table 6.5. In this table all respondents are taken together. Their answers to the question as to whether or not there is conflict in their firms are then tabulated against the reasons they saw for conflict, so far as these can be categorised.

As can be seen, of forty-four men who did see 'two sides in the company', twenty-eight (over three-fifths) blamed it on historical

Table 6.5 Co-variation of answers to questions concerning existence of conflict in the firm and reasons for conflict

Do you see two sides in your firm?	All	*1* Social class, historical attitudes, educational system	*2* Managers or managed, unions	*3* Wage-bargaining cash nexus	*4* Communications, large plants, agitators, militants	No reply/don't know/other
Total answering:	106	16	14	20	40	16
(a) Yes	44	15(94)	13(93)	6(30)	6(15)	4(25)
(b) No	41	1(6)	1(7)	2(10)	27(68)	10(63)
(c) Can't generalise/ don't know	21	0	0	12(60)	7(18)	2(13)

attitudes and so on or the inevitable tensions between managers and men or unions and management. Those who did not see conflict in their own firm blamed conflict in industry on communications, the size of plants or, in a few cases, agitators and militants. Of the twenty-one who could not generalise about their own firm, twelve saw it as a variable factor occurring, for example, at times of wage-bargaining.

This pronounced pattern means that the explanations as to why there are two sides in industry vary both with the size and type of firm a man heads. These are, however, highly interrelated variables, since outside the City there are relatively few large firms that have no manufacturing plants whatsoever. Tables 6.6 and 6.7 show this.

In these tables we see that it is the heads of the largest companies, but more so the manufacturing companies, who are least likely to see conflict as caused by communication, large plants, militants, agitators or similar reasons. (Those in smaller companies were less likely to answer.) These men look to other factors to explain conflict; factors which, to a degree, may be seen as beyond their control. Conflict may be viewed as written into the fabric of the British life: as inevitable between managers and the managed, or where there are trade unions, or else as occurring at times of wage bargaining. However, it is only the first group - those who see conflict as due to the British class or educational system, historical attitudes and so on - who would see tension in industrial relations as an enduring feature of company relationships. That is 50 of the 90 (58 per cent) of those giving classifiable answers, would probably view conflict as amenable to good management. A further twenty would expect conflict only at times of wage bargaining.

That the distribution of attitudes has, apparently, some connection with the kinds of firms men work in is not surprising.

Table 6.6   Reasons for conflict in the firm — by sector

	All	Manufacturing	Service	City
Number	106	54	31	21
Answers given				
1 Historical attitudes/ educational system/class	16(15)	10(19)	5(16)	1(4)
2 Managers and managed/ management and unions	14(13)	10(19)	2(6)	2(10)
3 Wage-bargaining/cash nexus	20(19)	13(24)	4(13)	3(14)
4 Communications/large plants/ militants/agitators	40(38)	15(28)	15(48)	10(48)
Other/no reply/don't know	16(15)	6(11)	5(16)	5(24)

Table 6.7   Reasons for conflict in the firm – by size of firm

	All	Size of firm – number of employees			
		Up to 1,000	1,000 to 4,999	5,000 to 14,999	15,000 or more
Number	106	16	20	25	45
Answers given					
1 Historical attitudes/ education system/class	16(15)	1(6)	3(15)	4(16)	8(18)
2 Managers and managed/ management and unions	14(13)	1(6)	2(10)	2(8)	9(20)
3 Wage-bargaining/cash nexus	20(19)	2(13)	4(20)	4(16)	10(22)
4 Communications/large plants/ militants/agitators	40(38)	7(44)	7(35)	10(40)	16(36)
Other/no reply/don't know	16(15)	5(31)	4(20)	5(20)	2(4)

Other researchers have also indicated a relationship between shop-floor workers' attitudes and size of plant (for example, Ingham, 1967; Indik, 1963, 1965), and, indeed, managerial attitudes and size of organisation (for example, Porter, 1962-4). Presumably top management's attitudes and expectations are formed by experience, even if that is somewhat indirect. However, the direct relationship between the personal backgrounds of the men who were interviewed and their attitudes to conflict is weak. It was found that 60 per cent of those with shopfloor management experience saw two sides in their firms, compared to 39 per cent of those without this experience, but the number of those with any such experience is so small that it would be wrong to draw firm conclusions from it.

Apart from what appears in the tables, there emerges from discussions on industrial relations an enormous stress on communication. [2] As we have seen, employees in the lower levels of the firm, or outside the core, are regarded as being uninterested in the firm's objectives, or unsophisticated in their understanding of them. However, if they are told what is going on, especially when it comes to making changes that affect them, then it is felt they will be 'reasonable', that is, compliant.

'Communications' arises in more specific ways. First, there is one of the most widely held theories of top executives which sees the large plants in which many employees now work as being conducive to industrial unrest. Such a connection has, of course, been made by social theorists from Marx on, but some businessmen took it further. Ideally, the maximum size of an industrial factory, it was often said, was five hundred, because then the manager

could know every one of the employees personally. It was often
noted too that five hundred is the size of an army battalion. This
concern with personal relationships may be seen as paralleling the
situation of the interviewees themselves, who cannot hope to have
personal relationships with everyone in their firm, and in some
cases have given up any pretence of doing so.

One should point out that this belief in the desirability of small
plants rarely has practical consequences. Those interviewed
thought relationships would be better in small firms and in small
factories, but, with exceptions, they had sought to expand their
firms, and often their plants, wherever it was thought it would
generate more profits. Despite the problems it brings, they themselves are controlled by other forces: 'economies of scale' and 'if
you don't expand you decline'.

Communications has been given an impetus from another direction. During the period over which interviewing took place, inflation pushed up the absolute value of profits, whilst often leaving the companies concerned no better or even worse off in real
terms. But in time of wage restraint, and a Labour government in
power, such profits are vulnerable to attack. Hence there was a
widespread campaign to inform employees of the need for profits,
and the uses of them. The message, however, is put across by
indirect methods - advertisements to the public at large, company
newspapers, or simplified versions of the company reports. The
author left interview after interview clutching such documents -
evidence of the chairman or managing director's earnest desire to communicate. Early in 1977 in fact there was a competition
for the best set of annual reports for employees - it had two hundred entries. [3]

6.6 MULTIPLE IMAGES OF THE FIRM

A man's image of society is often taken to be a partial reflection
of his view of the relationships in the workplace. Thus a tendency
to label all bosses, and authority figures as 'them', to be contrasted to 'us', amongst manual workers has been taken to be a
reflection of workplace relationships on the one hand as well as an
indication of an embryonic class consciousness.

In practice, the position is found to be more complex, and in
the case of top businessmen it appears to be very much more so.
Businessmen as a group did not show any single view of the firm.
Quite possibly the position they adopt is contextually variable.
For what was not verified was Winkler's (1974) statement of directors that 'their attitude as revealed in everyday behaviour was
very strongly "us" v. "them" or an extreme form of the pluralist
conception', even though much of the rest of his paper was quite
believable.

Certainly there are some businessmen who take the attitude that
trade unions are now so strong that their members are well pro-
tected, and that top managers must pay their attention to middle

management. Taken further by a few businessmen, this can be
cited as a 'them and us' viewpoint. Here is one such statement
from one of the relatively few men who has his office on the factory site:
> 'We employ getting on for 20,000 in the UK. One is very
> conscious of the fact that these people's livelihoods depend
> to a degree on how we function. We're a bloody sight more
> aware of this than they [gesticulates out of the window] seem
> to recognise. You know I don't think they think that we care.
> But we *do* care. You know a new order means continuing work
> for them, and profit for us. So a double thing.'

This man says most of his workers care only about their wage
packet. But it's difficult to generalise. Many are Asians, it's hard
to communicate with them. And in one division, where most disputes occur, there are 'people who are determined to wreck the
joint'. He expects a 'we and they' attitude from the workforce:
'Why, I suppose because they seė me driving home at night in a
Jaguar, and they've got to catch the bus.'

Yet this man is unusual, both in his physical proximity to the
workforce, and because his largest division does have particular
labour problems. In many cases the size of companies, and the
separation of the directorate from the labour force allows for more
inconsistent attitudes, for multiple images of the firm. A summary
of the evidence from this chapter allows us to trace these.

The primary image of the firm, and of work life, we saw, is that
of the company as a core, a willing management and an uninterested mass. This is the reflection of the chairman and managing
director's central concerns for much of the time with strategy,
policy and resource allocation. For these purposes they work with
a group that may vary from a few to two hundred top managers.
Some of this group they see, they know of them by name and of
their careers. They may gather them together to tell them of the
ruling coalition's plans and objectives for the firm. If bargaining
goes on over strategy it is within the coalition, or, to a lesser
extent, within the core company.

Beyond the core the interviewees do not expect understanding
of the company's aims and policies, except very broadly the need
for investment and profit. The expectation, however, is of compliance, and of order. Operations are assumed to proceed smoothly,
and the larger the firm the more justification the top executive
has for delegating operational control, and industrial relations
matters.

The conception of the firm here may to an extent be called
'unitary' as Fox (1966) described it. Certainly managers do believe
that the interests of all unite in the long-term success of the firm
and Fox was right to draw attention to the military metaphors of
the firm, since to the extent that businessmen used any metaphors
these were the most common. However, as we saw in chapter 4,
there may also be a more pertinent reason than any overt expectation that the firm should be controlled like the army. That is
that for a number of men the army was their first, and for some

their most important, experience of man management.

Thus it would be said that a factory should have less than five hundred men, the size of a battalion in the army. On the setting of objectives that 'one would not expect a lance corporal to have the same tactical objectives as a battalion commander', and on employee participation: 'the general has to decide if he is going to advance on a broad front - he consults his brigade commanders, the platoon sergeant consults his platoon.' In the company, like the army, there are officers and men. But in the factory 'the foreman is more powerful than the works manager because he is the sergeant major of the army.' Yet the rank of the foreman proved difficult to fix, sometimes he was a warrant officer or a lieutenant, sometimes only a sergeant or corporal.

However, businessmen's images of their firms are more complex than this. Industrial troubles over two centuries, and a hundred years of trade unionism cannot be ignored. A majority, however, regard conflict within the firm as avoidable - due to such factors as poor communication, large plants, misguided militancy and so on. Those most prone to experience such conflict, however, are more likely to view it as something beyond their control - the result of British class attitudes, of history, of the educational system, or else as sporadic and associated with wage-bargaining.

It is plausible that when confronted with opposition or conflict from below in practice top businessmen take up somewhat harder attitudes. They may see misguided, misinformed or ignorant workers as harming their pursuit of their strategic plans; or else presume that lower management has failed in its job. This too may result in seemingly inconsistent views of shopfloor or other lower grade workers. Catch businessmen at different times, or in different situations, and they may be found using generalisations or stereotypes of workers which may even be downright contradictory (cf. Winkler, 1974).

In all this Fox's 'pluralist' ideology in practice seems rather rare. That employees at all levels have their own rights and interests which have to be reconciled is certainly accepted. But there seems no enduring desire to view the firm as a set of competing coalitions. Rather conflict is seen either as a failure (which is the unitary point of view) or else as just sporadic, or out of the businessmen's hands. To the extent that competing interests are recognised they are so only within the context that maintains that all share the same long term interest. Indeed Fox himself makes a similar point in his more recent writings (1973, 1974).

6.7 ISSUES: (1) TRADE UNIONS

In the light of what has been said it is worth considering briefly how, and why, top businessmen react to more concrete issues. For brevity, I summarise only the general run of big business opinion on these, attempting to relate it to what has gone before. First - what about trade unions: are they necessary, who should join and why?[4]

The basic position of the majority of top executives may be said to be one that accepts the principle of unionism, and accords to trade unions a legitimate place. This we saw also in the review of the literature of business ideology in chapter 1. Businessmen's images of the firm reveal clearly what they expect the role of the unions to be. Unions should accept that in the long term all have a vested interest in the success of the firm, and that the pursuit of profit is in the interests of all.

Granted that unions do this (and the onus is expected to fall on their leaders), then unions are accepted as legitimate. More than that, unions are accorded a definite purpose, a function, by businessmen. Unions are desirable, it is held, for all groups where one could not negotiate directly with every person individually.

This definition of the purpose of unions has several advantages. First, the principle of a union is accepted without there being any hint that employees need protection, or gain more, by being part of a collective body. Rather, the arrangement is presented as one of convenience for both parties - top management and employee. Second, the limits of a trade union's interest are clearly defined: bargaining on wages and conditions in lieu of top management meeting each individual. Other issues - consultation and participation, especially where it could impinge on strategic planning - can be defined as outside a union's provenance. Third, at a time when unionisation has spread beyond groups other than manual workers and may well go on spreading, it makes sense of this phenomenon by defining just how far unionisation should spread.

Thus, one should expect resistance to trade unionism per se to be strong only in comparatively small firms. But in larger firms there is a point in the managerial hierarchy at which those at the top feel unionisation would be undesirable. Unionisation should stop some way below the level at which those at the top can know and negotiate (or settle) salaries and conditions on an individual basis - in effect, a return to the core company. As to actual negotiation with union leaders, company policy obviously varies considerably, some firms liking to handle all such negotiations at the centre, others preferring to negotiate on a plant-by-plant basis. But those at the very top, one suggests, are unlikely to concern themselves with such matters - their task is strategy.

6.8 ISSUES: (2) EMPLOYEE PARTICIPATION

Businessmen's images of the firm are reflected also in their views on employee participation. If we consider the widely canvassed idea of putting shopfloor and other workers on the board then the responses of those interviewed are not surprising. Since the company for some purposes is seen as a core grouping of those who are interested, informed, qualified and trusted to participate on strategic issues, and a mass who are none of these, then the idea of putting a few workers on the board can be seen as pointless.

(And indeed there is a relatively low level of support even amongst some trade unionists for the idea.) Alternatively the idea of a balanced board, or one with a majority of employees, can conjure up quite a different picture of relationships in the company and the idea will be regarded with great apprehension. From one point of view, putting workers on the board serves no purpose; from the other it is seen as turning the boardroom into an arena of conflict and debate, which, from such accounts as we have, it is not. In the words of the chairman of the largest firm in this study: 'If it's a minority of workers it's a waste of time, if it were a majority it would be a disaster.'

However, employee participation can take many forms, and businessmen often express themselves as being responsive to, or advocates of, calls for greater participation. It is, however, of interest to explore the limits that are put on this, as they appeared in this study, and to do so I will set out first my own definitions of four related concepts. I recognise that my definitions are not necessarily accepted ones. I take:

(a) Industrial democracy to be a system in which either the workers of productive enterprises own them and elect representatives to run them; or by election or other voting procedure elect the management; or run the enterprises through periodic meetings. In such systems the employees as a group control the enterprises, though they may not own them; they may partly own them, or the state may own them. Into this group would be placed the Scott Bader commonwealth, worker co-operatives, and Yugoslavian enterprises.

(b) Employee participation: a system in which by some means or other workers have some say in deciding how decisions are to be taken; or are present at discussions or meetings at which decisions are discussed or taken. Into this category would be placed all systems in which some workers sit on the boards of enterprises, but cannot ultimately control them. This would include the proposals of the Bullock (1977) Committee.

(c) Consultation: by consultation in this context I mean a process in which before management takes decisions it asks the views of interested parties, by informal means or through formally constituted bodies. But in a consultative process management reserves the right to take decisions, and to decide over which issues it will consult.

(d) Communication: a process in which management tells people what it is doing, and why, and sometimes what it is going to do.

Clearly, there is no clear demarcation line between these concepts. Each level shades into the one above. But these definitions may be helpful in what follows.

To sum up the attitudes of the interviewees as a group one may say that virtually all believe strongly in the virtues of communication, and that businessmen are making greater efforts than they have done in the past to communicate. There is some belief, but it is not so widespread, in consultation, and where it exists it is firmly held that 'people should be consulted over the things that

concern them'. The businessmen interviewed did not appear to
favour participation, and they did not feel there was a demand
for it. They certainly did not conceive of industrial democracy as
being desirable or practicable as it has been defined above.

Again these conclusions are in line with what has been said in
this chapter. But in the discussions it was found that the phrases,
industrial democracy, participation, consultation, involvement and
communication, were used so interchangeably by top businessmen
that almost no systematic analysis of the type used elsewhere is
applicable. One doubts that the muddle is completely accidental:
by seeing participation as consultation businessmen can declare
themselves in favour of more of it, without committing themselves
to anything that would restrict management prerogative. The CBI
evidence to the Bullock Committee reflects this; at one stage for
example, they state that

A fundamental principle, therefore, on which proposals for
greater employee involvement in company affairs must be
based, is that participative arrangements must be designed
to fit a company structure, and not vice versa. (Department
of Trade and Industry, 1977, p.30).

In the next paragraph we see that the participative arrangements
refer in fact to consultative agreements, and we are told the CBI
favours this approach. Later the CBI spells out its options, and
the committee themselves follow the semantic confusion now generated, by their statement that:

The CBI believe that the main focus of attention at present
should be below Board level participation. What is needed in
their view is a gradual organic development of industrial
democracy from the shopfloor upwards.

Of course, the confusion of words is not confined to the CBI, or
businessmen, but it is convenient for them. The minority report
of the business members of the Bullock Committee expresses their
views well. The board is seen as the 'apex of a company's management team' (not, as it is elsewhere, a group arbitrating on and
judging management). Employee representation on such boards
would be disruptive, dilute management expertise and introduce
collective bargaining to the boardroom.

Crucially, too, of course, the minority report opposed the putting of trade union representatives on boards. This must be seen
as one of the most problematic areas of the majority report, and in
the discussions of employee participation (which occurred before
the publication of the report) director after director pointed out
the iniquities of having only trade union members and not all employees represented on the board. Indeed, there were only two men
who were in basic agreement with the TUC's 1974 suggestions.

Altogether it is clear, as the minority report to the Bullock Committee confirms, that businessmen are opposed to any diminution
or dilution of management power. However, it would be wrong in
saying this to leave the impression that British businessmen's
efforts at greater communication or consultation were not genuinely
meant or serious. I believe that they were, and although there is

still a contrast in the methods used to communicate to top managers (calling all the top X together for special briefings) and those used for other groups in the firm, which tend to take the more indirect form of company newspapers or special versions of the annual report, they do spring from a genuine conviction that people want to know more about what is going on in the company. (The use of TV films, or elaborate systems of briefing groups are attempts to go further than the indirect methods.)

It was a belief of many of those interviewed, and likewise expressed in the Bullock minority report, that consultation needed to start at the bottom and be about issues that concerned shopfloor workers. It would be no use, it was felt, simply taking workers from the shopfloor and moving them to the top of the company. And certain firms had gone a long way in trying to extend consultation from the shopfloor upwards. Such systems begin of course, with the works council, but on top of this some firms had, by their chief executive's account, developed either regional councils or councils for subsidiary firms to which delegates from the lower councils were sent. It would be wrong to deny the good intentions behind those moves, or that they were regarded by the chief executives themselves as significant and important steps in trying to improve relationships within their firms.

6.9 CONCLUSION

I suggested in this chapter that top businessmen of large companies may operate with multiple images of the company. The most frequent consequence of the top businessmen's views of the firm is the contrast between the 'core' company and the mass. The core may be thought of as relatively well-informed, involved, personally known to the directorate and trusted. There is ignorance of what the mass of the company is like. They are assumed, in the absence of other evidence, to concur with top management's objectives, to be compliant. Images of groups outside the core - of shopfloor workers, or clerical workers - may be culled from a number of relatively indirect sources, and may invoke or involve various stereotypes - of deferentials, of workers tied only to the job by their wage, of union members, of militants who are politically motivated, of 'decent chaps'.

Different images may be invoked in different situations. The firm may be a hierarchy to some, or a series of concentric layers to others, or it may be a series of 'them and us' relationships: of 'resource allocators and others' - the 'core firm and others', 'managers and others', 'non-union members and others'.

Only a minority of those heading firms employing more than 1000 expected their ordinary employees to understand or share their objectives for the firm. But equally, only in manufacturing companies and the larger companies did a majority clearly feel there were two sides in the company, though quite large proportions were unsure or unwilling to generalise. Explanations for

conflict seem to vary with the type of company a man works in
and, to a lesser extent, the size of the firm; but the largest group
among those interviewed felt that conflict could be avoided but for
the communication problems engendered by such factors as large
plants; or the work of agitators and misguided militants. And another sizeable group of respondents saw conflict as sporadic and
related to wage-bargaining.

I have tried to show that the businessmen's attitudes to their
firms, and beliefs about relationships within them, are related to
their attitudes to trade unions, and employee participation. Businessmen's attitudes to the firm are rarely of a 'pluralistic' kind,
that is regarding the firm as a set of coalitions or groups with
their own distinct interests. And, correspondingly, their attitudes
to unions and participation are fundamentally pragmatic, and
attempt to give a functional place to unions and participative
arrangements within the framework of an (assumed) consensus in
the company.

In the next chapter we will look outside the company and examine businessmen's views of society more generally and, specifically, their views of social class and social status. Businessmen's
views of their firms as ordered hierarchies, of a 'core' grouping,
meeting and discussing centralised policy, of an informed elite and
a compliant mass, might suggest a similarly elitist view of society.
As we shall see, in terms of social class or status this does not
prove to be the case.

7 NOT A SOCIETY PERSON, NOT AT ALL SNOOTY: businessmen's views of class and status in Britain

'Back in my hotel, I wait at the crowded cocktail bar for my trade union guest, who is immediately identifiable since he looks so different from the other clients, mostly businessmen. I had vaguely expected him to look different, but not quite so startlingly.... When the waiter comes to take our luncheon order, there is a bit of difficulty, since the menu rather baffles my guest, who is clearly unaccustomed to its fancy dishes. But he is not in the least bit embarrassed; nor is the waiter at all snooty.'
Peregrine Worsthorne: 'Capitalist Midlands, Classless Cambridge', 'The Sunday Telegraph', 5 June 1977

'I'm not a society person. If it were not for my job I'd be completely unknown.... Many of us could read of some high junketing at some high place in the papers without recognising any of the names of the people who attended or knowing who they were or what role they had.'
Merchant banker, interviewed June 1974

7.1 INTRODUCTION

Earlier I discussed the problems associated with investigating meaning systems,[1] and pointed out that they were likely to be even greater in the case of businessmen. I suggested there that businessmen are a group which conceivably has diverse experience and background; whilst being a group that shares a common occupational position and the concomitant roles that go with this. They can also be considered to be split by one major structuration of class; that of owning or not owning capital on a large scale.

Thus, depending on one's viewpoint, businessmen are part of the ruling class, or some businessmen are part of the ruling class; alternatively they are a high status group, though again, perhaps, one with far-reaching power. These conceptions all bring similar difficulties: for example, how does one expect a privileged group in a capitalist society to view its own position? To accept the existence of itself as a class or high status group is to accept the possibility of class opposition, or public disavowal of that status. To consistently deny the existence of class or status or community in any sense may be to destroy the basis of group cohesion on which the continuing privilege and power of the group may to some extent depend. It is to this and a number of related topics that this chapter is addressed.

7.2 OUTLINE OF THE CHAPTER

In practice, and to some extent in contrast to the other data, the data relating to businessmen's images of society proved difficult to analyse, and I have been led to approach them from several different angles. It may be helpful therefore to give an outline of the course of the analysis.

I begin by describing the methodology adopted in the interview (section 7.3). I then attempt to give some idea of how the businessmen I interviewed discussed social class by describing and commenting on just one interview (section 7.4). I then describe the range of answers received from the respondents in terms of the number of classes they see (7.5); the criteria on which they divided one class from another (7.6); the way in which they saw the upper class or other high status groups (7.7); and the positions to which they assigned themselves in the class structure (7.8).

In sections 7.9-7.11 I break off from the overview of the interviews to discuss one specific aspect: that is, why businessmen conceive of only a small upper class which, in turn, is not seen as a ruling or governing class, and to which most of them do not consider they belong. I consider it important to discuss these particular topics in order to understand the limitations on the extent to which elite groups in advanced industrial societies can develop consciousness of their elite status and cohesion in action.

In section 7.12 I make a comparison of the 'images of society' held by top businessmen with those discussed in other sociological research in Britain. I then attempt to account for the variation which I observed amongst the viewpoints of the businessmen in this sample (7.13); in particular I compare 'capitalists' (family businessmen and entrepreneurs) with 'managers' (or bureaucrats). I also make similar comparisons between groups using more complex measures of family background.

However, these attempts to analyse the data statistically, it should be said in advance, did not prove successful, and I conclude that this kind of analysis is unlikely ever to be successful. Although one can find distinctive reactions amongst some small groups of respondents, the majority construct their images of society by drawing together certain well-worn ideological themes with their own personal experience. In section 7.15 I analyse the distinctive discussions of social class that took place with four groups of respondents: first, men I call 'sociological sophisticates'; then those men who had been highly socially mobile; third, the traditional upper class, and lastly, a group who consider themselves to stand right outside the British class structure.

In section 7.16 I discuss six themes that recur throughout the images of society of businessmen. And, in 7.17, by way of conclusion, I ask whether businessmen's images of society are indeed 'status models'; I suggest that they are to no greater extent than are those held, for example, by manual workers, but that business-

men's desire to de-emphasise social class in society prevents them
developing a class consciousness in the fullest sense.

7.3 METHODOLOGY

It was assumed, and in a number of cases this proved correct,
that businessmen would not be keen to talk about social class.
Therefore, as will be seen from the interview schedule (Appendix
1), unless it arose spontaneously it was usually the last major
topic discussed. In practice, something around the last third of
the interview would be devoted to it. The topic was raised via an
introductory statement of form: 'People talk of there being classes
in British society - what is your own view of this?' A series of
prepared and spontaneous questions were then used to follow this
up. In a minority of cases, the topic arose naturally in the course
of discussion, and was followed up as soon as it was possible to
do so. Occasionally, a statement reported in the press by some
public figure (for example, statements by Jack Jones of the TGWU,
or Chancellor Schmidt of West Germany) could be used by way of
introduction.

Nevertheless, in a substantial minority of cases raising the issue
of social class appeared to cause a certain amount of tension, or
unease in the respondents. There is no way of knowing, or quan-
tifying, how strong this feeling was, but it was clear that it existed, and that it was felt most strongly amongst those born into
a high social status grouping (for example, hereditary peers), or,
at the other extreme, those who had experienced some significant
social mobility.

Tension manifested itself in a number of ways: a small group
indicated their annoyance; and three, after making rudimentary
answers, stopped the interview at this point. (One of the three
said: 'Why are you asking me this, you're writing a Fabian tract,
I'll shut up.') Others asked the purpose of such a question, or
stated their doubts about the relevance of it to other sections of
the research. Again, men who had been quite articulate and keen
to give their answers on other topics, would 'dry up' or have to
be coaxed through the discussion on class.

Contrastingly, there was a small group who were willing, or
positively eager, to talk on this topic. These again included some
of those who had experienced high upward social mobility, and
those men who were foreign-born.

Despite the problems, once the topic had been broached, and it
was clear that the interviewer was not going to engage in political
rhetoric, or 'put one over' the respondent, a reasonable amount
of questioning covering the existence of social class, of the factors
determining it, of social mobility, and of differences of wealth and
status was managed.

The reasons behind the tension that a discussion of social class
and status creates, appear to be:
(a) The reaction of any high status group when the question of

its status is raised. As we shall see class, for most respondents,
is a matter of the status system, not only of objective relationships. Even so, simply raising the issue is to raise the whole
system of inequalities in society, and to confront the group in
question with the possibility that its position is not legitimate.
Most resented by the businessmen was any implication that their
position in the company was not earned, and one of the most frequently volunteered statements was one to the effect that there
are 'men of all types on our company board'.

(b) A second reason would seem to be that raising the issue of
class to some extent deflated the role of the businessman in the
interview situation. This might be described as 'experienced businessman informing naive university researcher'. Businessmen are
not experts on social class, and do not pretend to be, but one or
two clearly suspected the researcher was testing their knowledge
against his own. Thus at one stage one man said: 'Well, I'm no
sociologist, which I guess you are.....'

(c) A third reason appears to be that although the British are
highly status conscious it is not the 'done thing' to talk about it.
Class or status may also depend on a range of indefinables, such
as accent, and the right school, rather than, say, earning power,
and thus be difficult to put simply into words, other than phrases
such as 'he's not one of us'. Equally, the British may so frequently
have been accused of being class conscious that they are unwilling
to make overt reference to it.

(d) Finally, it is clear that to some businessmen the very seman-
tics of class imagery are associated with the political left, and
thus to raise the issue of class can be seen as raising a political
attack. This is most clearly seen in the case of the phrase 'working class'. The businessmen frequently objected to this, because
of its implications that there was a class that did not work. In
their own descriptions of society they would quite often refer to
'those who work with their hands' or to 'artisans'.

7.4 HOW BUSINESSMEN SPOKE OF CLASS

The majority of sociological accounts of perceptions or images of
class consist of tables of percentages, or labelled pictures, that
sum up the patterns that were found amongst a group of respondents. (Exceptions are Nichols, 1974; and Lane, 1961). I utilise
the same methodology here but hope also to convey to the reader
the style and content of the interviews: the words the respondents
used, their phrasing, the ambiguities, and the points they were
keen to make. As in previous chapters, therefore, I include a
number of verbatim extracts from the transcripts.

But, in order to give an overview, I begin by following through
just one interview. Whilst every interview was different, this one
is fairly typical of a certain kind of respondent, who is neither
part of the aristocracy, but neither can be said to have had to
struggle to achieve his position in his company. He is classified in

this study as a bureaucrat, but his father was, in fact, the managing director of the same company before him. He had a minor public school and Oxbridge education.

We begin at the stage of the interview at which the subject of class was first raised.

(Q. I would like to ask your views on some more general social issues, and begin by asking: people talk of there being classes in British society. What is your view of this?)

'There certainly were, and - there still are to some extent - a class society is merely another way of saying somebody lives in a somewhat different manner, has different methods of leisure, ways of behaving, sometimes different ways of talking. In so far as there are still differences of emphasis, yes, there are still classes.'

(Q. You say there were, and still are ....?)

'There were and still are, but whereas in the past such differences were remarked upon, or were noticed, or did in fact cause a division - nowadays although those differences are still there, though I would have thought in a less marked degree, people are not anywhere as concerned about drawing the lines as they used to be.'

These statements were typical of those encountered: class is accepted as existing, but the lines of demarcation are said to be 'blurring', or people are at any rate 'less concerned' about drawing them. Class is seen primarily as a difference in lifestyle. The interview then continues:

(Q. How many do you think there are?)

'Difficult to say. I think I know what it was in the thirties. The so-called upper class, middle class divided into two, and then I suppose you had the so-called lower or working classes.'

(Q. Do you still see an upper class in British society?)

'In some respects there are certain people who seem to have the same kind of attributes as they did in the thirties. I think they're possibly fewer than they were. There do still seem to be a few around.'

(Q. Well, what sort of people are there?)

'Well, take the Marquis of Bath.'

(Q. I don't know the Marquis of Bath.)

'No, nor do I. I would suggest some of the big landowners and the country house chaps. Well take the Duke of Devonshire, I suppose - no, I'm not one of them. I'm not a big landowner and I'm not a country house chap but they have existed in the thirties and they still exist.'

(Q. This remnant of the aristocracy and the landowners?)

'Yes, the remnant of the aristocracy.'

(Q. But you don't see yourself coming into this section?)

'I don't think we've ever come into that category.'

(Q. Even though you're the head of a large company?)

'Yes.'

Again statements such as these were often encountered. The
upper class still exists but is shrinking, and the man in question
disassociates himself from it, for the upper class is the aristocracy.
In the next section the respondent suggests certain other recur-
rent themes: class is not based on income as such, but there is a
line between manual and white-collar workers because the former
rarely move up into the ranks of the latter.

(Q. This division - the working class and the middle class -
does that still exist?)

'Yes. I think that exists really rather more than the other one
still. They've diminished. They're not helped by chancellors
redrawing the lines.'

(Q. How?)

'On cash - anybody over £8,500 a year.'

(Q. You think?)

'It's divisive.'

(Q. Would you draw it at £8,500?)

'You can't draw the line on salary, because the young people
get less than the older ones - I don't really draw the line
nowadays very much. Though there is still a line because the
employees on the works - the manual workers - rarely get
through into the managerial class as it were.'

(Q. They're unable to make this transition?)

'They don't seem to make this transition. Whether they're able
to or not I'm not sure, or whether they're even given the
chance to do so, I'm not entirely sure.'

(Q. Is it them or their children you'd expect to find coming
through into the middle class?)

'I'd expect their children to.'

(Q. Do you think they will?)

'I do. I expect their children to be a very different kettle of
fish and that the lines will become more blurred. That's the
hope.'

The above extract has one slightly unusual feature: the man in
question is aware that employees from the works rarely 'get
through into the managerial class', but he professes himself as
unsure whether they have the ability or 'whether they're even
given the chance'. He apparently regards this aspect of company
life, of giving people the chance to make 'the transition' as outside

his knowledge or responsibility (he is chairman of the main board).
He then professes his hope that there is now greater social mobility between generations. In the final extract he reaffirms the
importance of education, and points out that some of the directors
on his board did not go to public school, but he evades the question of whether there is equality of opportunity.

(Q. It is as easy for the son of a manual worker as it would
be, say, for your own son?)

'Well, it's much easier [than it used to be] - with the
education system. Oh no, it wasn't as easy in the past.
Your education prevented you. And you weren't given that
opportunity if you hadn't had that education.'

(Q. It does appear that a majority of the directors of large
companies have been to public school. Is this simply the
result of this?)

'Yes, - I suppose that's true. I'm told it is. I certainly did.
There are one or two directors on our board who didn't go
to public school. There are two who pushed themselves up
with really poor education. If they can do that with that
system they're really good people.'
In order to analyse the interviews it is necessary to make some
categorisation of them. By way of example, the respondent above
would have been classified as having a three-class model of
society: upper, middle and lower or working. His own position by
inference is middle-class; and the upper class is apparently seen
as being the aristocracy or large landowners. The differences of lifestyle and taste; but occupation and education are referred to as
being respectively indicators of class and important aids and barriers to social mobility. This again was typical; it was particularly
difficult to segregate the signs of class from the causes of it as
they were perceived. I now turn to an analysis of the sample taken
as a whole.

7.5 THE NUMBER OF CLASSES PERCEIVED

In looking at the businessmen's accounts of class in society I look
at four different aspects in turn: the number of classes which they
perceived, the criteria on which they base their separation of one
class from another, the existence or not of an upper class, and
their own position within the class system.
Of the 130 men interviewed, just four denied the existence, so
far as they could see, of a system of stratification beyond the
'objective' gradations of income or wealth. Fifteen men, though
they were willing to discuss the topic, spoke in such ambiguous
terms as to make it impossible from the resulting data to work out
what picture they had of stratification in Britain. Sixteen of those
interviewed presented society as a continuous hierarchy, or social

class ladder, or in the words of two respondents, a spectrum.

The remainder - 95 - of the 130 (73 per cent) were aware of class as a system with discontinuities. Ten men did not precisely define the number of classes. From the remainder of the answers, however, it became clear that a single major division of class/ status is seen as dividing society. Respondents might divide off further an upper class, but this was invariably seen as relatively small. Further divisions of the middle or upper classes might be made to give four, five (or in one case) six classes, but these were refinements made by a minority. In other words the class view of the majority can be pictured as one of the following variations of the same theme, as in Figure 7.1.

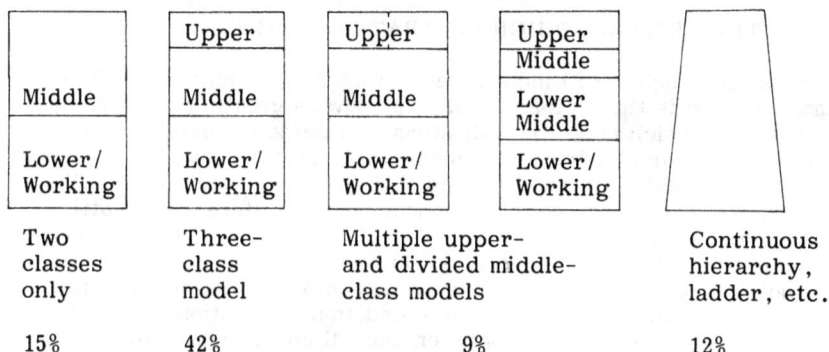

	Upper	Upper	Upper
			Middle
Middle	Middle	Middle	Lower Middle
Lower/ Working	Lower/ Working	Lower/ Working	Lower/ Working
Two classes only	Three-class model	Multiple upper- and divided middle-class models	Continuous hierarchy, ladder, etc.
15%	42%	9%	12%

(Pictures drawn by *author*, not respondents)

Classes, but no clear picture: 8%
Class denied (4 men):   3%
Answer not classifiable: 11.5%

Figure 7.1   Models of class in Britain

It can be seen that the three-class model is the most frequent single image, and was given as their image by 55 of the 111 (that is, half), who clearly perceived a stratification system.

And in many respects the models with multiple upper classes are not very distinct from the more straightforward three-class models. Thus, the respondents fall into three groups: first, those who see two major classes, those who see basically three, and those who see not classes but a continuous hierarchy. As an example of the latter there was the insurance company director who said:

'Yes I do [see classes]. These days they're largely economic. I think the hereditary aristocracy as part of the class system .... well, I suppose it still exists, but it doesn't seem to me very important in the total context.... I think this [social class] is particularly evident in housing. If I think of the area in which I live, which perhaps is not typical, and perhaps is unduly class conscious, there are quite distinct, sort

of economic groupings of housing - ranging from council
houses up to the largest detached mansions standing in
several acres of ground. This is a very obvious form of
economic stratification.'

(Q. So the old terms, working class, middle class, upper
class have lost their meaning?)

'I would have thought so to a considerable extent. You can
still fit stereotypes in any of these classes but I think the
dividing lines which used to exist are much more difficult if
not impossible to define.'

7.6   THE CRITERIA WHICH SEPARATE CLASSES

The second aspect of businessmen's images of society which is examined here is the factors which they saw as creating or forming
class, and which could be indicators of a person's class. A whole
range of personal attributes which might create social divisions
were mentioned, but six occurred with particular frequency. They
were: income/wealth; education; occupation; differences of attitudes and values; ability/intellect; and hereditary status or family
background. Far less frequently mentioned, but of some interest,
is holding power or authority in society and mention of these is
included in Table 7.1. It may be noted that occupation here refers
most often to a distinction between manual and non-manual workers.
In referring to education, some respondents mentioned the public
school system, or private schools generally, others referred to
the level of education that people had achieved.
   In addition to these respondents referred to a diverse range of
other attributes including: joining a trade union or not joining;
housing; manners; lifestyle; leisure interests; accent; 'who you
mix with' and 'who you vote for'. However, these lesser criteria
were almost invariably mentioned together with at least one of the
six main ones (1-6) which are shown in Table 7.1, p. 177.
   It will immediately become apparent from this table that the
majority of respondents who gave any basis for class would mention two or more criteria.
   This is exemplified by the chairman of a small, predominantly
service family firm, who was a hereditary peer, and educated at
Eton and Cambridge. Asked the standard question on class he
replied: 'Good Marxist theory and all that?', and after further
prompting, leading to 'do you see classes in society?', he goes on:
'Not in a strict sense. I mean you get groups of people whose
   incomes, tastes, backgrounds and what you will are roughly
   similar; you get other groups where they're quite different.
   This is due to a variety of causes. There obviously is a difference between the chap who works on the shopfloor, and the
   chap who works in an office. They are different animals. They
   are doing different kinds of things and their outlook's bound
   to be different. You may call it class, you may not. I don't know.'

Table 7.1   The basis of class

	All	Chief executives[a]
Total number of men interviewed	130	90
Numbers whose answers can be classified	112	77
Number seeing, as basis of class		
1 Income/wealth	36(32)	26(34)
2 Education	50(45)	34(44)
3 Occupation	40(36)	26(34)
4 Attitudes/values held by members of different groups	35(31)	24(31)
5 Ability/intellect	16(14)	9(12)
6 'Status', family background, position in local community, etc.	15(13)	11(14)
7 Power/authority	6(5)	4(5)

a This column is for chief executives of manufacturing/service firms.

Figures in brackets are percentages, based on the total number of men giving any basis for stratification.

Though the above model draws on a number of attributes to define class, it lacks the stress on education that characterises many. The latter is seen in this quote from the chief executive of a large bank. This man, the son of an MP, public school and Oxford educated, adopts a similar model with only slightly different criteria and terminology.

'It largely is a matter of educational background, I think, and on the whole those who have reached the old matriculation standard are the bourgeoisie one way or another. They have an in-built love of property. They like owning their own houses. They don't like anything that attacks that. They don't like seeing property values declining at the moment at all. They don't like equally an inflation that doesn't have tax escalating with it .... I think they feel common interests in protecting the advantages they achieved by education.'

(Q. So your employees would largely come from a class united by common interests, shared educational background and certain attitudes to property?)

'I think we have; I would have to disregard the messenger staff who would regard themselves more as artisan.'

(Q. So you would see an artisan class as well as a bourgeoisie?)

'I do see it - in factories, if you go to heavy engineering factories, where you still have effectively a blacksmithery - forging is a very good example. The manual worker involved in forging - it's still entirely an artisan piece of work and you couldn't expect and shouldn't expect in my view a man who is tremendously physically strong and has to put up with intolerable heat all day to regard himself as middle class, however smart his house....'

Aside from those who mentioned the six main determinants of class there was a very small group (four men) who had a power/ authority model. Although the six main attributes were often juxtaposed no patterns or associations emerged clearly within them. For example, it was not even possible to demonstrate that ability and intellect were more frequently mentioned with education than they were with any of the other four main attributes.

7.7 THE UPPER CLASS

The criteria for defining the upper class generally differed from those used to define the principal forms of stratification in Britain. Instead, the criteria were either having a hereditary title and probably land in the country, or simply being wealthy. The upper class were not presented as having distinctive occupations, education or attitudes, except to the extent that they were seen as having rural occupations such as farming, or were caricatured as being in the stately home business. Sometimes they were also associated with certain leisure interests such as hunting or shooting.

A majority of all those interviewed, and a greater percentage of those who gave a classifiable answer on the topic, saw a small but distinctive upper class. Table 7.2 summarises the findings.

Table 7.2   References to the upper class

Number interviewed	130
Number of respondents clearly referring to an upper class	76(58)
Number denying the existence of such a class	13(10)
All other[a]	41(32)

a These would include men who present society as a continuous hierarchy, deny the existence of stratification of a class/status type, or would not give an answer.

Figures in brackets are percentages based on the number of men giving an answer.

An attempt was made in the interviews to obtain some idea of what sort of people come into the upper class as businessmen see it. From all the groups mentioned, the aristocracy and the very wealthy, which for most respondents meant much wealthier than they were, emerge as by far the most frequently included. The other groups, occasionally said to be either in or on the fringes of the upper class, included politicians, civil servants, some businessmen, and artists and entertainers. However, as the next table shows, of those definitely seeing an upper class, that is 76 respondents, fifty-six or 74 per cent specifically included the aristocracy, thirty-two (42 per cent) mentioned the wealthy, and twenty-one (28 per cent) referred to other groups. Thus 43 per cent of *all* respondents saw the aristocracy as part of an upper class, and a quarter so viewed the very wealthy.

Table 7.3   Groups which constitute the upper class

Total interviewed	130
Number mentioning any upper class	76
Number mentioning the aristocracy	56(74)
Number mentioning the wealthy/very rich	32(42)
Other groups mentioned	21(28)

Percentages, in brackets, are based on the 76 men who definitely saw an upper class.

7.8 SELF-ASSIGNED CLASS

Quite clearly, the class to which a person assigns himself is dependent to some extent on the model of class that that person holds. Getting respondents to 'label' themselves was frequently the hardest part of the interviews; and where men were unwilling to speak freely about class in general, or denied the importance of stratification, or where they pictured class as a more or less continuous hierarchy it was unusual to obtain any self-assigned class position. Thus, the next table which records the frequency with which men assigned themselves to different classes, is largely drawn from those who had previously referred to models of society with either two or more distinct classes. It will be seen that, of 79 men giving an answer, just ten (13 per cent) saw themselves as 'upper-class'. By far the greatest number preferred the label 'middle-class'.

Table 7.4   Self-assigned class of businessmen

Number answering	79
Number saying working-class	2(3)
Number saying middle-class	67(84)
Number saying upper-class	10(13)

Figures in brackets are percentages.

7.9 NO RULING CLASS?

The observations made so far on businessmen's views of the class
structure, were they to be taken at face value, could potentially
have important implications for theory concerning class, and class
or elite consciousness. Let us assume for one moment that the
respondents had no desire to deceive the researcher, but gave
replies which honestly reflected their own image or picture of
society. Then one must immediately point to the diversity, and
the complexity, of the range of answers found here. There could
hardly be said to be a dominant train of thought with respect to
class. There seemed no common agreement about how members of
different classes were to be known or recognised. And whilst a
three-class (working, middle, upper) model of society was the
one most frequently encountered, the majority of those adopting
it deliberately placed themselves in the middle grouping and thus
aligned themselves with the middle class.

Taking a rather simplistic view of the nature of society, and of
the relationship between the structure of society and subjective
perceptions of it, one might immediately ask: how can a ruling
class be said to exist if a group of what, *prima facie,* would
appear to be members of it both fail to agree on whether it exists,
on its nature, or who its fellow members are? How can such a
class develop Meisel's (1962) three Cs - group consciousness,
coherence and conspiracy - when its members cannot or do not
identify closely with one another?

In chapter 3 I set out two arguments concerning the kind of
data presented here. The first is that I failed to interview a sufficient number of people who clearly were members of the upper
class: or, more importantly, that where I did they told deliberate
lies about their views of society. The second argument would
maintain that the perceptions of members of society tell us little
about the structure of society; and whether a ruling class recognises its existence is irrelevant to how it behaves.

I will not rehearse these arguments, and the counter-arguments
again. Rather I will state my own explanation regarding the statements of businessmen concerning class which is as follows: whilst
elements of elite perspective were evident amongst the viewpoints
of the respondents they did not emerge clearly and regularly when
they were talking of class. Part of the reason for this is that the
businessmen were to an extent trapped by the terminology of
class. They (and by implication other people in our society) have
an inherited understanding of what the terms upper class, middle
class and so on mean. This understanding could not be dispensed
with, even though the respondents made it clear that so far as
they were concerned, the groups most usually seen as upper class
had largely lost the role and functions that such a label might
imply.

Thus, even those who included the aristocracy amongst the upper class, would often disparage it with phrases like 'merely
fringe stuff', 'very small', 'no longer important' or 'insignificant'.

Likewise, the wealthy would be characterised as 'those who spend big', 'people with too much money and not enough culture', 'the jet set' or 'cafe society'.

Businessmen do not, for the most part, place themselves amongst the two major upper-class groupings because in their eyes they meet neither of the important criteria. They are not aristocrats or members of the landed gentry and although, as we have seen, they are wealthy by ordinary standards, the majority of bureaucrats do not consider themselves as wealthy. They regard themselves as salaried employees, men who have to work for a living. Asked to say what they would consider as wealth, they would either name sums which could not be obtained in Britain from salary alone, for example, £1,000,000, or £500,000, or say that a wealthy person is one who does not have to work for a living, or give any thought to how much he spends.

That group which by consent of those interviewed was the one best qualified to be considered as upper-class in the conventional sense, that is, members of the landed gentry and aristocracy, was the group least willing to assign themselves to a place in the class/ status structure. (As we saw only ten men said they were upper class.) Even then they did it reluctantly: thus we have the peer who said he had 'one foot in the upper class, one foot in the middle', and the family businessman who stated:

'I have great difficulty in knowing who the upper class is. One thing I can say is that I see a group that doesn't worry about these things. At other levels, I see all sorts of strains, people trying to get in; and a lot of people worried about people getting in, and trying to preserve their status....'

(Q. Are you in the upper class?)

'Well, in so far as I am not concerned about my social position, I am not worried.... there is nowhere above me that I see that I want to get to, yes. I can't see another above me.'

Of course, most of the entrepreneurs and family businessmen would qualify for (and accept) the title of wealthy, but the peculiar nature of the British social class system with its emphasis on title and background means that many of these can exempt themselves from the upper class as such. For example:

'I still feel that the background of our family, with my father right from the youngest days I can remember when he first gave me a Borough bank account with only £5 in it, we had to tithe that income and each of us decided how to dispose of that one-tenth of it. That feeling is still with me. I like to think that I can get on with anybody in the country.'

(Q. You don't think of yourself as upper-class?)

'Certainly not. The fact that the Queen saw fit to make me a knight doesn't change me as .... I realise what other people feel that having been given an honour of that sort you're a changed person.' (family businessman - large company)

There is, however, another aspect to the denial of upper-class position that emerged from the interviews and deserves comment: wealth is often associated with frivolity, display and excess and members of the business elite have something of a dislike or distrust of this. Their values make them suspicious of conspicuous consumption. Further, they seem to feel that some groups who might be thought of as part of the 'jet set', such as pop singers or footballers are over-rewarded. Thus, one bureaucrat defined the upper class as 'those who spend big'. He was later asked whether he mixed in his non-work life with what he had earlier defined as the middle class. His reply was:

'I suppose in practice yes, for this particular reason, and that is that on my father's side we're of Northern Ireland descent, who as a matter of tradition if you like would not be the sort of people who would want to act big whatever.. .. and who would regard with the utmost contempt the sort of situation we've had round our way, Esher, in Surrey, quite a lot, where you've got a chap down the road who's bought a big house, he's spent a lot of money converting it into something even finer, new swimming pool and so on, and was obviously on a different social stratum to us. I mean he'd never have thought of inviting us there, and we'd never have thought of accepting if he had, he comes in quite a different class. Chap went bankrupt the following year. I mean, I dare say I could have bought the fellow out quite easily. But because he comes into the big spender class, big spender whether you've got the money or it's borrowed, he therefore, his whole sort of thing, I mean if he had a party he had dozens of chaps in white coats serving out drinks, this sort of thing, which no matter how much money I had I wouldn't do.' (bureaucrat - small service firm)

However, the dislike of those who 'spend big' is not confined to those of the middle ranges in family social status; those from the traditional elite, those who might well be considered to be upper-class, shared it, though in a form, as indicated in this next quote from a merchant banker, that smacks of disdain for the nouveau riche:

'In London before the War when you went out and dined in a restaurant you would always meet somebody you knew. Nowadays, when you go out you don't meet anybody you know, and in most cases I'm not at all sure you'd want to know them - you know, the jet set, millionaires, film stars and so on.'

(Q. Are they the upper class?)

'No, I don't know, they're outside it.'

(Q. Where do you come?)

'Because of my foreign origin I'm in a curious position, but my family have been landowners for many years and are well

known in the City, so I'm on the fringes of the upper class.'
(bureaucrat, chairman - merchant bank)

The attitude of many bureaucrats is that the antics of the upper
class are something apart from them. Their own lives are similar
to many of their managers below them. Thus, the bureaucrat head
of a large trading firm, asked to define the upper class said:

'Such a difficult thing to define - but if you went to one of
these eating places, Annabel's, say, or Les Ambassadeurs,
you would find there wealthy people from overseas, some of
the dwindling aristocracy, and some people from the City,
they would form part of the upper class.... But you know
it's a full-time job being rich, you have to work so hard safeguarding your money, ... most of them talk about it the
whole time, what they should do about it and so on - it's the
sole topic of conversation..... But there is also an Establishment and that's a rather different thing.'

As in the last quote, directors in industry would sometimes
place members of City firms in the upper class. And, in common
with the general pattern, although some such men placed themselves there, others disagreed, such as the banker, with whom
the next section of interview was recorded:

(Q. How many classes do you think there are?)

'In today's society, it's very difficult to say, isn't it? One
sees so little at the top of the pyramid.'

(Q. Some people would say you were at the top?)

'Well that would be ridiculous, wouldn't it? Oh, absolutely
ridiculous. I'm not a society person. If it were not for my
job I'd be completely unknown ..... I'm not a socialite ....
I regard myself as a member of the middle classes.... Let's
talk about the top of the pyramid. I don't suppose things
have changed much here since Proust's day really, Many of
us could read a notice of some high junketing at some high
place in the papers without recognising any of the names
of the people who attended or knowing who they were or
what role they had.'

7.10 THE LOW STATUS OF BRITISH BUSINESSMEN

Two groups then were perceived as publicly held in high status
by these respondents: the traditional aristocracy, regarded as
being of waning importance but still having cachet, and the more
obvious of the wealthy. In contrast, many businessmen themselves
tended to feel that as businessmen they were held in rather low
esteem. There are two dimensions to this: first, they compared
their position unfavourably with that of men in equivalent positions in other countries, and second, they compared themselves
with models of what directors in large companies used to be like
in the past.

These comparisons, however, are not just ones of status:

monetary comparisons enter into both dimensions. There can be no doubt that Britain's top directors receive less in financial remuneration than do their counterparts in most European capitalist countries and the United States. The directors of multinationals are particularly aware of this, as some pay their subordinates in other countries more than they receive themselves. Since businessmen tend to feel that people are, or should be, 'paid what they are worth' in terms of the market, they inevitably feel that the market is undervaluing them, and that this is in some way a reflection of public esteem.

This aspect of businessmen's current position emerged only partially in the earlier interviews. In the second half of the study it was discussed more specifically, when the respondents were asked how they thought the social position of a director in their companies compared with that of men in the same positions before the last war.

Those who answered tended to be far more aware of differences within the company than outside. They put forward a version of the managerialist thesis from the point of view of a participant, which emphasised changes in the responsibilities, management style and wealth of the top men of industry.

Frequently, those interviewed said that the companies they now ran were either very much bigger than they had been before the war, or in some cases bigger than any company was before the war. This gave them, they felt, far greater responsibilities, the difficulties of which are exacerbated by changes in public and governmental attitudes, both nationally and internationally.

At the same time a change in management style was emphasised. The men who headed companies in the past were pictured as highly autocratic, and certainly as being unapproachable by the ordinary employee. One of the directors summed it up by saying: 'When I first came here, when the chairman got in the lift everyone else got out. Nowadays the secretaries might get in the lift with the chairman without even realising who he is.'

This statement may say rather little for the communicative ability of the present chairman, but does convey the sense of distance from the mass of employees that directors were said to have in the past.

Contrastingly, it was thought that the modern director operates with a different management style. He communicates and consults far more, and is far less able to decide what to do and then order it to be done.

Another aspect of the low esteem of the businessmen, especially of those in manufacturing, is that of the generally low status of business management in Britain as a career. This was of practical concern as they felt that industry was not able to recruit people of sufficient calibre. The dislike of industry, compared to the professions is somewhat traditional in Britain, as one of the family businessmen illustrated from his own experience. [2]

'When I got married in 1950 my father-in-law was a Major General. And in a very disparaging voice he was heard to

say "＿＿＿＿'s in trade". We have made the fatal mistake
in this country of thinking that industry is dedicated to
making profits without thought of human values, that we
stop at nothing to make a profit, that we squeeze the
workers into the dirt, and that sort of thing. While I think
that image has changed in the last twenty-five years or so
just go round any university - and ask the undergraduates
where they want to go. The last place they want to go is
industry.'

The final factor that is seen as giving the British businessman
a low status is that of the generally poor performance of British
industry compared to that of its foreign competitors. Those interviewed saw management as blamed for this, in some cases, though
they would apportion the blame wholly or partly elsewhere.

It would be interesting to test out these ideas concerning the
status of industry, and business, and of business managers, to
see what foundation they have in public attitudes. What is clear
is that, although businessmen themselves have more urgent and
pressing concerns, they do perceive themselves as being a lower
status group than they feel they should be. In contrast, for example, although the landowning aristocracy is seen as having
gradually lost political power and influence, they are thought to
retain a position in public esteem as a status elite.

Another comparison that was occasionally made was that of the
modern director with the 'captains of industry' of the past. Here,
as those interviewed often recognised, the comparison may not be
of like with like. For the captains of industry were often entrepreneurs or tycoons with a huge personal stake in their businesses.
Nowadays, although a number of such men do run companies
amongst the top 250, and indeed may be the business figures the
public hears most about via the gossip columns, they are not the
men who run the very largest corporations, sit on the representative bodies such as trade associations or the CBI, and present
business to government.

The bureaucrats therefore made specific reference to the fact
that they were far less well off than directors used to be, and
sometimes linked this to misconceptions by the public. Thus the
head of the biggest firm in this study said that: 'Before the war
the directors of this company were very wealthy men. You used
to see a line of Rolls Royces round this building. You won't see
any now.' Similarly the head of a massive pharmaceuticals firm
said:

'The chap who is head of a large company nowadays probably
is a manager of a public company. Before the war it was more
likely that he would be an owner, or part owner of the business.'

(Q. Do you think people are aware of this?)

'No, they are probably not. That's why you get these references in the media to this deplorable term, the boss, an
opprobrious term. That term comes from the days when the

man who headed an industrial company was the old style iron-
grinder ..... I'm a professional manager, a technocrat, I don't
suppose the mass of people would see me that way. To them
I'm just the bloke who runs ————.'

7.11 STATUS IS NOT THE SAME AS POWER

Extrapolating from their own statements, it seems that businessmen feel their own status in British society is lower than it should
be. An outmoded, small, even irrelevant aristocracy retains public prestige. So, too, do certain more obvious members of the
wealthy; of 'cafe society', or the 'jet set', groups which, in one
of the few sociological discussions devoted to them, Alberoni (1972)
has called a 'powerless elite', a group which has charisma which
does not translate into power.

The respondents made a number of contrasts between the status
of elite groupings, be they the very rich, the aristocracy or the
jet set, and the power that such groups have. Thus one retired
executive said: 'Using Lord Goodman's words it's influence that's
the thing - I mean you can be a multi-millionaire but if you've no
influence you're of no importance'. And a banker who was quoted
earlier in this chapter contrasted the status of the aristocracy
with the power that they now have:

'The landed aristocracy are obviously of diminishing importance in this country, what do you think? ..... And if it
were not for the fact that some of them do hold public office
of one kind or another we would probably know nothing of
them; they don't really seem to play an important part in the
life of the country.'

Another of the bankers was one of the few men in this study
whose image of society could be classified as a power model. Society for him was 'the narrow strip of people who take responsibility',
with below them the non-commissioned officers, and 'the men who
go along'. This man's family appeared in 'Burke's Landed Gentry',
but as he saw it: 'The old upper class has really disappeared
altogether - they've gone off into the amateur world with the
Junkers in Germany .... and the Grandees in Spain. I think they
really are now quite insignificant.'

From the statements of the kind I have quoted above it is possible to put together an explanation of why businessmen decried
the importance of the upper class, and so frequently denied their
own position in it. They were, in effect, distinguishing between
status and power. Thus they could label the aristocracy, together
with some of the wealthy, the jet set, cafe society or whatever, as
merely status groupings of dubious importance. Some of them preferred a different phrase, the establishment, to describe the
central, informal power grouping that they see in Britain.

7.12 CLASS IMAGERY COMPARED

I have stated that the businessmen themselves did not assign themselves to a high position within the British class structure, but usually saw themselves as part of a largish middle-class grouping, one of two major classes. One might ask, therefore, whether top businessmen have a distinctive view of class, one that is quite clearly different from that of other groupings, and which might, perhaps, be identified as an elitist viewpoint.

In this section, therefore, I compare the findings of this study with those from studies which have been made of other occupational and social groups. In the comparisons that follow I refer only to studies of British society, so as to avoid the complications that comparisons across cultures would introduce, and I look exclusively at studies of urban groups, for again it is urban industrial society that is probably most relevant to businessmen.[3]

A number of contrasts are apparent between businessmen and other groups. Most businessmen claim to see themselves as middle-class, with a minority seeing themselves as 'upper-class'. Previous descriptions of social class imagery reveal a diversity of view as to where big business directors come in the British social class system. The affluent workers of Luton (see Goldthorpe et al., 1969c) appear to have placed the very rich, rather than businessmen per se, as a separate upper class, but, in something of a contrast to their other views, they also mentioned the aristocracy very frequently. Moorhouse (1976) found a similar pattern in his study of (mainly) manual workers in Barking. Brown and Brannen (1970), in contrast, report that shipbuilding workers did see 'bosses', presumably meaning industrial company directors, as an upper class; whilst Scase (1974) reports that over half of the English factory workers he studied mentioned company directors as belonging to the upper class, compared to 42 per cent referring to the aristocracy, and 20 per cent referring to the rich. Thus there is something of a contrast in that, whereas many manual workers would place business directors as part of an elite grouping, businessmen themselves would tend to deny that they hold such a position.

These similarities and contrasts must be understood in conjunction with the picture that the different groups hold of society as a totality. An interesting observation may be made here, which is that the largest group of the top businessmen in this study adopted three-class models, with only 9 per cent differentiating four, five or six classes. In this respect businessmen are similar to manual workers, and their images of society differ from the model of middle-class images of society propounded by McKenzie (1975). The latter suggests that it is a middle-class (that is, presumably white-collar) characteristic to differentiate relatively many hierarchical graduations. One might, however, see the hierarchical, one-class model that was found amongst some businessmen as corresponding to McKenzie's multigraded model, but this was one that was adhered to by only 12 per cent. It should be mentioned that there is little evidence comparable to that obtained from studies of manual workers to support McKenzie's contention. However, the respondents in this study do form a notable contrast to the industrial supervisors, reported in a recent study by Child, Pearce and King (1980), where some 42 per cent of those interviewed were found to hold class images involving four or more classes (although, overall, a three-class model was the single most commonly held type).

We may also note that the findings do not confirm the observation by Winkler (1975) that the directors he observed held modified 'us and them' images of society. In the abstract the majority of the businessmen studied here did not hold such images; but we may also note that no group of manual workers has yet been studied in which such images are the *most* frequently reported. Even the shipbuilding workers studied by Brown and Cousins[4] (who according to the implications of Lockwood's, 1966, theoretical discussion should be relatively close to the ideal type of proletarian worker) in fact held two-class models in only around a third of cases. Amongst shipbuilding workers, in fact, three-class models were the most common.

It should also be noted that although the 'affluent workers' of Goldthorpe's study have been usually reported as seeing society as predominantly of one class differentiated by consumption standards, the most common picture reported in Goldthorpe et al. (1969, p. 148) is a three-class model, but these workers tended to shrink the upper or lower classes, giving a very large central or lower class.

Indeed, it would seem that the three-class model permeates British class imagery; almost as though it is embedded in the very language. Indeed, at the risk of inventing explanations, one may suggest that this, in fact, is the case – that when respondents seek words to describe the social structure, the words that common parlance provides them with are those of upper, middle and lower, or working. What respondents then do is to stretch these terms to fit their own circumstances. Thus, the affluent workers, concerned to deny the importance of the traditional white-collar, or craftsmanship, distinction conceive of a very large central class differentiated internally only by consumption. Other manual workers, such as those studied by Cousins and Brown, do the same – seeing themselves as part of the largest of all the classes, though in four-fifths of cases the shipbuilding workers saw themselves as part of the bottom class. In contrast, foremen concerned to assert their status in the face of diminishing rewards relative to manual workers, and an eroded role in the authority structure, may wish to invent more than three classes, to draw additional divisions within which to give themselves a distinctive niche. Contrastingly, again, the concern of top businessmen is, if anything, the reverse: rather than show themselves as overly concerned with the intricacies and complexities of the British class system, they play down their position, placing themselves as part of one relatively large sub-group of society, the middle class.

One sees more obvious differences between businessmen's class

models and those of other groups when one turns to the discrim-
inants of class position. A constant feature of recent studies of
manual workers has been the importance that such groups attach
to income, standards of consumption, or to a lesser extent wealth.
Different commentators have put a different interpretation on this:
Goldthorpe et al., for example, see it as significant of the 'instru-
mental' orientation of the affluent worker; whereas Moorhouse
(1976), amongst others, argues that frequent mentions of money
by respondents are not incompatible with 'power' models of society,
or at least a realisation of inequalities of power. Whatever the
interpretation, in the studies by Goldthorpe, Moorhouse, Scase,
Cousins and Brown, and Child et al., money in some form is always the most frequently mentioned divider of one class from
another.

The businessmen studied here form something of a contrast.
Whilst it seems unlikely that, had they been specifically questioned
on it, they would not have accepted that income/wealth and class
position were associated, when they came to try to pin down for
themselves what created class, the businessmen interviewed in
this study were much more likely to mention education in some
form (45 per cent), slightly more likely to mention occupation (36
per cent), and about as likely to point to differences of attitudes
and values (31 per cent, see Table 7.1). Why there should be this
contrast is not entirely clear, but one reason did suggest itself on
the basis of the interviews. The businessmen who were interviewed
were trying to accommodate their models of class to certain changes
in society, most notably, as they saw it, the blurring of class
boundaries, caused by the achievement by some groups of manual
workers of high wages which would allow them styles and standards of consumption previously attainable only by white-collar
workers. Similarly, businessmen perceive new channels of social
mobility (via the universities); and changes in the attitudes of
some white-collar groups (for example, towards unionisation).
Thus, in the face of such changes, they come to perceive the difference between the two major classes as no longer being such
clear definables as income or the kind of work you do, but being
also education (where and to what level) and the attitudes and
values you hold. I will enlarge on this theme below (section 7.16).

7.13 VARIATIONS IN IMAGES OF SOCIETY

I have described the images of society held by top businessmen,
and have compared them with those held by other groups. Can
one, to any extent, account for the variation that occurs within
them? Are there, in fact, several types of business outlook?

In chapter 2 I reviewed the various descriptions that we have of
businessmen and directors, from which a variety of potential influences, of career, schooling, type of industry worked in, and
so on, could be perceived. However, reference back to the discussion of chapter 1 reminds us that the primary structuration of

social class in an industrial society is the ownership, or lack of it, of capital in some form or other. That there can be a clear distinction between controllers of industry who personally own considerable personal capital and those who do not is, as we saw, the foundation of the ownership and control debate.

The first examination made of the data was, therefore, to see if there were clear distinctions between the three types of businessmen distinguished throughout this study, that is, between bureaucrats, family businessmen and entrepreneurs. What I have done is to classify the statements which the respondents made about class and tabulate them against the three types of respondent. The results are shown in Tables 7.5, 7.6 and 7.7 on pages 191 and 192.

The tables reveal no very striking differences between the 'capitalists' and the 'managers' and certainly none that can be easily explained. For example, five out of twenty capitalists called themselves 'upper-class', compared to five out of fifty-nine bureaucrats; but this still leaves the vast majority of both groups calling themselves middle-class. Similarly, the capitalists turn out to mention ability and occupation more, and income/wealth less than the bureaucrats, but not to such an extent that the differences were statistically significant.

Drawing on the theory in chapter 2, I then searched for a number of possible connections between individual career experience and social background and the present outlook of the respondents on class. For example, I have made comparisons of the views of men who work in 'City' firms with those in manufacturing and service industries. I have looked at the effect of the size of company, using different measures. I have compared men who have worked in different functional positions in the past, by comparing those who have had experience of shopfloor management with those who have not. In all these cases the resulting tabulations have not brought out any notable, or indeed, statistically significant relationships; and I have not thought it worthwhile to reproduce them here.

I also tried one more attempt at prediction, by tabulating the answers concerning class against the classifications of the social index proposed in chapter 4. The index gives a crude measure of the extent to which the personal circumstances of the respondents have changed in their lifetime.

The tabulation of the number of classes that respondents perceive produces no pattern of any interest and is not reproduced here. The table (Table 7.8) of the self-assigned class against status position produces at least a predictable pattern: the two men, the only men in fact, who call themselves working-class come from backgrounds which fall in the social status index into the upwardly mobile group. The greatest percentage of men, six out of twenty-one (29 per cent) who call themselves upper-class come from Group I - the aristocrats and men who attended Clarendon schools.

Looking at the attributes on which class or status is seen as

Table 7.5 Variations in images of society as seen by different types of businessmen

Type of Respondent	All	Bureaucrat	All 'capital'-holders	Family businessman	Entrepreneur
Number	130	96	34	24	10
Number giving no classifiable picture	18	13	5	4	1
Number referring to classes but not specifying number	10(9)	6(7)	4(14)	1(5)	3
Number who see a hierarchy/ladder	16(14)	11(13)	5(17)	4(20)	1
Number who see four or more classes	12(11)	10(12)	2(7)	1(5)	1
Number who see three classes	55(50)	42(51)	13(45)	9(45)	4
Number who see two classes only	19(17)	14(17)	5(17)	5(25)	0

Percentages, in brackets, are based on those who do give a classifiable answer.

Table 7.6   Self-rated class by type of respondent

	Bureaucrat	Family businessman	Entrepreneur	All
Number of those giving an answer	59	15	5	79
Ranking:				
Working	2(3.5)	0	0	2(3)
Middle	52(88)	11(73)	4(80)	67(85)
Upper	5(8.5)	4(27)	1(20)	10(12)

Table 7.7   The bases of stratification as stated by different groups

	Bureaucrat	Family businessman	Entrepreneur[a]	All
Percentages of each group stating as a basis of class/status:				
1 Income/wealth	34	20	33	32
2 Education	44	45	55	45
3 Occupation	27	50	22	36
4 Social attitudes and values	32	25	44	31
5 Ability/intellect	10	15	33	14
6 Status/background	12	10	22	13
7 Power/authority	6	0	11	5
Numbers on which % are based	83	20	9	112

a Clearly percentages in this column are based on very small numbers, and they are put in for purposes of comparison only.

On a comparison of the three groups, using a chi-square test, there was no significant statistical difference at the 5 per cent level.

being based (Table 7.9), some interesting contrasts arise. The upwardly mobile group particularly mentioned attitudes and values (60 per cent); income and wealth (53 per cent) as discriminators of class. At the other end of the scale, education was particularly mentioned by group I (50 per cent), and group II (48 per cent),

Table 7.8   Self-rating of class by family background

	All giving self-ranking	Position on social status index			
		Group IV (Up. mobile)	III	II	I (Elite)
Number	76	11	14	30	21
Ranking					
Upper-class	10(13)	1	1	2	6
Middle-class	64(84)	8	13	28	15
Working-class	2 (3)	2	0	0	0

with the other attributes given rather less prominence. Education is also thought to be important by group III, and this group mentions few differentiators of class altogether compared to the other groups.

It would be easy to invent explanations for the few trends apparent here; for example, that the upwardly mobile do not see education as important because they have been mobile without a public school education, and in some cases without formal education beyond the minimum leaving age. This group is also highly aware of differences of attitudes and values, of culture, perhaps because they have had to adapt to these as they have succeeded in their business careers.

However, it must be admitted that this form of statistical patterning does not really highlight particular differences between sub-groups within our sample, except that it does suggest that amongst the upwardly mobile, and amongst those born into the elite groupings, are the men who are most conscious of social class and status and who perceive it the most distinctly. But, in fact, this was apparent from the interview material in any case; and I will return to amplify and demonstrate this point below (section 7.15).

Internal Patterning
The discussion of chapter 2 suggested rather more than that businessmen's background and experiences would shape their perceptions of social class. It also suggested that the term 'meaning systems' would comprise perceptions about the firm, and the local community, as well as about society as a whole. One might expect, perhaps, that a person who took a 'them or us' or two-sides view of the company, would see a similar division within society more generally.

The data here, however, does not support this contention. For when we look at the attitudes which businessmen expressed towards

Table 7.9   The bases of class by family background

	All	IV Upwardly mobile	III State school	II Public school	I Traditional elite
Total which can be tabulated	107	15	24	42	26
1 Income/wealth	34(32)	8(53)	3(13)	15(36)	8(30)
2 Education	47(44)	3(20)	11(46)	20(48)	13(50)
3 Occupation	32(30)	6(40)	4(17)	13(31)	9(33)
4 Attitudes/values	39(36)	9(60)	9(38)	15(37)	6(22)
5 Ability	13(12)	3(20)	2 (8)	6(15)	2 (7)
6 Status/background	15(14)	1 (7)	3(13)	5(12)	6(20)
7 Power	5 (5)	1 (7)	0	1 (2)	3(11)

Figures in brackets are percentages. Corrected Chi-squared for stating income or wealth as a basis, as opposed to not stating it, shows significant differences at the 5 per cent level.

the employees in their firms, and their perceptions of class/status, we find a number of obvious anomalies. These may be seen in the next two tables. In Table 7.10, the number of social classes perceived by the businessmen are tabulated against whether or not they saw 'two sides' in their firms. No distinct patterning is apparent; indeed, what is noticeable is that four men who said they did see something of a 'them and us' situation in their companies pictured society as a graduated hierarchy; with four of the same group seeing four or more classes, and five men who saw society as just two major classes, did not see two sides in the company.

Table 7.10   Answers to question: 'Do you see two sides in your company?'

	Yes	No	Don't know/ can't generalise	All
	43	41	21	105
Number of classes perceived in society				
Four or more	4	4	3	11
Three	19	18	8	45
Two	6	5	4	15
No clear number/class denied, etc.	10	7	5	22
Graduated hierarchy	4	7	1	12

Since the distribution of answers to the question about two sides in the firm was related to the reasons given for conflict within the company, it is not surprising that no relationship is apparent in the next table (Table 7.11).

I accept that the numbers in the cells in these tables are too small for statistical purposes. Nevertheless, they do serve perhaps to show that the consistencies of viewpoint which were suggested were not apparent amongst this group of businessmen.

7.14   RE-EXPLAINING CLASS IMAGERY

These statistical attempts to account for how people come to hold certain images of society have little success. This may be disappointing, but, in retrospect, there are several clear reasons why the approach was unlikely to produce significant findings, even had classification of respondent's answers been straightforward and simple.

The first reason is that the elements of the images which people held are separated from one another, that is, the number of classes

Table 7.11   Reasons for conflict within the firm

	Class/historical attitudes, etc.	Trade unions/ managers and managed	Wage-bargaining	Large plants, communications, trouble-makers	All reasons
	15	14	20	36	85
Number of classes in society:					
Four or more	0	2	4	2	8
Three	9	5	5	19	38
Two	1	3	3	6	13
Graduated hierarchy	3	2	1	4	10
No clear number/class denied, etc.	2	2	7	5	16

is separated from the causes of class, from the perceived membership of the upper class and so on. In practice, however, these
were presented by respondents as totalities, and should perhaps
be examined as such.

Second, each aspect of the men's experience is taken in isolation
and examined; yet the men themselves were able to draw on a
variety of different experiences in constructing their pictures of
society. In other words, there was not just a group of men whose
fathers were family businessmen, and those who weren't; a group
who had been to public school and who had not, a group who had
worked in close contact with manual workers and a group who had
not: rather, there were men who were family businessmen, who
had also been to public school, and had also supervised factory
production, and so on.

Thus, even assuming that the men interviewed here held relatively stable and permanent images of society which were connected directly to their experiences, it would be a very complex
task to unravel these connections. This being the case, it is not
surprising, perhaps, that both I and other workers have encountered a multiplicity of images of society. A further complication,
much noted in the literature, lies in the fact that images of society
may not be stable at all, but vary from context to context.

I believe also that there is another explanation of some relevance,
which is that part of the multiplicity of images of society encountered stems from the fact that social class is not, in fact, important
in any real and everyday sense to most of the men who were
interviewed. The conceptions that they put together were thus
largely abstract ones, assembled for the occasion, that is, for the
interview. The elements themselves remained relatively stable;
that is, a high proportion of the men who were asked about social
class referred to a two- or three-class structure, most referred
to education, occupation, income or attitudes as class dividers,
and so on. But what differed was the way in which these elements
were assembled.

Thus, a better approach to class imagery may be to discuss
those small groups of men who had very definite ideas on social
class, to whom it was more than an abstract topic; and then to
discuss the structured and recurring elements on which the majority of the businessmen drew in constructing their class models.

I distinguish four groups for whom the topic of social class did
seem to have a real and definite impact: those men who had been
highly upwardly mobile; those I call the 'sociological sophisticates';
the traditional upper class; and a group one may call the 'outsiders'. I will try to demonstrate these distinctions.

7.15 SOME DISTINCTIVE VIEWS OF CLASS

Sociological Sophisticates
By and large we do not expect businessmen to offer images of
society that as descriptions of society have the same depth of

observation and precision that sociologists themselves can offer.
But businessmen are a well-educated and widely experienced
group, and a minority, in talking of class, made descriptions of
the differences between the working and middle class that were
in essence as finely elaborated as those to be found in the sociological literature.

This group may be called the 'sociological sophisticates'. The
sources of their knowledge appear to be: either first-hand knowledge gained through political work, particularly on local councils,
or in one case in the personnel field, or, alternatively, reading
of social history or sociology. The works quoted included the
'Affluent Worker' studies (once) and 'Uses of Literacy' (twice).

Here is one man talking, who apart from being chief executive
of a manufacturing firm, is a local councillor.

'I am involved in this in an area which has a very large GLC
estate. A massive one - like round here (this office) you've
got these tower blocks. You've got tens of thousands of
poeple all living in the same way - not necessarily at the
same material level, because there are some who are quite
well off, and some who are very hard up. But they are living
in a sort of environment where the general expectation of
what you are and what you are going to do is low. That is a
class of people living in that way .... I think it's really the
way in which people live. It's the environment, the expectation of life and all that which means that the youngster on
the estate is going to go to a school on the estate and his
horizons are not going to go beyond that, going on a school
bus, and what they do at weekends - it's down to the local
supermarket, and if there's any sport then it's on the school
fields or it's on this, or it may even be a football club but
it's not very far away, and it's the same people going there
all the time. This forms a class - it forms an identity of
people all the same - and they regard others as different.
They don't have to be a different colour or a different creed,
they are just different.'

This account may not come across in sociologist-style prose, but
it is unusual for its description of working-class life, and the
recent and direct acquaintanceship with the working class that
produced it.

Here is another example from the personnel director of a large
multinational firm:

(Q. So you seem to be able to distinguish the middle class and
working class - even though you say the distinction means
nothing?)

'Well, it is partly a voting distinction. Partly an income distinction which is now becoming blurred. Partly an occupational
distinction and partly a social one. If one looks at the networks, as I understand you're a sociologist, you see a different pattern of networks and behaviour and this is quite
important in the personnel world, because you find that so
called working class wives tend to consort with other working

class women rather than their husbands socially. Whereas
the middle classes, meaning more particularly better educated
people whose husbands have managerial occupations, you find
there's greater geographic mobility, and husbands and wives
tend to share intellectual and cultural pursuits rather than
being separated except around the dinner table or in bed.
Which is really quite interesting; you know I worked in the
steel industry in Wales, people who sought employment when
you probed why they wanted to come and work, it was because
their wives were Welsh women and at some stage in her life the
Welsh woman likes to be near her mother. And so the man is
being dragged back to his wife's town of origin, and forced to
get employment there. One found this was largely but not
entirely a working class phenomenon - middle class people
tended to be more mobile. The distinctions are becoming
blurred.'

The 'sociological sophisticates' are a tiny minority - I would place
only six men in this study in this category - but it is important to
record their existence, for clearly it would be wrong to assume
that all top businessmen are, and have been, isolated from contact
with lower status groups. The sophisticates may well be the 'one-
man chains', that Winkler (1974) refers to - the men that other
directors consult when they want to know about working-class
attitudes. The other group with first-hand knowledge is the highly
upwardly mobile, but their experience is a more personally significant one.

The Highly Mobile
Whilst the majority of those interviewed could afford to take a detached view of class, insulated as they are from class boundaries,
there were some groups for whom the question carried a particular tension, most obviously, the 'highly mobile'.

It will be recalled that this group, although in the terms of this
study highly mobile, were drawn largely from a skilled manual or
routine white-collar home background (see chapter 4, section 4.2).
And in terms of this definition there were just eighteen of them.

They tended to react to questions on social class in one of two
ways: they either denied completely that it was of any importance
or were highly aware of it and its effect on them and spoke at
some length about it. These would seem to indicate alternative
ways in which one feels one has had to make adaptations to succeed in one's business or social life.

Thus, the managing director of a large service group who had
been the right-hand man of an entrepreneur (whom he described
as a 'wheeler-dealer type') for some twenty years, clearly felt that
he had not had to make such adaptation.

(Q. Do the terms working class, middle class, upper class
have a meaning for you?)

'They're used, but in my opinion they've long outlived their
usefulness.'

(Q. Did they ever have a meaning?)

'They probably did - about a hundred years ago. I don't think that in the circumstances in which we find ourselves today that these meanings apply. People do use artificial rankings, for example, the aristocracy, but that's only a minute classification. Most people socially are able to mix freely - I can - I go to the board of [————— Bank], then to a business lunch, then to a pub - I don't have any problem anywhere.'

Of course, one way in which one's career in the hierarchy of a company will not be impeded through lack of education, social grace, or connections, is to have begun it oneself. Just one of the entrepreneurs could be classified as highly mobile, and he produced a response denying the significance of class.

This man provides an interesting example of how the upwardly mobile can embrace the values of the group they move into more vehemently than the group itself. Born the son of a greengrocer, he left school at thirteen, and within a few years had entered business for himself. Over a long period he has gradually built up a large multinational company. He makes no secret of his origins; but is known for his opposition to the trade unions, and his support for such groups as Aims of Industry (now Aims). In the interview he evades the topic of class, with such statements as 'it is a class society, I think the people who try to make it more of a class society are the socialists'; 'people don't look up as they used to'; 'I hope class is going if not gone.'

At the end of formal questioning, he was tackled more informally about his views.

(Q. You came up from the bottom, from a fairly poor home, and you had your own business in Lancashire in the 1930s. You must have seen a lot of poverty and hardship. Yet now you are clearly opposed to socialism, and to Labour policies. How is that?)

'I did come from a poor home - but there wasn't hardship. People talk of there being slums, there weren't slums, the houses were perfectly good. It was what the people made of them. Our house was always kept clean and well maintained. We had no hot water ... but the house was fit to live in. It's what people make of them... What has socialism done for people? It doesn't produce wealth; it's private industry that does that.'

(Q. Many people would see a contribution in alleviating poverty, the National Health Service, the Social Services and so on?)

'It wasn't a national health service, they took it over - the socialists don't understand that only private industry creates wealth.'

Here the meaning system of the 'respectable working class'/lower middle class appears to have been grafted on to business ideology, to produce an amalgam more uncompromising than that of many of the traditional elite.

On occasion in denying class the upwardly mobile could produce statements in which they defined a picture of class whilst also denying its existence. Consider this statement from the assistant managing director of a retail group, himself the son of a railway-man:

'Well, it still exists. And having come up from the so-called working class, and I still consider myself working-class – I don't know what it means frankly. You know if one talks of working class, middle class, upper class, I don't know what it means except as snobbery whether it comes from one end or the other.... I don't think those terms have very much relevance except to the individual who wants to consider himself upper class. Does it mean he dresses better, has a million in the bank, or what, I've no idea. And middle-class, he is a professional man or doctor, does he live in a better neighbourhood, does the working-class man have a council house? I don't know.'

Contrastingly, other men who had been upwardly mobile testified to the effect that it had had on their lives. They were highly aware of differences in attitudes between different social classes. The son of a minor public service employee, now a director of a huge multinational, defined class this way:

'Yes, there are groups in society who identify with each other very clearly, and it's very difficult for these groups to have a sensible conversation with each other because their philosophy and ethos is different.... There is a group of people who, by their character, probably don't save, believe in collectivism rather than individualism, probably are not of high intellectual achievement, probably but not always. And there's the stockbroker belt, the Highgate – whatever you wish to call it. The upper middle class which is more competitive, is selective, has more wealth, has more educational achievement but is not necessarily public school.'

This man says his parents come from the lower middle class. He has also pointed out earlier that he has lost his Lancashire accent over the years, and says:

'It would be very difficult for someone who went to a secondary modern or the D-stream of a comprehensive to change rapidly enough to end up at the top of this company. I think there are a lot of problems. I can think of one man I know, who started off as a barefoot newsboy in the East End of London. He's an able man and obviously very pushy, but it's been a hell of a stretch for him. Whatever we say about it, there is a barrier; if your voice doesn't sound right, or if you go drinking in the evening instead of playing golf – it does make a difference. And it pulls the wife with him as well, and it's much more difficult for her.'

This revealing comment on the problems of social mobility was echoed by another of the highly mobile who headed a small service company, but had made a great deal of money, and had been Lord Mayor of London.

'I think there is a social class here which is created by education. May I put it to you personally. I've already explained my background. I found it very difficult to make progress in certain areas of life when I'd achieved a certain degree of financial progress because of my background. But as you know I went into civic life because I felt a need to express myself other than in business, and as a result of my progress, shall we call it, in civic life, I have been able to make entry into every aspect of social life. That was the result of being successful in finance, and having the time to devote to it, and the rewards all came after I was 45 to 50.'

The Traditional Upper Class

If class is problematic for those who have experienced high upward mobility, it is problematic in a sense also for the social elite, the traditional upper class. They have to come to terms with charges that they owe their position to nepotism, going to the right school and the old boy network, and these may even come from other businessmen. Of course, they may ignore such attacks, putting them down to the 'envy, hatred and malice' of misguided socialists, but in the interview there was no escape. There were several ways of reacting: the first was to align themselves with the middle class, to present themselves as really 'managers' or 'meritocrats'. Thus one merchant banker, whose family had run the bank for over 200 years and who was a member of the aristocracy, declared that he had: 'one foot in the upper class, one foot in the middle class', because, 'I think a lot of my values are professional. I think that I tend if I may put it in a flippant way, to think that the upper class consists of 25 dukes, and that the rest of us are middle class.'

Likewise, a family businessman of enormous wealth, asked if he was a member of the upper class, said:

'Yes - in Morayshire I am. They think I'm mad, I think they're mad.'

(Q. Why is this?)

'They think anyone who doesn't have to earn a living, as I don't actually, is mad to go and do so. And in the same way I feel they have no pride in achievement, because they don't actually do anything. They're living in the past.'

In these statements, though class is defined, its importance is denied, at least for the respondent, whose values he says are of achievement, efficiency and enterprise. Another man with an Eton-Oxbridge-Guards background said:

'For my generation of management what we are concerned with is people's professional ability - and the difference is the people you regard as being efficient, successful, committed in their own field - and the fact that Sir William Armstrong was from the Salvation Army - the fact is that William got himself

into that position, that's what counts - and I think this is
the view of my generation in business.'

(Q. This is the meritocratic view?)

'That's right.'
An alternative reaction when interviewed, however, is simply to
refuse to talk about class. The man may or may not give some indication of knowing what class refers to but then the interview is
curtailed. Thus, just as the discussion was getting underway in
one interview, it came to:

(Q. It is wealth that creates classes?)

'Wealth is the starting factor: it's the main thing. It's hereditary and everything else if you want to start talking about
upper classes. You may want to live in a certain style but if
you haven't got the money you can't.'

(Q. Is it only money?)

'I haven't really thought about it. *I'm not interested in class.*
I'm not class conscious.'

(Q. Do you see an upper class?)

'A small one.'

And the questioning went no further.
Amongst the 130 men interviewed, the numbers of the traditional elite who reacted in a distinctive way to the topic of class was
nine.

The Outsider
The last small group with a distinct attitude to class one may call
the outsiders. They are men who were born, and often educated,
outside Britain, and they therefore take what they consider to be
a detached view. To some extent one can add here members of
some minority racial or religious groups who see class as irrelevant to their own position, for example, the Jewish family businessman who stated:

'I'm Jewish and Jewish people are able to move through
society in many ways - but so far as having the education
goes - and make no mistake Jewish people set a high value
on education - we're looking for other things - and it's not
that sort, i.e. class prejudice, of prejudice we're worried
about.'

The foreign-born men saw Britain as very class conscious compared with other countries. They mentioned particularly the
public school system, and its divisiveness as they saw it. Their
account of class was clearly autobiographical. Depending on circumstances, they could see themselves either as shunned by the
upper or upper middle class because of their foreign origins, or
else as classless because their background could not be identified.
Thus, the head of a small service company said:

'I think one of the great advantages of being a foreigner,

although I don't consider myself a foreigner for most purposes, is that for this purpose I am classless. I am upper-
middle-class, but it means nothing because I don't share
the background of the upper middle class to any extent.
Although to some extent - I've been to their universities
and I live in Hampstead, and I look down on people who
drive Rover cars. But that's very superficial. What's more
important is that I'm classless.'
Contrastingly, a German-born entrepreneur, asked about the
constraints on his ability to meet business objectives said: 'Myself, personally - if you want to touch on a delicate point I've
always got a sort of complex about my foreign origin - about my
inability to speak English as well as you do.'
Another foreign-born man showed a similar concern for the
nature of the upper classes and the impossibilities of entering it:
'When I go to my club which is the Reform here, or I go to
the House of Lords for lunch, everybody treats me very
nicely, but I know, and you feel, this slight invisible barrier.'

(Q. You still feel there's this thing about being a foreigner
and not going to public school?)

'Yes definitely. It's not strong like anti-black or anti-
semitism, but it's there. Let's get back within these four
walls to (——————— ———————) with Eton, the Guards, an MC,
a most perfect English gentleman; he's very nice to me but
he's not with me as if I am one of them.'

(Q. Is this really so - the Warburgs, for example, must now
be accepted?)

'Sigmund Warburg is 72, of German Jewish origin, a brilliant
banker, highly admired. I'm also admired in the country and
in industry, but being admired for your work and success
and being accepted in the country home at the weekend is a
great difference. Not I don't mind because I've got my family
and my friends. But one must bring it out because between
the educated [public school] class and the workman's class
in the mind of the workman I am in the ——————— class - he
makes no difference between the ———————class and me. It
is a terrible gap and it will take at least a generation to close
it.'

(Q. So there's two classes - the educated and the workman's
class?)

'Well, there are three classes aren't there, although I always
find the middle class terribly difficult to define, because I
know a lot of people who are not workmen by any means but
who are not the upper middle class .....'
But the outsiders, again, comprise only a small group among British businessmen; in this study there were seven of them.

7.16 THE THEMES OF CLASS IMAGERY

Aside from these minority groups, as we have seen, the responses
of this sample of businessmen taken as a whole could not be easily
analysed and do not fall into simple patterns, nor could they be
related to the past or present experience of the men who were
interviewed.

What one can say of businessmen, however, is that their images
of society do reveal certain themes, which recur over and over
again: themes which are perhaps indicative of strongly held beliefs about the nature of British society. Some of these have already
been alluded to, but in order to summarise and encapsulate them,
I will now take a specific look at the more important ones. The
major themes of business class imagery as I see them are as follows.

Class is Disappearing
Two apparently contradictory beliefs recur throughout the images
of society of businessmen. The first is that there will always be
inequalities of status and reward in society, the second that class
differences as traditionally conceived are disappearing, or that
class itself is on the wane. Often these ideas can occur in the
statements of the same man, but they are not necessarily irrecon-
cilable.

We have already seen some examples of the theme that class
distinctions are disappearing, or that class is less important in
modern-day Britain than it was in the past. There are several
different aspects to it: for some, it turns on the idea of there
being greater opportunities for social mobility than there used to
be; for others, increasing affluence, especially among manual
workers, is thought to have led to increasingly similar standards
of consumption and lifestyle. The most frequent portrayal of this
is in the matter of holidays, in which manual workers are pictured
as taking their holidays in the same foreign locations as the businessmen themsleves. (That many manual workers take holidays
abroad is not to be doubted but some businessmen gave the impression that the British mix more on the beaches of Spain than
they do in Britain.) Thus one managing director put it that: 'the
janitor is going to Majorca for his holidays, whereas I'm trying to
work out if I can afford to take the wife and kids and the answer
is I can't.'

To illustrate how the lines of class are seen as blurring, here
are the statements of the relatively young (forty-six) managing
director of a small manufacturing company. He himself had a minor
public school and Cambridge University background:

(Q. People talk of there being classes in society. What do
you think?)

'Yes, I think there are, I think they're getting very much
less. I think it's almost into two groups really. There's quite
a change in that those two classes are not so rigidly separated
as they were before - it's quite possible to move from the

lower to the upper one. I think so much of society though is
controlled by people with a certain education, social background, property owning experience. These people naturally
stick together, not necessarily for gain, political advantage
or anything else, but because they find each other's company
more acceptable.'

(Q. So there are two classes?)

'Yes, one can go into the refinements of super public schools,
Oxbridge and so on. I don't think that's very relevant. I
don't think there's an upper class, upper middle class, lower
middle, working class as there was. I think there's a line
much further up near the top which is a kind of mixture out
of what was the middle class and upper class, and this is true
in certain situations and in certain institutions it is quite
marked.'
As we can see, class is blurring - yet class persists.

A Second Theme: *The Inequality of Man*
This apparent contradiction between the picture of class as per-
manently with us and that of class as disappearing is the result
of the director's picture of the transformation of the social system.
We are generally held to be moving towards a meritocracy; thus,
it is the old class distinctions based upon hereditary position,
accent, and where you were educated, which are thought to be
breaking down. The meritocracy is seen as a kind of ladder along
which the individual's status (and income) will be related to his
education, ability, training and position in occupational hierarchies.
This is the ideal which businessmen see society moving towards,
and in this sense class will remain. Nevertheless, the predominant
picture of the class structure remains that of two classes. The
lower, which is partly the less educated, consists mainly of manual, routine clerical or shop-workers, is non-managerial, more
prone to unionisation and differs in tastes and leisure interests to
the upper, better educated, potentially managerial group. In a
sense here slightly differing images of society can be held even
by the same person because they express not only ideals of society,
but also changes in society.
   What the meritocrats share with almost all the other businessmen
is a belief that promotion in the company is by merit, and tied in
with this, the view that 'we all work for the company', 'we're all
workers now'. The chairman, now retired, of one of Britain's ten
largest companies put his views this way:
   'I firmly believe there'll always be a class system. The only
   thing that changes is the criteria by which the classes are
   defined. It used to be by brute force - the survival of the
   fittest. What happened then, blood, I suppose, inheritance.
   Now I suppose we're into the era of the technocrat. I think
   there'll always be a class system so long as babies are born
   with unequal intelligence into an unequal environment....
   No, I think ability will always qualify someone to be better

than someone without it. So even if they start level they
will become an upper class.'

The Importance of Education
Class and inequality are maintained by success in occupational
hierarchies; and that, in turn, follows from inequalities of intellect and ability. Yet it was also accepted by many businessmen
that rather more is needed. Specifically, what is required is the
right education, and upbringing, which in turn indicate attitudes
which themselves differentiate social classes. Thus, as we saw
earlier, in talking of social class, businessmen refer more frequently to education than to any other attribute, and in this they
differ from other groups in British society who see differences in
class first and foremost in money terms. Here is just one example
of how businessmen emphasise the part education plays in the
social structure:
    'Yes, I think there is a class structure. It's largely edu-
    cational now. It's got nothing at all to do with background
    and income. I think we are moving from an inherited kind
    of class structure to an educational class structure where
    unless one gets into a particular educational system at a
    particular age, you are locked out for the rest of your life.
    I think we have swapped one situation where one's academic
    achievement didn't mean a goddam thing, as long as you had
    the right father, to another where your achievement in the
    educational system is going to precondition largely what
    happens in the rest of life. We're between the two systems.'
Because education is so important, we should not be surprised
that not only top businessmen, who can afford to fairly comfortably, but many others of the middle class, strive so hard to give
their children private, and preferably 'public school', education.
Though I did not enquire, I have no doubt that the vast majority
of the businessmen interviewed had educated their sons at least
at public school. Yet at the same time, the importance of education
in the class structure is seen as leading to a more socially mobile
society.

Society is More Fluid
Businessmen liked to emphasise that society is much more socially
fluid than it was once, say, before the war. Anyone can be
socially mobile if they get the right education, and since anyone
with sufficient ability can go to university, so it is thought, anyone with ability and drive can make it to the top of the company.
Directors consistently stressed the openness of promotion to the
boardroom. When asked why it was that a majority of directors
were from public school, a very frequent response was to suggest
that this would no longer be so (or assert it was not so), or to
quibble over the definition of public school. On two occasions the
man being interviewed declared that a majority of his board were
not from public school, then checked through them only to discover that a majority in fact were.

However, the businessmen did see it as more difficult for the son of a manual worker both to get to university, and to get to the top in industry. The reason for this they ascribed to the effects of home influence, believing that middle-class parents would provide a more stimulating home life and one more conducive to academic success. They ascribed the success of the public schools to this, rather than any particular benefit of the schools themselves.

Thus, directors tend to believe society to be more open than it is. They are constantly aware of, and can name, those top businessmen who have come up from lower social strata. This belief in the openness of society leads them generally to feel that class would wither away - if only it were allowed to.

Class is a Political Weapon of the Left
The stumbling block from this point of view is the political left-wing, whether in the guise of the Labour party, or leading trade unionists. They are seen as using class to 'stir people up', to create 'envy, hatred and malice'. As one man said: 'It seems to me I hear a lot of talk about class from the left, but very little from the political right.'

Businessmen in particular resent the term working-class, since for them it conjures up an opposition between such a class and a leisured class with which they would be mistakenly lumped. Directors were sensitive to misconceptions of boardroom life, of it being 'all Rolls Royces, cigars and three-hour lunches', of 'fat men, living off company profits'. They did feel such misconceptions to be fairly widespread.

This notion of class, as a concept sustained and used by the left, could sometimes be applied also to the concept of the two sides of industry. Here, for example, is the statement of a family businessman:

'I reject this two sides of industry story. We were getting on so well in the 1950s and early 1960s. After the war, the war did a hell of a lot to break these class barriers down. When I was working on the shop floor you weren't aware at all of any distinctions. Such distinctions are in people's heads.... Society was becoming more affluent and the so-called class war was being ended or so it seemed. But in the last two to three years, politicians and the left wing have seen fit to whip it up again. Even in Australia which was always a classless society, we've seen this being created in the last two or three years. And this does affect us in business.'

Awareness of Other Views of Class
Yet although the left wing, or the agitators, are seen to use social class as a weapon, businessmen did in some cases show some awareness of hostility from below, and of rather different attitudes from their own workforce. Only a minority specifically said so, but there were at least some who perceived that other groups, most specifically manual workers, did not share their own conception of society.

Thus, one of those men who took a meritocratic view of society said:

'One of the things the shopfloor never liked me to say was that I was one of them once.'

(Q. They don't like that?)

'No, no - it cuts across their mores, you see - that you can't do it.'

(Q. There's just the bosses and us?)

'That's right. It's as perceived.'

And the retired chairman quoted above, who 'firmly believed' there would always be a class system, echoed this comment.

'I've argued with our shop stewards that the - board consists wholly of workers. They all look at me with dumb dissatisfaction on their faces.'

(Q. They don't agree with that sort of thing?)

'No, because they see it as a class deal; but the way in which they define class, I don't know, it's the authoritarian class.'

(Q. Those who have management authority?)

'Yes, yes. The authoritarian powerful class rather than anything derived from wealth or inheritance.'

And on a few occasions reference was made to the 'them and us' attitudes which sociologists have associated with the traditional worker. For example:

'There is an us and them attitude, too much of it. When I'm doing political canvassing, the number of people who say "I'm not going to vote" - those who say "they're all in it for what they can get out of it." There is this attitude, a working-class attitude. "Them" are the people who organise things - the council or council officers, the government, and management, the bosses in any form. "Them" are always supposed to create a jolly good environment for "us".'

7.17 CONCLUSION

At the beginning of this chapter I warned that it would be lengthy and somewhat complex in content. I doubt that at its conclusion readers will dispute this. Let me try, therefore, to draw together some of the strands from it and come to some conclusions about businessmen's views of class and status.

At a simple level we may conclude that businessmen hold what sociologists have usually called 'status' or 'prestige' models. That is, that rather than picturing society as two basically opposed groups, they tend to see it either as a more or less continuous hierarchy, or else as several classes, most usually three or sometimes four. In addition, these classes are not divided on some crude basis, such as 'workers and us'; 'the mass and us', but

rather class/status divisions are seen as differences of attitudes
and lifestyle resulting from a number of factors such as differences of income, education, occupation and family background.
It is important to remember also that respondents do not draw
the distinctions between class and status which are made by sociologists.

It has proved impossible to relate the businessmen's views of
society in any simple way to their present or previous work situation, to their personal ownership or otherwise of capital, nor
to the other aspects of their social background which were examined. I shall consider the implications of this for sociological
theory in chapter 9.

However, at this stage I wish to ask simply whether the implications of what are called 'status models' have been correctly
anticipated in the literature. The contrast that is usually drawn
is between the 'us and them' attitudes of the traditional manual
worker, and the 'deferential' attitudes of some kinds of manual
workers, which in turn is sometimes conflated with the middle-
class 'prestige' model of society. Actually, research on this issue
(see chapter 2) suggests that manual workers of the traditional
type appear, in fact, to be a minority group, even in the communities in which they might be expected to be most prevalent.
Contrastingly, when we analyse businessmen's attitudes, we find
that their (middle-class) viewpoints quite frequently contain elements that suggest a clear division between classes. To be sure,
this is not a division between 'bosses and others', that is, the 'us
and them' relationship seen from the other side, for the upper of
the two groupings comprises groups other than bosses, but
neither is it merely the division of society into a series of levels,
with people on each level being variously worthy of deference.

The sources of the businessmen's images of society are not
'local social status systems' of the kind described by Stacey et al.
(1960) and others. That is, they are not the result of living in a
small community where people's whole life history and family background are well known to other members of the community. They
are only status models of society to the extent that they do not
put primary emphasis on either a person's market and/or monetary
income position (except to the extent that education is seen as
giving some groups a better placing in the market) or a simple
division between 'bosses and men'. Rather, they contain both
objective factors and the perceived results of these such as attitudes, tastes, interests and lifestyles.

Very often these models do not view society as hierarchical
structures of varying statuses; rather, they incorporate a sharp
discontinuity between, in effect, the working and middle class. An
upper class may be recognised, but it is characterised as small
and declining; whereas the major discontinuity is viewed as persistent.

It would be somewhat surprising if this was not the case. Top
businessmen studied here are quite different from, for example,
the lower grade clerical staff, or small shopkeeprers who have

formed the basis for most previous conceptions of middle class
social imagery. Such an elite is not concerned about maintaining
its status in the face of encroachments on it by groups of manual
workers, nor do members of it worry about whether to join a staff
association rather than a union. Equally they are not concerned
to define the minutiae (as they would appear) of differences between respectable and rough working class, between skilled,
semi-skilled and unskilled workers, or between people who live in
one part of a London suburb and another.

Shielded as they are from what they see as the major division
of class structure, having some access both to the traditional
upper class, and (as we will see in chapter 8) to national centres of
power, businessmen must largely glean their conceptions of class
from sources, most notably the mass media, which may well present a picture, ultimately, of 'two nations'. A number of features
of British society reinforce this: for example, a constant friction
seems apparent between the TUC and CBI; more than other European nations, political life has been dominated by two major
parties; approximately half the working population is now union-
ised; approximately half own their homes, and so on.

Now, as we saw in chapter 6, it was not the case that the businessmen took an 'us and them' view of relationships in the firm.
To judge from the interviews, this was not their habitual stance.
However, the continuities in their images of society do present a
picture of two groups which differ, and differ not only in the jobs
they do, and their educational backgrounds, but also in their
aspirations, attitudes and tastes as well. It would not be surprising if directors regarded the mass of the workforce as a group
with which close personal identification and communication would
be almost impossible, and that in situations where conflict from
below is perceived (for example, strikes, go-slows or other forms
of industrial unrest) their attitudes may harden towards a conflictual, an 'us and them', perspective.

Whether or not this is so, it was clear that a number of those
interviewed were aware of such attitudes amongst some manual
workers towards higher management. It was most obvious in those
cases where respondents specifically contrasted their own view of
society with that of such workers.

Thus, I suggest that the dominant image of society amongst
businessmen contains a specific contrast between two major groupings, the middle and working class. And these are two groups
that could be said to have competing interests: the middle class,
being individualistic, concerned to promote the free market for
those with skills, and training (or capital), which is to their
benefit; the working class devoted to the collectivist ideal, seeing
its future in union action, and in the extension of the umbrella of
the state, which, by its intervention in the economic sphere, may
create the conditions in which collectivism is most successful.
(Though businessmen might not draw such conclusions overtly.)

I make this suggestion despite the fact that the majority of businessmen apparently see a three-class, not a two-class, model of

society. As we have seen, the three-class model of society is the one which has appeared most often amongst respondents' images in a number of studies including this one. However, I would argue that the very terminology available to people to talk of social class, that is working, middle and upper, tends to make such a finding inevitable (see section 7.12 above). Many of the respondents made it clear that the group they understood by the term upper class was not an important or influential one; it was, in a sense, outside the mainstream of society. Whilst the aristocracy and the very wealthy would be seen by most people as being of the highest status, the people many businessmen seem most to admire were certain other leading businessmen (for example, Sir Arnold Weinstock). We might represent this situation as in Figure 7.2.

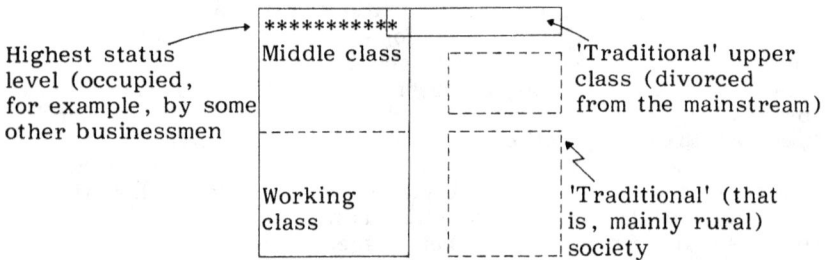

Highest status level (occupied, for example, by some other businessmen

Middle class

Working class

'Traditional' upper class (divorced from the mainstream)

'Traditional' (that is, mainly rural) society

Figure 7.2   Businessmen's 'picture' of society

If businessmen's social class/status image of society is fundamentally a two-class one, then it partly explains why the majority do not regard themselves as part of an 'upper class' which is a cohesive social, economic and political elite. The term 'upper class' does not apply to such a group. And indeed, it was when I began to make a specific investigation of the businessmen's picture of power that it became clear that the term 'establishment' much more nearly conveys for them a power-holding group (see next chapter).

Yet, although the respondents held to a large extent dichotomous models of society, there are important factors that mitigate against their holding class models as such. A fully developed two-class model of society implies the possibility of conflict between the classes, of divergent interests between them; and of unequal life-chances experienced by members of each.

But businessmen were often keen to stress the need for social cohesion or unity, especially at the level of the firm. They did so too in the context of the distribution of income and wealth, where an often expressed opinion was that 'we should get on with making a bigger cake and worry about sharing it later.' They regarded talk of class as coming from the left, and as being intended to cause social unrest.

Thus, businessmen exemplify the problem facing a privileged group in a democratic capitalist society. There is a bar to the extent to which class consciousness can be developed. A privileged group cannot enter into open class warfare, and whether or not members of it recognise the existence of classes, they must at the same time disavow the importance of them. Thus, their reaction to change that threatens their position may not be class-based and may, in fact, be largely piecemeal and pragmatic, despite the abundant opportunities for cohesion and conspiracy identified by the elite theorists.

I have tried to bring together the strands of thought contained in this and the previous section in one diagram (Figure 7.3). This identifies the most important, the core beliefs, of businessmen. The connecting arrows in the diagram serve simply to show how beliefs and ideas can be linked up to be reinforcing. But, as can be seen, there is a contradiction between the set of beliefs in the lower half of the diagram and those in the upper half. The set at the top maintains that there is a class system, and that for social or other reasons there always will be. The set at the bottom suggests that class is withering away in favour of an open merit-ocracy. How the tension between the two sets is resolved in practice, and communicated in an interview, is, I suggest, mould-ed by the businessmen's personal backgrounds, previous life experiences, and intellectual and cultural influences.

Men have unequal talents

A belief in the inequality of man

Men will become unequal in achievement and personal development despite efforts to make them equal (source: an amalgam of common sense, social Darwinism, and a reaction to misunderstood socialism)

Inequality will always exist

Awareness of certain dichotomies: Political 'left' and 'right'/Labour v. Tory/TUC v. CBI/unionised and non-unionised /managers and employees /those who own homes and those who do not/the middle class and the working class (source: personal experience, literature, media)

Class/status will not decline
Class persists

Class should decline

Core beliefs meet at a point of potential tension

Exact form of respondent's explanation of class dependent on own life history, and awareness of inequality, plus other personal beliefs

INTERVIEW

Lines of class/status are blurring

Income differentials are declining. We are all more prosperous; workers have much which once only the middle class had – e.g. consumer goods, cars, foreign holidays (source: media)

Class as a status system based on 'old school tie', accent, snobbishness is declining (source: personal knowledge)

Notions of the meritocracy and a more open class structure

There is equality of opportunity in business; promotion to higher management is open on merit (source: management ideologies)

Educational opportunity, notably university education is open to all (source: fact, as interpreted by businessmen)

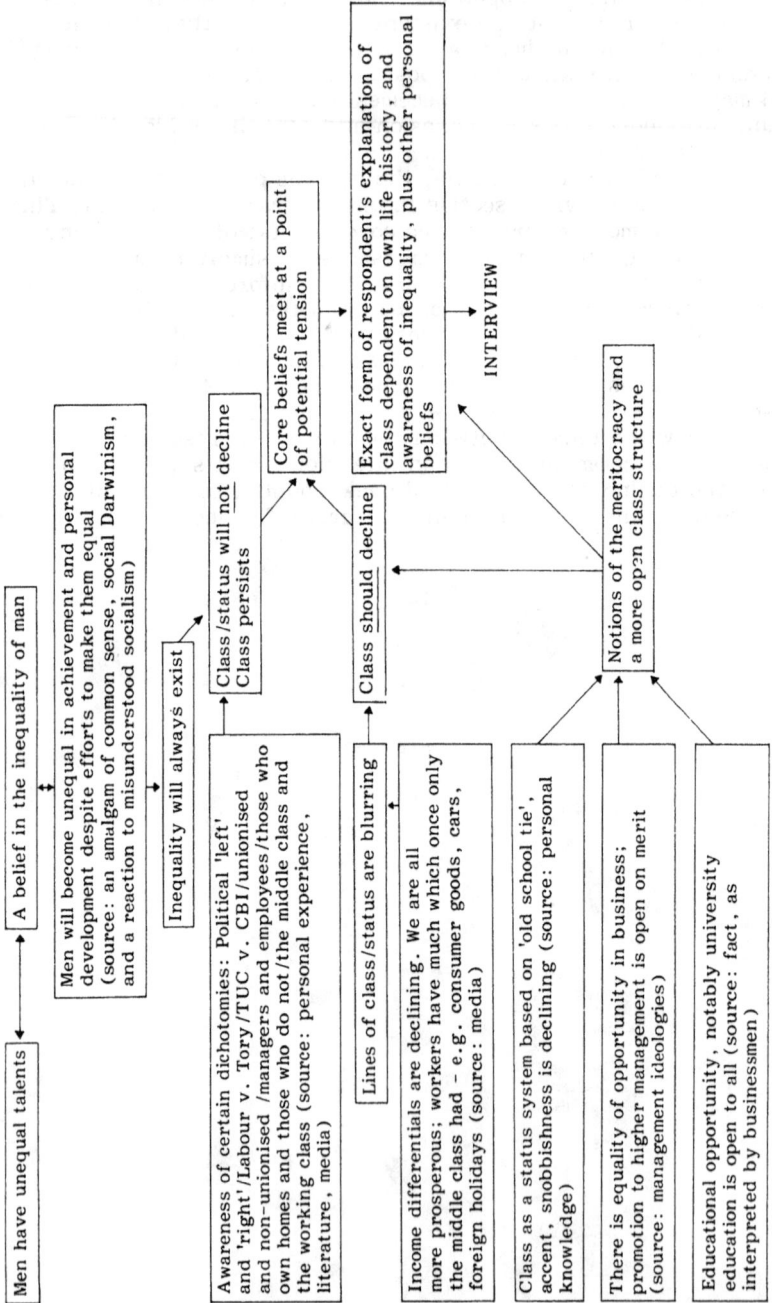

Figure 7.3   An outline of some core beliefs of top businessmen

8 AN UNINVENTED LOBBY:
the business picture of power in Britain

'Whitehall tends to invent a lobby even where none exists.'
J. Bruce-Gardyne and N. Lawson, 'The Power Game', 1976

8.1 INTRODUCTION

As I discussed above, it seems that the business elite, a group to whom theorists of many persuasions have ascribed great power, tend to view themselves as holding a position within the class/status structure no different from the sizeable group which they see as constituting the middle class. Where they accept the existence of an upper class, they distinguish it on criteria, such as having aristocratic connections, that are irrelevant to their position qua businessmen.

These findings should certainly not be misunderstood; most of those interviewed were well aware of their 'responsibilities *within* the firm', or put another way, the power their position gives them; and whether or not they played down their status, and its associated trappings, a number certainly showed signs of under-standable satisfaction at having reached the upper echelons of their companies.

Yet it did seem that the interview discussions of class and status lacked a dimension. For whatever the businessmen said about class and status, they might still be a power-holding group of great importance. Hence the decision was made (see chapter 3), to include in the remaining interviews a series of questions specifically concerned with businessmen's responsibili-ties and power vis-à-vis the state. This was done in the full realisation of the controversies that surround the study of power, and that the number of resulting interviews on the topic be even smaller than those of the study as a whole, and thus make it even more difficult to draw strong conclusions.

This chapter is concerned with how businessmen view power in Britain. By putting the evidence of the interviews together with statistical evidence on some points I shall develop here a number of hypotheses concerning the relationship between the business elite, and certain state elites, in particular, government min-isters, other MPs, and civil servants.

As I stated in chapter 1, I regard it as legitimate to regard the 'state' as consisting of a number of separate elites : the heads of government, the administration, police, security forces,

and so on. There is still much work to be done on the interplay
and relative influence of these (for example, on the influence of
senior civil servants compared to ministers). The concentration
in this chapter on three particular groups, and the consequent
lack of attention to the relationship between the business elite
and, say, the military elite, comes from an appreciation of the
groups that businessmen themselves regarded as important for
their purposes.

Because I am concerned here to examine how businessmen see
power in Britain, I am not concerned to demonstrate that businessmen and state officials share the same class background, have the
same education and cultural background and interests, share the
same pursuits, clubs and so on. Such evidence is available elsewhere,[1] and is taken for granted here. I have not taken a range
of pre-selected decisions and asked who was involved in taking
them and the nature of the outcome, nor did I set out to demonstrate how businessmen prevented issues from reaching the
decision-making arena. Rather, the approach here has been to
try to identify the forms of political and influential action open to
businessmen as they see them, the range of issues which involve
them, and to give some pointer to the types of action preferred
by them.

The interviews covering these topics, it will be recalled, were
held with nineteen main board directors, nine retired chief executives, and forty-two full-time chief executives, who, with four
exceptions,[2] headed industrial and commercial firms in the top
250 by turnover (or the top 180 wholly British-owned firms using
dual criteria). The statistical data presented here is based on my
sample of firms, rather than a fuller sample of British firms, because it was easiest to collect such data for firms which were
actually part of the study.

8.2 OUTLINE OF THE ARGUMENT

We may identify the following ways in which businessmen can
wield power in, or exert influence over the state apparatus:[3]
1 by directly gaining office as an MP, and more so, as a cabinet
minister, or else in local politics;
2 (a) by holding high position in the civil service; or
(b) by participating on Royal Commissions, committees, the
boards of nationalised industries, 'quasi-autonomous government
bodies', and on the adjuncts of these at local level, for example,
Area Health Boards;
3 (a) by holding high position in a political party (in Britain
very often the Tory party), by participating in party activities;
(b) by funding a party;
4 by access to or ability to influence those who hold positions
set out in 1-3, which in turn can come about through:
(i) private connections, formed through family, kinship, educational, social and other contacts; or indirect networks of these

using intermediaries;
(ii) shared 'class' interests, assumptions, or other cultural
definitions which further direct contact between state officials
and heads of private firms; or
(iii) shared objectives which produce the same result (for example,
national economic success); or
(iv) situations of mutual interdependence, for example, civil
servants requiring the assistance of businessmen;
5 blackmail, bribery, crude force in various forms. Such methods
will not be considered (which, in view of what has been revealed
of the behaviour of some firms since the study began, may be
considered an oversight).

The argument here will be that businessmen have moved, over
the course of this century, and can be expected to move further
in the same direction, from a situation in which they were frequently in positions in which they themselves took political
decisions, (that is, were members of government or MPs) or were
highly interlinked with such people, and one in which they could
certainly count on a set of shared objectives and assumptions
by people in such positions, to a situation in which they have to
attempt to influence those in such positions, often by direct
approach to them. In other words, much more than in the past,
they have become lobbyists. However, they are assisted in this
to some extent by increasing involvement by the state in economic
and business activity, which creates a situation of mutual interdependence between state officials and businessmen.

In terms of the typology set out immediately above, I am suggesting that whereas businessmen could, in the past, influence
state activity through channels 1,2,3 and 4 (i) they now utilise
4(iii) and (iv). However, 2(b) continues to provide an important
range of contacts between businessmen and state officials.

The period 1974-6 was a particularly good one in which to be
investigating these issues, since the manner in which the Labour
government was returned to power, and the policies which they
proposed, suggested at least the possibility that this would be a
more radical government than that of the 1964-70 period. At the
very least, a period when Labour is in power provides a much
better test of Marxist or power elite theories, since the kind
of evidence furnished in support of these in the past - drawn on
the basis of shared educational backgrounds of government MPs
and businessmen, shared club membership, family interconnec-
tions, MPs' business interests, and the position of MPs or cabinet
ministers on the boards of leading companies - is all too easy to
find when a Conservative government is in power.

8.3 NATIONAL VERSUS LOCAL POLITICS

The first hypothesis I will put forward here is that the business
elite are less likely to be involved in affairs of a local or regional
nature than they formerly were. If they do become involved with

politics it is increasingly likely to be in the form of action at a
national level, and, furthermore, to centre on London. It no
doubt remains true as others have shown (for example, Stacey
et al., 1975; Musgrove, 1963; Pahl, 1965) that managers, administrators and higher professionals continue to dominate local politics
and local voluntary associations. These people are not synonymous, however, with those at the very top of large companies.

The present situation contrasts somewhat with previous times
when captains of industry frequently did take a major role in the
activities of their neighbourhood. There are several reasons
which may be suggested for the change.

Far and away the most important is simply lack of time. As
companies have grown, and become more sophisticated, so being
a main board director appears to be regarded more and more as a
full-time occupation. Those employed full-time at the top of firms,
according to all estimates (see Young and Willmott, 1973; Copeman,
Lingh and Hanika, 1963; Child and Macmillan, 1972), probably
work longer hours than almost anyone else in the firm. In addition, as firms develop into multinationals, those at the top must
spend a considerable part of each year overseas, and this is
highly disruptive of any regular outside commitment.

There are, however, other reasons. In chapter 4 I indicated
that large companies seem increasingly to desire a London, or at
least south-eastern, headquarters. This means that top businessmen, in turn, live to a large extent in the south-east, where there
is, in any case, a relatively high concentration of managers, professionals and other white-collar groupings. There are simply
more of the kind of people who do get involved in such activities
around to do them. As we saw, there are parts of London, such
as areas of Belgravia and Knightsbridge, where so many top
businessmen live that if even one in ten competed for a place on
the local council, it would be readily filled. Businessmen's concern with national affairs may also reflect a realisation of an
undercurrent of centralisation of political decision-taking. Stacey
et al. (1975), for example, point out that many important decisions
affecting Banbury are taken quite outside the town.

Allied to such changes would appear to be a change in the businessman's view of himself. When the great industrialists of the
nineteenth century - the Cadburys, Rowntrees, Pilkingtons, and
the like - took a leading part in local affairs, they were adopting
a similar position to that of the local landowner or member of the
landed gentry, often in a rural context. Indeed Coleman (1973)
indicates that part of the drive to succeed in commerce was to be
able to mix with such groups, and to play the role of gentleman.
This tradition appears to be going. Businessmen's comments on
their non-company activities entirely supported these arguments.

At one stage the seventy men on whose views most of the arguments in this chapter are based were asked whether they felt
that businessmen such as themselves had any particular responsibilities outside the company. It was not always easy to get those
who answered to talk in terms other than of their responsibilities

as directors to serve the interests of shareholders, employees, customers and all the communities in which the firm operated - that is, the balancing interests ethos, as discussed in chapter 5. Those who did split fairly equally into three groups giving answers as follows:

(a) businessmen have no greater responsibilities than any other citizens in their private affairs;

(b) businessmen have no greater responsibilities, but they bring to outside activities skills, experience and knowledge that most people do not possess, and thus may prove valuable participants in outside activities;

(c) businessmen have a clear responsibility to involve themselves outside the company.

Answers of types (b) and (c) are not always easy to distinguish in practice, but this is of lesser importance here. What the answers do indicate is support for the argument above that the business elite's involvement outside the firm has changed in nature. Here, first, is a family businessman talking of his predecessors:

'They had a special place in the community. In those days they had more power. They were a very enlightened family. Put a lot of time and money into the community. Their position in the community was one of great power . . . the family had a position in the community which no one else approached. Now it's completely gone. Now we're just doing different jobs running the company.'

Another family businessman put it rather similarly:

'I think the big difference is that looking in terms of my family they were very much involved in local government - they provided a Mayor of ——, they sat on many of the committees of the city council, they gave the land for the hospital. The big difference now is we've become more compartmentalised. It's now not possible to have influence of that kind in several different fields, (a) because the job is more demanding and (b) because it's unacceptable anyway. The last member of the family who stood to be an MP was defeated by one of our own work people.'

One of the bureaucrats whose father had also been chairman of the same company pointed to the switch from local to national activity:

'[Before the war] my father was a large fish in a small pond, and indeed seemed to be quite big in the area. And had I should think in the area a very considerable influence. But outside in the wider world, no - probably he was not known. I suppose now, the company's larger, the men don't change - but they don't necessarily appear big in the community they live in, because they're not always there, or they're not there a lot of the time. But they do appear bigger in the larger world.'

(Q. So your father would have been known locally, whereas you'd be better known nationally?)

'That's right - you give up a certain amount of contact locally, and exchange it for a wider notoriety, if that's the word, outside.'

We shall see below that there has been something of a change in the nature of involvement at the national level. This, I will suggest, is more likely to involve activities of relevance to the firm itself, or business in general. Part of the reason for this is that businessmen feel their jobs to be extremely demanding. As one bureaucrat, director of a large multinational, said:

'I feel that if you do the kind of job I do it's very difficult to have a consistent role in the community. I would very much like to be an MP or a member of Camden Council, but such political activities as I had I felt obliged to give up because I just didn't have the time. So, weighing it all up, I feel that if I can do a good job in the company, and look after my family it's about as much as I am physically and mentally capable of. So this really means that effective work in the community will have to wait until I'm retired.'

These remarks seem to reflect a changing pattern of involvement by businessmen in national and local politics and voluntary associations. They suggested the following hypotheses:

(a) for a variety of reasons members of the business elite are less likely than they would have been in the past to take part in local affairs, political or otherwise;

(b) More importantly, they would play a lesser role in national politics, either as MPs or in party politics;

(c) However, more everyday evidence suggests that a range of bodies now exist which give businessmen access to and potential influence upon politicians and civil servants. Amongst these are the NEDC, the CBI, various business-government committees, the boards of nationalised industries and a whole range of what are called QUANGOS, or quasi-autonomous government organisations. One may suggest that this kind of activity is as strong or stronger than ever.

8.4 THE CHANGING NATURE OF POLITICAL INVOLVEMENT

To attempt to verify these hypotheses, I examined all the voluntary and political activities of chairmen and managing directors of firms in this study. Their activities were examined in the years 1925, 1950 and 1975 to see what trends were apparent.

The reason for taking firms in this study was that they gave a limited sample of firms to examine, and reduced the total amount of data-collection, since data had already been collected on the present-day heads of the firms. The sample, however, is clearly not a representative one of British industry: it is, for example, very heavily weighted towards very large firms. This, however,

is not a failing, since it is the heads of these that are most likely
to have political influence. A more serious criticism would be that
although the large (that is, top 100 and top 250-101 by turnover) firms of 1975 are adequately supplied, these were not in
many cases the large firms of 1925, or 1950. This would be a most
damaging failing of the methodology were the argument the
reverse of what it is: that is, that direct political or local involvement had increased. In fact, the methodology underestimates the
involvement of top businessmen in 1925 (and 1950), the more so
because many of the very large enterprises of those days - for
example, the railways or the steel companies - were then private
but now fall outside the sampling frame.

The methodology is as follows: from the 'Stock Exchange Yearbook' of 1975, 1950 and 1925, and other reference works, I
established who were the chairmen or managing directors of firms
in the study. From 'Who's Who' I established their various political
commitments and I have tabulated the results below to show the
lessening involvement in some areas and maintenance in others
in absolute terms. I draw conclusions on the basis of absolute
figures only, as percentaged figures grossly exaggerate the
involvement of past generations (because businessmen appear to
have been less likely to be in 'Who's Who').

The areas taken for consideration are as follows:

1 Being a Justice of the Peace
2 Sheriff, Lord Lieutenant, Deputy
  Lieutenant of town or county
3 Serving on hospital boards,
  university councils
	All types of
	local
	voluntary activity.

4 Serving as a county or town councillor 5 Being a mayor	Types of local political involvement.
6 Being a Member of Parliament	National political activity.

7 (i) Serving in the civil
  service in wartime
  (ii) Being in the civil service
  before entering industry
	Experience giving
	possible channels
	of access to
	civil service.

8 Serving on Royal Commissions,
  Government committees, e.g. the
  NEDC, NRDC, nationalised industry
  boards, Bullock committee
	Channels of
	access to MPs, etc.

9 High position in the FBI, or the CBI, e.g. member of Grand Council	Political lobbying forum.

10 Having a seat in the House of Lords

Table 8.1 Involvement of the heads of large firms in political and voluntary activities at three points in a fifty-year timespan

Commercial and industrial firms: 88 in 1975

		1925	1950	1975	Notes
Number of men on whom there is information		40	52	111	
Activity					
Local voluntary	1 JP	13	7	2	Majority were chairmen
	2 Sheriff, Lieut., D.L.	6	5	7	
	3 Hospital, University Boards	2	3	7	Includes Area Health Authorities but not school boards
Local political	4 Town/County Councillor	3	3	4	
	5 Mayor	2	0	1	
	6 MP/candidate	9(1)	4	2(1)	Figures in brackets are unsuccessful candidates. Main figures include both
National political and lobbying	7 Civil service { wartime / peace	5 / 1	9 / 0	2 / 6	
	8 Government committees	9(38)	15(45)	33(84)	Figure in brackets is approx. total committees by all men
	9 FBI/CBI	0	3(2)	9(2)	Member of Grand Council ( ) = presidents
	10 Seat in Lords	4	7	4(3)	Figures in brackets life peers
	11 Non-activists	16(40%)	27(52%)	65 (59%)	Figure in brackets is % based on men for whom there is information

Table 8.2 *Involvement of the heads of a sample of merchant banks, insurance companies and property companies in political and voluntary activities over a fifty-year timespan*

		1925	1950	1975	Notes
Number of men on whom there is information		13	16	33	Almost all are chairmen
Activity					
Local voluntary	1 JP	4	2	1	
	2 Sheriff, Lieut., D.L.	4	5	4	
	3 Hospital, university boards	1	2	2	As Table 8.1
Local political	4 Town/County Councillor	0	1	1	
	5 Mayor	0	1	1	
	6 MP/Candidate	1	1(1)	1(1)	As Table 8.1
National political and lobbying	7 Civil service { wartime	0	1	1	
	{ peace	1	2	2	
	8 Government committees	3(4)	3(10)	7(13)	As Table 8.1
	9 FBI/CBI	0	0	0	
	10 Seat in Lords	3	5	4(1)	As Table 8.1
	11 Non-activists	7	9	22	

Table 8.3   Political and voluntary involvement of heads of all firms in interview study over a fifty-year timespan

		1925	1950	1975	Notes
Number of men on whom there is information		53	68	144	
Activity					
Local voluntary	1 J.P.	17	9	3	
	2 Sheriff, Lieut., D.L.	10	10	11	
	3 Hospital, university boards	3	5	9	As Table 8.1
Local political	4 Town/County Councillor	3	4	5	
	5 Mayor	2	1	2	
	6 MP/candidate	10 (1)	5 (1)	3 (2)	As Table 8.1
National political and lobbying	7 Civil service {wartime	5	10	3	
	{peace	2	2	8	
	8 Government committees	12(42)	18(55)	40(97)	As Table 8.1
	9 FBI/CBI	0	3 (2)	9 (2)	Positions only held by men in commerce
	10 Seat in Lords	7	12	8 (4)	As Table 8.1
	11 Non-activists	23	36	87	

Activities 4-9 are taken as being a clear sign of political influence or involvement. So, as a final classification, men lacking
any involvement in these are called 'non-activists'.

The results of these investigations are shown in Tables 8.1,
8.2 and 8.3. These tables are the summary tables on which
trends can most easily be seen.

Despite the lacunae in the data that result from the lack of
information on the men who headed the firms in the study in
earlier periods, the trends in them certainly appear to support
the hypotheses put forward and would suggest that an investigation of the heads of a larger sample of large firms over time
would be rewarding.

We see from the tables that although more is known about
more men in 1975, involvement in local or political affairs is at
best maintained or else falls off in absolute terms. The two exceptions are hospital and university boards, where businessmen
seem to participate as much as ever (but then there are more
university boards than ever for them to sit on) and government
committees, where just as many men as ever are involved. Also,
we note the growth of the FBI and more recently the CBI as a
form of political activity.

The most striking changes are the fall off in the number of men
who are MPs and who are JPs. In 1925 firms in this study or their
forerunners provided nine MPs, two of whom were cabinet ministers, and one unsuccessful candidate. In 1975 the figure is just
three candidates of which only one was successful and actually
entered parliament. This particular man had to give up his seat
to resume his business career. The fall in the number of JPs I
interpret as a reduced involvement by businessmen in local
affairs, although the number of sheriffs, etc. and councillors
has kept fairly steady.

 The tables also reflect other social changes: industry (or
possibly certain sectors) appears to like to have a quota of men
who have been in the civil service: but whereas in previous
times these were men who served during wars on a temporary
basis, there now appears to be a certain amount of deliberate
recruitment of career civil servants. Likewise, although the
firms between them produced eight men entitled to sit in the
House of Lords in 1975, four of these were life peers.

The figures thus support the principal contention that direct
political office holding especially as MPs by members of the
business elite has fallen away. They thus contrast with studies
(for example, Guttsman, 1963) that show that a continuing high
proportion at least of Conservative MPs are company directors. I
suggest that, in fact, were one to investigate the latter, the vast
majority head comparatively small firms, many of them family
businesses. [4] In many cases they may have a greater affiliation for
and understanding of the self-employed than of the men who run
the massive firms that now dominate the economy (and who in turn
probably dominate the CBI). It seems that it is not the case,
where it once quite possibly was, that the command posts of both

industry and the state are held by the same men.[5]

It is of some importance to note that in the table above only around a third to half of businessmen are apparently active in any era, and the figure for 1975 is the lowest of the three. Yet this figure contrasts with the interview data, in which it tran-- spired that all but four of the seventy men had engaged, or were engaged, in some kind of contact aimed at influencing politicians or civil servants. Remove the nineteen directors from the seventy, all of whom were so involved, and we are still left with only four out of fifty-one (that is, less than 10 per cent) of chief executives of large companies who did not admit to some kind of informal political contact, influence or lobbying. Clearly what can be learnt from reference works is only a guide to the total span of business's political activity.

So far as the figures presented above go, the main objection to them remains the fact that firms which are large nowadays may have been comparatively small in 1925 or 1950. Likewise, firms that were relatively large then may have declined compared to other firms in the study. It might be suggested that it was always the heads of medium sized or smaller firms who took an active part in politics, and thus the data reveal no change. The author's own view is to doubt this. For one thing, it might be asked why, among forty men from commercial firms in this study, there were nine MPs in 1925, whilst the sample of nineteen firms from out- side the top 250 by turnover had only one ex-MP as a chief executive in 1975.

It should also be pointed out that the mode of control of large companies may have changed over time, and that some firms now classified as bureaucrat-controlled might have been family bus- inesses, or even entrepreneur-controlled in 1950 or 1925. How- ever, there was no evidence that family businessmen had in 1975 or in the past any greater propensity than bureaucrats to be involved in politics or local affairs. Rather, the figures suggested similar types of change amongst both groups, though the numbers being handled here are very small.

8.5 THE BUSINESS ELITE AND POLITICAL PARTIES

No discussion of businessmen and politics can ignore the Con- servative Party. Indeed, it may be argued that the Conservative Party is fundamentally devoted to the interests of capital holders and the upper middle classes, and that many business- men's major political involvement will be that of supporting the Party.

There is clearly some truth in the argument but the position is more complex than it seems. First, although the Conservative Party had, until 1969, been the most successful party in electoral terms for over a century, it was, until comparatively late in the nineteenth century, a party of the landed gentry and nobility. It

did not originally give support to business or doctrines of
laissez-faire capitalism. Historically, this was more the role of
the Liberals and a number of the businessmen who were heads of
companies in 1925, and who were, or had been, MPs, were
Liberals.

Nevertheless, the Conservative Party's success has been to
transform itself first into the 'natural' party of capitalists, and
latterly of managers, administrators and professionals also. It
receives support from business, and thus potentially acts as a
channel of business influence. Presumably to some extent also,
the greater the financial contribution, the more say a businessman may have. On the other hand, not all businessmen are themselves Tories (several of those interviewed supported the
Liberals, and at least one (socially mobile) man voted Labour),
and many may not wish to advertise their feelings to their unions
or their workforce.

In addition, supporting the Conservatives financially may be a
good move when they are in power, but rebound when a Labour
government comes in. Support may then waver for, as one director, of an engineering multinational, said: 'we've reduced our
contributions to the Conservative party, not because we've
changed our attitudes but because it's a wasteful way of exerting
political influence. There we were paying all that money while an
Industry Bill was being prepared under our noses.'

Thus it is interesting to examine variations in support for the
Tories. Here we are considering the actions of companies rather
than individuals. Sampson (1971, p.117) has remarked in this
regard: 'The Tories depend (it turns out) on relatively few banks
or big companies: most of the great corporations, like Shell,
Unilever or ICI, gave nothing, but a handful of the next biggest,
usually with a strong family tradition or a Tory politician on the
Board, gave quite large slices.'

Sampson also points out that companies may choose to give their
money not only to the Conservative Party but also to a number of
'curious propaganda organisations' which exist to counter socialist
or communist principles.

Using only the companies in which the chief executive was interviewed, the pattern of support both for the Party and for the propaganda organisations was examined (see tables 8.4 and 8.5). Of
those named by Sampson - British United Industrialists, Economic
League, Aims of Industry, Common Cause - Aims of Industry, now
renamed Aims for Freedom and Enterprise,[6] seems to be emerging
as the best supported.

Table 8.4, which categorises companies according to size, is in
line with Sampson's view, though Chi-squared tests do not show
the results to be statistically significant at the 5 per cent level.
Tendency to support the propaganda organisations appears to be
directly related to size of company. The City companies are also
big political givers; but whereas the banks give directly to the
Tories, the insurance companies tend to prefer the propaganda
organisations.

Table 8.4   Political and other donations by firms in the study – by size of firm

	All	Top 20	Top 21-90	Top 180-91	Below top 180	City firms
Number on which there is information	99	7	35	22	17	18
Giving to Conservatives	28(28)	0	15(43)	5(23)	2(12)	6(33)
Giving to 'propaganda' organisations	29(29)	3(43)	12(34)	6(27)	1(6)	7(39)
Giving to either	47(47)	3(43)	22(63)	9(38)	3(18)	10(56)

Table 8.5   Political and other donations by type of control

	All	Bureaucrat	Family businessman	Entrepreneur
Number	99	65	24	10
Giving to Conservatives	28(28)	16(23)	9(38)	3(30)
Giving to 'propaganda' organisations	29(29)	20(31)	8(33)	1(10)
Giving to either	47(47)	32(49)	12(50)	3(10)

Figures in brackets are percentages.

It is possible that a fuller investigation would produce more significant relationships between size and political giving, or type of control and political giving. The figures adduced here give some indication that around thirty-four out of sixty-four firms from the top 180 British companies give to either the Tory party or one of the propaganda organisations, and a similar percentage of City firms make such donations. Put another way, it appears that almost half of all firms feel they can do well enough without making such gifts. Part of the reason for this is that although businessmen do generally prefer to see the Conservatives in power, any picture of the Tories automatically acting in the best interests of business, or business having no influence over Labour politicians is grossly over-simplistic. This becomes

clear when we turn to consider what businessmen said about the
relationship between them and successive governments.

That the business viewpoint and Tory Party philosophy are far
from the same thing may someday be demonstrated when a history
of the Heath government with fuller access to all sources, is
written. The story appears to have been one of disillusion on
both sides. In 1970 businessmen seem to have felt they were
getting a government highly favourable to, and appreciative of,
business interests. The composition of the government suggested
this, as did the government's intentions: to cut taxation, to
support market capitalism, promote expansion and deal with the
deterioration of British industrial relations.

The reality was rather different. The 'no lame ducks' policy
was abandoned in some notable cases. The expansionist policy
brought with it high inflation, and subsequent pay policy. The
industrial relations legislation rather than promoting industrial
peace had the opposite effect.

To what extent was Heath doing what industrialists wanted?
The prevailing feeling amongst those interviewed, who were of
course speaking in retrospect, is that though many shared his
aims, many were also unhappy about the methods and tactics
adopted in achieving them. Many businessmen felt that the government did not use their advice, or consult them sufficiently. A
number echoed the feelings of one who said: 'I've been to
Chequers twice for lunch with Heath but you know, throughout
lunch he never mentioned, he never said, What do you think
about what the government is doing? - or the reaction of your
workers, like any intelligent leader would.'

The directors and chief executives from commercial firms also
tended to feel that the Heath government was closer to the City
than to them, and one or two pictured Labour as being close to
the unions, the Conservatives to the City, with them left unloved
by either party.

Thus it was the City influence which was blamed by some for
the Tories' handling of the Industrial Relations Act, and its consequent disruption. Further, the City was blamed for the final,
and from the Conservative Party point of view, disastrous, confrontation with the miners. As one chairman of an engineering
company put it:

'I don't think Edward Heath was well advised to listen to the
City. . . . I mean, one could go on about that: I was with him
the week before the election and he told me he wasn't going to
call an election. . . . He could have got the miners back to
work more quickly without an election and stayed in power. But
he didn't do it, because he was rolled upon. . . . He was rolled
upon by the Party, and the _____ the - people in the City, I
think, who said we just can't go on like this, we can't go on
with the country working at half time; but it was silly because
that had all been done and the goal was in sight, actually. His
nerve was broken, I think.'

There were those, however, who were apparently ready to take up the same battles again. Thus one peer, head of an industrial firm, who sat on several City boards, said:

'If the Conservative government is ready to tackle the unions. . . . which Heath in 1974 set out at putting over as the issue of that election but failed to press home, which is why he lost, I think. . . . If the government will tackle the unions, then, OK, I would vote Conservative. Last time the Conservative government got in they leant over backwards to win and woo the unions to no avail and antagonised the Conservative part of industry who put them in.'

I have indicated earlier, the changing mood of businessmen during the period of interviewing, and this has to be borne in mind in considering the view that businessmen took of their relationships with government. The earlier interviews took place in 1974, when there was much talk among businessmen of 'trade unions holding the country to ransom', and so on. But by the time of the interviews on which this chapter is based, late 1975, early 1976, there were obvious signs of a change of mood, re-flecting, as one said, their view 'that the unions were beginning to take responsibility'. Some certainly felt that strong lobbying was required, for as one director remarked:

'Well some people see it differently - you could take the view that we've seen it all before - the Attlee government, the Wilson government of 1964 were going to change the world, and it all got lost in sheer inertia, and things went on much as before. But you could take the view that this government is a much more grave thing.'

But in another company, in the same period (mid-1975) a director went so far as to say: 'I think they [businessmen] influ-ence the government because there can be no doubt that now we are having a Conservative government, aren't we? In the policies that are being adopted.' And by the time the last of the inter-views were done confidence seems to have returned. The first stage of a pay policy had been completed. and a second nego-tiated. The Industry Act had gone through, and the N.E.B. set up, but even in April 1977 only one planning agreement - that with Chrysler UK - had been signed. Businessmen were worried about their cash flow, and from the government side about price control, management salaries and the Bullock Committee; but once again they seemed to have learned to live with Labour.

8.6 PERCEPTIONS OF POWER UNDER A LABOUR GOVERNMENT

I have suggested that businessmen participate directly in politics to a lesser extent than in the past, and that they cannot depend on the support of a particular party to guarantee that what they want will be transmitted into political action. The traditional party of business has not been successful enough: and even when in power does not necessarily respond to business needs.

The result of this, therefore, is that, perhaps more than in the

past, businessmen are forced to be lobbyists. The direct questioning of business directors was intended to ascertain the extent,
methods and success of lobbying, most particularly, of course,
when a Labour government was in power.

In very general terms, I would summarise the business view of
power in Britain as follows: the government, that is, in practice
the cabinet plus senior civil servants, controls business, not
business the government. From the business point of view, the
power game is not a balanced one, for trade union leaders are
conceived as having a significant vetoing effect on government
action.

In effect, whereas union leaders have power, industrialists and
financiers have influence in government affairs. The men interviewed in this study did not feel that they could in any way press-
urise the government; except perhaps by publicising the adverse
effects of government activity.

It may be mentioned that some heads of multinational companies
were tackled on the possibility of threatening to divert investment if the government failed to co-operate; but though diversion
of investment was seen as a probable result of a poor climate for
business, no chief executive thought this could be used as a bargaining counter. Several reasons were given: first, investment
cannot be diverted overnight, and in any case the effects of such
diversion might only be felt in a few years time when the party
in power had changed. Second, it is difficult to do, since the
Treasury keeps tight control on the outflow of capital (though
this would no longer be a factor). Third, the threat of such
action invited retaliation.

Leaving aside trade union leaders, the power-holders, as businessmen saw it, are the cabinet ministers and senior civil servants - very roughly, under-secretary level and above. Local
government issues, apart from obtaining planning permission for
offices or factories, were of relatively minor importance to them.
Nor were MPs outside the cabinet accorded much power, though
there were thought to be situations in which access to them could
be useful.

Those interviewed claimed to be far from happy about the
effects of government on them and their companies. They accused
both politicians and civil servants of knowing far too little about
business. Though the intellect of top civil servants was never
questioned, their first-hand knowledge of the particular industries
they deal with was: in particular the tendency for civil servants
to move to new areas every two to three years, was criticised.[7]

There have been efforts since the early 1960's to move industry
and government closer, on the lines of the French indicative
planning system. But British businessmen still drew unfavourable
contrasts between their position and that of their French, German
or even American equivalents. A particular complaint was of the
enormous volume of legislation aimed at industry. The result of
these factors is that much business activity in relation to government is negative - aimed at correcting or preventing courses of

action rather than steering government in a desired direction.

In the more detailed consideration of businessmen's interaction with state officials that follows, I will consider in turn three questions:

(a) What issues bring businessmen, politicians and civil servants together?

(b) How do businessmen attempt to influence the state officials?

(c) How effective is this from the business point of view?

8.7 THE ISSUES

Aside from the general discussion, those interviewed were asked to give examples of particular issues over which they had tried, or were trying, to influence the government. The responses seem to fall broadly into four main issue-areas, with a fifth, at present less important. These were:

(a) the content of government legislation;

(b) the provisions of the budget: fiscal issues and government spending;

(c) areas of regulation determined outside parliament:
Board of Trade regulations: monopoly control, the application of wage control;

(d) broad areas of government policy and decision-making, most notably economic strategy;

(e) an additional small category may be added of 'international issues', an area which may be of increasing importance in the future.

To illustrate the full range of topics over which those interviewed claimed to have approached government I have listed all of them under the five headings in Table 8.6.

Table 8.6   Total list of issues mentioned by businessmen

(Seventy men were asked about this from sixty-two companies. Four men specifically said they and their company had not attempted to have any contact or influence. Seventeen others, although they spoke in general terms, did not produce examples. Therefore, these issues come from forty-one companies.)

In this table issues of current (1974-6) concern are signified by (C), those from before this period by (P).

1 *Legislation*

1.1	Consumer Credit Act	(P)	
1.2	Regional Development Act	(P)	
1.3	Finance Acts (and see below)	(C)	
1.4	Weights and Measures legislation – Metrication Bill	(C)	
1.5	Industrial Relations Act – closed shop legislation	(C)	
1.6	Prices and incomes legislation	(C)	6 men referred to this (see also 3.11)
1.7	Industry Bill – especially planning agreements	(C)	
1.8	Petroleum Bill	(C)	

Table 8.6   Total list of issues mentioned by businessmen (continued)

1.9	Policyholders Protection Bill	(C)
1.10	Dock Labour Act	(C)
1.11	Nationalisation of Aircraft/Shipping	(C)

2 The budget/provisions of the Finance Act/government spending

2.1	Tax concessions in the budget on investment	(C)	
2.2	Taxation of middle management	(C)	6 men referred to this
2.3	Taxation of profits realised from stock appreciation	(C)	2 men referred to this
2.4	{ Purchases by government for defence purposes	(C)	
	{ Purchases by Post Office	(C)	

3 Interpretation of government regulations; the operation of nationalised industry etc.

3.1	Government restrictions on housebuilding	(P)	
3.2	Failure by a company to pay customs import duty	(P)	
3.3	Buying of a steelworks from a nationalised industry	(P)	
3.4	Import of foreign agricultural products	(P)	
3.5	Import tariffs—export licences, chemical industry	(C)	
3.6	Restriction on amount of foreign construction of North Sea oil rigs	(C)	
3.7	Import quotas on TV tubes	(C)	
3.8	Board of Trade regulations affecting insurance companies	(C)	
3.9	Planning permission for a new factory	(C)	
3.10	The operation of planning law affecting retail sites	(C)	
3.11	Provisions of the Price Code	(C)	2 men referred to this
3.12	Food subsidies	(C)	
3.13	Will British Leyland build foundries for car parts – or will an outside company?	(C)	

4 Miscellaneous government policy

4.1	Economic policy	(C)	Matters for consultation and discussion between government and industry
4.2	Employee relations and the Bullock Report	(C)	
4.3	The level of investment in British industry and the causes of it	(C)	
4.4	Businessmen going along with Ministers and civil servants on trips abroad	(C)	
		(C)	

5 International affairs

5.1	Tariffs on entering EFTA	(P)
5.2	EEC regulations regarding monopoly	(C)
5.3	EEC legislation	(C)

This list is clearly not an exhaustive list of the issues which concerned businessmen at the time of the interviews nor even of those concerning the men who were interviewed. But it does give an idea of the very wide range of issues with which business is concerned: regional policy, housing, economic policy, taxation, industrial relations, insurance, subsidies, import quotas - all areas of wide public significance which are also areas in which businessmen feel their firms have a major stake and where they, in turn, have a major concern in getting their viewpoint across to government.

8.8 CHANNELS OF INFLUENCE

There would appear to be five major ways of influencing government. These, however, are not interchangeable: it is very much a question of horses for courses. The methods are:
(a) *Via personal contacts* - utilising friends, members of clubs, people known from civil service days, fellow directors, etc. It was often said that this is the most effective method. People in government quite naturally tend to be more prepared to talk to, have lunch with, or meet formally with, people they already know. As was pointed out earlier, there has always been among the leaders of industry, a number of men who have spent some time in the civil service (See Table 8.3). In the past these tended to be men who had spent a period in the civil service during the war: now they are recruited direct.

Reliance on private contacts alone, however, no longer appears to form the basis of much contact between government and business. Nor, indeed, does it appear to guarantee enough contact. The reasons are clear: on both sides there is a far greater desire than in the past to talk to the other side. The administration is so involved with controlling, regulating and encouraging industry that it has to know what is going on there. The issues are more complex than they were in the past. At the same time, the number of men who can comfortably operate as go-betweens is proportionally less. Politics and business are full-time occupations.

Much has been made in the literature of shared clubs, and interlocking directorates as means of inter-access. These may be ways by which businessmen can communicate with one another, and come to common viewpoints over certain issues which concern them. But as means of contact with politicians or civil servants they are just not adequate. Although the extent of the interlocking directorships amongst the large corporations has been well-demonstrated by other researchers, (see chapter 1) the extent of interlocking with the government in power has not been shown to be similarly great in Britain. The same applies to the 'exclusive' social clubs: as we saw earlier, only around 40 per cent of businessmen are likely to be members of such clubs, and in any case, Labour politicians often do not favour them. Nor should it be assumed that civil servants do. Chapman (1970) found that only

four out of the thirty-five members of the Administrative Class
whom he interviewed were members of such clubs (though they
would have been younger than the businessmen studied here).

Personal contacts are very useful where they exist and to show
just how useful, I have reproduced a series of case studies in
Appendix 2 which show the variety and range of such contacts.
Businessmen certainly cultivate them. But, in themselves, they
seem to be too haphazard a method of influence. Thus only four
men mentioned this as the way of influencing government: and
all were members of what were called earlier the 'social elite'
by background, and it may be that this group did depend on
such contacts to a far greater extent in the past.

(b) *By direct approach.* Because businessmen see cabinet
ministers and senior civil servants as the men with power, extensive reports were made of their attempts to influence these groups
by direct approach. Inviting one to lunch, or getting invited, is
the most usual way. (By all accounts some civil servants and
ministers must spend most days at business lunches.) Ministers
and civil servants are open to such approaches.

Contacts formed this way may be called 'semi-formal'. They are
not the informal kind mentioned in the last section, but they
are not as formal as approaches by trade associations or the CBI.
A minister going to lunch may discuss general or specific topics,
of great or no relevance to the businessmen concerned.

This appeared to be the most widely used form of lobbying.
However, it has its limitations. For one thing, cabinet ministers
and civil servants will only go to lunch at the bigger companies.
Further, though discussions at such luncheons can be used to
put across a general viewpoint (for example on price control, or
management salaries), only in certain circumstances may a company lobby in this way on its own behalf. It was often asserted
that, 'It is not good to be thought to be speaking only for your
own interest'. or 'Civil servants like to preserve their neutrality'. [8]

(c) *The CBI.* The CBI is the most public of the business lobby
methods. It is the national voice of business on major political
policy decisions. However, at the time of the interviews, there
was widespread dissatisfaction with the effectiveness of it. In
practice, it was the most frequently cited way of exerting political influence, though views of it ranged from 'Bloody useless' to
'the only way we've got'. [9]

The dissatisfaction was only partly to do with the actual personalities or efficiency of the organisation. Rather, it stemmed
from its very nature: the CBI represents, supposedly, the views
of all companies, large and small. Its members include both private
industry and the nationalised industries. In this situation, many
of the respondents pointed out the difficulty of getting a united
viewpoint. It was believed, probably not without reason, that
large companies, and indeed a small clique of representatives
from such companies, dominated CBI policy. Thus the CBI represents big business - but that is not all industry. Further, it
has to come to a united viewpoint in situations where there may be

real divisions between sectors of the business community: between producers of goods and retailers, for example.
(d) *Trade Associations*. Contrastingly, trade associations were accepted as a useful way of putting across the point of view of companies in a particular sector.[10]
(e) *Publicity*. Businessmen can resort in certain situations to the use of the mass media in an attempt to win public opinion to their side. There are a number of media open to them: the annual report, newspaper interviews, TV appearances, and so on. In practice, businessmen rarely saw these as a method of directly influencing government. There are several reasons for this amongst them: (a) businessmen see themselves as ineffective users of the media; (b) their view of power sees a small group of men at the head of the nation (a model, perhaps, drawn from business enterprise). To influence, one must influence them. Paradoxically, some men did suggest that politicians were only interested in getting votes, but they themselves did not think of directly affecting issues this way. I return to this below.

Now, as already remarked, some of these methods of influencing government are seen as more appropriate in some situations than others. Further, it was accepted that one's message was far more likely to be well received if one spoke for a particular sector of industry. To take an example: one head of a building firm interviewed said that his company was much affected by the demand for housing, itself liable to be affected by government policy. The firm, although large, could not make a direct approach to government. The man said:

'When I was President of the Builders' Federation in 1965 we wanted to influence government in its attitude to housing. We went to talk to the minister, Crossman at that time, to say that the industry had the capacity to build very many more houses than it was being allowed to build at that time, and pressed for restrictions to be relaxed – and we succeeded.'

However, the 'collective voice' can be applied by individuals. Thus, for example, a director of a very large company said:

'The CBI has a very heavy job to try and compete with the sheer flow of legislation, so we have to try to get directly involved. For example, at the committee stage of a Bill recently we got hold of a Conservative MP and pumped a few ideas into him. He had some ideas of his own, some of them good, but it was ours he put across in the discussion.'

When it comes to more specific issues, however, the company must make a direct approach to the minister involved, or civil servants. Thus the chairman of a food company said:

'Shirley Williams controls the price of bread: we've been in a loss making situation for about a year; over the last year and a half we've been educating Shirley Williams and Fred Peart. Either of them could give a run-down on the state of the food industry and the problems of it. All things being equal they would both agree to ease restrictions and put us in a sensible position. But they go to cabinet – if they want to start altering

the price code the unions want to alter voluntary restraint and
so they haven't been able to.'
These contacts can easily be made, especially if the company
is large enough. Yet there are situations when personal friendships accomplish what other contacts fail to do. One retired M.D.
related how he utilised a personal friendship with a civil servant
(Ted) when his company had inadvertently failed to pay customs
dues:

'I was M.D. of [——]. . . . [——] had been breaking the law.
We hadn't been paying something, customs or something or
other. We'd made a mistake. And those characters wanted
hundreds of thousands of pounds off us. So I spoke to Ted,
and said, look we've made a mistake .... And he said ....
"Get in touch with so and so, and go and see him, say you're
terribly sorry. I'll speak to him before you do." The upshot
was, we didn't pay anything.'

Because the method used varied with the issue it is impossible
to generalise as to which will be most effective. Respondents were
asked to state which methods they had used (Tables 8.7 and 8.8),
and no particular preferences or differences amongst different
types of company emerged, except for the important but unsur-
prising principle that the larger the company, the more direct its
access to those in power, especially cabinet ministers. Smaller
companies may have to make greater use of their local MPs or
other politicians.

Table 8.7 How different types of company attempt to influence government

	Type of control		
	All	*Bureaucratic*	*Family/Entrepreneur*
Number giving answer	57	37	20
Via access to			
Cabinet ministers	16(28)	12	4
Other politicians, esp. MPs	12(21)	8	4
Civil servants	16(28)	12	4
Through the CBI	19(33)	14	5
Trade associations	19(33)	10	9
Other*	13(23)	8	5

*Other would include the use of personal contact, access via the British Institute of
 Management, Institute of Directors, NEDO, etc.

(Chi-squared tests show no significant difference between groupings.)

It would be wrong, however, to make much of an inference from

Table 8.7 since respondents were asked which methods they did use; they were not probed on the ones they did not mention. Thus not mentioning the CBI is not a clear indication that a man does not see it as a channel of business opinion. We may assume that business men use all the channels they believe are available to them. The next table, however, indicates that certain are not thought to be open to some, but are to others, i.e. access to cabinet ministers (Table 8.8).

Table 8.8   Type of access to political decision-makers – by size of company

Size of company:	Total	Top 20	Commerce 21-90	91-180	Finance
No. giving a classifiable answer	57(100)	6	29	19	3
Access via					
Cabinet ministers	16(28)	5	7	2	2
Other politicians	12(21)	2	7	3	0
Civil servants	16(28)	2	10	2	2
The CBI	19(33)	3	8	8	0
Trade associations	19(33)	1	10	6	2
Other	13(23)	1	4	7	1

From this table we see that men in the largest top twenty companies specifically mentioned contact with a Cabinet minister in five out of six cases; yet only seven of the next twenty-nine largest companies mentioned this, and a further two of the next nineteen. Middle size companies (in terms of this table) seemed to use civil servants and politicians more than ministers.

Men in the largest companies mentioned more channels of influence on average (the six men mentioned fourteen, that is, 2.3 per company) than companies in the other size ranges. (forty-six from twenty-nine companies, approx 1.5 per company, and twenty-eight from nineteen companies, approx 1.5). It seems reasonable to infer that very large companies do have more channels of influence, and are thus more influential than those in the next size ranges. Clearly, the numbers of men appearing in the cells of these tables are small for statistical purposes. Nevertheless, the trends they indicate are at least in line with what common sense would suggest.

8.9 HOW SUCCESSFUL IS THE BUSINESS LOBBY?

Again, there can be no single answer about the success of businessmen's lobbying. To sum up the feelings of these respondents they were that: so far as preventing or altering major pieces of

legislation goes, if a political party is pledged by its manifesto to
do something then nothing can be done to stop it altogether. However, much can be done to influence the drafting by civil servants
of legislation - to affect the exact provisions of particular bills.
As we have seen, too, a certain amount can be done on particular
regulations - that is, the interpretation of existing law.

Contrast these two examples: much was written in the Press
about the nationalisation of shipbuilding and aircraft. Corporations
affected by this have used all means to publicise their case, but a
chairman whose company was to be affected drastically by the Act
stated: 'There's no use getting in a lather of fright about it. The
Labour party came into power pledged to do it, and it will do so.
But we have made it clear we think it a bad thing.' Contrastingly,
the insurance industry was not particularly pleased with the
Policyholders Protection Bill, brought before Parliament after the
notorious failure of some companies. The industry took the view
that if people bought cheap insurance from companies which subsequently failed, the successful companies should not be forced
to pick up the pieces, but an insurance company director said:

'Let's take the Policyholders Protection Bill which is now before
parliament. The Bill that's before Parliament is very different
from the one that was originally drafted. In this case the industry
and government got together . . . the government thought the
protection ought to be wider than we did . . . we've reached a
compromise situation.'

In the next table (Table 8.9) I have taken twenty issues, some
of which have been discussed, and indicated both the channel of
influence and the outcome from the business point of view. This
may give some picture of how business influence works on different issues and the variability of its success.

It will be clear that there were several major issues of general
concern to industry (as opposed to particular firms or sectors)
during the period of the interviews. One of these was the fact
that inflation pushed up company profits artificially, simply
because of the stocks of raw material which the companies held.
This was resolved fairly early on, by the chancellor making
special concessions on corporation tax.

The other issues were price control and the taxation of middle
and higher management salaries. Industry found it much harder
to get what it wanted here. So far as the latter issue goes, it was
a continuing concern of managers right throughout the period of
the interviews. Chairmen made constant references to it in their
speeches. Large companies produced evidence on it to the Diamond
Commission (1974). Surveys were done, academics wrote about it.
From what they said in the interviews, it would appear that businessmen never lost an opportunity to express their feelings on
the topic to government ministers. Finally, the chancellor did
make tax concessions in his budget of April 1976.

On price control, the politics were even more difficult from the
Labour government's point of view. Whether they wanted to allow
price rises or not, price control was seen as necessary if the

Table 8.9   The outcome of twenty issues on which business tried to influence government

Issue	Method of access	Outcome
Committee stage of Bill	Company invites Conservative MP to lunch	MP puts forward company's ideas in committee
Consumer Credit Act	Mail Order Trade Federation meets civil servants	Some success
Government regional policy	Company chairman persuades CBI – who put case to government	Failed
Closed shop legislation – as it affects press	Company chairman and newspaper editors see ministers	Failed
Industry Bill – planning agreements	Large company directors see Benn and Wilson on 2 occasions	Some success claimed
Petroleum Bill	Company chairman meets ministers/civil servants	Some success
Shipbuilding/aircraft nationalisation	All methods and widespread publicity	Failed
Policyholders Protection Bill	Industry managers work with civil servants	Limited success
Budget concessions – tax relief on investments	Company chairman meets senior civil servants at Chamber of Commerce party, 'lectures' them	Measures appear in budget (chairman claims credit)
Relaxation of Building Regulations (1965)	Head of trade association meets minister	Success
Agricultural subsidies	Company chairman meets relevant ministers	Some success
Price of bread	Company chairman meets relevant ministers	No success
Price Check Scheme	Trade association and various chairmen meet minister	A success for Industry?
Import quotas on foreign agricultural produce (Mid 60's)	Chairman utilises contacts from civil service formed in war	Success
Import quotas on TV tubes	Chairman goes to prime minister	Failed
Board of Trade Regulations – Insurance	Insurance company managers argue with civil servants	Success
Company fails to pay customs duty	M.D. uses personal contacts with civil service	Duty waived
Company purchases furnace from British Steel	Chairman goes to chancellor of the exchequer	Success
Company wanted to build foundries, instead of British Leyland	Company chairman meets Lord Ryder and other members of the NEB	Unresolved at time of interview
Price Control – foundry products	Chairman goes to minister	Failed

unions were to agree to wage restraint. A number of chairmen,
particularly in the food industry, recounted their efforts to influence Shirley Williams, (who is widely admired amongst them). Yet
here, as on many issues, they were not sure of their success.
Mrs Williams appeared to understand their problems, they said,
but maintained that the cabinet would not accept price rises.

Finally, after fairly continuous lobbying for two years, a certain amount of success was claimed; though for obvious reasons
business did not publicise it as such:

'Well, let's be fair - this price check scheme; we did a deal. . . .
We agreed not to say it was just window dressing, which it is;
and [they] agreed not to make it, let us say, an indictable
offence if any of us were not carrying it out to the letter of
the law. It really was as bad as that. This scheme is just a lot
of malarkey.

The position is: Shirley Williams has told us that she sees from
the figures she knows, it's not price control that has kept prices
down in the food trade but competition. But she can't get that
over to the trade unions, while she is getting agreement from
the trade unions over wage control, she must retain price control.'
(Head of large supermarket chain)

Businessmen, then, do have considerable influence. They
believe they have little effect on the overall legislation programme,
but they can affect the content of legislation, and they have an
impact, too, on the conduct of the administration.

Yet, overall, it must be said that businessmen saw themselves
as losers in the power game. Each of the seventy interviewed was
asked which groups had the most power: the civil service, the
unions, the City, or businessmen in industry. They found it a
difficult question to answer. There was no doubt in their minds
that the elected ministers held the ultimate power. And virtually
everybody saw both the civil service and the leaders of the big
unions as more powerful than businessmen. As to which of the
latter groups had more power, opinions varied.

Again many saw the City as a powerful group, but those interviewed did not seem clear just how powerful it is. They could not
put all the groups together on a simple measuring scale of power.
There was, though, a strong feeling that the City institutions
along with the Bank of England were groups that a government
could not afford to ignore.

8.10 THE MASS MEDIA

In chapter 1 I discussed the role of the business elite as creators
and sustainers of ideology. The obvious way for them to do this
is through the mass media. It is therefore of some interest to note
that businessmen felt that they had lost out in the struggle to put
their point of view across in the media.

Many observers have claimed that the media in a capitalist

society are far from neutral, and national daily papers in particular have been thought to support the *status quo*. It would be
wrong to think that businessmen saw these or the other media
this way. Rather, they saw positive action as necessary to put
across a desirable view of themselves. For example, the infla-
tionary boom of 1973-4 led to some very high increases in gross
profits, at a time when wage restraint was being asked for by
the government.

Naturally, the papers commented on this. From early 1974,
therefore, there were grave attempts by companies to explain,
via newspaper advertisements, 'the need for profits'. Indeed,
during this time businessmen complained often during interviews
that profit had become a dirty word, or 'profits are the seedcorn
of the future but people don't realise this'.

But the respondents were less concerned with the newspapers
as a medium for their message than with television. Rightly or
not, they ascribed to TV enormous influence and power to affect
the mass of people. And it was on TV in particular that they felt
business loses out. Almost all the men interviewed said that
businessmen did not appear often enough on TV; many said that
when they did appear, they were poor performers. Many, too,
criticised themselves in this respect.

The reason is, so they said, that businessmen are 'doers' not
'talkers'. They are not naturally eloquent. Asked to speak against
a politician or a trade unionist they would lose out. The nature,
too, of TV discussions was thought to mitigate in favour of the
pithy exchange and rhetoric, not elaborate explanation of the
complexities of the business world. The result of all this was, to
use a phrase that cropped up more than once 'the case for free
enterprise has gone by default'.[11] Further, the effect of speaking
their minds on certain issues would provoke an unpredictable
reaction from their own workforce.

The respondents compared British businessmen badly in this
respect with their counterparts in America, where, it was said,
industrialists took a more public stance, spoke out on national
issues, and put across the business case. In future they foresaw
a much bigger role for businessmen.

This point is made simply to counteract the somewhat simplistic
view from some quarters that businessmen can simply use the
media for their own ends. From the business perspective the
reverse is thought to be true - the media are thought, if anything,
to have a left-wing bias.

8.11 THE ESTABLISHMENT

In the last chapter I indicated that the 'upper class' was seen by
businessmen as unimportant, somehow divorced from the mainstream of society. In this chapter I have indicated the relatively
formal view of power they took, in which cabinet ministers and
civil servants are presented as the real power-holders in Britain,

and the group whom businessmen must attempt to influence through lobbying.

However, past observers of British political life have often drawn attention to the importance of an informal network of influence based on social contact and position, within the power structure of Britain. Perhaps the most used term for this informal grouping is 'the establishment', a name given to it by Henry Fairlie (see for example Fairlie, 1955a, b and c).[12]

I have suggested in this chapter that informal connections are extremely valuable, and are probably the most effective methods of influence where they can be used (see also Appendix 2), and if businessmen use other methods it may well be only because they have to, because informal methods are either not available or seen as inappropriate.

Although no systematic questions were included in the interviews, the term 'establishment' was used by some businessmen, and this allowed for some exploration of what the term meant to them. It appears to have several meanings. For some, it meant no more than a different name for the upper class, or received dogma.

From the majority, I would estimate around two-thirds, however, came a different impression. The establishment to them meant power; and power in Britain means cabinet ministers and civil servants. The business establishment is those businessmen who are consistently influential as a group, they know one another and they know the men in Whitehall and Downing Street. This group overlaps and interlocks with a City establishment, and with trade union leaders and other groups.

Here is a definition of the establishment, by the chairman of the third biggest company in this study:

'There is a group, mainly gyrating around Whitehall, that do seem to be in on many of the national decisions, and I suppose that of course includes politicians; it includes the leading civil servants, it includes bankers, it includes the heads of big companies, it includes quite a number of academics, important journalists, and I suppose you could say that happens in any society. They're certainly not there by birth as they may have been in the past; but they are there by virtue of doing key jobs, and they seem to meet one another, and to turn up at the same meetings, and the same dinners, and to turn up at the same get togethers. And of course in that group one must include trade union leaders. They're certainly in the establishment - the top 3, Mr Jack Jones, Mr Hugh Scanlon, Mr Len Murray - certainly one sees them and they're in the establishment, no doubt about it . . . . That there is a clique of people manipulating things, that's not so - but there are a group of people who turn up wherever important decisions are being taken.'

This man saw himself as 'on the fringes' of the establishment. His definition was relatively precise. Other men found it harder to define, some mentioning the City particularly, others the civil servants. Another man, who saw himself as sometimes 'in', some-

times out of the establishment, said it was:
'a thing which is not the upper class but has an element of
upper class about it, but has been very flexible and has
extended its boundaries and embraced others to respond to the
situation it finds itself in.'

(Q. Who comes into it?)

'Well nobody ever knows because it's not defined. It's that
area that has influence on society; on law-making and the like,
by cross consultation, it has a lot of influence on appointments,
very frequently public appointments, indeed even possibly
ministerial appointments by advice and consultation. Now people
flit in and out of the establishment. The establishment is a very
real thing, no doubt about it, it's a very interesting thing.
People flit in and out according to whether they're "in" or
"out".'
Other men, perhaps themselves less involved with the establishment, tended to see it as based in the City: one man quoted Jim
Slater (a friend of his), 'You never meet the establishment till
you've done wrong.' Slater, of all people, should know (see also
Appendix 2).
Those perhaps most involved pictured the establishment as
composed of different groups, which overlap: an industrial
establishment, a City establishment, the union leaders, the civil
servants, the politicians.
It was not hard for them, either, to think of figures who are
in it, Lord Aldington: a former minister, deputy Chairman
of the Conservative Party, Chairman of Grindlay's Bank, of
Sun Alliance, deputy chairman of GEC, and a director of Lloyds
Bank, a man who links politics, the City and industry; Lord
Greenhill: a former head of the diplomatic service, a governor
of the BBC, a director of BP and of British Leyland, also of
Warburgs, the merchant bank, of an insurance company and
British American Tobacco; Lord Plowden: former civil servant,
Chairman of Tube Investments, and so on.
The establishment is an elite of influence. They come from
people who are already elites within certain institutional spheres:
unions, business, the City and government. Yet they do not
monopolise influence; many other men who are chairmen of large
companies can have access and influence when occasion demands.
The findings here are very much in line with recent research
conducted in Britain by Mougel (1978). Mougel sent questionnaires to and interviewed a mixed group, including aristocracy,
gentry, politicians, businessmen, public school headmasters and
university dons. Questionnaires were completed by 138 of those
approached, and 53 were interviewed.
Mougel found that 85 per cent accepted the existence of the
establishment, 68 per cent saying they were members of it. The
most frequently chosen (by 64 per cent) definition of the establishment was 'the whole group of people in power'. The composi-

tion of the establishment, as viewed by Mougel's respondents, reflects the findings among businessmen reported here. The power-holders, and percentages mentioning each were said to be: government ministers and senior civil servants (81.5 per cent); bankers (81 per cent); High Court Judges (81 per cent); businessmen (78 per cent); High Anglican clergy (61.5 per cent); top university dons (58.5 per cent); senior doctors (55 per cent); senior army officers (54 per cent) and MPs (42 per cent). Not on the list presented by Mougel, but spontaneously added by 20 per cent, were trade union officials.

Reverting to the business point of view, it seems that the establishment has changed with time. It no longer consists of people with a known commonality of interest. Union leaders and politicians may well be arguing for different things. For union leaders, however, to spend too long in this situation has obvious problems if they are not to become cut off from the rank and file. The peculiar result of intermixing amongst the establishment is that a number of chairmen were better able to recount what Jack Jones or Clive Jenkins had told them recently than what any of their own workforce were thinking, or what their own experience had taught them about industrial relations.

The establishment, then, is not there by birth so much as by position; not everybody welcomed that or thought it was good for the country; said one entrepreneur:

'The developed society, the integrated society, started to decay I don't know when, but the decay was complete really when Macmillan went . . . . That, I think, is the root of our troubles. This is my own view - I've not heard it anywhere else. But when the establishment such as it is somehow drifted away from the core and force of public affairs then you've got trouble. And this is what has happened . . . . The mainstream of affairs is political and civil service. The establishment is bits of the financial and aristocratic hierarchy who basically get on with their work. But they are detached from the main stream of events. And industry, I'm sorry to say, manufacturing industry, doesn't really tie into it either. Now it used to: we had great social mobility. The successful industrialist could become a member of "society" and therefore influential to the establishment. The establishment was very important in politics but not now.'

But this was an extreme and unusual view from a man who bemoaned the passing of the entrepreneur and the family proprietor. The more usual view was that the nature of the establishment has changed, and whilst many of its members do not hold political office, they are influential none the less.

8.12 SUMMARY AND CONCLUSIONS

In this chapter the involvement of the heads (chairmen and chief executives) of large companies in interaction with the state elite was examined, and certain hypotheses developed. It was suggested that their direct political involvement, and involvement in certain sorts of local activity, has declined in the course of this century. Thus, there is probably less overlap than in the past between the personnel who comprise the state elite and those who comprise the business elite. At the same time, though businessmen continue to support the Conservative Party, they have not found this recently to be an effective way of instituting their wishes in state decision-making.

Businessmen regard themselves as at a disadvantage in the context of political power. Ultimate power in national politics lies with a small group of cabinet ministers and a similar sized body of senior civil servants. Yet over this group it was the trade union leaders who had most influence at the time of interviewing; and they were perceived as making better use of the media, particularly T.V.

Despite this, most of those interviewed recognised that they can influence national decision-making. Quite possibly they tended to underestimate this. Evidence was collected from their own statements that showed an extremely wide interest and involvement in policies and decisions concerning economic policy, wage and price regulations, taxation, insurance, excise duties, housing, defence spending, the operation of nationalised industries, as well as the more obvious areas of the Industry Act, industrial relations legislation and industrial democracy.

Influence exists on three levels according to how large a firm the man in question heads. But the strategic nature of the firm in relation to the state is also important: in other words, the state involves itself with certain industries more than others, for example, it does involve itself with motor cars, defence and agriculture, does not with restaurants or office equipment, and in the former industries a businessman has greater access to decision-takers.

At the lowest level, the heads of smaller firms have little access to decision-makers: they must work through the trade associations if they are to be effective at all. The CBI is seemingly dominated by large companies. Small companies can go to local MPs in areas where they have factories or offices: but the influence of MPs themselves varies greatly, and some businessmen clearly felt that the MPs they had access to, other than government ministers, were of little influence.

The heads of larger companies have direct access to senior civil servants and the best placed MPs. They dominate the CBI, and, one suspects, the trade associations. Even within this group, however, there is a further division, and perhaps only the heads of the biggest ten to twenty firms have direct access to senior ministers.

Beyond these levels there was perceived to be a group of men who have a more informal effect on power and decision-taking, a group to which one may apply the term 'the establishment'. To be a member of the establishment depends on many factors; one must head a firm of sufficient importance, of course, but, partly through inclination, not all the heads of the largest firms are involved; reputation is important, so to some extent is one's hereditary background; those who come up the company quickly and know other members of the establishment through other channels have a better chance of being noticed. But, granted some means of access, this is not essential. What is essential is to want to belong: an acceptance of an invitation to sit on one government committee, or body, can lead one to an invitation to be involved in others; and to dinners at this or that function, meetings in Whitehall and so on.

These conclusions are obviously drawn on the basis of limited evidence; and perhaps should be considered more as hypotheses for further work. The direction to which the conclusions here lead, however, is one that suggests that sociologists have tended to exaggerate the importance of shared class background, and of personal connections, of shared education, interlocking director-ships and shared social clubs amongst elite groups, even if these are taken only as indicative of shared sets of attitudes.

Rather, I would suggest that it may be a necessary feature of advanced capitalism that contact of the kind so frequently re-ported in this study occurs, and especially in Britain where the national economic performance, which depends on the performance of business, is consistently compared with that of other countries, and where political debate has come to centre on how this perform-ance can be improved.

The result would seem to be that elites on all sides are anxious for contact with one another. As the state seeks to control more and more, so the state officials must know more, and must be more open to approach. Civil servants are conscious of a need to meet with and listen to the heads of business. They are urged by the media, as well as by businessmen to do so. Thus, as Bruce-Gardyne and Lawson (1976) remark, 'Whitehall tends to invent a lobby even where one does not exist.'

However, this does create a dilemma for those who value the democratic process. On the one hand, it has been maintained, for example, by Shonfield (1965), that Britain's poor economic per-formance compared to other nations is partly the result of the failure of co-operation between government and industry. On the other hand, it is clear that much is being decided by elite group-ings which have not been elected. Trade union leaders are the group to whom the charge is most usually applied, as their posi-tion is somewhat public, but as we have seen, top businessmen are ultimately similarly placed. The result is that the specific content of much legislation, the interpretation of it and even its enforcement, become subjects for covert negotiation.

It may be true that a certain elected elite - ministers and those close to them - have the upper hand in this process. But the role of the mass of the public becomes that of deciding which group of negotiators is to hold power for five years. As Edelman (1967) expresses it, politicians make largely symbolic appeals to the voters, and engage in symbolic battles with one another, then,

whilst in office, they begin anew the processes of opinion formulation, reception of lobbyists, and negotiation.

Not only does the picture drawn here correspond badly to the
democratic ideal, it corresponds badly also to the pluralist perspective: for clearly those businessmen who have access to politicians can hardly be considered representative, even of business: rather, they represent big business - the massive, often
diversified and multinational corporations, whose heads formed
the bulk of the respondents in this study. As individuals they
may well be representative of the better-off sections of the middle
class, but certainly not all of it, and, indeed, are likely to be
little interested in the small shareholder (except that they may
personally be in that category).

It is hard to see how the balance of interests that Dahl, Rose
and other pluralists see, can be struck. As we have seen, access
to state officials by the directors of larger companies, in commerce
and the City, is direct and seen as legitimate. And whilst not all
directors by any means engaged in making such contacts, there
are a lot of such businessmen. If one were to assume that only
directors from the top 100 commercial firms, top twenty merchant
banks, top twenty insurance companies, could have access to
senior civil servants, it is hard to think of any other outside
pressure grouping that is so numerous. Businessmen may be the
most influential grouping on senior state officials, not because of
the extensive social contacts they have been viewed as having,
though these exist and are used as well, but because there are
so many of them, and they work actively at such contacts, and
the contacts are viewed as legitimate and necessary. It is perhaps an open question as to whether that is a peculiar feature of
British capitalism, or of Western capitalism, at this stage, or a
necessary condition for advanced capitalism to function.

9 CONCLUSION

9.1 INTRODUCTION

In setting out the objectives of this study I emphasised its exploratory and evolutionary nature. The objectives were therefore rather open: to investigate the possibilities of access to the business elite; to examine businessmen's meaning systems; and to investigate thereby some aspects of their behaviour as controllers of business firms and political influentials.

In this chapter I try to bring together and summarise the findings; take a more critical look at them, and draw out some implications. The chapter is organised into four sections, looking in turn at:
(a) the assumptions of the study;
(b) the main findings;
(c) the implications for future theory and research;
(d) the implication outside of sociological debate.

9.2 THE ASSUMPTIONS OF THE STUDY

In undertaking any piece of research it is necessary to make certain assumptions as to the relevant universe to be researched, the variables to be investigated and the methodology to be used. As far as possible, one draws on previous research, and the theory one is investigating, but at some stages hard decisions are required to make research practicable. I made several presumptions in this study, and it is worth considering how these stood up in practice.

The first assumption was that there is an elite among businessmen, a group whose members, while essentially doing the same tasks within the firm as other businessmen, take part in these and certain other activities in a way that makes them significantly different from the majority of company directors.

I specified the top directors in the bigger firms and financial institutions as the business elite. I claimed that it would not be satisfactory, therefore, to study men in lower managerial positions, or heading small localised companies, if we wished to generalise about the business elite.

I still hold that this assumption is justified, and to add to my earlier arguments would point to some of the evidence which is presented here. In chapter 4 which is the family background, education, training and career paths of the men in the study were discussed. The data confirmed the findings of previous studies: the businessmen were very likely to come from families where the father was in a high-status occupation; to have attended a public school, and an Oxbridge college, and to have obtained professional qualifications. In all aspects of their recruitment it seems likely that they differed from much of lower management or the heads of smaller firms.

When I discussed the role of the director in chapter 1, I pointed out his distinctive role in the allocation of capital, and for strategic planning and policy-formation in the company. The discussions with respondents in this study confirmed that, as far as they could specify them, they did see these as the distinctive features of their jobs. And some even stated that not all members of the main board would have such roles. Thus, although managers lower down in the companies might be involved in these tasks, it may still be argued that research among them would not throw the same light on the distinctive role of main board members.

I also ascribed to the business elite potential for exercising political power or influence, and the, admittedly limited, examination of businessmen's attempts to lobby civil servants and politicians did indicate that the access they had to such people varied with their personal standing, connections and the size of firm they headed.

Thus I would claim that the available evidence does suggest that there is an elite even among men with the title director, and that it would not be satisfactory to study men in managerial roles, or heading smaller firms if one were interested in the beliefs and values of this elite. However, this does not mean that the business elite can be specified by any simple criteria or that all men in similar positions play the rules ascribed to the business elite in chapter 1. But in that chapter I suggested the size of firm a person heads as an obvious variable which would affect their beliefs and attitudes and there was some evidence for this in the empirical findings.

I put forward two other propositions as to variables which would be important: first, the ownership position of the businessman; and second, the type of company he or she headed, specified in terms of its activities.

These raise more difficult issues. I derived the categories of bureaucrat, family businessman and entrepreneur on the basis of the discussion of the ownership and control debate. I gave an individual location within these categories to each businessman interviewed. I discussed some of the objections to the use of such categorisation in chapter 1: for example, that bureaucrats may be fronts for control that is exercised by wealthy individuals, banks or financial institutions, or that all businessmen are by other standards wealthy men, with most of that wealth held in industrial capital, and thus sharing common interests.

I cannot fully answer these objections. I did, however, show (chapter 4) that family businessmen as classified here were more likely to have attended elite educational institutions, and to have had different career paths, from the bureaucrats. There were also enormous differences in the wealth holdings and relative income levels of the family businessmen and entrepreneurs on the one hand and the bureaucrats on the other. Whereas the bureaucrats were very largely dependent for their incomes on their salaries, the two other groups derived much more of their income from their invested wealth.

Nor was there any evidence of 'hidden control' of the firms headed by the bureaucrats interviewed; though it must be admitted that there was no specific line of questioning that would reveal this. The respondents did refer to the influence of the financial institutions on them, and I did interview the heads of some such institutions. The conclusion, for what it is worth, is that some financial institutions could probably exercise greater control than they do, and what perhaps needs explaining is why they do not intervene more in practice (see section 9.4). Likewise, I did not become aware of the non-executive directors as exercising control over the chief executives interviewed in this study to any significant extent.

Yet it must be admitted that it was not possible to demonstrate clear distinctions in outlook and perception on many topics between family businessmen, entrepreneurs and bureaucrats; indeed I argued (in chapter 5) that in regard to the overall objectives and aims of businessmen such distinctions were not important.

However, it was noted that businessmen themselves were aware of these distinctions. It clearly did enter into their perceptions of themselves and of their own behaviour in some cases. Bureaucrats could maintain they were salaried managers, as much an employee as everyone else; family businessmen that they had a special feeling for their firms, and a commitment to longer-term objectives than their managers might be expected to have (chapter 5). Thus, although I now regard the ownership and control debate as something of an empty one, I would be unwilling to see the distinctions of ownership position abandoned in future studies of businessmen.

The importance of the type of company a person heads was shown to a limited extent in chapter 6, where perceptions of conflict in the firm were related both to the size and nature of the company. Nevertheless, it should be said that there are great difficulties in classifying firms adequately, even using the three rather broad groupings (manufacturing, service and finance) adopted here. Further, one might ask whether it is the personal experience of the businessman himself that counts, or the history of the firm, for it is evident that the two are liable to be related. I was not able to study men in different functional departments within their firms, nor to adequately compare chief executives in distinct sectors (for example, engineering with hotels). This must remain as a possible area of future research.

The final assumption, if one may call it that, was that open-ended interviewing would be the most appropriate methodology for examining the beliefs and attitudes of businessmen. In this regard there is no point here in going once again through the arguments concerning the sincerity of the respondents, or whether or not attitudes measured in this way are or are not a reflection of 'true' attitudes, which were put forward in chapter 3.

The problems of handling interview material collected in this way will by now be obvious to the reader, if they were not before. Classifying the answers of sophisticated respondents is not easy, especially as the answer to any one question should be seen in the context of those that preceded it, yet the classification has to be done if any sort of pattern is to be discerned in the data. In the circumstances, it is not surprising that with a sample of this size statistically significant patterns or correlations are found so seldom.

But let me end this section on an optimstic note. The methodology was chosen as being the most likely to obtain access to the largest cross section of those who truly constitute the business elite. In its defence it should be said that it did give access to 130 men of high position in the business world who spoke relatively freely about issues that could be, and sometimes were, of a sensitive nature. I doubt that any other method would give such a result on such a scale within any feasible timespan.

9.3　THE FINDINGS OF THE STUDY

Who are Top Businessmen?
I alluded to some of the findings of the study in the previous section. Risking some repetition I will summarise them in more systematic form.

I began the study by asking just what sort of people are the leaders of British industry. Here the evidence confirms and extends previous studies. From the examination of businessmen's background and careers (chapter 4) it became apparent that a majority of those interviewed were likely to have spent the greater part of their educational, working and social lives in a white-collar milieu. We saw that they were very likely to have fathers from white-collar occupations, to have attended public schools, and to have obtained university degrees or professional qualifications. Their paths upwards through their firms had involved contact with manual workers for only a minority of those interviewed - the majority had risen via sales, marketing or finance. Most have spent a long period in management, ending with, on average, twelve years on the board at the time of interview. Most live in the south-east of England, and such evidence as we have indicates that their friends and neighbours come very much from managerial and professional occupations.

Yet the data in chapter 4 indicate a division within the business elite that is clearly related to the ownership of capital. Entre-

preneurs and family businessmen have had different careers
from those of the bureaucrats, and as a generalisation it may be
said that they are usually very much wealthier. As already noted,
whereas the salaries of the bureaucrats could be quite clearly
related to their incomes, but not to their wealth holdings, the
incomes of the two 'capitalist' groupings were related statistically
to their wealth holdings, but not to their salaries; and this
seemed to indicate that the distinction between bureaucrats
and others was a valid one, which might have further predictive
use.

Views of the Firm
In chapter 5 I examined the businessmen's views of the firm itself, looking first at the purely economic role of the men at the
top. I showed that many top directors now attempt to conceptual-
ise the objectives that they have for the firm in a way which reconciles the long-term interests of all the principal groups associated with it. Although I distinguished carefully between capitalists and managers in the sample, a distinction recognised by the
interviewees themselves, I found no evidence for a deviation
from the traditional goals of capitalism. Profit remains the aim
and measure of success. The difference is only the emphasis on
the long term, and the reconciliation of this with the interests of
employees, customers and other groups.
   It is assumed by business directors that most people within the
company accept this logic. The men at the top may be regarded
as surrounded by a core company - the group with whom they
can hope to have some personal contact. I suggested that for
most purposes a psychological boundary exists around the core,
and that beyond it the rest of the firm is not a living, daily,
reality. The directorate themselves recognise that only a small
group can know and understand the aims and plans they make
for the company.
   When they do turn their attention to the rest of the firm, they
expect that the further one goes down the firm the less the
understanding of the objectives, and the less the interest in
them. At the same time, it is assumed that most employees share
a broad consensus with the men at the top. Overall this conception of the firm fits best within Fox's (1966) notion of the unitary
view of the firm. But top businessmen do not, as Fox suggested,
reject trade unionism, rather they ascribe to unions a functional
role, for managers as well as members. Unions are necessary for
any group so large that managers cannot bargain with them on a
personal basis. They are a convenience for both groups. From
this point of view, conflict is either avoidable - the result of
poor communication, large plants, misguided union militancy or
political activism - or else, amongst businessmen who are most
prone to experience it, it may be ascribed to factors beyond
management control including the British class system, associated
historically entrenched attitudes, the educational system, or
simply the periodic need to bargain over wages.

In the simplest terms, then, power, status and reward are seen to parallel one another in the firm, or are supposed to. Businessmen do not, at least in the abstract, view the firm as a set of coalitions or conflictual groups, except to the extent that top managers compete for resources. The role of the board is primarily strategy-formulation and resource allocation. Although there was much stress by the interviewees on communication, and some references to the increased need for participation, the general expectation would seem to be that plans will be made above and go smoothly into operation below.

Class and Status
As regards the class and status system of Britain, it was found that a majority of those interviewed did see distinct classes, and in effect referred to one major division within them. This is essentially the division between the lower or working class and the middle class. An upper class consisting of those with an inherited title or great wealth may also be added.

Society is split, then, into two groupings, at a boundary which, it is felt, is becoming increasingly difficult to define. The extent and nature of one's education was most frequently mentioned as the factor determining a person's class, but the most common view was one which pictures class as the cumulative or reinforcing effect of several factors, chiefly education, the job one does, one's standard of living, and the attitudes and values one holds.

A majority of those interviewed placed themselves within the middle class. They maintain there is no link between them and the aristocracy who by tradition are the upper class and remain so. Nor, for the most part, do they count themselves as wealthy. Even within the middle class, businessmen feel they have no particularly high status, for they remark on the traditional dislike of the British for industry as opposed to the professions or civil service. Again, businessmen lack the aura of glamour in the public eye attached to the 'jet set'. Only a few very well known businessmen are thought to rate highly in public esteem.

It was also noted that some of those interviewed were aware of, and set alongside their own conceptions of society, alternative models associated with the working class. We are dealing, then, with a group whose view of society is relatively sophisticated and not susceptible to simple explanation.

Power and Relationships with State Officials
In the business view of the distribution of power in Britain the higher officers of the state, most notably cabinet ministers and top civil servants, are seen as the dominant groupings. Businessmen have little realisable power vis-à-vis these groups, but they can have access to them, and thus can exert influence. Businessmen take what is perhaps a conventional view in seeing the heads of the larger trade unions as being more powerful than they

are. The extent of the perceived influence exerted by the
heads of City institutions did not emerge clearly from the interviews.

The hidden and informal nature of the exercise of power at the
national level was recognised by many of those interviewed, and
the presence of some business figures amongst the major wielders
of influence was accepted. But it is the size of the firm one heads,
and its strategic importance for government policy, that seem to
be seen as leading to an influential position, as much or more than
personal contacts or an elitist social background.

Altogether, then, the businessmen interviewed did not betray
much awareness of being part of a social class, or status elite,
that is also a power elite. To some extent this was to be expected:
businessmen are not likely to claim to be part of a ruling class able
to inherit and perpetuate its wealth over generations. And, not
surprisingly, there are indications that the perspective of those
theorists who have been called managerialists - who picture large
companies as run by managers who arbitrate between capital,
labour and consumers - is becoming incorporated into the thinking
and statements of businessmen themselves. I return to these
issues below.

9.4 IMPLICATIONS FOR THEORY AND FUTURE RESEARCH

Preamble
Having summarised very briefly the findings of the research, I
wish to turn now to consider some of the implications of this
study for current theory and future research. In doing so I shall
make further reference to the main body of findings. The four
areas considered are:

(a)   ownership and control;
(b)   images of society;
(c)   beliefs and ideology;
(d)   businessmen and the state.

Ownership and Control
Direct study of businessmen produced little evidence to suggest
that the managers of large industrial and commercial firms had
objectives which differed from those ascribed to traditional
capitalists, irrespective of their personal ownership position. If
top businessmen need to rationalise or defend their behaviour at
all then they find it perfectly possible to do so from within a perspective that sees all parties as benefiting from the pursuit of
profit. Even those men who specified their objectives in terms of
growth made reference to growth of profits in the majority of
cases.

As I suggested above, I can no longer regard the ownership and
control debate in the terms in which it has been traditionally conducted as having central importance for sociological theory. There

are however, a number of other issues which need further investigation.

The first of these concerns the short-term objectives of businessmen. I suggested, following other writers, that they probably attempt to achieve a steady year-by-year increase in profits.
Yet, although I even encountered a few men who went so far as
to say they deliberately manipulated profits to achieve this, it
must be accepted that I was not able to present full evidence to
back up the hypothesis. Thus, there remains a need to study
whether businessmen do set out to achieve such year-by-year
increases.

The most useful evidence here would be longitudinal, that is,
evidence of businessmen's reaction to changing market situations:
do they try to move payments from year to year to smooth out
the flow of funds? Do they invest more in good years, or put
aside more for depreciation and so reduce reported profits? Do
they, in bad years, look for ways to boost profits, through lay-
offs of employees, cost-cutting or accounting changes?

Another point of importance requiring investigation concerns
the position and role of non-executive directors. My own view,
not dissimilar to that of some previous writers (for example, Mace,
1971; Pahl and Winkler, 1974), is to doubt the importance of non-
executive directors as the 'watchdogs of capitalism'. But much
more direct evidence is required on this point, and here I suggest
it would be possible to set up some comparative studies. For instance, comparison could be made of boards with a high proportion of non-executives from City firms with those with a different
balance; or the behaviour of non-executives in firms dominated
by a single chief executive (for example, an entrepreneur) could
be compared with those where this was not the case. Again, since
some boards have taken steps to alter the role of the non-executive
to make it a more active one, it would be interesting to compare
such firms with those run on more traditional patterns.

The basis for my view of businessmen's short-term aims was
first, that the pursuit of a year-on-year increase in profit would
be a relatively simple route to the objective of maximising long-
term profits, and also that this would be what was expected by
the group which acts as the jury for chief executives, that is,
the financial journalists, stockbrokers' analysts and possibly the
analysts of the institutional investors.

Three points for further research arise from this hypothesis.
First, there is a need to study the interaction between the chair-
men/chief executives of commercial firms and members of these
groups: how often do they meet? In what circumstances? What
information does the chief executive supply? Does this go beyond
that supplied to other shareholders? What criteria are applied to
judging the performance of firms by members of the groups we
mentioned?

Second, it must be accepted that this study contains only a
small group of directors from what is, in fact, a very mixed sector,
that is, the City, which contains banking, property, insurance,

pension funds, and investment institutions. An extension of this work to investigate the objectives for the firm of the executives of these groups is required. At the same time, research is needed into what exactly the institutions look for from the industrial and commercial firms they invest in. I suggest that life insurance or pension-fund managers are committed to providing a steady flow of payments (to holders of insurance or pensioners). Whilst they may hold a mixture of investments, as a hypothesis one might say that they would most wish to hold those giving a steady flow of dividends, rather than those subject to a more volatile performance.

A third suggestion for future research reverses the usual sociological hypothesis concerning the institutions. It asks why, if as Prais (1976) states, such institutions now hold 40 per cent of all equity capital, a percentage that is likely to go on increasing, they do not take a more interventionist stance than they do. For I did, in fact, encounter a number of chief executives who expressed the view that the institutions could benefit British industry by intervening more than they do at present.

A number of reasons can be suggested for the lack of apparent intervention. In no order of importance they are: that such institutions, the banks and insurance companies, have business other than direct investment, and their executives devote the major part of their time to this, for this is what they have been trained for; that men in financial companies do not feel they have the necessary knowledge or experience to intervene directly in the strategic planning or policy-formation of, for example, a manufacturing firm, and that when they do intervene it is when things have clearly gone wrong and then to replace personnel at the top of the company; that they regard themselves as investors, protect their investments by keeping them small and spread between firms, and lack the necessary co-ordination or mechanisms to intervene directly; that intervention exists, is widespread, but is not apparent; that the consensus between company executives and the executives of financial institutions is so complete that intervention is not necessary. And finally, that the institutions are afraid to reveal themselves as a locus of capital holding or power because this would make them obvious targets in any future nationalisation programme. All of these remain as hypotheses; all, I maintain, require further research if we are to fully understand the workings of capitalism in Britain.

Meaning Systems

I gave above a description of the findings concerning meaning systems, or, more particularly, the images of class and status held by businessmen. I shall extend that description here, but also discuss how such meaning systems can be related to the objective situation of individual businessmen.

Being dissatisfied with the explanation given for the content of middle-class meaning systems, especially when applied to elite groups, I put together my own picture of the sources and influences on businessmen's thinking.

Fundamental among these, of course, is the relationship of the businessman to capital, as expressed in the divisions between the bureaucrat, family businessman and entrepreneur. Then we have the social background from which the person has come as indicated by their parent's occupation, and then a whole range of influences over the course of a lifetime which may influence a person's thinking. First, there is education, and here the contrast between public school and other values is emphasised, but both university and management education may also be important. The kinds of company one has worked in, and the positions one has held, may possibly influence one's views of relationships within the firm, and so within society more widely. Then there are the effects of community life, and of other contacts external to the firm, such as those made for political reasons.

Finally, businessmen are inevitably subject to a number of cultural influences, most obviously business ideology as it is developed by spokesmen and groups organised to protect their interests, the ideology of the Conservative Party, the counter-ideologies of socialist parties, and the influences of the mass media.

Throughout the study I looked for correspondences between the objective situation of individuals and the subjective perceptions of these. I have laid out on the next page those few that were apparent, and the limited success in establishing such correspondences is obvious.

However, laying out the findings in this way makes one point clearly. That is, that there appears to be no particular link between businessmen's views of their firm and their wider views of society, nor of the 'objective' factors that structure these. I indicated in chapter 5 that the company may be viewed in different ways at different times. So far as the direct personal contact of the men at the top goes, the company may be seen as a core, a very small part of the whole. At other times it may be viewed as a pyramid of responsibility and authority; and on other occasions as management and others (or, even, as 'us' and 'them').

The view of class taken by most respondents was separate and not clearly related. Most frequently, society was not pictured as a hierarchy, but rather as being split by a major cleavage. Yet this, in turn, was not between a small ruling group, whether class or elite, and the mass, but between two comparatively largish groups, the middle and working class. The upper class are not seen as a ruling class. Power in Britain is certainly viewed as inequitably distributed, but the greatest concentration is seen to result from the power held by the authorised holders - state officials. Though a certain informal power or influence grouping was recognised by those probably best positioned to know about it, the heads of bigger companies, the route into this is not seen as depending primarily on wealth or on status attributes.

It is important, therefore, to note that it was not clear how experience of the work environment directly contributed to busi-

nessmen's images of society; nor, aside from those I called
sociological sophisticates, who are a relatively small grouping,
how their community experience does. Not only do businessmen's
views of the firm appear to have a variable and ambiguous nature,
but there was no particular convergence apparent between the
beliefs and opinions held by individuals about their company, on
the one hand, and society more generally, on the other. At the
extreme, there were men who accepted a clear separation between
management and employees in the company, whilst picturing
society as a hierarchy of status, with others taking a reverse
view - seeing the company as a hierarchy with a broad consensus
between management and employees, but society as being two
distinct classes. (And there were of course a range of viewpoints
within these extremes.)

(a) The firm

Size ───────────────→	Businessmen's perceptions of:
+	the extent of sharing of ob- jectives
Type of firm ───────────→ respondent heads	likelihood and nature of indus- trial conflict
(that is, manufacturing v. service, etc.)	Explanations of causes of con- flict

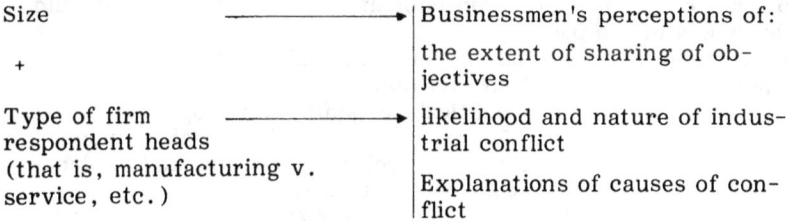

(b) Class and status in society

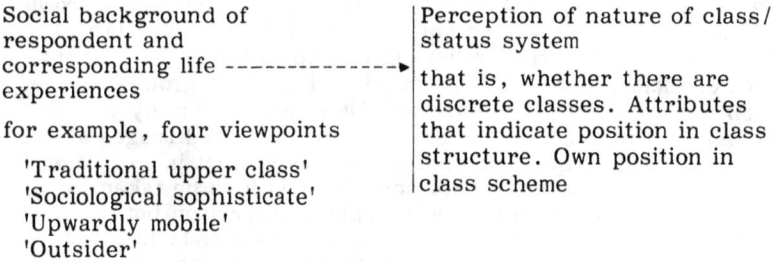

Social background of respondent and corresponding life ─ ─ ─ ─ ─ ─ → experiences	Perception of nature of class/ status system
	that is, whether there are discrete classes. Attributes
for example, four viewpoints	that indicate position in class structure. Own position in class scheme
'Traditional upper class' 'Sociological sophisticate' 'Upwardly mobile' 'Outsider'	

(c) Nature of power in Britain

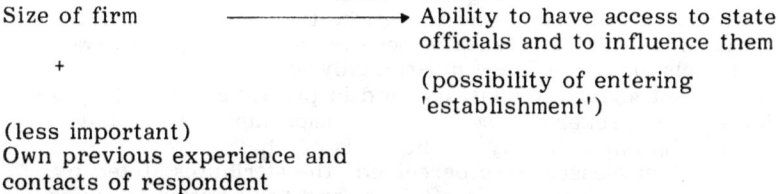

Size of firm ─────────────→	Ability to have access to state officials and to influence them
+	(possibility of entering 'establishment')
(less important) Own previous experience and contacts of respondent	

Figure 9.2 Some empirical findings of this study
This diagram indicates statistical connections, and the arrows
are not intended to suggest more than possible causal links.

Having pointed to the diversity of forms which the pictures of stratification could take among those interviewed, I should also restate the central beliefs and assumptions which businessmen have in common. These were (chapter 7):

(a) Class is disappearing, class distinctions are lessening, class in the traditional sense is withering away;

(b) Yet, because men are inherently unequal, there will always be a stratification system of some kind. Differences of class and status will always reappear no matter what you do to try to eradicate them.

(c) Because we are moving towards a meritocracy, in which people's class position will depend more and more on their success in occupational hierarchies, it is more important than ever to get the right start, to get a good education.

(d) And because education is now available to all, and anyone with brains and energy can get to university; and because in business companies promotion is open to all, society is more fluid than it was in the past.

(e) Although society is more open, although class should be withering away, conflict and tension is stirred up by the Left. The Left uses class as a political weapon to stir people up.

Despite the presence of such shared beliefs, the discussion of meaning systems here reveals problems of theory and explanation that go beyond the concerns of this study.

The 'problem' is that of explaining how such meaning systems or 'images of society' are created, or how they come to be patterned. The same difficulty has arisen in a number of previous studies, such as those of Brown et al. (1972) (see also Cousins and Brown in Bulmer, 1975); Blackburn and Mann (1975) and Hiller (1975a and b). Amongst the researchers cited, up to fourteen different images of society have been distinguished amongst groups of manual workers, and Blackburn and Mann found so many that they were led to question the existence of patterned images at all.

Indeed, the first question that one raises is what is an 'image of society', and at what level of specificity is it to be taken to exist? One may take as a simple example a comparison between two interview respondents, one of whom splits society into two classes, the first class consisting of those who do manual work, the second of those who work in offices, and another respondent who splits society into those who are managers or are elsewhere in positions of authority, and those who take orders. Are these to be taken as distinct images of society, or are they both two-class models and therefore fundamentally similar?

How we set about the analysis, and in particular the categories which the researcher chooses to see as important, will clearly affect the findings. Simply on the basis of whether, and how many, distinct classes were perceived, the attributes stated by the respondents as the basis of class, and the position to which those interviewed assigned themselves, one might well have concluded that amongst the business elite there are even more images of society than have been found amongst manual workers.

Nevertheless, the difficulty faced here is similar to that raised by the studies of the traditional worker and other groups referred to above. Lockwood's (1966) paradigm attempts to relate the work and community circumstance of the traditional worker to his own perception of these circumstances and society more widely. When researchers find fourteen distinct images of society, are we to conclude that they failed to look for the common elements in these apparently diverse images? Or is it rather that, had the researchers taken a large enough sample, and investigated such factors as religious experience, union membership and union ideology, experience of downward mobility, membership of voluntary associations plus any others found to be relevant, that a more complete paradigm relating the image of society or the 'meaning system' of the traditional worker to his circumstances would result? This study poses the same questions with a group whose life situation is entirely different.

The previous section raised also the problem of the internal consistency of images of society. In the case of the traditional worker, at least as pictured by Lockwood, experience of work life and community life are reinforcing, in such a way as to give a picture of both work and the social world more generally as 'us' and 'them'.

A possible interpretation of the position of the business elite is of a parallel situation. The elite are to an extent isolated from contact with all but a narrow stratum of society, both in the world of work and, quite possibly, outside. One might expect a similar 'us and them' attitude to those outside their own narrow circles, and this, at least, is Winkler's (1975) interpretation of directors' behaviour. (Cf. the theoretical discussion by Archibald, 1976.)

Yet the examination of directors' lives and thinking reveals no such internal consistency: pictures of the company and relationships in it are not paralleled by similar pictures of society, and further, there is apparent a certain amount of ambiguity of attitude towards industrial relations, on the one hand, together with far more complex thinking about class and power in society than any simple model can contain, on the other.

These findings appear to suggest that people find it perfectly possible to live with ambiguous, partly conflicting or even inconsistent beliefs about the world of work and society as a whole. This would be a further piece in a jigsaw of findings in recent years which suggest that the images of society held by individuals are very likely to be ambiguous, inconsistent and contextually variable. Some of the evidence was reviewed in chapter 2, in particular the paper by Mann (1970), who suggested that manual workers take a different stance on concrete issues concerned with inequality or industrial action than is implied by the abstract conceptions of society that they put forward when interviewed. Likewise, Platt's (1971) discussion of research on workers in Luton suggests a more complex state of affairs than that put forward in the main reports of the 'Affluent Worker' project (Gold-

thorpe et al., 1969). Nichols (1974), in a detailed discussion
of the attitudes of ten foremen shows the inconsistencies and
ambiguities in their class imagery; and Moorhouse (1976) shows
that some aspects of images of society show variation over
time.

All this indicates that there are severe limits to the extent to
which the content of images of society can be explained. This
does not mean, however, that the investigation of subjective
views of class, status and power is not worthwhile. To take the
study presented here, it seems doubtful that we would ever be
able to explain why some men choose to say that class position
depends very largely on an individual's income or wealth, whilst
others will state that it really comes down to the education one
has received.

Indeed, at the present time, and accepting that respondents
are fully aware that certain kinds of education and educational
achievement confer higher earning power, it is not even clear
that these are distinct viewpoints, still less why one man emphasises one, another the other.

Yet I would maintain that there were certain findings in this
study of top businessmen, for example, their affiliation with the
middle class, their dislike of conspicuous show, their beliefs in
the openness of society and the extent of opportunity for social
mobility, the view that power is firmly concentrated in the hands
of state officials, which do provide useful insights into their
central values and beliefs.

One further point may be made here. It may be suggested that
a group develops a coherent, consistent, and well-thought-out
meaning system on issues on which it feels particularly involved,
possibly because they form part of its responsibilities, or its
claim to material goods, prestige or power, or because it is
threatened in some way. The business elite can be said to be
some way away from the boundary of class or status which members of it see as definitive. Thus class and status are genuinely
not issues of importance for them in everyday life. Hence, there
may be no coherent business viewpoint on the topic of class,
whereas there is a much more developed one on other matters.
This returns us to the conception of ideology, which I take up in
the next section.

Meaning Systems and Ideologies
In the first chapter I suggested that it is useful to maintain a
distinction between the meaning systems of a group and the ideologies expressed on its behalf. I defined business ideology as
those ideas expressed on behalf of the heads of business enterprises which seek to justify or explain their position in relation
to the enterprises and society as a whole.

In accordance with this distinction, I hold that the study
presented here has been an examination of the meaning systems
of the business elite. We expect to find, and do find, considerable
diversity in such meaning systems, though we can also look for

the common elements within them.

We expect less diversity in ideology. A major purpose of ideologies is to convince groups other than the ones creating or propagating them. They are not likely to do this if they sound different or say quite clearly different things each time they are stated. Of course, ideologies may contain internal ambiguities or inconsistencies or even divisions of opinion, but in general we expect spokesmen to attempt to work towards statements of group opinion that are acceptable to the group themselves, but that can be stated on different occasions and in different contexts and still sound familiar to the group, and to those the ideology is aimed at.

It was further suggested in chapter 1 that elements of ideology can be incorporated into meaning systems. When they are, we expect to find the adherents of them making use of elements of the ideology in their own thinking; using the conventional language and statements of the spokesmen and doing so almost without thinking. This process is most obvious and is quite natural in those who are themselves spokesmen.

It follows from the conception advanced here that we cannot infer the content and nature of an ideology from a summation or distillation of interview answers. There are several reasons for this, most importantly that those who emerge as spokesmen for a group may be those who are best fitted to writing or speaking on its behalf, but not necessarily the most typical. Since ideology is publicly expressed, it may be more rational than the group themselves are; alternatively, it may make appeals to public emotion or sentiment that group members would not make.

Nevertheless, on the basis of the interview answers, statements about ideology of two kinds are possible: one can make some generalisations about the kind of ideology likely to emerge from a group at a given time - its style, tone, and underlying values. Second, one can point out where ideology has been incorporated into the thinking of a group in a more or less straightforward manner.

Two features of current business ideology are apparent from the study here. The first is the highly pragmatic tone of business thinking. Looking through the quotes in the preceding chapters (and this despite the fact that one is always tempted to quote the extreme or striking phrase rather than the representative one), one notes the almost complete absence of references to such themes as 'rights of property', 'keeping to one's station in life', being 'born to rule', 'God's intentions', 'the law of the survival of the fittest', or similar phrases which might have been found in the statements of businessmen in previous times. Nowadays the acid test of an idea often appears to be no more than whether or not it will increase the efficiency and wealth of the nation, the latter being conceptualised as the level of GNP. (No doubt Britain's lagging economic performance compared to other nations is partly responsible for this.) This test can be applied to such topics as curbing the power of the unions, taxation, government legislation, industrial democracy, and the redistribution of wealth.

Likewise, on the issue of social class one finds references to inequalities of ability which can never be eradicated, and to the idea of the emerging meritocracy, especially within the firm, which will again promote efficiency. A public school system is defended as much on the basis that removing the schools will place greater strain on an overloaded state system, as on the rights of parents to purchase education.

The second point, a corollary of the first, is that where ideals enter they are of the negative kind stressing the disadvantages of socialism. Reactionary has become so much a term of abuse that one hesitates to apply it, but it should not be forgotten that a conservative ideology is a reaction to trends that appear to threaten existing social relationships, and in that sense business ideology is reactionary.

The bedrock of the pragmatic and reactive business ideology is the nature and condition of existing Marxist nations. Any change that suggests a move towards the limitation of the autonomy of capitalist controllers or capitalist institutions can be suggested as being a move towards socialism, and a move along a route to Soviet-style communism. The kinds of political change favoured by business ideology, in contrast, are whatever is thought to increase the wealth of the nation.

If we turn to the second aspect of ideology, that is, the extent to which it is incorporated into the thinking of practitioners, then there is some variation. I have already put the view that beliefs about social class do not stem from a coherent ideological base. Social class is possibly not a topic of great importance to businessmen as businessmen, nor is it one on which there is much public debate, and in such debate as there is, businessmen are not a group who play a natural part per se. Thus, for example, it would strike most people as very strange if a president of the Confederation of British Industry were to appear in some public context to give his views of the class structure, the rights and obligations of different classes, the extent of class conflict and so on.

In contrast, when one examines attitudes concerning the objectives of the firm, and the roles of members of the board, then ideology is discernible. The ascendant one would appear to be the 'managerial ideology', which might be termed, as it was earlier, 'the ethos of balancing interests'. When we ask businessmen about their objectives for the firm, we find answers couched very often in very similar language, and repeating a very similar message. We can find similar statements in the writings of some theorists, and the public statements of some business spokesmen. Clearly, there has been a process of public formulation and reformulation of these statements.

The ideology of 'balancing interests' maintains that in the long term the interests of all groups concerned with the firm - shareholders, employees, customers and the public at large - are

served by the success of the company. The pursuit of profit
thus serves the interests of all. Those who run the company are
in the position of balancing the interests of all groups connected
with it - but they do so only in the short term. If the interests
of all are correctly balanced then in the long term the firm will
prosper. This ideology has been described here as an ideology
of balancing interests, rather than a managerial ideology, because it is as well and frequently expressed by family owners,
and even entrepreneurs and financiers, as by managers.

In the first chapter it was pointed out that this ideology has
been stated in varying forms for some time now in both Britain
and the United States. What emerges from this study is the
extent to which the ideology has entered the thinking of practitioners themselves. However, it is an open question as to
whether this has a tangible effect on behaviour.

One aspect of business ideology not so far mentioned is the
tendency to accept what has been done as unchangeable, although
adherents of the ideology may resist further encroachments or
developments of the same sort. We see this with regard to the
role of the state and to industrial relations.

In contrast to businessmen in the past (and Heilbroner (1964)
remarks on the same point), businessmen now accept the role of
the state in providing certain social and welfare services and in
playing an interventionist role in the economy. But they are
likely to regard any expansion of either role with suspicion. Likewise, in the realm of industrial relations, the rights of employees
to belong to trade unions are now widely accepted amongst the
heads of large companies, but, as was remarked earlier, unions
are ascribed a functional role within the firm. A trade union is
not seen as necessary for the protection of employees, and certainly not as the expression of class interests, but as a desirable
institution where an employer cannot bargain with each employee
on an individual basis.

Yet in the area of industrial relations, ideology is not as well-
developed as might be expected, granted the attention it receives
in the media. Very few persistent themes stand out, and taken
together they do not constitute a coherent framework of beliefs
and attitudes. Almost any businessmen will tell you that trade
unions in Britain now have too much power, but in itself this
can hardly be said to be ideology.

Again, as I have said, the very diversity of the situation that
companies are in prevents a unified ideological viewpoint emerging. We note some concepts that recur with relative frequency -
the importance attached to communication, an increased awareness of the need for participation - but little more.

However, the exploration of businessmen's beliefs and values
makes it easier to understand their distrust of industrial democracy. From the business elite's point of view such schemes have
no point, since the interests of employees are already, almost
automatically, safeguarded. Further, in terms of businessmen's
current normative touchstone - the question 'will it increase the

wealth of the nation' - industrial democracy is potentially disruptive and therefore, quite simply, counter-productive.

Businessmen and the State
One aspect of the continuing debate over the existence of a ruling class, a power elite, or competing elites, concerns the relationship of businessmen to state officials. Conclusions from this study must be drawn with caution, both because of the small number of men interviewed on this topic, and because of the problems of placing too much reliance on reports of behaviour. However, it does lead to some hypotheses which may form the basis of future investigation.

I suggested first that businessmen who form part of the business elite are less likely than they were in the past to hold a political office. Thus we must look past the statistics which show the composition of the parliamentary Tory Party over several decades as containing a consistently high proportion of business directors, and ask whether there has not been a hidden change in business involvement in that time.

If, as I believe, there has, then we now have a situation in which those businessmen who head large companies must influence state activities either indirectly, through the Tory Party, or through pressure groups, most obviously the CBI and the trade associations, or through direct access to cabinet ministers and civil servants.

This research looked at the direct access that businessmen have, and concluded that there was, in fact, quite considerable access through a variety of channels, although businessmen had only mixed success in achieving their aims. The question must then be posed: in a period of Labour government why should businessmen have such access? Why should ministers and civil servants see them and sometimes be persuaded by them?

I am not convinced by arguments that rest primarily on the importance of shared personal contacts, whether formed at school, university, in the course of a career, or in shared club membership. I would argue, on the contrary, that what is required is a study that looks at the three main groupings in the processes of power and influence, that is, the politicians, civil servants and businessmen. It needs to look at what each hopes to get from encounters with the other, and what resources, either as sanctions or as rewards are perceived as being available to each group. This approach would treat the encounters as open-ended bargaining situations, rather than foregone conclusions.

9.5 MORE EVERYDAY ISSUES

The main concern of this chapter, as throughout this book, has been with the implications that this study has for sociological theory and research. However, in the next two sections I wish to

consider two topics that are of perhaps of wider interest than
to sociologists alone; they concern the class consciousness of
top managers, and what I called here the 'balancing interests'
ethos.

Are Top Management too Class-conscious?

A question that this study may pose once more in the mind of the
reader arises out of a generalisation that is sometimes made about
the British. That is, that as a society we are concerned about
the refinements of class and status to a far greater degree than
people in other Western countries. The generalisation is sometimes levelled particularly at British managers, with the implication that if they were not so class-conscious, Britain would have
more successful industrial companies and thus be more prosperous.[1]

In considering this I would begin with the general observation
that charges that the British are particularly concerned with
class may be based either on a lack of firm comparative evidence,
or on observation of certain superficial aspects of British life
which, in practice, are not as important as they appear. In the
latter regard, one may mention the fact that Britain still has a
monarchy, a hereditary peerage with law-making powers, and an
elaborate system of titles and decorations. It also has a private
school system, which, as we have seen, provides a high proportion of those who succeed to elite positions. Finally, as is often
remarked on, in Britain speech is a very clear guide both to the
background and current status of the speaker.

In practice it is yet to be demonstrated that these aspects of
British life do distinguish the country in a real sense from other
Western capitalist countries. It is not clear that titles, whatever
they may derive from, are more important in Britain than elsewhere. Nor is Britain alone in having a private school system.
Baltzell (1958) and Domhoff (1967) have pointed out the efficiency
of American private schools in providing members of what Baltzell
calls 'an American business aristocracy'. Further, since in most
Western countries the children of professional and managerial
workers do better in the education system, and in subsequent
careers, it is difficult to separate this factor from the specific
one of having attended private school. Most Western democracies
seem similar to Britain in that those of similar wealth, income or
occupational prestige live in similar neighbourhoods, and if commentators such as Whyte (1957) are to be believed, pressure to
move to an area appropriate to one's status may be stronger on
American managers than it is on British ones. And with respect
to accent, Giles and Powesland (1975), in a comprehensive review
of the literature, have shown that accent is taken as a guide to
social status in several Western cultures, notably in Canada and
the United States. Taking the more fundamental inequalities -
those of wealth and power - Britain appears similar to other
capitalist societies in the extent of inequality that exists.

But what of the men at the top of British industry; are they perhaps more conscious of class than their compatriots? As I have already suggested, in fact, class or status may be of relatively less importance to the men who were interviewed in this study, simply because their own high status is so little to be doubted.

Certainly, though, some of the upwardly mobile did point out that adaptations of speech, dress and behaviour are necessary for those who wish to reach the very top. In this they were saying in layman's terms, what Bourdieu and Passeron (1977) have said in a more elaborate and academic way of the French educational system. The majority of those interviewed were inclined to emphasise the openness of promotion to the boardroom, maintaining, for example, that public school education per se was not taken into account in making top management promotions.

Since study after study has shown that a majority of top directors have been to public school, this could be taken with a large pinch of salt. But in saying this the interviewees could be perfectly sincere without it radically affecting the composition of boardrooms very much in the future. Looking and sounding right may be important for promotion at all levels and in this public school boys may be at an advantage whether or not anyone actually knows what school they attended. And promotion in future may well depend on the possession of educational qualifications, such as a university degree, a professional qualification, or a business degree, which those who have attended public school may, for whatever reason, be in a better position to obtain.

But there is one aspect of British culture that is reflected in the composition of the business elite which could be considered to be truly damaging. That is the tendency for certain career routes to lead to the top of companies rather than others. This was well demonstrated here. It is clear that experience of production management, or engineering management, or handling industrial relations has generally not been the experience in the past that led to the very top positions. This may well have been observed by those ascending the ladder, or contemplating entering industry. Correspondingly, those at the top may prefer to keep out of industrial relations matters, and fail to understand exactly what goes on and what needs to be done on the shopfloor.

This may also be a symptom of a much wider distrust of manufacturing industry in Britain in general, and of entering the production side of it in particular, which may mean that the more able choose to enter other specialities, either inside or outside industry. At the moment these generalisations rest on inadequate evidence, but if Britain's future prosperity depends on its ability to raise shopfloor productivity, as many now feel it does, then the lack of experience at the very top may be cause for disquiet.[2]

Can Directors really Balance Interests?
In the previous section I recalled the ideology of 'balancing interests' which was discussed in chapter 5. According to this ethos, the board of directors balances in the short term the

interests of disparate groups connected with the firm. The director reconciles these interests in the light of what is best for the firm in the long term, and in doing so discharges his social responsibility. In the long term, the interests of all parties coincide. And the current occupants of seats on company boards are those best fitted to the task, for they have risen through the firm, they have the years of experience, they understand the necessities and complexities that are involved.

So runs the current strain of business ideology, and I tend to believe that most businessmen are sincere and honest in stating their adherence to it. This is not to say that the evolution of such beliefs over the years has not been as a result of attacks on the unilateral power of directorates to pursue profit at the expense of employees, or at cost to the environment, and so forth. But the ideology, now evolved, appears to be sincerely held.

Nevertheless, a critical evaluation of the effects of such an ideology in practice is perhaps excusable here. For although this study does not allow firm conclusions to be drawn about the be- haviour of businessmen, it should not go unremarked that the ideology allows almost any action to be justified in practice, for almost any action can be said to be in the interests of some group or other, at least in the long term. Thus, if a firm fails to pay a dividend (actually an unlikely course), it can be justified on the grounds that retained profits are reinvested and will lead to bigger profits later. If shoddy goods are sold, or margins are high, then the consumer still benefits, for reinvestment leads to better and cheaper goods later. If the company pollutes, then even this can be justified for pollution control costs money and lower profit means less wealth has been created for the nation.

The issue can perhaps best be seen in relation to plant closures, redundancy and the acquisition or divestment of parts of the company. Despite redundancy pay, and various state provisions, losing a job does cause people considerable hardship, and having a factory or firm bought or sold causes employees at the very least worry or uncertainty. Nevertheless, men who presented themselves as strong believers in the importance of safeguarding employees' interests, went ahead during the course of this study with such operations.

Who then benefits from the business elite's attempts to balance interests? The question may be answered by considering with whom the elite have contact. I suggested earlier the notion of a 'core company', consisting of those with whom the very top man can have personal contact. Whatever happens, it seems unlikely that the interests of this group will be disregarded, no matter how other interests are balanced.

When, in the earlier interviews, I asked chief executives what gave them most satisfaction in their work (the question was later dropped), the most frequent replies were: (a) seeing the firm succeed and grow; and (b) seeing younger men one has picked out succeed and develop in the firm. If these were translated to 'seeing the firm succeed' and 'seeing members of the core firm prosper' it would convey my own view of the concerns of the directorate.

I put these views in a report sent to the interview respondents themselves. I wrote there:[3]

A director who gained a main board place in 1960, may correctly point to the fact that in 1975 the company employs as many men at higher wages. Yet after fifteen years of home and overseas investment, the balance of which may have changed; of merger, takeover, rationalisation, divestment and occasionally lay-offs and redundancy, a roll-call of those now working for the firm may look very different. . . .

Every top director will know a number of people who have been promoted, expanded their responsibilities, and in other ways prospered and developed during his tenure on the board, and he rightly regards their progress with satisfaction. Those un-knowns who have been made redundant, retired early, or are working for an entirely different company from that of fifteen years earlier may have less cause for satisfaction.

To raise these arguments is not to question the good faith of top businessmen nor to argue for inefficiency and uncompetitive-ness. Rather it is to ask whether the new ethos, the idea of the socially responsible company is likely to be sustained in practice. Is it reasonable to expect managers orientated through-out their careers to profit, return, or sales targets, when they step on to the board to begin to balance the competing interests that come together in the public company?

To be honest, one must point out that most of those who received the report chose to make no comment about it. Such reactions as there were covered the whole range of business ideology.

As one would expect, several of those who wrote in reply disagreed with the passage quoted above, one going so far as to call it cynical. Two agreed completely with it, though without giving their reasons, but from what they had said in the interviews their views would approximate to those of Friedman (1962) and Hayek (1960) that it is positively subversive for businessmen to pursue social ends, and that the free enterprise system only works correctly if they rigorously pursue maximum profits. One well-known businessman, who took the report to be an expression of the Friedman-Hayek viewpoint, sent a paper of his own arguing the case for directors to give attention to social responsibility.

Another spokesman took a slightly different line, and one which I suspect reflects the views of many of the silent majority who did not comment on the report. As this man saw it, I had

put too much emphasis on the idea that directors seek to justify their actions. The whole emphasis is finding an optimum solution . . . it is inaccurate to imply that any action can be justified. Some actions are never justified. For instance inaccurate or mis-leading information must never be given knowingly. . . . You imply criticism of the 'relative autonomy of top management'. The main responsibility of managers is to optimise the use of resources available to them. To carry out this responsibility they need to have authority to take decisions.

Here is another current of business thinking. It draws our attention to the purely technical tasks of management, and in essence reaffirms the concept of the manager as the neutral professional, concerned not with profit or growth per se, but with the optimum use of resources. As to whether this neutral professionalism is adequate protection for the interests and rights of employees, customers or other members of society is one that society as a whole must decide through the available political processes.

9.6 IN CONCLUSION

Partly because they were the author's own interests, partly because, as I have sought to show, they are inextricably linked, this book has brought together a number of issues which are often kept separate in sociological research: the study of meaning systems (or images of society), the study of business ideology and elites more generally, the study of political influence and power within society. Even so, taking the study of the business elite alone, it is clear that there is much still to be learnt.[4]

I have indicated some of the more direct implications that stem from this research in this chapter, but there are others again which should not be forgotten.[5] We still have very few studies based on first-hand observation of directors at work, and almost none of them outside. Whilst sociologists have lived in and experienced the lives of people in urban and rural working-class districts, and sometimes middle-class ones, life among elites has to be reconstructed from political or other memoirs or journalistic investigation and all too often it is the millionaire, tycoon or playboy who attracts attention rather than the less flamboyant heads of the majority of British companies. There are, of course, obvious difficulties in obtaining an inside view, and it may be that it could only come from someone who had themselves climbed the corporate hierarchy, by which time the person in question might no longer be a sociologist.

Yet if there is much to be done on the business elite, there are other elites which are even less investigated: the values, attitudes and interaction of the civil service, military, judiciary and even the educational elites have received very little systematic attention.

Increasingly, establishment opinion in Britain seems to be dominated by the need to solve the country's economic problems, which are at least now recognised to be the result of the chronic failure of its manufacturing industry. As a result, and this is, of course, a purely personal observation, it seems to be accepted that all social and political reform should come to a standstill. This, in turn, leaves elite groupings free from threat and out of public scrutiny. At such a time, sociologists have a role to play in continuing to examine and question the structure of the society which supports them. And yet, currently, there seems to less empirical reserach conducted than throughout most of the post-war period, and the more radical the politics of the social scientist the more likely he or she is to be engaged in the discussion and dissection of the work of other theorists. That too seems to be to be a retreat into a conservatism of a kind; and so the pious hope on which I conclude is that the cause of elite studies is not totally lost.

APPENDICES

1 THE INTERVIEW SCHEDULE

Name: Number:
Title: (Member of landed gentry/aristocracy:

Personal information

Position in company: Bureaucrat/family busin./entrepreneur
Nationality at birth: Married/single/

Children: Son(s)   Age:
              Daughter(s)
Place of residence:

Salary (gross, from this position, 1975 figure):

Shareholding (in present firm, end-1975 values):

Stated wealth holding:
    (Recode from end of interview)

Clubs (from 'Who's Who', etc.):

Recreations (stated):
List known outside directorships:

Membership of government bodies, etc. (with dates):

Company information

Name of company:
Manufacturing/service/insurance/merchant bank/property
Control type: bureaucrat/family/entrepreneur
Size (position in top 180 British firms in terms of assets and
    turnover)

Turnover:	1974:
	1975:
Profit:	1974:
	1975:
Assets:	1974:
	1975:

273

Number of employees (1975):   Britain:
                                 Total:
Multinational?:
Main areas of business:

Other comments:

The interview

1 *Career*: We do of course know (from 'Who's Who') some of your
life history, Mr/Sir/Lord————, but to give us a fuller picture
could you please trace briefly for us your career starting from
when you left secondary school.

Record and check following information is obtained:

Name of secondary school:
(Check: is that private?)

Age left:
University?   Name:
               Degree subject read:
               Class of degree (if possible):

Professional training:
Qualification obtained:

Armed forces experience:

First job after full-time education:
Then, with approximate dates:
        Companies worked for: Positions held:

N.b.   Age of obtaining main board appointment:

Finally ask:
Did you have any formal management training:
(Obtain details)

If not apparent:
What was your father's occupation:
(At age sixteen)

2* The first thing I should like to discuss with you is the question
of the responsibilities of the director: what in your view are the
primary responsibilities of the main board director in a company
such as this?

3* For bureaucrats (others go to Q4): Although you have some
shares in your company, these are clearly only a small part of
the total shares in circulation; would you like to hold more shares?

If you did, do you think this would affect your view of your responsibilities?

Do you know of companies where the directors do behave differently because they do have larger shareholdings?

Bureaucrats: go to Q5.

4* For family businessmen/entrepreneurs:
You have an obvious personal stake in this company, how much difference do you think this makes to the way you view these objectives?

5* (Probe) To some extent the responsibilities you have outlined could be said to be the responsibilities of any senior manager, in what ways do you see the main board director's responsibilities as differing from those of a manager?

6 What would you see as the principal objectives you and the board have formulated for the company at the present time?

7 Now, taking the objectives we have discussed, I should like to ask to what extent other groups in the company would understand these objectives, and to what extent they would share them.

First of all, what about the other members of the board, would they see them as you do?

8 And what about members of management, would they understand the objectives? Would they share them? (Probe how far down are they understood/shared?)

9 And what about employees outside management - would they understand these objectives? Would they share them?

10 We sometimes hear talk of the 'two sides' of industry. Do you see two sides in this company?

11 Accepting your answer to the (last) question, some people feel that there is an inevitable tension in the workplace because some people control, and others are controlled. What is your view on this?

12 Let us turn now to the trade unions; do you see trade unions as having a useful role to play in the situation of your own company, and what is that role?

(Probe for: unions for white-collar workers; for managers?)

13* Coming back now to the position of the director: so far as you can compare, how does the influence and social position of a man heading (this company/a company of this size) compare today with before the war?

14* Looking outside the company, do you think that people in your position - that is the heads of large companies - have a useful contribution to make to the way the country is run?

15* There must be times when the business community or parts of the business community wishes to affect the thinking and actions of government. To what extent do you feel they are able to do this?

(Probe: Over what sort of issues? What are the most effective methods? Examples?)

16* How do you think the influence of businessmen - like yourself - compares with that of other people or groups, for example:
(a) trade union leaders
(b) civil servants
(c) heads of financial institutions/the City?

17 (Finally) I would like to ask your views on some more general social issues, and begin by asking you; people talk of there being classes in British society, what is your view on this?

Establish the following:
If there are classes: How many major ones? On what are they based? Where do you come? Who comes in the upper class?

If there are no classes: Do the terms working class, middle class, upper class have no meaning?

Do you see a historical meaning?

What replaces them?

If not mentioned: What is the position of the aristocracy?
                                        The rich?

(Ask all) It does appear that a majority of the directors of large companies have been to a public school. Why do you think this should be?

How easy or difficult, then, would it be for the son of a manual worker to climb to your position in the company?

18 One question on a topical issue: what is your opinion on the proposed legislation on wealth and gifts tax?

19 (Ask if time) There has been much talk of employee participation in management; could you give me your views on this?

Who should participate? How?

Workers on the board?

20 (Ask all) Could you please look at this card and indicate in which range your total income from all sources, before tax, falls? Please just give me the letter which would identify it (note letter).

And using this card could you please indicate in the same way your total wealth, so far as you can estimate it. (Note letter.)

Close interview.

It should be noted that the original schedule contained questions which were later dropped. Questions marked with * were asked of only seventy respondents. See chapter 3.

2 ON THE USE OF PERSONAL CONTACTS IN ONE'S CAREER AND IN INFLUENCING GOVERNMENT

Perhaps the area most hidden from public view in business and political life is the way in which personal contacts - friendships, business associations and so on can be utilised in gaining business or political objectives.

It would be difficult in any research to give any systematic indication of how important such contacts are, compared to other, more formal, methods. Certainly, the impression given by the respondents in this study was that whilst they are very effective where then can be used, they are not essential.

However, to indicate the variety of ways in which they can work, set out below are five case studies, three drawn from interviews with retired chief executives, two from those with other chief executives. They are intended to illustrate a range of situations with regard to personal connections, and thus include some men who revealed a great number of such connections during the interviews. There were others at the other extreme, who revealed and appeared to have, almost no personal connections that would be useful.

Case 1

The first case is a man, J., with a huge range of personal contacts. This man claimed to know 'almost everybody in the so-called establishment'.

He was born in 1904; his family had a small business, but his father died, and he did not enter the business, leaving his uncle and cousins to carry it on instead. His close family was contrastingly poor, he says, and suggested this might account for his own ambition. At the age of twenty he went abroad to run a small factory in South America, a post obtained through a family con-

nection. Returning to England five years later (1931), he obtained
a job in a business whose main controller was an MP, rising to be
managing director of a subsidiary at the age of twenty-nine.

At the end of the war, now aged forty-one, J. took over as
M.D. and then chairman of the main company. In this post he
employed an eminent scientist as consultant to the company:
later the scientist in turn suggested J. as a suitable businessman
to sit on the NRDC. Whilst on the NRDC, J. met a merchant banker,
the chairman of a merchant bank which later merged. This
banker was also a director of an ailing public company in a
different sector from J.'s previous experience and asked J. to
take over as chairman, which he did in 1954. It is this public
company, (_____), which J. headed until his retirement,
building it into a large multinational group.

On his own board, J. came into contact with men who recommended or asked him to sit on three other large public company
boards (all of firms in the top 200 by turnover). On two of these
he claims he played a part in removing the chairmen and bringing
replacements in. The board memberships in turn gave him a
number of contacts in the banking field (Lazards, Hambros,
Rothschilds) and with insurance companies (Eagle Star, Prudential).
He claims to have played a part in the successful efforts of the
institutions to remove the head of Vickers and replace him with
Lord Robens and a new M.D.

J.'s interests were very much in the Arts. He was on the Arts
council, and on a special board to progress the building of the
National Theatre. It is here, he claims, he used his contacts in
business to great advantage to speed up the building of the (at
that stage) very late theatre. It is worth quoting his account:

'We couldn't get steel - two years delivery - I got it. I got
Monty Finniston, whom I know personally, to turn a special
factory over. I know Monty you see from the NRDC. Then we
wanted 500 motors - we'd forgotten to order them. GEC couldn't
do them, the ones from Crompton Parkinson wouldn't fit. We had
to get them from Weinstock. Well you have to be very clever to
get anything from Weinstock, even if you're a great friend of
his. I got them. They never waited for anything. They wanted
twenty-eight miles of electric cable, they'd forgotten to order.
BICC said everything's for export - two-year waiting list. I
got it. Everybody was astonished, Sir Max Rayne and so on -
they don't know people like I do. They needed 28,000 pop rivets
for the curtain - I don't know what they are, but I went to
what's his name, of GKN, chairman, just retired, and I got
them. Every damn thing they wanted, aluminium lifts from Tube
Investments. To be fair I couldn't have done it for my company,
but I knew every man who had the things we wanted.'

J's contacts are mainly in business: in the course of the interview he mentions twenty-seven company chairmen and bankers by
name. His account of his influence may be exaggerated (he certainly dropped more names than anyone else), but from the known
facts the incidents he related were not pure fabrication. However,

J. said he had made little attempt to influence politicians, though
he knows some. He has spoken to them, on some issues, but
thinks attempts to influence policy would be unsuccessful. 'Well
if I went to talk to Harold Wilson about this [high rates of super-
tax] he'd say, ''yes but we live in a democratic society, you
know, you think like that but you're an exception. There's only
100,000 of you in the country, or 50,000 or whatever it is. . . .''
I don't feel I'd get anywhere.'

Case 2

The next man, M., is of a very different kind. He was born the
son of the chairman of the London County Council, and the grand-
son on his mother's side of a peer. He went to Eton and Oxford,
leaving the latter after a year 'bored and broke' (his words). He
was retired when interviewed and chose to meet for the interview
at Brooks's club.
   Sometime during his Oxford days M. met Edward de Stein the banker
(on the football field). De Stein, also an Eton and Oxford man,
offered him a job in an industrial firm of which de Stein was chairman.
   After a while M. decided to change jobs and a relative found
him a job in a merchant bank. After the war M. moved to de
Stein's bank, and then became a director of the company which
he had originally joined at the bottom. Later he took over as
chairman. 'That was pure merit,' he said, perhaps a little defens-
ively.
   M. is presented here as a contrast: he felt he had little political
influence and thought that only chairmen of very large companies
such as ICI would have any political sway. However, during the
war he was in the Cabinet office and at one stage said:
   'I think the only influence that an individual can have is over
   the people he knows as personal contacts . . . I happened to
   work in the Cabinet office during the war and therefore got to
   know all the senior civil servants and so might have had some
   influence. But that sort of thing doesn't last - you drift apart
   or change jobs. For a very few years my friendships lasted
   with the people who emerged as top civil servants.'
   M. exemplifies a point of view found among several men with an
elite background: that influence operates through personal friendships (though he also said the City might have influence via the
Bank of England). It seems, though, that the old establishment
is breaking down somewhat and that personal friendships are no
longer an adequate method of lobbying (see chapter 8), and a
new approach is needed.

Case 3

The third man, S., was also in the civil service during the war,
but made much greater use of his contacts. S. went to grammar
school and Cambridge, then entered the retail trade. During the

war he was placed in the Ministry of Supply and here formed his contacts with civil servants. He ended up director of footwear and leather.

After the war S. entered the retail shoe industry, as M.D. of a chain of shops. After these were taken over by a well-known entrepreneur, S. left, and obtained the job of chairman of a small agricultural company. This firm later grew to be one of the top 200.

As S. said at one stage in the interview: 'The job of chairman of (_____) is a mixture of politics and commerce. In fact it's difficult to know which it involved more of. Agriculture is very political.'

As one example, S. quoted the situation in which imports of agricultural products from an EFTA country were threatening his company. S. used his civil service contacts, and the government were persuaded to negotiate an arrangement to limit the amount of produce brought into Britain.

S. said he had found Labour ministers more helpful than Conservative ones, and a Labour minister sat as a director on his board. A former civil servant took over from S. as company chairman.

During the early 1970s S. featured heavily in the popular press. At a time of wage restraint (under the Heath government), S. took a £16,000 wage increase as a result of a bonus scheme linked to the profits of the company. This was widely publicised ('I'm the most libelled man in England'), and one incident from this period sheds light on the relationship between business and the media. A photographer from the 'Daily Mail' went to photograph S.'s country home, and S.'s wife, while a reporter enquired in the nearby village for gossip. S., extremely affronted, told his stockbroker, who in turn happened to know the late Lord Rothermere. The stockbroker telephoned Rothermere to complain, but the newspaper proprietor's reply left no doubt of his own interests: 'Well I know it's terribly nasty, old chap, but that young man's selling newspapers.' (Rothermere's supposed remark bears a striking resemblance to that made by his uncle, Lord Northcliffe; referring to the late 1890s Lewis and Maude (1949) remark that: 'The new popular press showed that the domestic market included not only the well-to-do but the lower middle and working classes, even down to the poorest.' When a group of industrial magnates called on Northcliffe to complain of the way he handled their case in a strike, he retorted: 'Well, gentlemen, the ha'pence of the working class are as good as yours - and there's a damn sight more of them.') S. was libelled on a radio programme 'Any Questions'. The cabinet minister on S.'s board spoke to Charles Curran about the incident and he asked to meet S. The ultimate result of the meeting was that S. himself made several radio appearances.

Though S. did have connections in business, he is more notable for his civil service contacts. He knew a number of MPs, but was in little doubt that backbench MPs had little influence. Contact with ministers was required if one was to usefully affect government; and 'it is no good convincing the minister if you haven't convinced the civil servants as well.'

Case 4

The next two cases are more straightforward, and perhaps more typical of the majority of bureaucrat-chairmen and entrepreneurs. Case 4 is that of B., public school educated, but with no other training and initially no particular connections in industry. B. began his career at the bottom of a large manufacturing company and has worked for it all his life.

After early training as an apprentice, B. was fortunate to come to the attention of the head of the company (a member of the founding family), and became his personal assistant. B. held various appointments, became M.D. in 1972, chairman in 1974. The group is one of Britain's largest 100 companies, but is based outside London.

It would be fair to say that B.'s contacts stem from his position as chairman of a large company. He said that industrialists do have influence, especially through their contacts with civil servants. He believed that he did influence a major decision, that of the Chancellor to allow tax relief on investment (Budget of 1975). B. thought this was worth a £1000 million to industry, and takes some credit for it. Whilst head of his local Chamber of Commerce he got the permanent secretary, under-secretary and deputy secretary of the DTI to a party at the Chamber of Commerce and gave them: 'a fair old bashing on the subject'.

This, he said, was a good way to put the point across: 'Because you've got to be very careful with civil servants, and why not – if you push your own company's point of view, they're entitled to say what are they up to. It's much better to do it as a group – the Chamber of Commerce, or the Trade Association or the CBI.'

It was B. who thought that Mr Heath had been pushed into confrontation in 1974 by the City. Yet his own contacts with the City are increasing; he offers this comment on the 'establishment':

'I suppose the establishment are the people in power who tend to come together and out of synergy, I suppose, reinforce each other. All right, an example – I'm a director of (_____) Bank. . . I'm damn sure if I hadn't been chairman of (_____) I wouldn't be on that board. And I could be just as good or bad a chap in another capacity and not be on the board of (_____) Bank, or not even be considered for the board. That sort of interlinking is a sort of establishment, isn't it?

And the board of (_____) Bank is a very good club. We meet once a fortnight and spend nearly a day; and, you know, a lot of my friends, and customers and competitors, we find ourselves having lunch together and we talk about things. I suppose that's an establishment, isn't it?'

(Q. That would seem to be the industrial establishment?)

'Yes, there are all sorts of establishments, I suppose . . . a
civic one, a government one.'

Case 5

The last case is similar, though the man, F., is an entrepreneur.
He took over a relatively small company some twenty-five years
ago and has built it up since into one of Britain's top 200. Just
over fifty when interviewed, he is unusual amongst entrepreneurs
in this study in having a public school background.

Though his company is large, however, he maintains that his
influence comes from the fact that he is a member of a nationalised
industry board. He got on to this simply because a minister had
heard of him, but this, in turn, gives him an entrée to the
'nationalised industry establishment', to use his phrase, the
group of men who run nationalised industries together with the
ministers and relevant civil servants. F. says that: 'One can
have influence but it's fairly sketchy. If you go out of your way
you can make contacts with ministers and civil servants, but
you've got to work at it.' One such contact, which F. did work
at, was the permanent secretary at the Treasury: F. met him at
a party, invited him to lunch, and now 'because he knows me,
when he wants to get together twenty or thirty businessmen to
consult with I'm included.'

Again he mentions that:
'The Conservative Party wants to make contact with the unions.
Heseltine got in touch with me, said he hadn't been round our
factories, so I fixed a visit for him. And he said could he meet
one or two of the union people - so now he owes me a favour.
That may be useful some day.'

These cases have been given only as examples of how personal
contacts can be formed and used. They come from a number of
experiences: in the case of M., a particular social background
and family connections. In the case of J., membership of a
government-sponsored organisation (NRDC) and outside directorships. In the case of S., previous experience as a civil servant.
F. draws on a variety of sources: meeting someone at a party,
direct approach by a shadow minister, and being recommended by
a member to the 'nationalised industry establishment'. B. is perhaps not truly a case study of the use of personal contacts, since
he used his position as head of a Chamber of Commerce. However,
both B. and F. show how position as a top businessman leads to
invitations to form further links, one with the City, the other
with politicians.

The case studies also indicate that to some extent it is a matter
of choice whether or not one forms interlinks with other elite
groups. M. has never really bothered, if his account is to be
believed. J. used his contacts extensively, but for business not
political purpose. Both B. and F., having begun to form outside
links, appear to be interested in forming more.

As stated in chapter 8, personal contacts are very useful.

However, size of company and personal reputation seem ultimately to count for more. Compare the accounts above with that related by one head of a company from one of the top twenty firms (in size). The chairman and other top directors of this group are not much involved with the CBI, nor do they have other directorships, apart from the chairman. The directors come from minor public, direct grant and state schools, and all have come up through the firm.

The directors of this company, like many others, were concerned about the effects of the Industry Bill, later the Industry Act. The chairman and another director requested, and were given, two meetings with Harold Wilson and with Mr Benn and senior civil servants. As a result, they believe they succeeded in modifying the Act, and the effect (eventual non-effect) of planning agreements. In this case, size and reputation were sufficient to give access.

NOTES

1 STRATEGISTS, IDEOLOGISTS AND INFLUENTIALS

1 See chapter 3 for fuller details of the sample. As it turned out, all those approached and eventually interviewed in this study were men. This was not a deliberate intention; it was simply an obvious though unexpected finding. For convenience I have usually referred to members of the business elite as men.

2 In the literature reviewed in Chapters 1 and 2 I pay little attention to the very extensive research concerned with the background of business leaders; for example, what percentage went to public school, what percentage belong to certain London clubs. This is because explicit comparisons are made in chapter 4, where this work is thoroughly discussed.

3 One might query the omission of nationalised industry directors. However, it should be pointed out that such men are simply not as free to take decisions as are the chief executives and directors studied here. Government clearly does intervene in the pricing policy, investment policy and employment policies of nationalised industries; and in any case some of these are in monopoly positions. Indubitably nationalised industry directors form part of the economic elite, but not that segment of it that I call the business elite. However, it may be noted that the study did contain four men who have headed nationalised industries at some stage of their careers.

4 I make this assumption despite Pahl and Winkler's (1974) claim that the term economic elite should only be used for those who allocate capital within the company. The problem is that somewhat prolonged investigation is necessary to establish just who is in the capital-allocating cabal, at least according to their research. Actually, this study does take account of this by concentrating on chief executives; I feel it unlikely that any significant proportion of these would not take resource allocation decisions.

5 Mintzberg (1973) carried out observational studies on five chief executives, three of them from business firms, in an attempt to evaluate what managers actually do. He concluded they had ten roles, which are common to some extent to all managers. They are: (a) the interpersonal roles of figurehead, liaison, and leader; (b) the information roles as monitor, disseminator and spokesman; (c) the decisional roles as entrepreneur, disturbance handler, resource allocator and negotiator.

6 The studies consulted were: Copeland (1947), Seymour (1954), Brown and Smith (1957), Institute of Directors (1961; 1964; 1968), Puckey (1969), British Institute of Management (1972), and Department of Trade and Industry (1977). Mace (1971; 1972) repeats this theory, but he argues that in practice most boards do not perform several of the functions imputed to them. He argues that only full-time executives can establish the objectives, strategies and policies of the corporation. He states that boards generally do not audit the performance of management, do not question the executive members, and only remove the chief executive in crisis situations.

7 In the revised edition (1967) of 'The Modern Corporation and Private Property,' Berle and Means produce evidence to show that whereas in 1929 the 100 largest American corporations controlled 44 per cent of net capital assets of all manufacturing firms, in 1962 the figure was 58.4 per cent. Work by Prais (1976) provides equivalent evidence for the United Kingdom. In this country the largest 100 enterprises produced some 5 per cent of manufacturing net output in 1909, 22 per cent in 1949, but 41 per cent in 1968. On current trends they could be producing two-thirds within ten to twenty years, depending on the type of projection.

8   The major British study is that of Florence (1961). He uses multiple criteria;
    to be owner-controlled a company had to have: (a) a single shareholder
    with 20 per cent or more of the votes; or (b) to be such that the largest
    twenty shareholders had 30 percent of the votes; or (c) to satisfy (a) or
    (b) if the shareholders were companies or in some way connected; or (d)
    to be one in which the directors had between them more than 5 per cent
    of the ordinary shares. Florence's conclusion for 268 companies is that two-
    thirds in 1951 were probably not owner-controlled.

9   A recent version of this idea suggests that finance control comes as a stage
    after a company has passed into managerial control (see Francis, 1980).

10 The reverse argument carried to extremes is used by Drucker (1976), who
    argues that since pension funds now own large amounts of American corpora-
    tions, and the funds, in turn, invest money provided by a very large sec-
    tion of society, America now has people's capitalism, or control of the means
    of production by the people.

11 The argument has been developed by Soref (1976), who found that upper-
    class directors were more likely to have outside directorships than were non-
    upper-class directors. Within their own firms they were just as likely to be
    on the executive committee as non-upper-class directors. Soref sees his
    findings as being in accordance with Domhoff's views, but he ignores the
    fact that among his sample there were always more non-upper-class than
    upper-class directors among both executive and non-executive directors.
    Thus, in practice, the non-upper-class men could outvote the upper-class
    men both in the executive committee and on the full board. The evidence
    from interlocking directorships is fully discussed in Scott (1979, ch. 4).

12 In repeating Brown's analysis, I treated 'financial control' as a disease -
    anyone who sits on the board of a financial institution is deemed to have
    caught it and thereafter to behave as a profit-maximising capitalist would.

    As Brown did, I examined the top 120 companies in 'The Times' 1,000 list.
    I separated out those companies where known entrepreneurs were chairman
    or chief executive, or where members of founding or controlling families
    were on the board. Then I separated out the subsidiaries of foreign multi-
    nationals. Finally, I examined all the directors on the remaining company
    boards, classifying them as co-ordinator-controllers if they had the
    financial control disease. Wherever such people were in the majority on the
    board. I classified the company as co-ordinator-controlled. The results of the
    analysis are set out in the table.

Dominant interest on board	Brown 1954	Brown 1966	Fidler 1976
Family/Tycoon	36	38	35
Co-ordinator	53	47	11
Managerial (British)	} 31	} 35	54
Managerial (overseas)			20
Totals	120	120	120

13 Nor are their examples convincing. From my own research I would dispute
    that Debenhams is an example of the intervention of finance control.
    Burmah, an example taken from Scott and Hughes (1976), though not
    referred to by Scott, could be said to contradict their point. Burmah was
    shown to be linked to six institutional holdings through shareholdings,
    directorships and management. Amongst such connections one may mention
    that of Lord Inchcape, who, aside from running the firm which bears his
    name, had shown his willingness to play an interventionist role as an out-
    side director in the P & O-Bovis saga in that he first blocked a bid by P
    & O for Bovis, then became chairman and carried out the same takeover
    (see the 'Sunday Times', 27 January 1974, p. 47). Burmah, then, is finan-
    cially controlled; Inchcape is the finance capitalist par excellence. Yet this

did not prevent Burmah from running into trouble when one of its insider directors bought too many tankers. Burmah was saved by the shares it held in BP, the price the government took for preventing it floundering completely. Lord Inchcape is reported to have remarked *à propos* of Burmah: 'a board of directors can only be as good as the information it receives.' This hardly squares with the picture of the interventionist financier. (On Burmah, see the 'Sunday Times', 5 January 1975, p. 52; 26 January 1975, p. 50; 23 February 1975, p. 50.)

14   For references to these and other studies see Taylor and MacMillan (1974). For a counter-example see Crenson (1971).

15   See also Bowman and Haire (1975).

16   Practitioners, however, may well disagree with this. See the views expressed in Bull (1972).

17   See also the chapter by Abell in Abell (1975).

18   They are: (a) normal management hierarchy; (b) crisis revelations; (c) consultation and bargaining; (d) one man chains, in which a single member of the board is taken to be in touch with the shopfloor; (e) personal service personnel; (f) past experience; (g) mass media; (h) attitude surveys.

19   This view is consistent with that suggested by Archibald (1976), who suggests that members of different classes feel threatened by one another and cope with the situation by withdrawal and avoidance.

20   Recent studies of television coverage of industrial relations suggest a strong tendency to view relationships in terms of two sides, to be interested only in situations of conflict, and to stress the inconvenience of strikes to the consumer. See, for example, Morley (1976), Glasgow University Media Group (1976).

21   This obviously limited discussion of Weber is based on 'Economy and Society', Weber (1968). I am aware of the recent claim (Scott, 1979) that Weber discusses only three social classes, and that the 'classes distinguished by property and education' are in fact a section heading, mistakenly translated. I am not in a position to decide on this, but Weber was clear about the importance of property as a determinant of class, and since the classes distinguished by property, etc. do not fit into the three social classes anywhere else, they must constitute a separate category. The only question is how many such classes there are, and whether or not they are all part of one major property-owning class, and here, of course, Weber's discussion is incomplete.

22   Giddens (1973), however, by his differentiation of the primary and secondary bases of class structuration, offers an explanation of how the possibility of infinite classes in Weber's theoretical scheme can reduce to three in practice. Giddens also stresses that people have to be conscious of class identity if the concept of class is to be a useful one.

23   See also Williams (1956) and Bell and Newby (1973).

24   Warner attempted to describe a status system for 'Yankee City'; but it is doubtful if anyone would attempt such an exercise for an urban community nowadays. See Warner and Lunt (1947); Warner, Meeker and Eells (1960) and, for a discussion of the problems of this approach, Gordon (1963).

25   A great measure of agreement was reported in the social ranking of occupations (see Hall and Jones (1950) and Moser and Hall in Glass (1954), and the NRDC study in Bendix and Lipset (1953)). Studies of certain subgroups of society, such as Young and Willmott (1956) and Stehr (1974) indicate a more complex picture, whilst Goldthorpe and Hope have raised grave doubts about the validity of these studies as measures of prestige. See their chapter in Hope (1972).

26   For example, the tendency for members of the working class to vote Conservative, studied by McKenzie and Silver (1968) and Nordlinger (1967) or the embourgeoisement thesis studied by Goldthorpe et al. (1968a; 1968b; 1969).

27   The thinking that led Lockwood to his scheme, particularly his debt to Bott (1954; 1971) and Blauner (1960), is discussed in the introduction to Bulmer (1975).

28 Fundamentally, deferential workers are the same as those so labelled by
Lockwood, whilst aspirational workers are those who perceive opportunities
for them personally of upward mobility, and Parkin's conceptualisation has
the strength of drawing our attention to the fact that social mobility is to
some extent a source of social stability by allowing the more able (and potentially the leaders) of the lower-class groupings to move out of their originating community.

29 Parkin might claim that his book represents a general discussion of the
nature of inequality and social stability, and that he is not offering a
detailed treatment of this particular area. Nevertheless, certain specific
problems do appear to have been ignored or treated only skimpily. For
example, Lockwood's privatised worker, the subject of a three-volume study
by Goldthorpe, Lockwood and co-workers, does not have a normative orientation that can be seen as a mixture of the three value systems that Parkin
discusses. Parkin's conception does have the virtue that it sidesteps the
major problem of Lockwood's, which is that it mixes structural factors
(community situation) and attitudinal ones. Bell and Newby have proposed
replacing the work situation variable by a measure of bureaucratisation (see
Bulmer, 1975). Another problem of Lockwood's model is that in the case of
the two types of traditional worker, the work and community situation
generate attitudes, but in the case of the privatised worker, attitudes
generate the situations. See the chapters by Brown and Daniel in Child
(1973).

30 Studies using a more structured approach are Runciman (1966); Butler and
Stokes (1969), and Lopreato and Hazelrigg (1972).

31 The different results obtained from research on different populations and
sub-groups is striking. For example, Hiller reports finding almost no
'privatised worker' conceptions whatsoever. Several authors, most notably
Bell and Newby, emphasise the ambiguities in their respondents' references
to class, status and related topics. Blackburn and Mann went so far as to
state that their respondents held no consistent political ideology, though,
as Lockwood points out (see Bulmer, 1975), this does not necessarily mean
they held no images of society.

32 Discussions of Althusser's general theories are provided by Kolakowski
(1971) and Callinicos (1976). His theory of ideology is discussed by Hirst
(1976) and McLennan, Molina and Peters in Centre for Contemporary
Cultural Studies (1978).

33 Witness, for example, the ire aroused by Campbell Adamson, director-
general of the CBI, for saying publicly what many businessmen at the time
had been saying privately about the Industrial Relations Act. See Grant
and Marsh (1977, p. 89).

34 Pareto's ideas are contained in Pareto (1935), though a more accessible
approach can be made through Pareto (1966). See also Aron (1968);
Bottomore (1966) and Meisel (1965). The extraordinary correspondence of
the central idea in Pareto's and Mosca's work, that of the elite and the mass,
and the idea of the circulation of elites, is said by Gregor (1969) to be due
to the fact that both men obtained these ideas from Gumplowicz.

35 Miliband's arguments and methodology are not fundamentally different from
those of many theorists who are not overtly Marxist. Duverger (1974), for
example, refers to Western societies as pluto-democracies - they are formally
democratic but power is held partly by the elected government, partly by
the owners of capital, as individuals or in the great industrial and financial
companies.

36 As Wolff (1968) argues is the case.

37 The pluralist view has not been much discussed using British evidence,
though an attempt has been made by Hewitt (1974). See also Morriss (1975)
and Hewitt (1976).

2 THE MEANING SYSTEMS OF TOP BUSINESSMEN

1   Again, see Rokeach here. Rokeach details several levels at which beliefs
    (and values) exist. Accepting this notion in principle, I should say that
    meaning systems as discussed in this book only really concern the middle
    levels. To fully understand individual action in a situation requires under-
    standing of all the levels.
2   See the discussion by Bulmer in Bulmer (1975).
3   Note that this refers to boardroom directors, not, for example, chief
    executives, although this study indicates that most chief executives have
    to an extent risen through the firm. See chapter 4.
4   Watson's article is contained in Gluckman and Devons (1964).
5   Apart from Whyte's study, see Spectorsky (1955) Seeley, Sim and Loosley
    (1956) and Riesman (1957). The field is surveyed by Thorns (1972).
6   Pahl (1965); Musgrove (1963, ch. 5, Musgrove demonstrates that in 'Midland
    City' professional employees and other middle-class groups continued to
    supply the leaders of voluntary associations even though they were often
    migrants to the town. One may doubt the political importance of some of the
    associations taken, however (for example, the scouts, guides, WVS), and I
    will show below that in certain areas of local law and political involvement
    businessmen are less involved than twenty-five or fifty years ago. See
    chapter 8.
7   See Coleman (1973) for a fascinating discussion of the desire by British
    businessmen to become members of the gentry.
8   See Wilkinson (1964), Weinberg (1967), Bamford (1967), Wakeford, (1969).
    Some useful material on boarding school life is also contained in Lambert
    and Millham (1968).
9   This transition seemed to be paralleled in the interview study by directors'
    accounts of their lives in industry. They would begin these accounts with
    such phrases as 'I began as the lowest form of animal life in XYZ company.
    . . .'
10 See also Buck (1971), especially later chapters. The use made here of
    McKenzie and Silver's analysis perhaps ignores the fact that the appeal of
    the party to the ordinary voter may be different to that which it makes to
    elites. In effect, the business elite have no alternative to vote for, and its
    specific ideology may not be important to them. However, I did find some
    businessmen who stood as Liberal candidates at elections, and one who
    claimed to vote Labour.
11 A comparative analysis of the two would be instructive, as American busi-
    ness appears to operate in a more favourable climate than does British. The
    businessman in America has higher rewards and is said to have higher
    prestige than does his counterpart in Britain.
12 For example Child (1969) shows that British management thinkers had
    already come up with many of the ideas of the human relations movement in
    the 1920s, although it was the 1940s before the ideas and writings of Elton
    Mayo were imported into Britain. Mayo's writings then gave 'human relations'
    an additional thrust.
13 This shift of values has also been remarked on by Riesman et al. (1950).

3 DESIGN OF THE RESEARCH

1   I mean to imply no criticism of later works by Rosemary Stewart, such as
    Stewart (1967; 1976).
2   Although Ellis and Child (1973) could find no evidence of a 'bureaucratic
    man' or 'bureaucratic personality' in large firms; rather they suggest that
    particular types of personality may enter or adapt to particular occupations
    or industries.
3   See also Bruce (1976).
4   One should, perhaps, accept the results of these comparisons with caution,
    granted that there are several methods of interpreting TAT tests. Henry's

system, though used very effectively by him, is apparently used by few other researchers (see Murstein, 1963).

5 Dexter and co-workers interviewed some 900 businessmen to obtain their attitudes to trade tariffs. See Bauer, Pool and Dexter (1963); and Dexter (1970) for much useful advice on elite interviewing. Kincaid and Bright, (1957) do report access problems, but Dexter suggests that they were interviewing businessmen on a subject (civil defence policy) of little importance to them as businessmen.

6 Nichols (1969) obtained co-operation from sixteen out of nineteen companies for his 'Northern City' study, but has pointed out to me that it took two years to obtain 65 interviews. John Child, who interviewed chief executives and other directors in a study of organisation structure (Child, 1972), has told me that there were some problems, not so much with obtaining access, but with the length of time required for the interview. On another front, Headey (1974) has obtained interviews with cabinet ministers and civil servants.

7 This is reminiscent of Clegg's attempts to ask formally about power within an organisation. Clegg gives an interesting discussion of the nature of, and acceptance of, the power that is 'embedded' in the very nature of organisations, or organisations as their members expect and perceive them to be. See Clegg (1975), especially ch. 4 and ch. 7.

8 Since the secret tape recording of Sir Richard Dobson at a dinner in which he referred to 'blackish people' and 'wogs', and questioned the beneficial effect of trade unions, remarks which led to his resignation as chairman of British Leyland, this might be harder to obtain. See 'The Times', 29 October 1977, p.1; 22 October, pp.1 and 2.

9 Jack Winkler, who had already made a study of directors. See the papers by Pahl and Winkler (1974) and Winkler (1975).

10 Ethnomethodologists would raise rather different criticisms, notably that all we are doing is taking the views of members of society and comparing them to our own so that, as Turner puts it: 'members thereby stand corrected as though they had intended to produce a science of their lives in the process of living them' (Turner, 1974 p.10). See also the chapter by Dorothy Smith in the same volume.

11 This is not, of course, by any means the only problem of Althusser's work, nor indeed the greatest. See the discussions for example in Kolakowski (1971) and Callinicos (1976).

12 Some businessmen can decorate their offices to a style not possible at home. One prominent insurance company chairman, classed here as a bureaucrat, took me up to the company boardroom, the interior design of which had been undertaken by himself and his wife. There round the walls were prime examples of modern British painting - a Hockney, a Ben Nicholson, a Francis Bacon - together with tapestry and sculpture with which I was less familiar. There was no way he could have afforded such things for his home (he said).

4 RESERVED SEATS: FAMILY BACKGROUND, EDUCATION, CAREER AND PRESENT LIFESTYLES OF TOP BUSINESSMEN

1 The Clarendon Commission of 1861-64 mentioned nine schools as 'significant of the position that a few schools had gained in the public eye'. They were: Eton, Harrow, Charterhouse, Merchant Taylors', Rugby, St. Paul's, Shrewsbury, Westminster and Winchester. The quote is taken from Sampson (1971).

2 However, Hall and Amado-Fischgrund's conclusion that 'professional and executive positions provide a channel of upward mobility over two generations' is not strictly correct, since no measure of occupational status currently in use places the professions below businessmen.

3 There were two viscounts, one earl, one other son of a peer, two baronets and eleven members of the landed gentry. The edition of 'Burke's Landed

Gentry' referred to is the 18th, published in three volumes (1965, 1969 and 1972).

4   A similar argument is made by Bourdieu and Passeron (1977) (see section two of 'Reproduction'). In their terms, the elite have 'cultural capital' and add to it through educational advancement. Others must acquire this capital, but the system is highly selective in allowing only the brightest to do so.

5   Correctly or not, the experience of some other countries is said to have been different in this regard. For instance, in a letter to the 'Sunday Times', Dr Jeremy Bray stated that 'Sabburo Okita, the veteran Japanese economist . . . gave it as his opinion that one reason for their success was that defeat in war removed a generation of industrial as well as military leadership and allowed fresh men and ideas to emerge.' See the 'Sunday Times', 1 February 1976, p. 60.

6   For some reason which was not apparent afterwards, both the interviewer and the interviewee accepted a peer and a duchess as occupations!

5 THE COMPANY COMES FIRST: THE RESPONSIBILITIES AND OBJECTIVES OF DIRECTORS

1   See Child (1969), p. 73 and p. 219. The other references are discussed in Professor Child's PhD thesis (Child, 1967). They are Rowntree (1920), Vyle (1922) and Elbourne, who is reported in the Journal of Industrial Administration, vol. I, 2 February 1921, p. 58.

2   Nichols made very similar observations to those made here, although he made no attempt to discover how widespread the 'ethos' is. See Nichols (1969) pp. 225-6.

3   Such a generalisation might not apply, in contrast, to top American executives. The top salary paid to a 'manager' in a US company in 1977 was £570,000, and this presumably allows the acquisition of quite large amounts of capital. See the 'Sunday Times', 17 April, 1977.

4   Perrow sees organisations as having five types of goal: societal, output, system, product, and derived. In his terms, the 'balancing interests' ethos that I discussed above implies that businessmen see no essential disjunction between these types of goal when pursued by the business company.

5   Much fuller evidence should be forthcoming from the Anglo-German project on growth and development of the firm directed in Britain by Child and Silberston and in Germany by Kieser. See Child et al. (1975).

6   The need for better non-executive directors is periodically raised by the British financial press. See, for example, 'The search for the Super-director', 'Sunday Times', 27 July, 1975; 'Wanted now a new breed of watchdog in the boardroom', 'Sunday Times', 21 August, 1977; 'Men who sit where the buck stops', 'Financial Times', 19 September, 1975.

7   It may stand as a comment that aside from the Lonhro meetings of the early seventies, the most exciting AGM reported in the press in recent years seems to have been that of the Derby County Football Club. See the 'Guardian', 10 November, 1976, 'Clouh casts a long shadow'. The exception to this is almost any AGM involving Mr 'Tiny' Rowland.

6 THE VIEW FROM MOUNT OLYMPUS: CONFLICT, CONSENSUS AND PARTICIPATION IN THE FIRM

1   The Royal Commission on Trade Unions and Employers' Associations (1968), the Donovan Commission.

2   This is echoed elsewhere. The CBI apparently has an Employee Communications Unit. See the 'Guardian', 20 June, 1977, p. 16. In 1977 this unit issued a thirty-two-page booklet on communications with people at work. This contained eleven key questions which senior managers should ask themselves regarding communication at work.

3   Reported on BBC Radio Four's 'Financial World Tonight'.

4   For a more detailed breakdown of answers on this topic see Fidler (1974).

7 NOT A SOCIETY PERSON, NOT AT ALL SNOOTY: BUSINESSMEN'S VIEWS
OF CLASS AND STATUS IN BRITAIN

1   These problems are discussed in greater detail in Fidler (1979).
2   Recent concern about the status of businessmen, especially those in manu-
     facturing industry, is reflected in Finniston (1980) and Mant (1977).
3   Indeed, it was obvious that businessmen's images of society were not based
     on reference to Plowman et al.'s (1962) 'local social status systems'. They
     were more more abstract and called on a wider frame of reference than
     such systems.
4   See Brown and Brannen (1970), Cousins and Brown (1975) or the paper by
     these authors in Bulmer (1975).

8 AN UNINVENTED LOBBY: THE BUSINESS PICTURE OF POWER IN BRITAIN

1   See, for example, the collections by Urry and Wakeford (1973) and
     Stanworth and Giddens (1974a).
2   The four were directors of merchant banks or insurance companies.
3   This typology is developed following Finer (1955).
4   Such an examination can easily be made by use of the 'Times Guide to the
     House of Commons' (1979) or Roth, Kerbey and Tench, (1975).
5   This might explain the feeling amongst businessmen that politicians of all
     parties have little understanding of business. Thus the business experience
     of even those politicians who are also businessmen could be disparaged, as,
     for example, by the entrepreneur who remarked of the last Tory government:
     'The man in the street might have said to himself the Conservative govern-
     ment contains John Davies, Peter Walker, Keith Joseph, all significant
     people with lots of business experience. In none of those, or any other cases
     was it true. Taking those three men: Peter Walker was an insurance sales-
     man, a good attractive personality, but nothing beyond that - not a tycoon.
     Keith Joseph is an immensely intelligent man and was a deputy chairman of
     Bovis for a time, but never, ever a businessman. John Davies was M.D. of
     one of the oil companies - Shell-Mex and BP, I think, which was a marketing
     job quite honestly. They had no business connections, and their business
     personalities didn't relate quite honestly to big business at all.'
6   And more recently renamed Aims.
7   Chapman (1970) states that the policy of moving civil servants from post to
     post every few years is, or has been, deliberate.
8   Nevertheless, on the basis of this study I cannot agree with the author of
     an article in the journal 'Multinational Business' who writes: 'The U.K. is
     indeed one of the most difficult countries in which to lobby effectively. . . .
     [But] little time is wasted on M.P.s who unlike U.S. congressmen have no
     power, while entertaining ministers tends to be a waste of time. Virtually
     all serious discussions involving ministers and large firms is conducted with
     at least one civil servant present. This is an unwritten rule in Whitehall.
     Moreover in many key areas of interest to multinationals, policy has been
     made almost wholly by two or three key civil servants - Treasury officials in
     the case of exchange controls, and Ministry of Fuel and Power (now DTI)
     officials in the case of energy policy, especially oil' ('Economist' Intelligence
     Unit, 1972). Businessmen did not see entertaining ministers, at least in the
     sense of inviting them to lunch or dinner, as a waste of time, though they
     did say one could never be sure if one had got one's point across success-
     fully. It was certainly regarded as important to influence the civil servants
     as well as the minister, but the 'unwritten rule' was not mentioned. On the
     question of oil, in fact North Sea oil, a businessman said he had found Mr
     Benn and his officials 'surprisingly helpful'.
9   For a full discussion of the CBI's role see Grant and Marsh (1977).

10 I have already emphasised that business has much to gain by influencing government. The trade associations go to the government with continuous requests. For example, 'The Times' of 25 April 1977 reported two of these: an attempt to prevent a Japanese company building a factory in Britain, and for protection against footwear imports.

11 For some further views on businessmen and TV see 'The BBC: is it biased against the boardroom?', in 'The Director', December 1975. This is an account of a meeting of Sir Charles Curran and five company directors. Curran commented in this on the problems of persuading industrialists to appear on TV. The directors, in turn, made it clear that a 'responsible role' for the BBC would involve it in emphasising the virtues of capitalism (Curran did not agree). Thus one said: 'I would agree that the public has got the message about the dangers of inflation but are you doing your job speaking up for the competitive system and showing how it can help defeat inflation?'

An Aims for Freedom and Enterprise brochure echoes the importance placed on TV as a medium by the businessmen interviewed here: 'In Western society the radicals have tended to grasp the great importance of television. Many of their activities have been designed to have visual impact on television rather than achieve anything specific. The protagonists of freedom and enterprise have got to master such techniques'.

12 Mougel (1978) traces the evolution of the term establishment.

9 CONCLUSION

1 Thus in a poll of European (non-British) company chief executives, reported in the March 1978 edition of the magazine 'Chief Executive Monthly', a majority thought British managers to be highly class-conscious.

2 See Mant (1977) for generalisations on this point and many similar.

3 This passage comes from an unpublished report direct to the interviewees. The views expressed are similar to those of Kaysen (1959).

4 Nichols (1969) ended his work with a dozen examples of areas where further empirical investigations were needed. Almost all still await such investigation.

5 With regard to corporate strategy and the development of firms in a changing environment there is the Nuffield-Aston-Berlin project in which interviews have been conducted in this country with both main board and subsidiary company directors in some twenty firms. The framework of this project is set out in Child et al. (1975); and some findings are given in Francis (1980) and Nyman and Silberston (1978). The political involvement of businessmen in Britain and the United States is currently being investigated by Michael Useem of Boston University.

BIBLIOGRAPHY

Aaronovitch, S. (1961), 'The Ruling Class', London, Lawrence & Wishart.

Abell, P. (ed.) (1965), 'Organisations as Power and Influence Systems', London, Heinemann.

Alberoni, F. (1972), The Powerless 'Elite': Theory and Sociological Research on the Phenomenon of the Stars, in McQuail, D. (ed.), 'Sociology of Mass Communications', Harmondsworth, Penguin.

Althusser, L. (1965), 'For Marx', Harmondsworth, Penguin.

Althusser, L. (1971), 'Lenin and Philosophy and Other Essays', London, New Left Books.

Althusser, L., and Balibar, E. (1970), 'Reading Capital', Harmondsworth, Penguin.

Ansoff, H.I. (1969), 'Corporate Strategy', Harmondsworth, Penguin.

Archibald, W.P. (1976), 'Face-to-Face: The Alienating Effects of Class, Status and Power Divisions', 'American Sociological Review', vol. 41, pp. 819-37.

Aron, R. (1968), 'Main Currents in Sociological Thought', vol. 2, London, Weidenfeld & Nicolson.

Bachrach, P. (1969), 'The Theory of Democratic Elitism', London, University of London Press.

Bachrach, P., and Baratz, M.S. (1962), The Two Faces of Power, 'American Political Science Review', LVI, pp. 947-52.

Bachrach, P., and Baratz, M.S. (1963), Decisions and Nondecisions, 'American Political Science Review', LVII, pp. 632-42.

Bain, G. (1977), In Defence of Bullock's Basic Thinking, 'Personnel Management', May, pp. 25-7.

Bain, G., et al. (1973), 'Social Stratification and Trade Unionism: A Critique', London, Heinemann (Warwick Studies in Industrial Relations).

Baltzell, E.D. (1958), 'An American Business Aristocracy', Chicago, Free Press.

Bamford, T.W. (1967), 'The Rise of the Public Schools', Sunbury-on-Thames, Nelson.

Bannock, G. (1973), 'The Juggernauts', Harmondsworth, Penguin.

Bannock, G. (1976), Higher Incomes and the Market System, 'The Banker', April.

Baran, P.A., and Sweezy, P.M. (1966), 'Monopoly Capital', New York, Monthly Review Press.

Baratz, M.S. (1956), Corporate Giants and the Power Structure, 'Western Political Quarterly', vol. 9.

Barritt, D.P. (1957), The Stated Qualifications of Directors of Large Public Companies, 'Journal of Industrial Economics', vol. 5, no. 3.

Bauer, R.A., Pool, I. de S., and Dexter, L.A. (1963), 'American Business and Public Policy', New York, Atherton Press.

Bell, C. (1968), 'Middle-Class Families', London, Routledge & Kegan Paul.

Bell, C., and Newby, H. (1973) 'Variation in agricultural workers' images of society, 'Sociological Review', May.

Bell, D. (1961), 'The End of Ideology', New York, Collier-Macmillan.

Bell, R., Edwards, D.U., and Wagner, R.H. (1969), 'Political Power: A Reader in Theory and Research', New York, Free Press.

Bendix, R. (1956), 'Work and Authority in Industry', New York, John Wiley & Sons.

Bendix R., and Houston, F.W. (1957), Social Mobility and the American Business Elite, I, 'British Journal of Sociology', vol. 8, pp. 357-69.

Bendix, R., and Houston, F.W. (1958), Social Mobility and the American Business Elite, II, 'British Journal of Sociology', vol. 9, pp. 1-14.

Bendix, R., and Lipset, S.M. (1953), 'Class, Status and Power', London,
Routledge & Kegan Paul.
Bentley, A. (1908), 'The Process of Government', Chicago University Press.
Berger, B.M. (1961), The Myth of Suburbia, 'The Journal of Social Issues',
vol. XVII, no. 1.
Berle, A.A. (1960), 'Power without Property', New York, Harcourt Brace
Jovanovich.
Berle, A.A., and Means, G.C. (1932), 'The Modern Corporation and Private
Property', New York, Macmillan (Revised 1967).
Betts, R. (1967), The Characteristics of British Company Directors, 'Journal
of Management Studies', 4,1.
Birnbaum, N. (1953), Conflicting Interpretations of the Rise of Capitalism,
'British Journal of Sociology', vol. 4, pp. 125-41.
Blackburn, R.M., and Mann, M. (1975), The ideologies of non-skilled workers,
in Bulmer (1975).
Blauner, R. (1960), Work Satisfaction and Industrial Trends in Modern Society,
in Galenson, W., and Lipset, S.M. (eds), 'Labour and Trade Unionism', New
York, John Wiley & Sons.
Bolton Committee (1971), 'Report of the Committee of Inquiry on Small Firms',
cmnd 4811, London, HMSO.
Boswell, J. (1973), 'The Rise and Decline of Small Firms', London, Allen & Unwin.
Bott, E. (1954), The Concept of Class as a Reference Group, 'Human Relations,
VII, pp. 259-85.
Bott, E. (1971), 'Family and Social Network', 2nd edn., New York, Free Press.
Bottomore, T.B. (1956), Some Reflections on the Sociology of Knowledge,
'British Journal of Sociology', 7, pp. 52-8.
Bottomore, T.B. (1965), 'Classes in Modern Society', London, Allen & Unwin.
Bottomore, T.B. (1966), 'Elites and Society', Harmondsworth, Penguin.
Bourdieu, P. (1973), Cultural Reproduction and Social Reproduction, in Brown,
R. (ed.), 'Knowledge, Education and Cultural Change', London, Tavistock.
Bourdieu, P., and Passeron, J.C. (1977), 'Reproduction', London, Sage.
Bower, J. (1974), On the Amoral Organisation, in Marris, R. (ed.), 'The
Corporate Society', London, Macmillan.
Bowman, E.H., and Haire, M. (1975), A Strategic Posture Toward Corporate
Social Responsibility, 'California Management Review', vol. XVIII, no.2, Winter.
Boyd, D. (1973), 'Elites and their Education', Slough, NFER Publishing.
British Institute of Management (1972), 'The Board of Directors', B.I.M.
Management Survey Report 10, London.
Brooks, J. (1971), 'Business Adventures', Harmondsworth, Penguin.
Brown, C.C., and Smith, E.E. (eds) (1957), 'The Director Looks at His Job',
New York, Columbia University Press.
Brown, M.B. (1968), The Controllers of British Industry, reproduced in Urry,
J., and Wakeford, J. (1973), 'Power in Britain', London, Heinemann.
Brown, R.K., and Brannen, P. (1970), Social Relations and Social Perspectives
amongst Shipbuilding Workers, 'Sociology', vol. 4, nos. 1 and 2.
Brown, R.K., et al. (1972), The Contours of Solidarity, 'British Journal of
Industrial Relations', vol. 10, no. 1.
Bruce, R. (1976), 'The Entrepreneurs', Bedford, Libertarian Books.
Bruce-Gardyne, J., and Lawson, N. (1976), 'The Power Game', London,
Macmillan.
Buck, P.W. (ed.) (1971), 'How Conservatives Think', Harmondsworth, Penguin.
Bull, G. (1972), 'Industrial Relations: The Boardroom Viewpoint', London,
Bodley Head.
Bulmer, M. (ed.) (1975), 'Working-Class Images of Society', London, Routledge
& Kegan Paul.
Burch, P.M. Jnr. (1972), 'The Managerial Revolution Reassessed', Lexington,
Mass., Heath.
'Burke's Landed Gentry' (1965, 1969, 1972), 18th edition, London, Burke's
Peerage.
'Burke's Peerage' (1970), 10th edition, London: Burke's Peerage.
Burnham, J. (1962), 'The Managerial Revolution', Harmondsworth, Penguin.
Butler, D., and Stokes, D. (1969), 'Political Change in Britain', London, Macmillan.

Butler, D., and Stokes, D. (1969), 'Political Change in Britain', London, Macmillan
Callinicos, A. (1976), 'Althusser's Marxism', London, Pluto.
Centers, R. (1949), 'The Psychology of Social Class', Princeton University Press.
Centre for Contemporary Cultural Studies (1978), 'On Ideology', London, Hutchinson.
Chandler, M. (1975), It's Time to Clean up the Boardroom, 'Harvard Business Review', vol. 53, no. 5, pp. 73-82.
Chapman, R.A. (1970), 'The Higher Civil Service in Britain', London, Constable.
Cheit, E.F. (ed.) (1964), 'The Business Establishment', New York, John Wiley & Sons.
Child, J. (1967), British Management Thought and Education, PhD thesis submitted at Cambridge University (published as Child, 1969).
Child, J. (1969), 'British Management Thought: A Critical Analysis', London, Allen & Unwin.
Child, J. (1972), Organization Structure and Strategies of Control: A Replication of the Aston Study, 'Administrative Science Quarterly', vol. 17, pp. 163-77.
Child, J. (ed.) (1973), 'Man and Organization', London, Allen & Unwin.
Child, J., Francis, A., Kieser, A., Nyman, S., and Silberston, A. (1975), The Growth of Firms as a Field of Research, University of Aston Management Centre, Working Paper series, no. 30, January.
Child, J., and MacMillan, B. (1972), Managerial Leisure in British and American Contexts, 'Journal of Management Studies', May, pp. 182-95.
Child, J., Pearce, S., and King, L. (1980), Class Perceptions and Social Identification of Industrial Supervisors, 'Sociology', vol. 14.
Christ, T. (1970), Thematic Analysis of the American Business Creed, 'Journal of Social Forces', December, 49, pp. 239-45.
Clark, D.G. (1966), 'The Industrial Manager: His Background and Career Pattern', London, Business Publications.
Clegg, S. (1975), 'Power, Rule and Domination', London, Routledge & Kegan Paul.
Clements, R.V. (1958), 'Managers: A Study of their Careers in Industry', London, Allen & Unwin.
Cole, G.D.H. (1950), The Conception of the Middle Classes, 'British Journal of Sociology', vol. 1, pp. 275-90.
Coleman, D.C. (1973), Gentlemen and Players, 'Economic History Review', Second Series, vol. XXVI, no. 1, pp. 92-116.
Collins, O.F., Moore, D.G., and Unwalla, D.B. (1964), 'The Enterprising Man', East Lansing, Michigan University Press.
Converse, P.E. (1964), The Nature of Belief Systems in Mass Publics, in Apter, D.E. (ed.). 'Ideology and Discontent', New York, Free Press.
Copeland, M.T. (1947), 'The Board of Directors and Business Management', Boston, Harvard University Graduate School of Business.
Copeman, G.H. (1955), 'Leaders of British Industry', London, Gee.
Copeman, G.H. (1959), 'The Role of the Managing Director', London, Business Publications.
Copeman, G.H. (1971), 'The Chief Executive and Business Growth', London, Leviathan House.
Copeman, G.H., Lingh, H., and Hanika, A.F. de P. (1963), 'How The Executive Spends his Time', London, Business Publications.
Cousins, J., and Brown, R. (1975), Patterns of Paradox; Shipbuilding Workers' Images of Society, in Bulmer (ed.) (1975).
Crenson, M.A. (1971), 'The Unpolitics of Air Pollution: A Study of Non-decision-making in the Cities', New York, Johns Hopkins Press.
Crewe, I. (ed.) (1974), 'British Political Sociology Yearbook', London, Croom Helm.
Cronjé, S., Ling, M., and Cronjé, G. (1976), 'Lonhro, Portrait of a Multinational', London, Friedmann.
Cyert, R., and March, J. (1963), 'A Behavioural Theory of the Firm', Englewood Cliffs, N.J., Prentice-Hall.

Dahl, R. (1958), A Critique of the Ruling Elite Model, 'American Political Science Review', vol. 52, no. 2, June.
Dahl, R.A. (1961), 'Who Governs?' New Haven and London, Yale University Press.
Dahrendorf, R. (1959), 'Class and Class Conflict in Industrial Society', London, Routledge & Kegan Paul.
Davies, A.F. (1967), 'Images of Class', Sydney University Press.
Department of Trade and Industry (1977), 'Report on the Committee of Inquiry on Industrial Democracy', Chairman Lord Bullock, London, HMSO.
De Vroey, M. (1975), The Separation of Ownership and Control in Large Corporations, 'Review of Radical Political Economy', vol. 7, no. 2, Summer.
Dexter, L.A. (1970), 'Elite and Specialised Interviewing', Evanston, North West University Press.
'The Director' (1965), The Anatomy of the Board, January.
'The Director' (1966a), The Director Observed, April.
'The Director' (1966b), The Director Observed Away from the Desk, May.
'The Director' (1975), The BBC: Is it Biased against the Boardroom? December.
Domhoff, G.W. (1967), 'Who Rules America?', Englewood Cliffs, N.J., Prentice-Hall.
Dooley, P.C. (1969), The interlocking Directorate, 'American Economic Review', vol. LIX, no. 3, June, pp. 314-23.
Drucker, P. (1976), 'The Unseen Revolution', London, Heinemann.
Duverger, M. (1974), 'Modern Democracies: Economic Power Versus Political Power', Hinsdale, Illinois, Dryden Press.
Earley, J.S. (1956), The Marginal Policies of Excellently Managed Companies, 'American Economic Review', vol. XXXXVI, no. 2, March.
Economist Intelligence Unit (1972), The Go-Betweens (Government Relations, otherwise known as lobbying), 'Multinational Business', no. 3.
Edelman, M. (1967), 'The Symbolic Uses of Politics', Urbana, University of Illinois Press.
Ellis, T., and Child, J. (1973), Placing Stereotypes of the Manager into Perspective, 'The Journal of Management Studies', October, pp. 233-55.
Epstein, E.H. (1969), 'The Corporation in American Politics', Englewood Cliffs, N.J., Prentice-Hall.
Fairlie, H. (1955a, b, c), Political Commentary, 'Spectator', 23 September, 30 September, 7 October.
Fidler, J.E. (1974), Attitudes as Ideology: How Chief Executives see their Companies, MSc thesis, presented at Imperial College, London.
Fidler, J.E. (1979), The beliefs, values and attitudes of British top business-men concerning class and class relationships, within the firm, and wider society, PhD thesis, submitted at the University of Aston, Birmingham.
Finer, S.E. (1955), The Political Power of Private Capital, I, 'Sociological Review', vol. 3, no. 2, pp. 279-94.
Finer, S.E. (1956), The Political Power of Private Capital, II, 'Sociological Review', vol. 4, no. 1, pp. 5-30.
Finniston (1980), 'Engineering Our Future: Report of the Committee of Inquiry into the Engineering Profession', Chairman: Sir Montague Finniston, Cmnd. 7794, London, HMSO.
Fitch, R., and Oppenheimer, M. (1970), Who Rules the Corporations?, Parts 1, 2 and 3, 'Socialist Revolution', vol. 1, no. 4, pp. 73-107; vol. 1, no. 5, pp. 61-114; vol. 1, no. 6, pp. 33-94.
Florence, P.S. (1961), 'Ownership, Control and Success of Large Companies', London, Sweet & Maxwell.
Fores, M., and Clark, D. (1975), Why Sweden Manages Better, 'Management Today', February.
Form, W.H., and Rytina, J. (1969), Ideological Beliefs on the Distribution of Power in the United States, 'American Sociological Review', vol. 34, no. 1, pp. 19-31.
Fox, A. (1966), 'Industrial Sociology and Industrial Relations: Royal Commission on Trade Unions and Employers Associations, Research Paper No. 3', London, HMSO.

Fox, A. (1973), A Social Critique of Pluralist Ideology, in Child, J. (ed.)(1973).
Fox, A. (1974), 'Beyond Contract', London, Faber & Faber.
Francis, A. (1980), Families, Firms and Finance Control: The Development of UK Industrial Firms with Particular Reference to their Ownership and Control, 'Sociology'. vol. 14. no. 1.
Friedman, M. (1953), The Methodology of Positive Economics, in 'Essays in Positive Economics', Chicago University Press.
Friedman, M. (1962), 'Capitalism and Freedom', University of Chicago Press.
Fry, G.K. (1969), 'Statesmen in Disguise', London, Macmillan.
Galbraith, J.K. (1952), 'American Capitalism: The Concept of Countervailing Power', New York, Houghton Mifflin.
Galbraith, J.K. (1967), 'The New Industrial State', London, Hamish Hamilton.
Geertz, C. (1964), Ideology as a Cultural System, in Apter, D.E. (ed.), 'Ideology and Discontent', New York, Free Press.
Getty, J.P. (1976), 'As I See It', London, W.H. Allen.
Giddens, A. (1973), 'The Class Structure of the Advanced Societies', London, Hutchinson University Library.
Giddens, A. (1974), Elites in the British Class Structure, in Stanworth, P., and Giddens, A. (eds) (1974a).
Giles, H., and Powesland, P.F. (1975), 'Speech Style and Social Evaluation', London, Academic Press.
Glasgow University Media Group (1976), 'Bad News', London, Routledge & Kegan Paul.
Glass, D.V. (ed.) (1954), 'Social Mobility in Britain', London, Routledge & Kegan Paul.
Glennerster, H., and Pryke, R. (1973), The Contribution of the Public Schools and Oxbridge, in Urry, J. and Wakeford, J. (eds), 'Power in Britain' (originally published as 'The Public Schools', Fabian Society, 1964).
Gluckman, M., and Devons, E. (eds) (1964), 'Closed Systems and Open Minds', Edinburgh, Oliver & Boyd.
Goldthorpe, J.H., and Hope, K. (1974), 'The Social Grading of Occupations', Oxford University Press.
Goldthorpe, J.H., Lockwood, D., Bechhofer, F., and Platt, J. (1968a), 'The Affluent Worker: Industrial Attitudes and Behaviour', Cambridge University Press.
Goldthorpe, J.H., Lockwood, D., Bechhofer, F., and Platt, J. (1968b), 'The Affluent Worker: Political Attitudes and Behaviour', Cambridge University Press.
Goldthorpe, J.H., Lockwood, D., Bechhofer, F., and Platt, J. (1969), 'The Affluent Worker in the Class Structure', Cambridge University Press.
Gordon, M.M. (1963), 'Social Class In American Sociology', New York, McGraw-Hill.
Gordon, R.A. (1961), 'Business Leadership in the Large Corporation', Berkeley, Los Angeles, University of California Press (reprint of 1945 edition).
Granick, D. (1962), 'The European Executive', London, Weidenfeld & Nicolson.
Granick, D. (1971), 'Managerial Comparisons of Four Developed Countries: France, Britain, United States, Russia', Massachusetts, M.I.T. Press.
Grant, W.P., and Marsh D. (1977), 'The Confederation of British Industry', London, Hodder & Stoughton.
Gregor, A.J. (1969), 'The Ideology of Fascism', New York, Free Press.
Gross, N. (1953), Social Class Identification in the Urban Community, 'American Sociological Review', vol. 18, no. 4, August.
Guttsman, W.L. (1963), 'The British Political Elite', London, MacGibbon & Kee.
Hall, D.J., and Amado-Fischgrund, G. (1969), Chief Executives in Britain, 'European Business', no. 20, January, pp. 23-9.
Hall, D.J., and de Bettignies, H-Cl. (1968), The French Business Elite, 'European Business', no. 19, October.
Hall, D.J., de Bettignies, H-Cl., and Amado-Fischgrund, G. (1969), The European Business Elite, 'European Business', no. 23, October, pp. 45-55.
Hall, J.R., and Jones, D.C. (1950), The Social Grading of Occupations, 'British Journal of Sociology', vol. 1, pp. 31-55.
Harris, N. (1968), 'Beliefs in Society', London, C.A. Watts.

Harris, N. (1972), 'Competition and the Corporate Society', London, Methuen.
Hayek, F.A. (1960), The corporation in a democratic society: in whose interest ought it and will it be run?, in Anshen, M. and Bach, G.L., 'Management and Corporation 1985', New York, McGraw-Hill.
Headey, B.W. (1974), 'Cabinet Ministers: The Roles of Politicians in Executive Office', London, Allen & Unwin.
Heilbroner, R.L. (1964), The View from the Top, in Cheit, E. (ed.), 'The Business Establishment', New York, John Wiley & Sons.
Heller, R. (1973), The State of British Boardrooms, 'Management Today', May.
Henry, W.E. (1949), The Business Executive: Psychodynamics of a Social Role, 'American Journal of Sociology', LIV, January, pp. 286–91.
Henry, W.E. (1956), 'The Analysis of Fantasy: The Thematic Aperception Technique in the Study of Personality', New York, John Wiley & Sons.
Hewitt, C. (1974), Policy Making in Postwar Britain: A Nation-level Test of Elitist and Pluralist Hypotheses, 'British Journal of Political Science', vol. 4, no. 2, April.
Hewitt, C. (1976), Pluralism in British Policy Making: A Reply to Morriss, 'British Journal of Political Science', vol. 6, no. 3, July.
Hilferding, R. (1910), 'Das Finanzkapital', Munich, Literarische Agentur Willi Weisman, trans. as 'Finance Capital' (1980), London, Routledge & Kegan Paul.
Hiller, P. (1975a), The Nature and Location of Everyday Conceptions of Social Class, 'Sociology', vol. 9, no. 1.
Hiller, P. (1975b), Continuities and Variations in Everyday Conceptions of Social Class, 'Sociology', vol. 9, no. 3.
Hindess, B. (1978), Classes and Politics in Marxist Theory, in Littlejohn, G., Smart, B., Wakeford, J., and Yuval-Davis, N. (eds.), 'Power and the State', London, British Sociological Association.
Hirst, P.Q. (1976), Althusser and the Theory of Ideology, 'Economy and Society', vol. 5, no. 4.
Hoggart, R. (1957), 'The Uses of Literacy', London, Chatto & Windus.
Hope, K. (ed.) (1972), 'The Analysis of Social Mobility', Oxford University Press.
Hunter, F. (1953), 'Community Power Structure', Chapel Hill, University of North Carolina Press.
Hunter, F. (1959), 'Top Leadership, U.S.A.', Chapel Hill, University of North Carolina Press.
Indik, B.P. (1963), Some Effects of Organizational Size on Member Attitudes and Behaviour, 'Human Relations', 16, pp. 361-84.
Indik, B.P. (1965), Organization Size and Member Participation: Some Empirical Tests of Alternative Explanations, 'Human Relations', 18, pp. 339-49
Ingham, G.K. (1967), Organization Size, Orientation to Work, and Industrial Behaviour, 'Sociology', vol. 1, no. 3, September, pp. 239-58.
Institute of Directors (1961) (1964) (1968) (successive editions), 'Standard Boardroom Practice', London.
Jay, A. (1967), 'Management and Machiavelli', London, Hodder & Stoughton.
Jay, A. (1972), 'Corporation Man', London, Cape.
Jervis, F.R. (1974), 'Bosses in British Business', London, Routledge & Kegan Paul.
Jessop, B. (1978), Capitalism and Democracy: The Best Possible Political Shell?, in Littlejohn, G., Smart, B., Wakeford, J., and Yuval-Davis, N. (eds), 'Power and the State', London, British Sociological Association.
Johnson, R.W. (1973), The British Political Elite 1955-1972, 'European Journal of Sociology', XIV, pp. 35-77.
Kamerschen, D.R. (1968), The Influence of Ownership and Control on Profit Rates, 'American Economic Review', LVIII.
Kaysen, C. (1960), The Corporation: How Much Power, What Scope?, in Mason, E.S. (ed.) (1960).
Keller, S. (1963), 'Beyond the Ruling Class', New York, Random House.
Kelsall, R.K. (1955), 'Recruitment of Higher Civil Servants in Britain', London, Routledge & Kegan Paul.
Kennet, J (1975), 'The Sociology of Pierre Bourdieu', Educational Review, vol. 25, no. 3.

Kincaid, H.V. and Bright, M. (1957), Interviewing the Business Elite, 'American Journal of Sociology', LXIII, 3, November.

Kolakowski, L. (1971), Althusser's Marx, 'The Socialist Register', pp. 111-28.

Krooss, H.E. (1970), 'Executive Opinion', New York, Doubleday.

Lambert, R.J., and Millham, S. (1968), 'The Hot House Society', London, Weidenfeld & Nicolson.

Lane, R. (1961), 'Political Ideology: Why the American Common Man Believes What he Does', New York, Free Press.

Lane, R.E. (1954), 'The Regulation of Businessmen: Social Conditions of Government Economic Control', New Haven, Yale University Press.

Larner, R.J. (1966), Ownership and Control in the 200 Largest Non-Financial Corporations, 1929 and 1963, 'American Economic Review', LVI, 4, September.

Lazell, H.G. (1975), 'From Pills to Penicillin', London, Heinemann.

Lee, J. (1922), 'The Social Implications of Christianity', London, Student Christian Movement.

Lentz, A., and Tschirigi, H. (1963), The Ethical Content of Annual Reports, 'Journal of Business', 36, October, pp. 387-93.

Lethbridge, D. (1975), The Top Skills of Top Management, 'Management Today', July.

Levine, J.H. (1972), The Sphere of Influence, 'American Sociological Review', 37, pp. 14-27.

Lewis, L.S. (1964), Class Consciousness and the Salience of Class, 'Sociology and Social Research', vol. 49, no. 2, pp. 173-82.

Lewis, R. and Maude, A. (1949), 'The English Middle Classes', London, Phoenix House.

Lewis, R., and Stewart, R. (1958), 'The Boss', London, Phoenix House.

Lockwood, D. (1958), 'The Black-Coated Worker', London, Allen & Unwin.

Lockwood, D. (1966), Sources of Variation in Working-class Images of Society 'Sociological Review', New Series, vol. 14.

Lopreato, J., and Hazelrigg, L.E. (1972), 'Class Conflict and Mobility', San Francisco, Chandler.

Lukács, G. (1971), 'History and Class Consciousness', London, Merlin Press.

Lukes, S. (1974), 'Power: A Radical View', London, Macmillan.

Lundberg, F. (1946), 'America's Sixty Families', New York, Citadel.

Lupton, T., and Wilson, C.S. (1959), The Social Background and Connections of 'Top Decision Makers', 'The Manchester School', vol. 27, no. 1, January.

McClelland, D.C., Atkinson, J.W., Clark, R.A., and Lowell, E.L. (1953), 'The Achievement Motive', New York, Irvington.

McClelland, D.C. (1961), 'The Achieving Society', New York, Irvington.

Mace, M.L. (1971), 'Directors: Myth and Reality', Boston, Division of Research, Graduate School of Business Administration, Harvard University.

Mace, M.L. (1972), The President and the Board of Directors, 'Harvard Business Review', March-April.

McGivering, I.C., Matthews, D.G.J., and Scott, W.H. (1960), 'Management in Britain', Liverpool University Press.

McKenzie, G. (1975), World Images and the World of Work, in Esland, G., Salaman, G., and Speakman, M. (eds), 'People and Work', Edinburgh, Holmes McDougall.

McKenzie, R.T., and Silver, A. (1968), 'Angels in Marble', London, Heinemann.

Mann, M. (1970), The Social Cohesion of Liberal Democracy, 'American Sociological Review', vol. 35, no. 3, June.

Mann, M. (1973), 'Consciousness and Action among the Western Working Class', London, Macmillan.

Mannheim, K. (1960), 'Ideology and Utopia', London, Routledge & Kegan Paul.

Mant, A. (1977), 'The Rise and Fall of the British Manager', London, Macmillan.

Margerison, C.J., and Elliott, C.K. (1975), Top Men's Self-Portrait, 'New Society', 22 May.

Marsh, D. (1976), On Joining Interest Groups: An Empirical Consideration of the Work of Mancur Olson Jr., 'British Journal of Political Science', vol. 16, no. 6, pp. 257-71.

Marsh, D. (1978), More on Joining Interest Groups, 'British Journal of Political

Science, vol. 18, no. 3.

Marx, K. and Engels, F. (1964), 'The Communist Manifesto', New York, Washington Square Press.

Marx, K., and Engels, F. (1968), 'Selected Works', London, Lawrence & Wishart.

Marx, K., and Engels, F. (1970), 'The German Ideology', London, Lawrence & Wishart.

Mason, E.S. (1958), The Apologetics of Managerialism, 'Journal of Business', XXXI.

Mason, E.S. (ed.) (1960), 'The Corporation in Modern Society', Cambridge, Mass., Harvard University Press.

Meisel, J.H. (1962), 'The Myth of the Ruling Class: Gaetano Mosca and the Elite', University of Michigan Press.

Meisel, J.H. (ed.) (1965), 'Pareto and Mosca - Makers of Social Science', Englewood Cliffs, N.J., Prentice-Hall.

Merton, R.K. (1957), 'Social Theory and Social Structure', Chicago, Free Press.

Meszaros, I. (ed.) (1971), 'Aspects of History and Class Consciousness', London, Routledge & Kegan Paul.

Miliband, R. (1969), 'The State in Capitalist Society', London, Weidenfeld & Nicolson.

Miliband, R. (1970), The Capitalist State: Reply to Nicos Poulantzas, 'New Left Review', 59, January-February.

Miliband, R. (1973), Poulantzas and the Capitalist State, 'New Left Review', 82, November-December.

Mills, C.W. (1956), 'The Power Elite', New York, Oxford University Press.

Mintzberg, H. (1973), 'The Nature of Managerial Work', New York, Harper & Row.

Mohr, L.B. (1972), The Concept of Organizational Goal, 'American Political Science Review', June, pp. 470-81.

Mond, Sir Alfred (later Lord Melchett) (1927), 'Industry and Politics', London, Macmillan.

Monsen, R.J., Jr. (1960), 'Modern American Capitalism: Ideologies and Issues', Boston, Houghton Mifflin.

Monsen, R.J., Chiu, J.S., and Cooley, D.E. (1968), The Effect of Separation of Ownership and Control on the Performance of the Large Firm, 'Quarterly Journal of Economics', 82.

Moorhouse, H.F. (1973), The Political Incorporation of the Working Class, 'Sociology', vol. 7, no. 3, September.

Moorhouse, H.F. (1976), Attitudes to Class and Class Relationships in Britain, 'Sociology', vol. 10, no. 3.

Morley, D. (1976), Industrial Conflict and the Mass Media, 'Sociological Review', New Series, vol. 24, no. 2, pp. 245-68.

Morriss, P. (1975), The Pluralist Case not Proven: Hewitt on Britain, 'British Journal of Political Science', 5, pp. 385-92.

Mosca, G. (1938), 'The Ruling Class', New York, McGraw-Hill.

Mougel, F.C. (1978), L'Establishment Britannique depuis 1945, 'Annales du Groupe d'Etudes et de Recherches Britanniques, Université de Bordeaux', Volume III.

Murstein, B.I. (1963), 'Theory and Research in Projective Techniques', New York, John Wiley & Sons.

Musgrove, F.H. (1963), 'The Migratory Elite', London, Heinemann.

Newbould, G.D., and Jackson, A.S. (1972), 'The Receding Ideal', Liverpool, Guttshead.

Nichols, T. (1969), 'Ownership, Control and Ideology', London, Allen & Unwin.

Nichols, T. (1974), Labourism and Class Consciousness, The 'Class Ideology' of Some Northern Foremen, 'Sociological Review', New Series, vol. 22, no. 4, November.

Nichols, T., and Beynon, H. (1977), 'Living with Capitalism', London, Routledge & Kegan Paul.

Nordlinger, E.A. (1967), 'The Working Class Tories', London, MacGibbon & Kee.

Nyman, S., and Silberston, A. (1978), The ownership and control of industry, Oxford Economic Papers, 30, 1.

Ossowski, S. (1963), 'Class Structure in the Social Consciousness', London, Routledge & Kegan Paul.
Packard, V.O. (1963), 'The Pyramid Climbers', London, Longmans.
Page, M. (1972), 'The Company Savage', London, Cassell.
Pahl, J.M., and Pahl, R.E. (1971), 'Managers and their Wives', Harmondsworth, Penguin.
Pahl, R.E. (1965), Class and Community in English Commuter Villages, 'Sociologia Ruralis', vol. 5, pp. 5-22.
Pahl, R.E., and Winkler, J.T. (1974), The Economic Elite: Theory and Practice, in Stanworth, P., and Giddens, A. (eds) (1974a).
Pareto, V. (1935), 'The Mind and Society', trans. A. Bourgiono and A. Livingston, New York, Harcourt Brace Jovanovich.
Pareto, V. (1966), 'Sociological Writings', ed. S. Finer, London, Pall Mall.
Parkin, F. (1971), 'Class, Inequality and Political Order', London, MacGibbon & Kee.
Parry, G. (1969), 'Political Elites', London, Allen & Unwin.
Parsons, G.F. (1972), The Giant Manufacturing Corporations and Balanced Regional Growth in Britain, 'Area', vol. 4, no. 2.
Parsons, T. (1957), The Distribution of Power in American Society, 'World Politics', X, 57-8, pp. 123-43.
Parsons, T. (1962), An Approach to the Sociology of Knowledge, in 'Sociological Theory and Modern Society', New York, Free Press.
Payne, G., and Ford, G. (1977), The Lieutenant Class, 'New Society', 21 July.
Pellegrin, R.J., and Coates, C.H. (1956), Absentee-owned Corporations and Community Power Structure, 'American Journal of Sociology', vol. 61, pp. 413-19.
Penrose, E.T. (1952), Biological Analogies in the Theory of the Firm, 'American Economic Review', 42, pp. 804-19.
Perrott, R. (1968), 'The Aristocrats', London, Weidenfeld & Nicolson.
Perrow, C. (1970), 'Organizational Analysis', London, Tavistock.
Peterson, R.B. (1971), Chief Executive Attitudes: A Cross Cultural Analysis, 'Industrial Relations', vol. 10, no. 2, May.
Pfeffer, J. (1972), Size and Composition of Corporate Boards of Directors: The Organization and its Environment, 'Administrative Science Quarterly', vol. 17, no. 2, June.
Plamenatz, J. (1970), 'Ideology', London, Pall Mall.
Platt, J. (1971), Variations in Answers to Different Questions on Perceptions of Class, 'Sociological Review', vol. 19, pp. 409-11.
Plowman, D.E.G., Minchington, W.E., and Stacey, M. (1962), Local Social Status in England and Wales, 'Sociological Review', vol. 10, no. 2.
Polsby, N.W. (1960), How to Study Community Power, the Pluralist Alternative, 'Journal of Politics', 22, August, pp. 474-84.
Polsby, N.W. (1963), 'Community Power and Political Theory', New Haven, Yale University Press.
Popitz, H., Bahrdt, H.P., Jueres, E.A., and Kesting, A. (1957), 'Das Gesellschaftsbild des Arbeiters', Tübingen, Mohr.
Porter, L.W. (1962-4), Job Attitudes in Management, I-VI, 'Journal of Applied Psychology', 1962, 46, pp. 375-84; 1963, 47, pp. 142-8, pp. 267-75, pp. 386-97; 1964, 48, pp. 31-6, pp. 305-9.
Poulantzas, N. (1968), 'Pouvoir politique et classes sociales', Paris, Maspero.
Poulantzas, N. (1969), The Problem of the Capitalist State, 'New Left Review', no. 58.
Prais, S.J. (1976), 'The Evolution of Giant Firms in Britain', Cambridge University Press.
Prandy, K. (1965), 'Professional Employees', London, Faber & Faber.
Prewitt, K., and Stone, A. (1973), 'The Ruling Elites', New York, Harper & Row.
Puckey, Sir W.C. (1969), 'The Board Room', London, Hutchinson.
Pugh, D.S., and Hinings, C.R. (eds) (1976), 'Organizational Structure, Extensions and Replications: The Aston Programme II', Farnborough, Hants., Saxon House.
Radice, H.K. (1971), Control Type, Profitability and Growth in Large Firms,

'Economic Journal', 81.
Raynor, J. (1969), 'The Middle Class', London, Longmans.
Reid, I. (1977), 'Social Class Differences in Britain: A Sourcebook', London, Open Books.
Riesman, D. (1957), The Suburban Dislocation, 'Annals of the American Academy of Political and Social Science', November.
Riesman, D., et al. (1950), 'The Lonely Crowd: A Study of the Changing American Character', New Haven and London, Yale University Press.
Rochester, A. (1936), 'Rulers of America', New York, International.
Roe, C.G. (1977), 'The Changing Role of the Chief Executive', London, Jean MacGregor.
Rokeach, M. (1968), 'Beliefs, Attitudes and Values', San Francisco, Jossey-Bass.
Rose, A. (1967), 'The Power Structure', New York, Oxford University Press.
Roth, A., Kerbey, J., and Tench, J. (1975), 'The Business Background of MPs', 1975-6 edition, London, Parliamentary Profiles.
Rowntree, B.S. (1920), The Aim and Principles of Welfare Work, 'Welfare World', vol. I, no. 2, February.
Royal Commission on Trade Unions and Employers' Associations (1968), London, HMSO
Royal Commission on the Distribution of Income and Wealth (1974), The Diamond Commission, London, HMSO.
Rubinstein, W.D. (1976), Wealth, elites and the class structure of modern Britain, 'Past and Present', 70.
Runciman, W.G. (1966), 'Relative Deprivation and Social Justice', London, Routledge & Kegan Paul.
Salaman, G. (1971a), Some Sociological Determinants of Occupational Communities, 'Sociological Review', 19, pp. 53-71.
Salaman, G. (1972b), Two Occupational Communities: Examples of a Remarkable Convergence of Work and Non-Work, 'Sociological Review', 19, pp. 389-407.
Sampson, A. (1971), 'The New Anatomy of Britain', London, Hodder & Stoughton.
Saxon, O.G., Jr (1966), Annual Headache: The Stockholders Meeting, 'Harvard Business Review', vol. 44, no. 1, January-February, pp. 132-7.
Scase, R. (1974), Conceptions of the Class Structure and Political Ideology: Some Observations on Attitudes in England and Sweden, in Parkin, F. (ed.), 'The Social Analysis of Class Structure', London, Tavistock.
Scase, R. (1975), Images of Inequality in Sweden and Britain, 'Human Relations', vol. 28, no. 3, pp. 261-77.
Scott, J. (1979), 'Corporations, Classes and Capitalism', London, Hutchinson.
Scott, J., and Hughes, M. (1976), Ownership and Control in a Satellite Economy: A Discussion from Scottish Data, 'Sociology', vol. 10, no. 1.
Scott, W.A. (1959), The Empirical Assessment of Values and Ideologies, 'American Sociological Review', vol. 24, no. 3, June.
Seeley, J.R., Sim, R.A., and Loosley, E.W. (1956), 'Crestwood Heights', New York, Basic Books.
Seeman, M. (1977), Some Real and Imaginary Consequences of Social Mobility: A French-American Comparison, 'American Journal of Sociology', vol. 82, no. 4, January.
Seider, M. (1974), American Big Business Ideology: A Content Analysis of Executive Speeches, 'American Sociological Review', vol. 39, no. 6, December.
Seymour, J. (1954), 'Company Direction: An Introduction to the Direction of Manufacturing Companies', London, Macdonald & Evans
Shackleton, J.R. (1978), Dr. Marsh on Olson: A Comment, 'British Journal of Political Science', vol. 18, no. 3, July.
Sheldon, O. (1923), 'The Philosophy of Management', London, Pitman.
Shenfield, B. (1971), 'Company Boards', London, Allen & Unwin.
Shonfield, A. (now Sir A.) (1965), 'Modern Capitalism', London, Oxford University Press.
Simon, H.A. (1964), On the Concept of Organizational Goal, 'Administrative Science Quarterly', 9, pp. 1-22.
Soref, M. (1976), Social Class and a Division of Labor within the Corporate Elite: A Note on Class, Interlocking and Executive Committee Membership of

Directors of U.S. Industrial Firms, 'The Sociological Quarterly', 17, Summer, pp. 360-8.
Spectorsky, A.C. (1955), 'The Exurbanites', Philadelphia, J.P. Lippincott.
Stacey, B. (1967), Some Psychological Consequences of Inter-Generation Mobility, 'Human Relations', vol. 20.
Stacey, M., et al. (1960), 'Tradition and Change', Oxford University Press.
Stacey, M., Batstone, E., Bell, C., and Murcott, A. (1975), 'Power, Persistence and Change', London, Routledge & Kegan Paul.
Stanworth, P., and Giddens, A. (eds) (1974a), 'Elites and Power in British Society', Cambridge University Press.
Stanworth, P., and Giddens, A. (1974b), An Economic Elite: A Demographic Profile of Company Chairmen, in Stanworth and Giddens, (eds) (1974a).
Stanworth, P., and Giddens, A. (1975), The Modern Corporate Economy: Interlocking Directorships in Britain 1906-1970, 'Sociological Review', vol. 23, no. 1, February.
Stark, W. (1958), 'The Sociology of Knowledge', London, Routledge & Kegan Paul.
Stehr, N. (1974), Consensus and Dissensus in Occupational Prestige, 'British Journal of Sociology', vol. XXV, no. 4, December.
Stewart, A., Prandy, K., and Blackburn, R.M. (1973), Measuring the Class Structure, 'Nature', 26.
Stewart, R. (1967), 'The Reality of Management', London, Pan.
Stewart, R. (1976), 'Contrasts in Management', Maidenhead, Bucks., McGraw-Hill.
Sturdivant, F.D., and Adler, R.D. (1976), Executive Origins: Still a Gray Flannel World? 'Harvard Business Review', vol. 54, no. 6, November-December.
Sutherland, D. (1968), 'The Landowners', London, Anthony Blond.
Sutton, F.X., Harris, S.E., Kaysen, C., and Tobin, J. (1956), 'The American Business Creed', Cambridge, Mass., Harvard University Press.
Sweezy, P. (1956), Power Elite or Ruling Class?, 'Monthly Review', VII, pp. 148-54.
Swingewood, A. (1975), 'Marx and Modern Social Theory', London, Macmillan.
Sykes, A.J.M. (1965), Some Differences in the Attitudes of Clerical and Manual Workers, 'Sociological Review', vol. 13, no. 3.
Taylor, B., and MacMillan, K. (1974), 'Top Management', London, Longmans.
Thomas, A.B. (1978), The British business elite: the case of the retail sector, 'Sociological Review', 26, pp. 305-26.
Thorngren, D. (1970), How do Contact Systems Affect Regional Development?, 'Environmental Planning', 2.
Thorns, D.C. (1972), 'Suburbia', London, MacGibbon & Kee.
Times Newspapers (1979), 'Times Guide to the House of Commons', London.
Tornquist, G. (1970), 'Contact Systems and Regional Development', Lund Studies in Geography, Series B, no. 35, Gleerup, Lund.
Tugendhat, C. (1971). 'The Multinationals', London, Eyre & Spottiswoode.
Turner, R. (ed.) (1974), 'Ethnomethodology', Harmondsworth, Penguin.
Turner, R.H. (1958), Life Situation and Subculture: A Comparison of Merited Prestige Judgements by Three Occupational Classes in Britain, 'British Journal of Sociology', vol. IX, no. 4, December.
Turner, R.H. (1966), Sponsored and Contest Mobility and the School System, 'American Sociological Review', vol. 25, no. 6.
Urry, J. and Wakeford, J. (eds) (1973), 'Power in Britain', London, Heinemann.
Useem, M. (1978), The inner group of the American capitalist class, 'Social Problems', 25.
Useem, M. (1979), The Social Organization of the American Business Elite and Participation of Corporation Directors in the Governance of American Institutions, 'American Sociological Review', vol. 44, August, pp. 53-72.
Useem, M. (1980), Corporations and the Corporate Elite, 'Ann. Rev. Sociol', 6, pp. 41-77.
Veblen, T. (1899), 'The Theory of the Leisure Class', New York, Macmillan.
Villarejo, D. (1961), Stock Ownership and the Control of Corporations, Parts I,

II, and III, 'New University Thought', Chicago, Autumn, pp. 33-77.

Vyle, G.C. (1922), The third factor in industry, 'Journal of Industrial Administration', vol. I, no. 12.

Wakeford, J. (1969), 'The Cloistered Elite', London, Macmillan.

Warner, W.L., and Abegglen, J.C. (1955), 'Big Business Leaders in America', New York, Harper.

Warner, W.L., and Lunt, P.S. (1947), 'The Status System of a Modern Community', New Haven, Yale University Press.

Warner, W.L., Meeker, M., and Eells, K. (1960), 'Social Class in America', London, Hamish Hamilton.

Watson, W. (1964), Social Mobility and Social Class in Industrial Communities, in Gluckman, M., and Devons, E. (eds) (1964).

Weber, M. (1930), 'The Protestant Ethic and the Spirit of Capitalism', London, Allen & Unwin.

Weber, M. (1968), 'Economy and Society', ed. G. Roth and C. Wittich, New York, Bedminster Press.

Weinberg, I. (1967), 'The English Public Schools: The Sociology of Elite Education', New York, Atherton.

Westaway, J. (1974a), Contact Potential and the Occupational Structure of the British Urban System 1961-1966, 'Regional Studies', vol. 8, no. 1.

Westaway, J. (1974b), The Spatial Hierarchy of Business Organizations and its Implications for the British Urban System, 'Regional Studies', vol. 8, no. 2.

Westergaard, J. (1975), The Power of Property, 'New Society', 11 September.

Westergaard, J., and Resler, H. (1975), 'Class in a Capitalist Society', London, Heinemann.

Whitley, R.D. (1973), Commonalities and Connections among Directors of Large Financial Institutions, 'Sociological Review', New Series, vol. 21, no. 4, November.

Whyte, W.H., Jr. (1957), 'The Organization Man', London, Cape.

Wildsmith, J.R. (1973), 'Managerial Theories of the Firm', London, Martin Robertson.

Wilkinson, R. (1964), 'The Prefects: British Leadership and the Public School Tradition', London, Oxford University Press.

Willener, A. (1957), 'Images de la Société et Classes Sociales', Berne.

Williams, W.M. (1956), 'The Sociology of an English Village: Gosforth', London, Routledge & Kegan Paul.

Willmott, P., and Young, M. (1960), 'Family and Class in a London Suburb', London, Routledge & Kegan Paul.

Winkler, J. (1974), The Ghost at the Bargaining Table: Directors and Industrial Relations, 'British Journal of Industrial Relations', 12, July.

Winkler, J. (1975), Company Directors . . . or Corporate Knights, 'The Director', January.

Winkler, J. (1976), Corporatism, 'European Journal of Sociology', vol. 17, no. 1.

Wolff, R.P. (1968), 'The Poverty of Liberalism', Boston, Beacon Press.

Wood, S., and Elliott, R. (1977), A Critical Evaluation of Fox's Radicalisation of Industrial Relations Theory, 'Sociology', vol. 11, no. 1, January.

Young, M. (1961), 'The Rise of the Meritocracy', Harmondsworth, Penguin.

Young, M., and Willmott, P. (1956), Social Grading by Manual Workers, 'British Journal of Sociology', vol. 7, no. 4, December.

Young, M., and Willmott, P. (1957), 'Family and Kinship in East London', London, Routledge & Kegan Paul.

Young, M., and Willmott, P. (1973), 'The Symmetrical Family', London, Routledge & Kegan Paul.

Zald, M.N. (1969), The power and functions of boards of directors: a theoretical synthesis, 'American Journal of Sociology', 75, pp. 97-111.

Zeitlin, M. (1974), Corporate ownership and control: the large corporation and the capitalist class, 'American Journal of Sociology', 79, pp. 1073-119.

Zeitlin, M. (1976), On class theory of the large corporation, 'American Journal of Sociology', 81, pp. 894-903.

INDEX

Abegglen, J.C., 56
Abell, P., 13n
ability, as a basis of class, 176-8, 192, 194, 206-7
achievement: as middle-class value, 42; need for, 55-6
'actor's frame of reference', 71
Adamson, Campbell, 30n
ages of businessmen interviewed, 98
agricultural subsidies, 240
Aims (of Industry, for Freedom and Enterprise), 200, 227-8, 242n
Aldington, Lord, 244
Althusser, L., 27-8, 73-4
Amado-Fischgrund, G., 59, 88, 90, 91
Ansoff, H.I., 120, 132
anthropology and company life, 53
Archibald, W.P., 14n, 261
Area Health Authorities, 216
aristocracy, 18, 244, 267; value system of, 44-5, 51; businessmen members of, 45n, 92-3, 218, 244, 254; seen as the upper class, 172-3, 178-81, 185-7, 212, 254; and the Conservative party, 216; American business aristocracy, 267; see also gentry; upper class
armed forces: businessmen's service in, 98-9, 115; as metaphors for companies, 99, 161-2
Armstrong, Sir William, 202
Aron, R., 32n
Arts Council, 278
aspirational workers, 21
assumptions of this study, 249-52
Attlee government, 230
attitudes (values), 37, 189; as a basis of class, 176-8, 192, 194, 208-9, 211
'audience', chief executive's, 139-42, 144, 256

Bachrach, P., 32-3, 36-7
Bacon, Francis, 76n
'balancing interests', ethos of, 49, 118, 135, 143-4, 218, 253; stated, 120; antecedants of, 120-1, 265; examples and incidence, 121-3; as ideology, 264-6; validity evaluated, 268-71
Balibar, E., 27, 73

Baltzell, E.D., 17, 267
Bamford, T.W., 46n
Bank of England, 241
banks, merchant and 'fringe', 75; see also financial institutions
Baran, P.A., 55
Baratz, M.S., 36-7
baronetage, members of, 92-3; see also aristocracy; gentry; upper class
Barritt, D.P., 91
Bath, Marquis of, 172
Bauer, R.A., 58
Beechams (company), 117
beliefs, centrality of, 39
belief systems, see meaning systems
Bell, C., 18n, 22n, 42-3, 46
Bell, D., 15
Bendix, R., 19, 29-30, 48-9, 61
Benn, Tony, 235n, 240, 283
Bentley, A., 33
Berger, B.M., 42
Berle, A.A., 6-7, 9, 15, 117
Betts, R., 91
BICC (company), 278
biology, 'new' and company life, 53
Birnbaum, N., 26
Blackburn, R.M., 22n, 260
Blauner, R., 20n
BOAC, 99
Board of Trade regulations, lobbying over, 232-3, 240
boardroom furnishing, 76n
boards of directors: cliques within, 4n, 9, 54, 134, 250; tasks of, 5-6, 54, 131-2, 250; objectives, 9-13; businessmen's views of tasks, 130-7, 145-6, 250, 254; sharing chief executives' objectives, 147-51
Bolton Committee, 124
bosses, 54, 187
Boswell, J., 56, 124
Bott, E., 19, 20n, 22, 39, 40
Bottomore, T.B., 3, 28, 32n
Bourdieu, P., 93, 94n, 268
bourgeoisie, 17-18, 26-7; see also capitalists; finance capitalists; family businessmen; entrepreneurs
Bovis (company), 9n, 141, 226n

Bowman, E.H., 12n
Boyd, D., 187, 188n
Brannen, P., 187, 188n
Bray, Dr Jeremy, 98n
bribery, of politicians, 70, 75, 217
Bright, M., 58, 67
British American Tobacco (now BAT Industries), 244
British Broadcasting Corporation (BBC), 242n, 244, 280
British Institute of Management, 5n, 237
British Leyland, 67n, 244; lobbying concerning, 233, 240
British Petroleum (BP), 226n, 244
British United Industrialists, 227-8
Brooks, J., 141
Brown, C.C., 5n, 121
Brown, M.B., 8-9
Brown, R.K., 187-9, 260
Bruce-Gardyne, J., 215, 247
Buck, P.W., 47n
budget, business lobbying concerning, 232-3, 239-40, 281
Builders' Federation, 236, 240
Bull, G., 13n
Bullock Committee, 221
Bullock Report (Department of Trade and Industry), 5n, 165-6; lobbying over, 233
Bulmer, M., 20n, 22, 23, 40n, 188n, 260
Burch, P.M., Jnr, 7
bureaucracy, 31
bureaucratisation, 22n, 55
bureaucrats (treated as a distinct group within business elite), 53, 57, 250-1, 258; personalities, 56; defined, 60; education, 83-4, 250-1; social status compared to family businessmen, 93-4; entry to careers, 95-7, 250-3; differentiated from other businessmen by income, wealth, 104-9, 115, 251-3; firms controlled by, compared with others, 124-6; view of firm compared with capitalists', 128-30, 143-4, 251; view of class compared with capitalists', 189-92
business, bad publicity for, 75
business elite: positions of those studied, 1, 64; defined and distinguished from other groups, 3-4, 53-7, 59-64, 249-50; roles of, 4-5; as managers, 5, 42-3, 49; in the ownership and control debate, 6-13, 15-16, 117-18, 143-4, 253; and industrial relations, 13-15, 145-67, 253; and class structure, 15-17, 24; as ideologists, 25-30, 42, 48-52, 258, 262-6; as political influentials, 31-7, 215-48, 250, 254-5, 266, 277-83;

meaning systems of, 41-52, 257-62; values as members of middle class, 42-3, 50-1, 257-8; contact with working class, 14, 43-4, 50-1, 60, 112-13, 114-16, 146, 252; values as members of upper class, 44-5, 50-1; values as ex-public schoolboys, 45-7, 51; and the Conservative party, 47-8, 50-1, 226-30, 258, 266; ethos of balancing interests, 49, 118, 135, 143-4, 218, 253, 268-71; personalities, 54-5; social mobility of, 54, 79-82, 87-8, 92-4, 115, 249-50, 252, 258, 268; education and training, 82-95, 101-2, 115, 249-50, 252, 258, 268; careers, 95-104, 115, 249-50, 252-3; service experience, 98-9, 115; management training, 99-100, 115; incomes and wealth holdings, 104-9, 251-3; community life, 109-12, 217-26, 252, 258; friends, 112, 116, 252; leisure interests, 113-14; objectives for companies, 118-24, 253; performances in running companies, 124-6; views on shareholdings, 127-30; views of responsibilities, 130-44, 250, 254; images of the firm, 145-6, 160-2, 166-7; expectation of sharing of objectives, 147-51, 253-4; views of 'core' company and conflict, 151-62, 253; views of company related to views of class, 154-9, 166-7, 193-6, 258-62; views on trade unions, 160-3, 253-65; views on participation, 163-6, 265-6; images of class, 171-83, 254, 257-62; status of businessmen, 183-6, 190-3, 254; views of the 'establishment', 183, 186, 212, 242-7, 258-9, 277, 281-2; images of class compared with other groups, 187-9; distinctive views of class, 195-204, 259; themes of class imagery, 205-14; changing political role, 216-26, 245-8, 266; lobbying, 230-41, 250, 266, 277-83; use of mass media, 236, 241-2; see also bureaucrats; directors; entrepreneurs; family businessmen; managers
business ideology, see ideology
business schools, 99-100
Butler, D., 22n

cabinet ministers: as businessmen's friends, 112; businessmen as, 216-17; power of, 231-2, 246, 254-5, 266; lobbying to, 234-8, 240-1, 242-5, 266, 280-3
Cadbury family, 60, 218
'cafe society', 186
Callinicos, A., 27n, 74n

Canada, speech in, 267
capital: allocation as a task of company
boards, 54, 131-7, 145-6, 250; cultural, 93, 94n; acquisition by managers, 104-9, 128-9
capitalism, development of, 6-13, 15
capitalists: and the Conservative
party, 226-8; finance, see separate
entry; see also family businessmen;
entrepreneurs; bourgeoisie
captains of industry, 49, 185
careers of businessmen, 95-104, 249-
53, 268; entry of bureaucrats to,
95-7; family businessmen and entrepreneurs, 97; service experience, 98-
9; management training, 99-100;
in-company experience, 100-3;
number of organisations employed
in, 130; age on main board, 103-4
Chamber of Commerce, 281-2
Chandler, M., 140
Chapman, R.A., 231n, 234-5
Cheit, E.F., 12
chief executive's 'audience', 139-42,
144, 256
Child, J., xv, 22n, 30, 48n, 49, 50, 56n,
58, 120-1, 125, 131n, 188-9, 218, 271
Chiu, J.S., 125
Chrysler UK, 230
City (of London) companies, see
financial institutions; finance capitalists
civil servants: as an elite, 32-4, 36,
215-6, 271; businessmen's experiences as, 101-2, 221-5; as businessmen's friends, 112, 279; as members
of upper class, 179; political influence of, in Britain, 216, 231-2, 234-
5, 237-8, 240-8, 254-5, 266, 279-83
Clarendon Schools, 83n; use in social
status index, 93; see also public
schools
Clark, D., 83
Clark, D.G., 90
class, ruling, 3-4, 31-4; businessmen's
lack of view of, 180-3, 255
class, social, 15-17; Weber's definition
of, 16; primary and secondary structuration, 17n; Conservative view of,
47; consciousness of, 73; businessmen's views on, related to view of
firm, 154-9, 166-7, 193-6, 258-67;
general view in outline, 169-70, 254,
258, 263-4; tension of discussing,
170-1; one interview in detail, 171-4;
class lines blurring, 172, 205-6, 260;
effect of social mobility, 173-4, 205;
importance of education, 174, 177,
207, 254, 260; number of classes
perceived, 174-6, 187-8; models of,
175, 180, 187-91, 258-9; basis of,

176-8, 189-92, 254; self-assigned
position, 179, 187, 189-94, 254; as a
status system (continuous hierarchy),
174-6, 187-8, 209-14; and the status
of businessmen, 183-6; variations of
viewpoint, 189-93; sociological sophisticates' view of, 197-9, 259; upwardly
mobile view of, 199-202, 259, 268;
upper-class view of, 202-3, 259;
outsider's view of, 203-4, 259; as a
weapon of the left, 208, 260; awareness of other views, 208-9, 254;
salience of, 268
class consciousness, 24-6, 73; of the
British, 267; of business elite, 267-8
Clegg, S., 66n
Clements, R.V., 61, 95-7
Clore, Sir Charles, 61
closed shop legislation, 232, 240
clubs, social, 47, 113, 216, 234, 247,
266
Cole, G.D.H., 18
Coleman, D.C., 45n, 218
Collins, O.F., 56, 97
Common Cause, 227-8
communication, businessmen's stress
on, 159-60, 163-6, 254, 265-6
community situation, 18-23, 210-11; of
businessmen, 42-5, 52, 109-16, 210-
11, 217-26
companies: control of, 6-10, 12-13,
125-6, 139-44, 251, 255-7, 284; small
and large compared, 55-6; types
defined, 60; classification by size
and type of control, 61; size related
to executives' salaries, shareholdings,
106-8; location of headquarters, 109-
12, 218; rates of return compared,
124-6; growth of, 137-8; contrasting
images, 145-6, 160-2; 'core' company,
145, 151-3, 163, 166-7, 253, 269-70;
conflict, 153-60, 166-7, 253-4; size
and type related to view of company, 154, 158-9, 250-1, 258-9;
view of company related to view of
class, 154-9, 166-7, 193-6, 258-62;
size related to view of class, 190;
political giving, 227-8; type of
control and size related to method
of lobbying, 237-8, 246, 250,
254-5
concentration of assets, 6
Confederation of British Industry (CBI),
211, 264, 281, 283; Employee Communications Unit, 160n; evidence to
Bullock Committee, 165; as a means
of political influence, 216, 221-5,
235-8, 246, 266
consciousness, false, 26-7
Conservative party, 45, 244, 266, 280;
working-class support, 19n; values

of, 47-8, 51; support of businessmen for, 226-8, 246; 1970-4 government, 226n, 229-30, 280, 282
consultation, in the firm, 163-6, 254; see also communication
Consumer Credit Act, 232, 240
contest system, 45, 51
Converse, P.E., 29
Cooley, D.E., 125
Copeland, M.T., 5n
Copeman, G.H., 88-91, 218
council, 'local', businessmen as members, 219-25
'core' company, 145, 151-3, 163, 166-7, 253, 269-70
corporatism, 47
Cousins, J., 188-9, 260
Cowdray, Lord, 60
Crenson, M.A., 11n, 37
Crewe, I., 58
Croda International, 61
Crompton Parkinson, 278
Crossman, Richard, 236
Curran, Sir Charles, 242n, 280
customs duty, 233, 237, 240
Cyert, R., 13

Dahl, R.A., 35-6, 58, 248
Dahrendorf, R., 15
'Daily Mail', 141, 280
Daniel, W.W., 22n
Darwinism, 'social', 48, 150
Davies, A.F., 22
Davies, John, 226n
Debenhams (stores), 9n
Department of Trade and Industry, 235, 281; see also Bullock Report
Derby County Football Club, 141n
Devons, E., 42n
Devonshire, Duke of, 172
De Vroey, M., 8
Dexter, L.A., 58
Diamond Commission (Royal Commission on the Distribution of Income and Wealth), 76, 109, 239
directors: tasks of, 5-6, 54, 131-2, 250, 254; Institute of, 5n, 58; observation of, 9, 14, 58, 271; businessmen's views of tasks, 130-7, 250, 254; influence of non-executives, 7, 10, 12-13, 139-40, 144, 251, 256; changing management styles, 184-5; working hours, 218; of nationalised industries, 3, 282; for full references see business elite and boards of directors
directorships, interlocking, 7-9, 12-13, 139-40, 144, 251, 256; as means of political influence, 234, 247
Distillers (company), 75
Dobson, Sir Richard, 67n

Dock Labour Act, 233
Domhoff, G.W., 8, 35, 267
Drucker, P., 8n
Dunkerley, D., xvi
Dunlop (company), 60
Duverger, M., 33n

Eagle Star Insurance, 278
economics, bourgeois, critique of this research (and reply), 71-2
Economic League, 227-8
economic elite, distinguished from business elite, 3
Edelman, M., 247
education, of businessmen, 249-50, 252; schooling, 82-4, 88-9, 91-3, 115, 249-50, 252, 258, 268; university, 83-6, 89-91, 115, 249-50, 252, 258; professional training, 86-7, 91, 94-5, 101-2, 115, 249-50; management training, 98-100, 115; importance, 174, 177, 207; as a basis of class, 176-7, 189, 254, 260; shared as a channel of influence, 247
educational elite, 271
Eells, K., 19n
Elbourne, 121
elite studies, characterisation, 58
elites, circulation of, 32n
elites, theory of, 3-4, 32-7, 249-52
Elliott, R., 14
Ellis, T., 56n
embourgeoisement, 19n
Engels, F., 1, 25, 26, 31
entrepreneurs: as a group within the business elite, 53, 57, 250-1, 258; personalities, 56; defined, 60; as members of marginal groups, 82; education, 83-4, 250-1; careers, 97, 250-3; ages on founding firms, 103; wealth and income differentiation from bureaucrats, 104-9, 115, 251, 253; rates of return compared with other control types, 124-6; view of firm compared with bureaucrats and family owners, 130, 134-5, 143-4, 251; view of class compared with bureaucrats and family owners, 189-92
establishment, 183, 186, 212, 242-7, 258-9, 277, 281-2
ethnomethodology, critique of this research, 69n
Eton, 82-4; see also public schools
European Economic Community (EEC), lobbying, 233
European Free Trade Association (EFTA), lobbying, 233, 280

Fairlie, H., 243
family businessmen, treated as a

separate group among businessmen
studied, 53, 57, 250-1, 258; defined,
60; education, 83-4, 250-1; family
background compared, 93-4; careers,
97, 250-3; wealth and income, 104,
109, 115, 251-3; rates of return
compared with other controllers,
124-6; view of firm compared with
other controllers, 127-8, 143-4, 251;
view of class compared with other
controllers, 189-92
Farrow, N., 89
Federation of British Industry, 221-5;
see also its successor, Confederation
of British Industry
Fidler, J., 163n, 168n
Finance Acts, 232-3
finance capitalists, 7-9, 12-13, 125-6,
139-44, 251, 256-7; practical definition, 60; education of City executives, 83-4; family background, 93-
4; careers, 97; as businessmen's
friends, 112; service to customer,
123-4, 143; view of class, 190; as
members of the establishment, 242-5
financial institutions: control of other
companies by, 7-9, 12-13, 125-6,
139-44, 251, 256-7; British (City)
companies' political donations, 227-8;
influence on government, 229-30;
power of, 241-5, 254-5; see also
finance capitalists
'Financial Times', 141-2
Finer, S.E., 216n
Finniston, Sir Montague, 184, 278
Fitch, R., 8
Florence, P.S., 6n, 125
food industry, lobbying by, 233, 236,
240-1
Ford, G., 88
Fores, M., 83
Fox, A., 13, 14, 50-1, 99, 161-2, 253
France, educational system in, 268
Francis, A., 7n, 125, 271n
Friedman, M., 71, 270
friends, businessmen's, 112, 115-16,
234, 252, 279

Galbraith, J.K., 11, 32
GEC, 244, 278
Geddes, Sir Reay, 60
Geertz, C., 28
gentry, landed, 45n, 218, 244; mem-
bers of, 92-3; and the Conservative
party, 226; see also upper class
Getty, John Paul, 78-9
Giddens, A., 4, 8, 17, 89, 90, 216n
Giles, H., 267
GKN, 60, 278
Glasgow University Media Group, 14n
Glass, D.V., 19n

Glennerster, H., 89
Gluckman, M., 42n
Goldthorpe, J.H., 19n, 22n, 79, 92,
146, 187-9, 261-2
Gordon, M.M., 19n
Gordon, R.A., 6
government, local, importance to
businessmen, 231
government purchasing, 233
government-sponsored committees, 221-5
grading, social, 19n, 72; of business-
men's fathers, 79-82, 92-3
Gramsci, A., 27
Grant, W.P., 30n, 235n
Greenhill, Lord, 244
Gregor, A.J., 32n
Grindlays bank, 244
growth of companies, 137-8
Gumplowicz, L., 32n
Guttsman, W., 90, 225

Haire, M., 12n
Hall, D.J., 59, 88, 90, 91
Hall, J.R., 19n
Hambros bank, 278
Hanika, A.F. de P., 218
Harris, N., 28, 47-8
Hayek, F.A., 270
Hazelrigg, L.E., 22n
Headey, B.W., 58n
Healey, Denis, 76
Heath, Edward, 74, 75, 229, 230, 281
Heilbroner, R.L., 12, 49-50
Heller, R., 59, 89, 90
Henry, W.E., 56, 57n, 119
Heseltine, Michael, 282
Hewitt, C., 35n
Hilferding, R., 7
Hiller, P., 22-3, 260
Hindess, B., 73-4
Hinings, C.R., 55-6
'hired deferentials', 112, 153
Hirst, P.Q., 27n, 73-4
Hockney, David, 76n
Hoggart, R., 19, 22
Hope, K., 19n, 79, 92-3
Hope-Goldthorpe Scale, used for father's
occupation, 79-82; limitations of, 92;
use in social status index, 93
hospital boards, businessmen serving
on, 221-5
housebuilding, lobbying over, 233,
236, 240
human relations, 48n, 50
Hunter, F., 35, 58

ideology, 25-30; and meaning systems,
29-30, 262-3; business ideology, 29-
30, 48-51, 258, 262-6; entrepreneurial,
48-9; 'classical', 49-51; managerial,
49-51, 204-6, see also ethos of

balancing interests; and company
life, 53
images of class, see class; images of
society; meaning systems
images of society, 15-24, 195-7, 257-
62; middle-class, 17-22, 187-8, 209-
13; upper-class, 17, 202-3, 259;
working-class, 19-24, 187-9; for
businessmen's images see class,
businessmen's views on; companies;
power
Imperial Chemical Industries (ICI), 60,
227, 279
Inchcape, Lord, 9n
income, as a basis of class, 176-7, 189-
94, 254
incomes, businessmen's, 104-9
Indik, B.P., 159
industrial democracy, 164, 265-6; see
also communication
industrial relations: businessmen's
role, 13-15; Royal Commission, 13,
146; television coverage, 14n;
businessmen's views on, 145-67,
253
Industrial Relations Act (1971), 30n,
74, 229, 232
Industry Act, 76, 227-8, 232, 240, 283
Ingham, G.K., 159
Institute of Directors, 5n, 58
institutional shareholders, see financial
institutions
insurance companies, see financial
institutions
intellect, as a basis of class, 176-8,
192, 194, 206-7
interest groups, and control of companies, 7-9, 12-13; see also directorships, interlocking
interviews, in this study, method of
obtaining, 62-4; design of schedule,
64-7; length, 67; tape-recording,
67; reproduction of extracts, 67-8;
problems of, 68-9, 252; sincerity of
respondents, 69-71, 252; context of,
74-6; description of, 76-7; schedule
reproduced, 273-7
investment analysts, influence of, 139,
141-2, 144, 256
investment: diversion by multinationals,
231; lobbying over, 233

Jackson, A.S., 120, 138, 139
Japan, economic success of, 98n
Japanese factory, lobbying over, 236n
Jay, A., 53
Jenkins, Clive, 245
Jervis, F.R., 54
'jet set', 182, 186, 254
Jewish businessmen, 97, 203
Jones, D.C., 19n

Jones, Jack, 170, 243, 245
Joseph, Sir Keith, 226n
journalists, financial, 139, 141-2, 144,
256
judiciary, 271
Justices of the Peace, businessmen as,
221-6

Kamerschen, D.R., 125
Kaysen, C., 10-11
Keller, S., 35
Kerbey, J., 225n
knowledge, sociology of, 28-9
Kolakowski, L., 27n, 74n
Kieser, A., 131n
Kincaid, H.V., 58n, 67
King, L., 188-9

Labour government, 74, 200, 240;
business lobbying, 217, 232-41, 246-
7, 266, 280; and trade unions, 229;
perceptions of power under, 230-2
Labour voting by businessmen, 47n,
227
Lambert, R.J., 46n
landed gentry, see gentry
Lane, R., 19, 171
Larner, R.J., 6
Lawson, N., 215, 247
Lazards bank, 278
Lazell, H.G., 117
Lee, J., 121
leisure interests of businessmen, 113-
14
Lenin, V.I., 8
Lewis, R., 18, 46, 54, 280
Liberal party, ideology, 227; voting
for, by businessmen, 47n, 227
Lingh, H., 218
Lipset, S.M., 19
Lloyds bank, 244
lobbying, 36, 217, 266; business view
of, 230-2; issues concerning business
elite, 232-4; channels of influence,
216-17, 221-5, 234-48, 250-5, 266,
277-83; success of, 238-41
Lockwood, D., 19-22, 40, 188, 261
London: businessmen living in, 110,
112, 218; transfer of company head-
quarters to, 110-12
Lonhro (company), 75
Loosley, E.W., 42n
Lopreato, J., 22n
Lords, House of, membership as a
channel of influence, 221-5; see also
aristocracy
Lukács, G., 26
Lukes, S., 37
Lundberg, F., 6
Lunt, P.S., 19n

McClelland, D.C., 55
Mace, M.L., 5n, 9, 133-4, 140, 256
McGivering, I.C., 50
Machiavelli, and company life, 53
McKenzie, G., 187-8
McKenzie, R.T., 19n, 47
McLennan, G., 27n
Macmillan, B., 218
Macmillan, Sir Harold, 245
MacMillan, K., 11n
magistrates, businessmen as, 221-6
management science, and company life, 53
management training of businessmen, 98-100, 115
managerial control of companies, 6-13, 124-6, 251, 255-7
managers: roles of, 5; distinguished from business elite, 5, 54, 249-50; sharing company objectives, 147-51; involvement in politics and voluntary organisations, 218; for businessmen in this study who were managers, see bureaucrats
Mann, M., 22n, 23-4, 260-1
Mannheim, K., 25, 28, 32
Mant, A., 45, 53, 184n, 268n
March, J., 13
Marsh, D., 30n, 235n
Marx, K., 1, 7, 15-17, 25-7, 31, 159
Marxism: and elite theory, 3-4; and ideology, 26-7; 'scientific', 26; and the state, 31; critique of this study, 71-4; 'economistic', 73
Mason, E.S., 10
mass media, and industrial relations, 14n; and lobbying, 236, 241-2
Matthews, D.G.J., 50
Maude, A., 18, 46, 280
Mayo, E., 48n
mayors, businessmen as, 221-5
meaning systems, 17-24; definitions, 19, 39; methods of researching, 22; and ideology, 29-30, 262-3; discussion, 39-41, 50, 257-62; see also images of society; class; businessmen's views on; companies; power
Means, G.C., 6-7
Meeker, M., 19n
Meisel, J.H., 3, 32n, 180
Members of Parliament: businessmen's friends, 112; businessmen as, 216-17, 219-27; power of, 231-2, 246, 266; in lobbying, 236-8, 240, 245-6, 280-1, see also cabinet ministers
meritocratic view: of firm, 51; of society, 203, 206-7, 260
Merton, R.K., 26, 28
methodology of this research, 58-9; critique of, 68-74, 252; ethnomethodologist's critique, 69n; economist's

critique, 71-2; Marxist critique, 71-4
Metrication Bill, 232
middle class, 15-18; images of society of, 17-22, 187-8, 209-13; values of, 42-3; and public school values, 45-6; major division from working class, 175, 254, 258; businessmen's self-assignment to, 179, 187, 254
Miliband, R., 3, 33-4
military, role within the state, 27, 33, 215-16; values of, 271
Minchington, W.E., 18
miners' strike (1974), 74
Ministry of Fuel and Power, 235n
Mintzberg, H., 5
Molina, V., 27n
monarchy, 267
Mond, Sir Alfred, 121
Monsen, R.J., 49, 125
Moore, D.G., 56, 97
Moorhouse, H.F., 187, 189, 262
Morley, D., 14n
Morriss, P., 35n
Mougel, F.C., xvi, 244
Murray, Len, 243
Murstein, B.I., 57n
Musgrove, F.H., 218

National Economic Development Council (NEDC / NEDO), 221-4, 237
National Enterprise Board (NEB), 74, 230, 240
National Research and Development Council (NRCD), 221-4, 278, 282
National Theatre, 278
nationalisation, 74; of aircraft/shipping, 233, 239-40
nationalised industries, directors of, 3, 282; as channels of political influence, 216, 221-5, 282
nationalism, 49
Newbould, G.D., 120, 138, 139
Newby, H., 18n, 22n
Nichols, T., xv, 11-12, 30, 49, 50, 58, 88, 90, 121, 171, 262, 271n
Nicholson, Ben, 76n
Nordlinger, E.A., 19n
North Sea oil: policy, 235n; rigs, 233
Northcliffe, Lord, 280
Nyman, S., 8-10, 271n

objectives, businessmen's for their firms, 9-13, 118-24, 253-4, 255-7; long- and short-term goals, 130-42, 256-7; expectations that objectives are shared, 147-51, 253-4
observation studies of directors, 9, 14, 58, 271
occupation as a basis of class, 176-8, 189, 192-4, 206-7, 210-11, 260

occupations, grading of, 19n
Okita, Sabburo, 98n
Oppenheimer, M., 8
organisational goal, see businessmen's
  objectives for their firms
outsider's view of class, 203-4, 259
ownership and control debate, 6-13,
  15-16, 117-18, 143-4, 255-7

Packard, V.O., 53
Page, M., 53
Pahl, J.M., 42, 95
Pahl, R.E., xvi, 4n, 9, 10, 14, 42-3,
  54, 58, 67n, 95, 110, 134, 139, 218,
  256
Pareto, V., 32
Parkin, F., 17, 19, 21, 29-30, 45
Parsons, G.F., 109
Parsons, T., 28
participation, employee, 163-6, 254,
  265-6
parties, political, 16; businessmen's
  participation, 216-17, 219-28; see
  also Conservative; Labour;
  Liberal
Passeron, J.C., 93, 94n, 268
Payne, G., 88
Pearce, S., 188-9
Peart, Fred, 236
Penrose, E., 72
pension funds, see financial institu-
  tions
Perrott, R., 44-5
Perrow, C., 131
personal contacts, use of in lobbying,
  234-5, 237-8, 250, 255, 266, 277-83
Peters, R., 27n
Peterson, R.B., 59
Petroleum Bill, 232
Pilkingtons, 109, 218
Plamenatz, J., 28
planning agreements, 230
planning permission, lobbying over,
  233
Platt, J., 261
Plowden, Lord, 244
Plowman, D.E.G., 18
pluralism, political, 32-3, 35-7; in the
  British case, 35n; conclusions
  concerning, 242-8, 254-5, 266
pluralist view of the firm, 13-15, 50,
  99, 162
plutodemocracy, 33n
P. & O. (company), 9n, 141
police, in the state, 27, 33, 215-16
Policyholders Protection Bill, 233, 239,
  240
politicians: among businessmen's
  friends, 112; and social clubs, 113,
  234; as members of upper class,
  179; business contact with, 234-5,

266; on television, 242; see also
  cabinet ministers; Members of Parliament
politics, business participation in: outline of argument, 216-17; business
  view of, 230-2; discussion of, 245-
  8, 254-5, 258-9, 266; see also lobbying
Pool, I. de S., 58
Popitz, H., 19, 22
population, drift to the south, 109-11,
  115-16
Porter, L.W., 159
Post Office purchasing, 233
Poulantzas, N., 3, 34, 37, 74
power: problems of conceptualising,
  35-7; need for among managers, 55;
  in models of society, 176-7, 189,
  258-9; differentiated from status by
  businessmen, 186
power elite, 34-6, 266
Powesland, P.F., 267
Prais, S.J., 6n, 141, 257
price check scheme, 240-1
price-makers and price-takers, 55
prices and incomes, lobbying over,
  232, 239-41
professional employees: prestige
  compared to businessmen, 82; as
  businessmen's friends, 112; involvement in voluntary organisations, 218;
  and the Conservative party, 226-7
'professional manager', 10, 139
professional training, among businessmen, 86-7, 91, 101-2, 249-50; related
  to social status, 94-5
profit: and managerial goals, 6, 9-13;
  and business ideology, 49; businessmen's views on, 118, 253, 256-7;
  reasons for profit as a goal, 119-21;
  impossibility of maximisation, 120,
  137, 139
proletariat, and ideology, 25-7
property boom, 75
propaganda organisations, 227-8
'Protestant Ethic', 26, 42, 49
Prudential Assurance, 278
Pryke, R., 89
'psychological boundary to the firm',
  151-3, 253; see also 'core' company
public schools, 267; values of, 45-7,
  258; numbers of businessmen attending, 82-4, 88-9, 91-3, 115, 249-50,
  252, 268; businessmen's opinions
  on, 174, 207-8, 264, 268
publicity, use in lobbying, 236, 240
Puckey, Sir W.C., 5n
Pugh, D.S., 55-6

questionnaire studies among businessmen, 59

Radice, H.K., 125
RAF, see armed forces
Rank Organisation, 75
rate of return, in companies of different control types, 124-6
Rayne, Sir Max, 278
Raynor, J., 18, 42, 46
reference works, problems of using, 78
Regional Development Act, 232
regional policy, lobbying, 240
Registrar-General's social class groupings, used, 79-82, 87-8
religious affiliation, and social class imagery, 261
Riesman, D., 35, 42n, 50n
Robens, Lord, 278
Rochester, A., 6
Rokeach, M., 39
Rose, A., 35-6, 248
Roth, A., 225n
Rothermere, Lord, 280
Rothschilds bank, 278
Rowland, 'Tiny', 141n
Rowntree, B.S., 121
Rowntree family, 218
Royal Commissions on the Distribution of Income and Wealth, 76, 109, 239; on Trades Unions and Employers' Associations, 13, 146
Royal Commissions, as a channel of political influence, 216
Royal Navy, see armed forces
Runciman, W.G., 22n
Ryder, Lord, 240

Sainsburys, 60
salaries, of chief executives, 105-8
sample, in this study, 64-5
Sampson, A., 227
Samuelson, P., 29, 49
Scanlon, Hugh, 243
Scase, R., 187, 189
Scheler, M., 26
Schmidt, Chancellor Helmut, 170
schools, contacts formed at, 266
school boards, businessmen serving on, 221-5
schools, public, see public schools
Scott, J., 8n, 9, 16n
Scott, W.H., 50
Scottish and Universal Investments (SUITS), 75
sectors of industry, importance of distinguishing, 53; defined here, 60
Seeley, J.R., 42n
Seider, M., 49
Sergeant, Patrick, 141
Seymour, J., 5n
Shackleton, J.R., 71
shareholding: control of companies, 6-7, 12-13; holdings of businessmen,

105-8; views on desirability of, 128-30
shareholders: influence on company boards, 140-1, 144, 256-7; directors' responsibilities to, see ethos of balancing interests
Sheldon, O., 121
Shell, 227
Shell-Mex, 226n
Shenfield, B., 11
sherriffs, businessmen as, 221-6
Shonfield, Sir A., 247
Silberston, A., 8-10, 131n, 271n
Silver, A., 19n, 47
Sim, R.A., 42n
Simon, H.A., 137-8
Slater, Jim, 244
Slater-Walker, 75
Smith, D., 69n
Smith, E.E., 5n, 121
social mobility: of businessmen, 54 258, 268; as shown by father's occupation, 79-82, 87-8, 92, 115, 249-50, 252; as measured by social status index, 93-4; service experience as a channel of, 98-9; related to view of social class, 190-3, 199-202, 259; and social imagery, 261
social status index: defined, 91-4; used to compare groups of businessmen, 93-4; related to university and professional training, 94-5; used to compare rates of return, 126-7; used to examine views of class, 190-3
socialism, businessmen's views on, 264
sociological sophisticates' view of class, 197-9, 259
Soref, M., 8n
South Africa, behaviour of British companies, 75, 141
Spectorsky, A.G., 42
speech as an indicator of class, 267
Spencer, Herbert, 48
spiralists, 42, 43
Stacey, M., 18, 210, 218
Stanworth, P., 8, 89, 90, 216n
state: definitions of, 27, 33, 215-16; power of businessmen versus, 215-17, 245-8
status: Weber's definition, 16; local social status, 18, 19n, 187n, 210; of businessmen, 183-6
status models of class, 174-6, 209-14
steelworkers, lobbying over, 233, 240
Stehr, N., 19n
Stewart, R., 54
stockbrokers' analysts, influence of, 139, 141-2, 144, 256
subsidies, lobbying for, 233
suburban life, 42-3

suburbs, businessmen living in, 43, 110, 112
Sun Alliance, 244
supervisors' view of class, 188
Sutherland, D., 44-5
Sutton, F.X., 29, 49
Sweezy, P., 55
Swingewood, A., 15

tape-recording of interviews, 67
Taylor, B., 11n
Taylorism, 50
taxation, lobbying about, 233, 239
'technostructure', 11
television: coverage of industrial relations, 14n; use in lobbying, 236, 241-2
Tench, J., 225n
Thorn, Sir James, 60
Thorngren, D., 109
Thorns, D.C., 42n
'Times Guide to the House of Commons', 225n
Tornquist, G., 109
Trade and Industry, Department of (DTI), 235, 281
trade associations, 236-8, 240, 246, 266, 281
Trades Union Congress (TUC), 211
trade unionists: on TV, 242; members of 'establishment', 242-5; power of, 247, 254-5
trade unions, 13; and company conflict, 154, 253-4; businessmen's views on, 160, 162-3, 230, 253-4, 263, 265; and effect on social imagery, 261
transcribing of interviews, 67
Treasury, 231, 235n, 282
Tube Investments, 60, 244, 278
Turner, R., 69n
Turner, R.H., 45

Unilever (company), 227,
unitary view of the firm, 13-15, 50-1, 99, 161-2, 253
university, 266, 268; attendance by businessmen, 83-5, 89-91, 115, 249-50, 252-8; subjects studied, 84-6; attendance related to family background, 94-5
university councils, businessmen on, 221-5
Unwalla, D.B., 56, 97
upper class: attitudes of, 44-5, 51; businessmen's views of, 172-3, 178-83, 185-7, 212, 254, 258; number seeing existence of, 175, 178; businessmen's self-assignment to, 179-83, 187, 190, 193, 254; status vis-à-vis businessmen, 184-6, 254;

upper-class view of society, 17, 202-3, 259
Urry, J., 216n
USA: and 'social Darwinism', 48; business ideology in, 48-50; speech style, 267
Useem, M., xvi, 271n

validity, of this research, 69, 71-4
values, centrality, 39
Veblen, T., 44
Vickers (company), 278
voluntary organisations, 43, 261; involvement of businessmen in, 217-26
voting, as an indicator of class, 176
Vyle, G.C., 121n

wage-bargaining, and conflict in firm, 155-9, 167, 253
wage control, 154; lobbying over, 232-3
Wakeford, J., 46n, 83, 216n
Walker, Peter, 226n
Warburg, Sigmund, 204
Warburgs bank, 244
Warner, W.L., 19n, 56
Watson, W., 42, 110
wealth, of chief executives, 104-9
'wealthy', as the upper class, 178-9, 181-3, 187, 254
Weber, M., 1, 16-17, 26, 31-2, 55, 73
Wedderburn, D., xv
Weinberg, I., 46n
Weinstock, Sir Arnold, 61n, 212n, 278
Westaway, J., 109-10
Whitley, R.D., 8, 89, 90
Whyte, W.H., Jnr, 42, 50, 55, 267
Wildsmith, J.R., 6
Wilkinson, R., 46n
Willener, A., 19, 22
Williams, Shirley, 236, 241
Williams, W.M., 18n
Willmott, P., 19, 42, 46, 110, 113-14, 218
Wilson, Sir Harold, 230, 240, 279, 283
Winkler, J.T., xv, 4n, 9, 10, 14, 17, 44, 47, 54, 58, 59, 67n, 102, 134, 139, 140, 146, 153, 160, 162, 188, 199, 256, 261
Wolff, R.P., 34n
Wolfson, Sir Isaac, 61
Wood, Sir Frederick, 61
Wood, S., 14
workers (manual): 'aspirational', 21; 'deferential', 20, 21; 'privatised', 20, 22n; 'affluent', 187-9, 261-2; traditional 'proletarian', 20, 187-8, 261; among businessmen's social contacts, 14, 43-4, 50-1, 60, 112-16,

146, 252; expectation that they share objectives, 148-51

working class, 258; as a major division from middle class, 175, 254; businessmen's self-assignment to, 179, 190; images of society, 19-24, 187-9, 210 views of businessmen in class structure, 187

Worsthorne, Peregrine, 168

Young, M., 19, 42, 46, 110, 113-14, 218

Zeitlin, M., 6-8

For Product Safety Concerns and Information please contact our EU
representative GPSR@taylorandfrancis.com
Taylor & Francis Verlag GmbH, Kaufingerstraße 24, 80331 München, Germany

www.ingramcontent.com/pod-product-compliance
Lightning Source LLC
Chambersburg PA
CBHW061133220326
41599CB00025B/4225